THE SECOND DISRUPTION

The Free Church in Victorian Scotland and the Origins of the Free Presbyterian Church

SCOTTISH HISTORICAL REVIEW

MONOGRAPHS SERIES

No. 8

THE SECOND DISRUPTION

The Free Church in Victorian Scotland and the Origins of the Free Presbyterian Church

JAMES LACHLAN MacLEOD

TUCKWELL PRESS

First published in Great Britain in 2000 by
Tuckwell Press Ltd
The Mill House, Phantassie, East Linton, East Lothian, EH40 3DG
Scotland

All rights reserved

ISBN 1 86232 097 7

British Library Cataloguing-in-Publication Data. A catalogue
record for this book is available on request from the British Library

Typeset in 10/12 Baskerville by
Aligra Lancaster
Printed and bound in Great Britain by
Cromwell Press, Broughton Gifford, Melksham, Wiltshire

for
JESSICA

Contents

Acknowledgements

This book could not have been completed without the help of a great many people, many of whom did so at considerable personal inconvenience.

First, I would like to thank all those who lent me valuable documents or who made such documents readily available. In particular I would like to acknowledge the kindness of the late Rev. Donald B. Macleod for lending me the unique *John Macleod Collection*; and Miss Jean Nicolson, who entrusted to me many of her precious early volumes of the *Free Presbyterian Magazine*.

Secondly, I must thank the staff of two libraries. The great bulk of my work was done at the New College Library, and without the constantly courteous, humorous, efficient and, above all, highly skilled help provided by the staff, this book would not have seen the light of day. Norma and Paul in particular have always been prepared to go far beyond the call of duty, and to them I say a heartfelt thankyou. In recent times, Jan Beckett and Diane Warren of Harlaxton College Library have been a constant source of friendly and efficient help and encouragement – it is much appreciated.

Thirdly, I would like to thank Dr Andy Ross, who supervised my Ph.D. work with patience, humour and wisdom, and Professor Stewart J. Brown whose wise advice turned this from a dissertation into a book. John Tuckwell's interest and encouragement has been long-term, and has been of enormous value to me. I also must thank Alison Grant, whose meticulous preparation of this book for print was accompanied by many helpful suggestions.

Fourthly, I must thank those friends and colleagues who laboured with me in and around New College these past few years. In particular my dear friends Rowan Strong, John Harrison, Otele Perelini, Bruce MacDonald, Tim Meadowcroft, Neil MacDonald and Martin Dotterweich. Your companionship and prayers made the experience an unforgettable one. May God bless you all.

Finally, I thank my Mother and my late Father for the initial inspiration and for the constant encouragement and motivation.

It goes without saying that the remaining errors of fact or presentation remain my own responsibility.

J. L. McL

Abbreviations

AGAFC	Acts of the General Assembly of the Free Church of Scotland
Book of Genesis (EBS)	Marcus Dods, The Book of Genesis (Expositor's Bible Series, London, 1888)
Book of Genesis (HBC)	Marcus Dods, The Book of Genesis: With Introduction and Notes (Handbooks for Bible Classes Series, Edinburgh, 1882)
FPM	Free Presbyterian Magazine
PDGAFCS	Proceedings and Debates of the General Assembly of the Free Church of Scotland
RSCHS	Records of the Scottish Church History Society

Introduction

The delegates were all gone, the members worn out with the fatigues of the previous day, and in the galleries there were, for the first time, empty spaces during prayers. For the first time, also, the hall was comparatively cool.[1]

On such an unprepossessing stage, at the end of a long and largely pointless debate[2] in the Free Church General Assembly Hall in Edinburgh, an event took place that was to have a very significant impact on Scotland's religious history. On Thursday 25 May 1893, an elderly minister, Donald Macfarlane of Raasay, came forward to read and table his formal protest over a piece of legislation called the Free Church Declaratory Act. This Act had been intended to ease the terms of subscription to the Westminster Confession of Faith. To Macfarlane, however, it meant much more than that: it changed the very nature of the Free Church, making it a Church in which he could no longer remain a minister. He now severed his connection with the Church he had served since his ordination in 1876. Macfarlane was followed out of the Church by his former school teacher, Donald Macdonald, minister of Shieldaig, and by a handful of students who had been intending to enter the Free Church ministry. They took with them many thousands of Free Church members and adherents, almost all of whom resided in the Highlands and the Western Isles. Despite early difficulties, the new Church survived and prospered. By 1900 there were seventy-five charges and mission-stations. It was initially named The Free Church Presbytery of Scotland, but within a short period of time had come to be known as the Free Presbyterian Church of Scotland. A Second Disruption had taken place, and yet another Scottish denomination had been born.

The story began fifty years earlier, at the Great Disruption of 1843. The Disruption of 1843 has been described as 'probably the most important event in the history of nineteenth-century Scotland and a major episode in the history of the modern Western Church',[3] and it was certainly an event that was both monumental and traumatic. One third of the ministers and perhaps half of the laity left the Established Church of Scotland following the prolonged bitter struggles of the 'Ten Years' Conflict'. This decade-long battle was between two parties in the Church

---

1 'The Declaratory Act in the Free Assembly', *British Weekly*, 1 Jun. 1893, p. 82.
2 It was described as a 'reiteration of stale arguments': ibid., p. 82.
3 S. J. Brown, 'The Disruption and the dream: the making of New College, 1843–1861', in D. F. Wright and G. D. Badcock (eds.), *Disruption to Diversity: Edinburgh Divinity, 1846–1996* (Edinburgh, 1996), p. 30.

of Scotland – the Moderates and the Evangelicals – and the most important issue that divided them at this time was patronage, the right of the landowner to nominate the parish minister irrespective of the wishes of the parishioners. Beyond that though, the two parties stood for two different religious perspectives: the Moderates tended to represent a rather restrained and worldly form of Christianity – 'broad minded, cultured, and undogmatic'[4] – while the Evangelicals, as their name suggests, were in favour of a more robust version, taking an interest in social issues, emphasising the importance of a personal conversion experience and stressing the seventeenth-century Calvinist theology of the Westminster Confession of Faith.[5]

From 1833 to 1843 though, the battle was concentrated on the issue of patronage – what the Evangelicals, led by Thomas Chalmers, saw as unwarranted interference by the State into the affairs of the Church. The civil courts argued that as an Established Church, the Church of Scotland, had to be subordinate to the law of the land; this especially applied to the matter of patronage, which the civil courts defined as a property right. If a local patron presented a certain minister to a parish living, the congregation was bound to accept him whether they wanted him or not. The complexities of this issue were argued through the civil courts all the way up to the House of Lords. The Evangelicals who opposed the perceived 'intrusion' of unwanted ministers became known as the 'non-intrusion' party, and they fought particularly hard over three famous cases, at Auchterarder, Lethendy, and Marnoch, where despite the decisions of large majorities of the male heads of family to reject the presented candidate, the civil courts insisted that the candidates be accepted.[6]

Furthermore, in 1843, the Court of Session declared as illegal the General Assembly's 1834 Chapels Act. This was an Act which had formally recognised the status of the extra churches that had been built over the years to ease the burden of overpopulated parishes – the so-called chapels-of-ease. Most notably, it had allowed their ministers and elders, who were mainly Evangelicals, to serve as members of all Church courts up to and including the General Assembly. Taken as a whole, the various decisions of the civil courts supported one principle. That principle was that Church courts' decisions were to be subject to those of civil courts, thereby fatally compromising the principle of the spiritual

---

[4] A. L. Drummond and J. Bulloch, *The Church in Victorian Scotland, 1843–1874* (Edinburgh, 1975), p. 1.

[5] S. J. Brown, 'The Ten Years' Conflict and the Disruption of 1843', in S. J. Brown and M. Fry (eds.), *Scotland in the Age of the Disruption* (Edinburgh, 1993), pp. 1–6. For a contemporary account, see R. Buchanan, *The Ten Years' Conflict* (Glasgow, 1852).

[6] Brown, 'Disruption and the dream', pp. 30–3; Brown, 'Ten Years' Conflict', pp. 10–20; Drummond and Bulloch, *Church in Victorian Scotland*, pp. 233–43; A. Stewart and J. K. Cameron, *The Free Church of Scotland, 1843–1910: A Vindication* (Edinburgh and Glasgow, 1910), pp. 1–9; T. Brown, *Annals of the Disruption; with Extracts from the Narratives of Ministers who Left the Scottish Establishment in 1843* (Edinburgh, 1893), pp. 20–48.

independence of the Church, particularly in the areas of ordination of ministers and church discipline.

After years of conflict, the Church of Scotland split in May 1843, with the non-intrusionists departing to form the Free Church of Scotland. In the words of one of their number, writing fifty years later:

> With Chalmers and Welsh at their head ... they marched, vanquished yet victorious, casting no longing, lingering looks behind, severed further at each step from the smile of royalty and the favour of the great, and, what was far more serious, from comfortable homes and venerable churches beautiful with the holiest associations of their lives ... One thought, and one only, sustained them: they had the approval of their consciences and the smile of their Master.[7]

Over one third of the Church of Scotland's ministers left, and they also took with them about half the lay membership of the Church; this was indeed 'disruption' on a huge scale – William Ferguson called it 'the most momentous single event of the nineteenth century' for Scotland,[8] while Michael Lynch called the Disruption 'a turning-point in Scottish history'.[9] The Highlands deserted the Established Church almost *en masse*, and in the Lowland cities a high proportion of people left too; in Edinburgh two-thirds, in Glasgow around half, and in Aberdeen it was nearly 70%.[10] What it did was shatter Scotland's religious equilibrium in a manner not seen since the Reformation and produce a new Church which, although national in focus, was very much concentrated in two loci – the urban centres of the Lowlands and the rural communities of the Highlands.[11] This reality, apparent from the earliest days of the Free Church's existence, was to be a fundamental factor in its gradual unravelling and the breakaway of the Free Prebyterians fifty years later.

For as the Free Church developed over the next fifty years, it became increasingly a middle-class Church that was dominated from the Lowlands, with almost all its most significant leaders being firmly rooted there. S. J. Brown argues that in the years after the Disruption, 'the Free Church became an increasingly middle class body',[12] while James Hunter has observed that it was 'ultimately dependent on the urban middle class of Lowland Scotland rather than the small tenantry of the Highlands'.[13]

---

7 W. G. Blaikie, *After Fifty Years or Letters of a Grandfather on Occasion of the Jubilee of the Free Church of Scotland in 1893* (London, 1893), p. 31.

8 W. Ferguson, *Scotland: 1689 to the Present* (Edinburgh, 1978), p. 313.

9 M. Lynch, *Scotland: A New History* (London, 1992), pp. 397–8.

10 C. G. Brown, 'Religion, class and Church growth', in W. H. Fraser and R. J. Morris (eds.), *People and Society in Scotland, 1830–1914* (Edinburgh, 1990), p. 320.

11 S. J. Brown, *Thomas Chalmers and the Godly Commonwealth* (Oxford, 1982), pp. 335–6; S. J. Brown, 'Martyrdom in early Victorian Scotland: Disruption Fathers and the making of the Free Church', in D. Wood (ed.), *Martyrs and Martyrologies* (Oxford, 1993), p. 323.

12 Brown, *Thomas Chalmers*, p. 346.

13 J. Hunter, *The Making of the Crofting Community* (Edinburgh, 1976), p. 105.

After the death of Chalmers in 1847 the Church became dominated by younger men like Robert Smith Candlish and William Cunningham, and as the years passed they were replaced by men like Alexander Whyte, James Denney, Marcus Dods, A. B. Bruce and Robert Rainy, of whom the overwhelmingly dominant figure was, without dispute, Rainy.[14] What all these men had in common was a locus in the Lowlands of Scotland, and it is clear that in the fifty years between the Disruption of 1843 and the Second Disruption of 1893, the Free Church became increasingly rooted in the language, manners and mores of the Scottish Lowlands, increasingly isolating that part of the Church which resided north of the Highland line, and increasingly becoming, in effect, two communions.

What made this particularly damaging was the fact that the Highlands were an indispensable component of the Free Church. The Highlanders had joined the Free Church in huge numbers at the time of the Disruption – Rainy's biographer, Patrick Carnegie Simpson, called it 'a tidal wave which, in especially the north and north-west districts, carried the population *en masse*'.[15] The situation was such that in the Island of Lewis, official Free Church figures showed that in 1874, out of a population of some 23,439, only 460 were not in the Free Church.[16] In 1894, Lord Overtoun could provoke laughter in the Free Church General Assembly when he pointed out that many Church of Scotland congregations in the Highlands numbered as low as two, and he went on to comment that

> to think of a minister, an educated, God-fearing man, being placed there at the public expense to look after two people, who presumably might be himself and his wife, did not give one the idea of the Established Church taking a great grip on the religious life of the Highlands.[17]

The high level of commitment in Lewis to the Free Church had a statistically devastating effect on the Church of Scotland – a fact that was amusingly illustrated by the Rev. Alexander Lee of Nairn in the General Assembly of 1882. He described the reply of one Lewis woman to the question of her catechist:

> the question put was – 'Well, my woman, can you tell me now what we are to understand by the term the invisible church?' To which,

---

[14] In the index of Stewart and Cameron's, *Free Church of Scotland*, Chalmers features 13 times, Cunningham and Dods twice, Drummond once and even the controversial William Robertson Smith only 6 times; Rainy features 58 times.

[15] P. C. Simpson, *Life of Principal Rainy* (London, 1909), i, p. 433.

[16] *PDGAFCS*, 1874, p. 130. One extreme example was the parish of Uig, Lewis, which had a population of 2,159. Its non-Free Church population was zero. Eventually Lewis was to have a considerable influence on the ministry also; by 1886 the Free Church had 26 ministers who were Lewis men: *PDGAFCS*, 1886, p. 183.

[17] Ibid., 1894, p. 158. The Assembly responded to this with 'loud laughter and applause'.

after due consideration, and with all that air of respect that our Highland people ever manifest towards their spiritual overseers, she gravely replied, 'Well, no, unless it be the Established Church.'[18]

Lee then added the comment: 'And, verily, as far as spiritual work and moral power is concerned, that answer most truly describes the condition of the State church not only in the Lewis but also throughout the Highlands generally.'[19]

The loyalty of the Highlands to the Free Church at the time of the Disruption had brought them many hardships. The Highlanders suffered for their loyalty to the Non-Intrusionist cause, and although it might not have been the 'reign of terror' of popular lore,[20] there is no doubt that a great deal of misery had to be endured by the Highlanders. Many people lost their jobs and their homes for supporting the Free Church, and sites for church buildings were denied, forcing Free Church members to worship in the open air – causing discomfort to all and perhaps even hastening the death of some. It is perhaps not surprising that the language and imagery of martyrdom was widely used: 'Something ... of the martyr-spirit was needed to meet the difficulties of that time. Man had not only to spend, but be spent, for Christ.'[21]

Undoubtedly people suffered for the principles at stake in the Disruption all over Scotland and beyond, but it was the Highlanders who captured the imagination most. The notion that the Free Church owed the Highlanders something in return for their fidelity and sacrifice in 1843 was stressed repeatedly in Free Church General Assemblies. The sentiment was well summed up by William Garden Blaikie, himself a veteran of 1843. Writing on the occasion of the Church's fiftieth anniversary in 1893, he said, 'The adherence of such masses of people in the Highlands, while a remarkable testimony to the Free Church, imposed on her a very serious obligation.'[22] Robert Rainy echoed this on becoming convener of the Free Church Highland Committee in 1883.[23] As early as 1870, the Earl of Dalhousie had said that he 'knew of none of their people that had so great claims on the Church as the Highlanders',[24] and over the years at the annual delivery of the *Report of the Free Church Highland Committee*, the peculiar attachment of the Highlands to the Free Church was something on which it became almost ritual to comment.

18 Ibid., 1882, p. 229.
19 Ibid.
20 Brown, *Annals of the Disruption*, p. 354.
21 Ibid., p. 382. S. J. Brown observed: 'Martyrdom played a vital role in defining the identity of the Free Church of Scotland': Brown, 'Martyrdom in early Victorian Scotland', p. 319.
22 Blaikie, *After Fifty Years*, p. 89.
23 *PDGAFCS*, 1883, p. 95.
24 Ibid., 1870, p. 140.

Over the years, speaker after speaker rose to pay tribute to the unique debt that the Church owed the Highlands and to the singular nature of Highland dedication to the Church. Ferguson of Kinmundy commented in 1878 that 'there was nobody truer to the Church than the Highland people',[25] a fact which, in the opinion of Thomas McLauchlan, left the Church with special responsibilities:

> I repeat what I have often said in this House, that the people of the Highlands have special claims upon this Free Church of ours. They adhered with singular unanimity in many parts in 1843, and they adhere to her firmly still.[26]

This massive Highland commitment to the Free Church was partly caused by 'sectarian intolerance', which made remaining in the Church of Scotland in some places seem like a sin,[27] and it was partly caused by the considerable pressures in a Highland community to conform to a religious norm.[28] It was also, however, the reaction of a peasantry embittered by the Clearances and the apparent acquiescence with which the Moderate clergy of the Church of Scotland had greeted these hated actions by Highland landlords; in this respect the Disruption in the Highlands was a response to 'deep-seated social antagonisms'.[29] But perhaps most of all the Disruption attracted massive Highland support because of the deep-seated affection in most of the Western Highlands and Islands for the Evangelical style of religion associated with the non-intrusionists who formed the Free Church. The Disruption in the Highlands was a political and social movement certainly – it might even have been, in Hunter's words, 'a class conflict'[30] – but it was more than that. It was a movement of people who favoured a particular type of Protestantism, who had seen that religion challenged in the Church of Scotland when the Moderates dominated, and who wanted to associate themselves with a denomination that unambiguously supported it. This attitude – the Highlanders' deep commitment to and willingness to defend a particular type of Protestantism – was to have an absolutely integral part to play in the emergence of the Free Presbyterian Church.

---

25 Ibid., 1878, p. 255.
26 Ibid., 1875, p. 188.
27 It also created the situation where at least one Free Church landowner refused to allow the Church of Scotland minister access to his island charge: A. I. MacInnes, 'Evangelical Protestantism in the nineteenth-century Highlands', in G. Walker and T. Gallagher (eds.), *Sermons and Battle Hymns: Protestant Popular Culture in Modern Scotland* (Edinburgh, 1990), p. 57.
28 'In this social setting dissent would cause severe problems. It would involve alienation from progressive developments in the island. It would involve the stigma of alienation from the dominant social group and, furthermore, it would involve ostracism from the community and bring shame on one's family. These, of course, were not inconsiderable factors in Lewis society': D. B. A. Ansdell, 'The 1843 Disruption of the Church of Scotland in the Isle of Lewis', *RSCHS*, xxiv (2) (1992), pp. 196–7.
29 Hunter, *Making of the Crofting Community*, p. 106.
30 Ibid., p. 104.

After 1843, as the Free Church became divided between two different understandings of Protestantism, that division exacerbated the pre-existing divisions between Highlands and Lowlands.

While the Free Church that emerged in 1843 was on the surface a strong and successful Church, with key areas of support in the Lowland towns and cities and in the Highlands, the dichotomy between these two regions would in time contribute to the weakening of the Free Church. Moreover, the world into which the Free Church had been born was one of almost unprecedented change. In 1889, looking back at the years since the Disruption, Professor Marcus Dods of the Free Church seminary, New College, Edinburgh, observed:

> It might be difficult to lay one's finger on any half-century in the world's history during which changes so rapid, so profound, so fruitful and so permanent have taken place as those which the past generation has seen ... Every department of human thought and activity has felt the touch of the new influences.[31]

The Free Church prided itself on being a cerebral communion; one scholar has called it 'as well-educated a church as any in history, laity as well as clergy'.[32] Free Church laymen held prominent places in the world of education, in both science and the humanities, in law, in medicine and in local government.[33] This meant that the Church could not wrap itself in the cloak of traditional Calvinism and shelter itself from the changes in society and academic thought. In a changing world, the Free Church felt that it in turn had to be a changing church. When the Free Church did respond to the changing world, however, one result was bitter internecine conflict. While the Free Presbyterian founding fathers themselves might not have realised it, the seeds of the Second Disruption were sown not just by ministers and theologians, but by a whole host of scientists, philosophers, social reformers and politicians.

This book looks at the tensions within the Free Church and divides the causes of the Second Disruption of 1893 into four main areas. It commences with a wide-ranging chapter that emphasises those aspects of the changing world which, directly or indirectly, most affected the Free Churchmen who left at the Second Disruption. The Free Presbyterians always stressed the absolute centrality of Scripture in their outlook, and the second chapter therefore examines the bitter divisions engendered

---

31 M. Dods, *Recent Progress in Theology: Inaugural Lecture at New College Edinburgh, 1889* (Edinburgh, 1889), p. 6.
32 R. A. Riesen, *Criticism and Faith in Late Victorian Scotland: A. B. Davidson, William Robertson Smith and George Adam Smith* (Lanham, MD, 1985), p. 221.
33 A glance at the roll of members of the 1893 General Assembly reveals the presence of the Professor of the Practice of Physics at Edinburgh University; the President of the Royal College of Surgeons, Edinburgh; the Professor of Conveyancing at Edinburgh University along with countless Writers to the Signet and Advocates; and the Lord Provost of Edinburgh: *PDGAFCS*, 1893, pp. viii–xxvii.

in the Free Church by two of the most significant areas of change in the nineteenth century, both of which could be interpreted as attacks on Scripture, biblical criticism and Darwinian science. Given that the Second Disruption was an overwhelmingly Highland affair, with over 90% of the early Free Presbyterian congregations located in the Highlands, Chapter 3 explores the central issue of the division within the Free Church between the Highlands and Lowlands. This is something which has been consistently underemphasised by the writers of standard Free Presbyterian histories, but which seems to be of great importance. Finally, Chapter 4 surveys the controversial movement towards revision of the Westminster Confession that was to be the final trigger of, and official justification for, the Second Disruption.

What emerges from this is that many of the questions that have been at the forefront of Free Presbyterian minds over the succeeding one hundred years were live issues at the time of their birth. As will be seen, for example, the revival of Roman Catholicism in Scotland was a source of controversy in the later decades of the nineteenth century and that has been a subject which has preoccupied the Free Presbyterians ever since.[34] Traditional Sabbatarianism was coming under pressure in the very years in which the Free Presbyterian Church was being conceived, and again that issue has remained very much alive with the denomination. Similarly, and probably more importantly, the two great areas of ecclesiastical debate which did most to produce a Disruption in 1893, the Bible and the Westminster Confession of Faith, produced a denomination which has been conspicuous in its tenacious defence of its understanding of these two documents in an uncongenial environment. Holding the Bible as a verbally inspired and inerrant text, while at the same time maintaining the Westminster Confession in its entirety, has become a badge of the Free Presbyterian Church. Coupled with an unbending stance on Sabbatarianism and on the Roman Catholic Church, these concerns, all very much alive at the time of the Second Disruption, remain integral to the Free Presbyterian identity today. Far though it has come in many ways since May 1893, the Free Presbyterian Church remains, for better or worse, very much a child of the era in which it was born.

---

[34] While the bitter dispute that split the Free Presbyterian Church in 1989 was a complex and multi-faceted one, the primary 'issue' was over conflicting attitudes to attendance at a Roman Catholic Requiem Mass.

CHAPTER ONE

The Changing World

Urbanisation

The Industrial Revolution originated in Britain, and it was in nineteenth-century Britain that its results were first most profoundly felt. London became the financial centre of the world and British industry, finance and commerce dominated world trade. The British Empire expanded rapidly, while the British model of parliamentary democracy proved influential throughout the world. For religion, though, danger signs were beginning to appear. Looking at a broad sweep of international religious history, S. S. Acquaviva said that

> at a certain point the influence of social life began to be negative for religion, so that [1] Almost all new social phenomena came to have a disintegrative effect on religious life; [2] A steady diminution of the influence of religion on secular life became evident. This was accompanied by the desacralisation of society.[1]

In Scotland this 'certain point' was beginning to be reached with the onset of industrialisation, a phenomenon of which Acquaviva stated that 'Everything concurs in indicating ... that religion undergoes a profound crisis in industrial society.'[2] While the nature of this 'crisis' is open to debate, and while the whole 'secularization theory' is currently being re-examined,[3] it seems clear that nineteenth-century Scotland experienced both industrialisation and a profound religious crisis.

In Scotland the direct effects of the industrial revolution, although not as rapid as often supposed,[4] were widespread and spectacular, giving rise to what has been called 'the Scottish Victorian economic miracle'.[5] The

1 S. S. Acquaviva, *The Decline of the Sacred in Secular Society* (Oxford, 1979), p. 37.

2 Ibid., p. 84.

3 Callum Brown and others have recently argued that many of the old assumptions regarding secularisation theory have to be re-examined. For an introduction, see S. Bruce (ed.), *Religion and Modernization: Sociologists and Historians debate the Secularization Thesis* (Oxford, 1992). And in the words of Donald Withrington, 'We should not ... equate the undoubted fact of increased non-church-going with a turning away from all religious belief and attachment ... In fact secularisation drew relatively little of its support from Scotland, throughout the latter half of the nineteenth century': D. J. Withrington: '"A Ferment of Change": aspirations, ideas and ideals in nineteenth-century Scotland', in D. Gifford (ed.), *The History of Scottish Literature*, vol. III (Aberdeen, 1988), p. 50.

4 Withrington, e.g., observes that it was not until the 1870s that a majority of Scots who worked were employed in non-agricultural occupations: ibid., p. 44.

5 S. and O. Checkland, *Industry and Ethos: Scotland, 1832–1914* (London, 1984), p. 12.

Checklands attributed this to a combination of the Union of 1707; 'the favours of nature'; the growth of a breed of industrialists, traders and bankers; and the effect of a religious value-system which laid stress on

> popular education, on individual responsibility, and on answerability to God for his gifts ... These virtues, so appropriate to survival under traditional Scottish poverty, could now work powerfully in the nation's escape from it.[6]

The results were dramatic, with Glasgow burgeoning into the second city of the Empire and fabulous fortunes being made in tea and textiles, ship-building and sugar. Between 1841 and 1911, Glasgow's population increased from 275,000 to 784,000; Edinburgh and Leith witnessed a population growth from 164,000 to 401,000; and Aberdeen and Dundee both increased from around 65,000 in 1841 to around 165,000 in 1911. In the century following 1830, the number of Scots living in towns of 5,000 or more doubled from one-third to two-thirds.[7]

It was, however, a time of greatly increased wealth for a few and increased poverty and squalor for many. As Christopher Smout expressed it:

> the success of textiles in the first phase of the industrial revolution is succeeded by the success of iron and coal in the second, then after 1860 by the triumph of steel, ships, jute, tweed and high farming ... [but] the age of great industrial triumphs was an age of appalling social deprivation, not, certainly without amelioration, but with no solutions for its terrible problems ... Unspeakable urban squalor, compounded of drink abuse, bad housing, low wages, long hours and sham education ... What was the point of all those triumphs of the great Victorian age of industry if so many people were so unspeakably oppressed by its operations?[8]

Small communities expanded to become sprawling urban centres and these urban areas contained some of the worst slums in Europe, which provoked in the middle classes mixed feelings of sympathy, revulsion and downright terror. It was not as if they could ignore this cancerous growth in their cities, for although they themselves may have decanted to peripheral and pleasant suburbs, they had to pass through urban slums if they wanted to worship at St Giles's in Edinburgh, go to offices

---

[6] Ibid., p. 12. And, as Ian Donnachie has observed: 'even the pioneers of economic and social history ... did little to modify the popularly held view that the secret of Scotland's greatness in the era of industrialisation was the enterprising Scot ... The "self-made man" ... is still regarded as the conventional hero of the Industrial Revolution and is not altogether a myth, yet the evidence of modern historical research suggests that he was in the minority': I. Donnachie, '"The Enterprising Scot"', in I. Donnachie and C. Whatley (eds.), *The Manufacture of Scottish History* (Edinburgh, 1992), p. 90.

[7] T. C. Smout, *A Century of the Scottish People, 1830–1950* (London, 1986), pp. 32, 41.

[8] Ibid., p. 2.

in the city centre, or attend the Universities of either Glasgow or Edinburgh.[9] J. M. E. Ross, in the biography of his father, the Free Church minister William Ross, thus described the Cowcaddens area of Glasgow in the 1880s:

> You pass through the entry of some towering tenement to find that ... you can pass through and out into what ought to be a garden or open space behind, to find that the open space has shrunk into a narrow courtyard and that there is another towering tenement on the other side of it, the one tenement robbing the other of its due measure of light and air.[10]

The young Hugh Miller was horrified by what he found on his initial arrival in the Edinburgh area in 1824:

> it is in the great towns that Paganism now chiefly prevails. In at least their lapsed classes – a rapidly increasing proportion of their population – it is those cities of our country which first caught the light of religion and learning, that have become pre-eminently its dark parts.[11]

Some Free Churchmen felt that their duty was not to involve themselves in political and social issues but to concentrate on the preaching of the Gospel.[12] He that won souls was wise, they believed, and if a minister was to do his best at that then he should not be spending his time worrying over working or housing conditions.[13] This

---

[9] Ibid., p. 29.

[10] J. M. E. Ross, *William Ross of Cowcaddens* (London, 1905), pp. 88–9. A. C. Cheyne referred to 'the destitution, crime, squalor and disease, all on a massive scale, which not only defied sanitary and moral control but even seemed to be undermining the very foundations of civilised life and Christian faith in Glasgow, Edinburgh, and the Central Lowlands of Scotland generally': A. C. Cheyne, 'Thomas Chalmers: then and now', in A. C. Cheyne (ed.), *The Practical and the Pious: Essays on Thomas Chalmers (1780–1847)* (Edinburgh, 1985), p. 15.

[11] Quoted in G. Rosie, *Hugh Miller: Outrage and Order* (Edinburgh, 1981), p. 40.

[12] Involvement in socio-political issues had aroused controversy in the past also; see, e.g., W. H. Marwick, 'Social heretics in the Scottish Churches', *RSCHS*, xi (3) (1953), pp. 228–30; D. H. Bishop, 'Church and Society: A Study of the Social Work and Thought of James Begg, D.D. (1808–1883), A. H. Charteris, D.D., LL.D. (1835–1908) and David Watson, D.D. (1859–1943)' (Edinburgh University, Ph.D. thesis, 1953), esp. pp. 1–104; and A. C. Ross, *John Philip (1775–1851): Missions, Race and Politics in South Africa* (Aberdeen, 1986).

[13] When even a relatively enlightened Free Churchman like W. G. Blaikie could express the views that the vast majority of the population were destined to be 'hewers of wood and drawers of water' – quoted in D. C. Smith, *Passive Obedience and Prophetic Protest: Social Criticism in the Scottish Church, 1830–1945* (New York, 1987), p. 193 – and that the Churches' role in helping the working classes out of their depressed state was 'to stand by and to shout encouragement to them' – in D. J Withrington, 'The Churches in Scotland, c.1870–c.1900: towards a new social conscience?', *RSCHS*, xxix (1977), p. 164 – it should perhaps not be surprising that the Free Church did not do more to respond to the problems of urbanisation. It is hard to visualise men who lived in parts of Edinburgh like Charlotte Square (Alexander Whyte), or Great King Street (Marcus

tendency was probably exacerbated by the fact that as the century progressed the Free Church was, in the Lowlands at any rate, becoming more of a middle-class Church.[14] Others, however, saw themselves as having a divinely ordained duty to do their best to help the poor in their midst, and became involved in what might be called urban mission. James Begg, for example, dedicated some thirty-five years of his life to the struggle against poverty both in the Highlands and the Lowlands.[15] Alexander Whyte sought to alleviate suffering during the Glasgow typhus epidemic of 1865, and later strove to recruit the office-bearers and teachers of his congregation for active social work. In following the example set by Thomas Chalmers, who had struggled against poverty during his time in two urban Glasgow parishes, the Tron and St John's, impressive work was done by such Free Churchmen as Dugald MacColl in the Glasgow Wynds and James Hood Wilson in Edinburgh's Fountainbridge.[16] There were many similar projects in other Scottish towns and cities, with the high-point of the Free Church's urban mission coming in the late 1860s and the early 1870s. By that point as many as sixty urban 'territorial' churches had been built, but by 1889 the number of such churches supported by the Free Church had dwindled to twelve as, in S. J. Brown's words,

> The Free Church increasingly withdrew from its commitment to achieving the Christian commonwealth, and began regarding itself primarily as a gathered Church of Christian individuals, 'holding the fort' in the midst of a sinful, secular society.[17]

It is clearly a complex issue, but it is evident that the urbanisation of Scotland, with all its attendant social problems, was yet another vexing backdrop against which the Free Church had to work out its position.

Dods), or Morningside (A. T. Innes) having a great deal of understanding for or sympathy with the urban – or rural – labouring poor.

[14] S. J. Brown talked of 'a membership proud of their strict work ethic and social status': Brown, *Thomas Chalmers*, pp. 345–6, and, more recently, he has pointed out that 'in urban areas the Free Church attracted prosperous middle-class congregations and rapidly gained respectability and influence': Brown, 'Martyrdom in early Victorian Scotland', p. 327; Callum Brown has described the late 19th-century Free Church as swiftly moving towards 'a liberal, middle class theology': C. G. Brown, *The Social History of Religion in Scotland since 1730* (London, 1987), p. 127; and Steve Bruce has argued that the eventual fracture of the Church was due in part to 'modernising influences on the urban middle class ... acquiring wealth, status, position and with them, travel, education and considerable opportunities to indulge the senses': S. Bruce, *No Pope of Rome: Militant Protestantism in Modern Scotland* (Edinburgh, 1985), p. 24.

[15] J. W. Rogerson, *The Bible and Criticism in Victorian Britain: Profiles of F. D. Maurice and William Robertson Smith* (Sheffield, 1995), pp. 61–5.

[16] S. J. Brown, 'Thomas Chalmers and the communal ideal in Victorian Scotland' in T. C. Smout (ed.), *Victorian Values: A Joint Symposium of the Royal Society of Edinburgh and the British Academy, December 1990* (Oxford, 1992), pp. 64, 70–3.

[17] Ibid., p. 74.

Intemperance

For churchmen, the situation was exacerbated by the influence of liquor. As early as 1839, a survey had shown Scotland to be well ahead of the field when it came to the consumption of spirits.[18] In the Cowcaddens area of Glasgow, for example, it was said that

> public houses abounded on every hand ... There were twenty-two public houses and licensed grocers within a minute-or-two's walk of the Church, while a more extended survey of the district soon disclosed more than 120 ... a district reckoned, and rightly reckoned, to be amongst the poorest parts of the city spent in twenty years on intoxicants about £2,600,000.[19]

Nor was the influence of alcohol in the inner city just a product of middle-class evangelical paranoia. A working-class journalist, writing in the *North British Daily Mail* under the pseudonym, 'the Amateur Vagrant', gave a moving account of the Garscube Road in Glasgow on a Saturday night around midnight:

> Prostitution and illicit drinking go hand in hand. Vice, crime, debauchery, poverty, destitution, misery, dirt, overcrowding and insanitation are written in large letters all over. The place is seriously and dangerously overbuilt. The greed of the landlord and the asinine stupidity of the Dean of Courts have turned it into a pandemonium and if ... [we] set the whole area on fire we would be doing God service.[20]

Even the *Contemporary Review*, not always sympathetic to conservative religion, commented picturesquely on the demeaning effects of alcohol, blaming it for

> nearly all the crime and misery in broad Britain ... there is not a soul living who does not know very well that there never was a pestilence crawling over the earth which could match the alcoholic poisons in murderous power.[21]

The *Edinburgh Review* quoted from a Commons Select Committee in 1873, which described drunkenness as a 'fertile source of misery, poverty, and degradation',[22] while a Free Church committee heard in 1886 of the scale of the problem in Glasgow:

---

18 The consumption of spirits per head per annum was 8 pints in England, 13 pints in Ireland and 23 pints in Scotland: A. Ross, 'The development of the Scottish Catholic community, 1878–1978', *Innes Rev.*, xxix (1978), p. 40.

19 Ross, *William Ross of Cowcaddens*, pp. 89–90.

20 Ibid., pp. 93–4: quoting 'the Amateur Vagrant' from the *North British Daily Mail.*

21 J. Runciman, 'The ethics of the drink question', *Contemporary Rev.*, lvi (Oct. 1889), p. 539.

22 'Drunkenness, abstinence, and restraint', *Edinburgh Rev.*, cxxxvii (280) (1873), p. 416.

On the second Saturday of May, 2,212 persons entered one public-house in the neighbourhood of our Glasgow theatres. Two-thirds of these were young men. On the previous Saturday, in one of the thoroughfares of the city, 2,943 persons entered one public house, more than one half entering after seven o'clock at night.[23]

The same report quoted the venerated minister, Robert Murray MacCheyne: 'Public-houses are the curse of Scotland. I never see "licensed to sell spirits", but I think it means licence to ruin souls.'[24] It was not until the 1890s that the churches began to renounce the habit of attacking intemperance as the root of all evil and began to see it as not only a cause but also a symptom of social ill-being.[25]

Although drunkenness was not confined to the West-Central industrial conglomerations and to the working classes, it was linked with the problems of industrialisation. To a man like William Ross, indus-trialisation was a direct and personal challenge, and to the Scottish Church in general it forced large-scale re-thinking about what the real issues were, and how these issues were being confronted. How much longer, it had to be asked, could the Free Church stick to the 'Old Paths'.

The Highland Situation

The Central Belt, then, experienced a remarkable and at times difficult transition into industrial society, accompanied by an almost unavoidable demographic explosion. The Highlands, too, experienced a quite different transformation during the late Victorian period. Demographi-cally the picture is extremely complex, as the combined factors of migration, emigration, clearances, new technology and economic pressures on both tenants and landlords all contributed to the 'push' and 'pull' effect on rural populations. With the exception of the Isle of Lewis, most Highland and Island communities experienced a decline in population between around 1830 and the closing decades of the nineteenth century.[26] The combination of the increased opportunities afforded by the expanding towns in the Central Belt and the difficulties associated with the decline of traditional Highland and Island occupations meant that the combined 'push' and 'pull' factors were at times very great. As Charles Withers has shown, though, there was a

---

23 'Report of Temperance Committee', *PDGAFCS*, 1886, App. XXII, p. 5.
24 Ibid., p. 2. The *Free Presbyterian Magazine* reported some 13 years later that Britain spent £154,480,934 on alcohol in 1899 and commented that: 'A plentiful crop of lost souls is no doubt reaped from this lavish sowing to the flesh': '£154,000,000', *FPM*, iv (3) (1899), p. 119.
25 D. J. Withrington, 'Non-church-going, church organisation and "crisis in the church", *c*.1800–*c*.1920', *RSCHS*, xxiv (2) (1992), p. 199.
26 Smout, *Century of the Scottish People*, p. 69.

geographical distinction between different areas of the Highlands in their migratory activities. From the southern and eastern parts of the Highlands migration was often permanent, while migration from the north-west Highlands and the Islands tended to be more temporary and seasonal.[27] It seems likely that these processes were increased in the wake of the Industrial Revolution, but as Withers pointed out, the paucity of statistics for the pre-1850 period make this difficult to quantify. What can be said is that from the 1840s onwards the population of the Highlands was in decline and that, with the slight exception of the 1870s, this decline continued into the twentieth century.[28]

It would be wrong, however, to suggest that all Highland population changes were gradual and part of a long-term, 'natural', process. The earlier decades of the century had witnessed the phenomenon of the Clearances which, whatever their origins,[29] had left a legacy of bitter resentment throughout the Highlands. The first wave of Clearances commenced around 1800 with the intention of repositioning the Highland population on the coast to make room for sheep, and at the same time providing a convenient supply of labour for the new and extremely labour-intensive kelp industry.[30] The second phase followed the potato famine of the 1840s; its purpose was to remove the Highlander out of the country altogether. The Gaelic poet Sorley MacLean has called Highland emigration 'the phenomenon of phenomena' in the nineteenth century.[31] It was the time when, according to J. M. E. Ross's account of his grand-father's experience in Kildonan,

> men and women, many of them worthy of better treatment, were turned out by a ruthless landlordism to make room for sheep, and their houses burned about their ears when they seemed to the authorities to be lingering unduly.[32]

The process was described in the Free Church General Assembly of 1878 by an indignant Bailie Campbell:

> the Highlanders ... were driven from the finest of the land – the fine straths and glens, which were now occupied by deer. They were sent

---

27 C. W. J. Withers, 'Highland–Lowland migration and the making of the crofting community, 1775–1891', *Scot. Geog. Magazine*, ciii (2) (1987), p. 76.

28 Ibid., pp. 76–7.

29 'Mass eviction', said T. M. Devine, 'was the culmination of the interplay of powerful demographic, economic and ideological forces': T. M. Devine, *The Great Highland Famine: Hunger, Emigration and the Scottish Highlands in the Nineteenth Century* (Edinburgh, 1988), p. 189.

30 The profitability of kelp was itself destroyed by the discovery of cheaper substitutes to use in the manufacture of soap and glass: S. Bruce, 'Social change and collective behaviour: the Revival in eighteenth-century Ross-shire', *British Journal of Sociology*, xxiv (4) (1983), p. 557.

31 J. D. Wood, 'Transatlantic land reform, America and the Crofters' Revolt, 1878–1888', *Scot. Hist. Rev.*, lxiii (1984), p. 79.

32 Ross, *William Ross of Cowcaddens*, p. 3.

away down to the sea, there to grow, on most miserable patches of ground, their potatoes and corn. This was not as it ought to be.[33]

Six years earlier, the Rev. William Rose of Poolewe had been even more unequivocal:

Deer and sheep; first sheep, but now deer, are supplanting our men. Now, on this deer-forest system I wish to remark that they are an unmitigated evil. A Highland proprietor is reported to have called them a great industry: I call them a great iniquity ... to have our people hunted from the land of their birth, either abroad, or to huts and hovels on the sea-shore, is what we cannot help looking upon with indignation ... the grouse and the deer-stalker, who, in order that his pleasure and passion be gratified, can continue to lay waste leagues of our glens and dales, is only an evil, and the whole institution ought to be laid under legal restrictions.[34]

This 'ruthless landlordism' was to be something that many people saw as a recurrent theme throughout the century, and it was another issue which made it difficult for the Church to confine itself solely to the spiritual sphere. Even Neil Cameron, one of the Free Church divinity students whose departure in 1893 led to the formation of the Free Presbyterian Church, felt that the land issue could not be overlooked. While no advocate of 'Highland Liberation Theology',[35] Cameron did touch on the subject of the Clearances in a sermon which appeared as early as the fourth issue of the *Free Presbyterian Magazine*. While referring to 'the bondage of Zion', Cameron observed that 'under iniquitous laws in this land families were evicted, and had to go to foreign lands to seek another home. Did not the children share the grief of their parents?'[36] He then proceeded to make a remarkable analogy when he talked of

the feelings of every true child of God, when Christ and His bride – the Church – their mother – are cruelly dealt with; the foundations of their house razed to the ground, and no room left for them, in some places, but the open fields or the sea shore.[37]

Cameron's apparent paralleling of the mistreatment of Christ and His Church and of the victims of the Clearances – in a sermon preached at the most ten years after the Land Laws agitation of the late 1880s – is a clear sign of how deeply ingrained was his Highland sense of grievance over these issues.

[33] *PDGAFCS*, 1878, p. 256.
[34] *PDGAFCS*, 1872, p. 312.
[35] See, e.g., D. E. Meek, '"The Land Question Answered From the Bible": the land issue and the development of a Highland theology of liberation', *Scot. Geog. Magazine*, ciii (2) (1987), p. 84.
[36] N. Cameron, 'Psalms lxxx. 12,13', *FPM*, i (4) (1896), p. 132.
[37] Ibid., p. 132.

Later, the Free Presbyterians produced a still more outspoken attack on the landlords. The *Free Presbyterian Magazine* stated in 1898 that

Strathnaver and the banks of the Kildonan river, and many other fertile spots, once the seats of a stalwart God-fearing race, are now silent haunts of sheep and deer. The money-grabbing instincts of the landlords proved stronger than the calls of humanity and patriotism, and they ruthlessly evicted hundreds of virtuous peasants, to lay the land under sheep. For why? in the eyes of the landlords at that time a fat pocket book was the most sacred of all earthly possessions.[38]

This is coming close to being a classic piece of social criticism, but the article did not stop there; it continued with what was an almost rebellious air:

It was a century ago that the spoilation was done, but it may chance that the reckoning day is not yet come. Well-built Highland crofters did not at the time seem so profitable a species of live stock as sheep or deer, but they proved excellent fighting material for Peninsular campaigning and feats of war at Waterloo. Our wars are not at an end – the worst of them is likely yet to come – and ... our supply of sturdy recruits is precarious. The sheep and deer which browse in Strathnaver will not avail to man the regiment in time of need, and when lords and ladies whose fathers spoiled the dwelling-places of a gallant faithful race, find their sumptuous town houses and country houses in danger of being burnt over them, they may have cause to reflect on the exact character of the divine judgement.[39]

The Clearances transformed the Highlands in an extremely traumatic manner; it should perhaps not be surprising that Highland churchmen should respond with strong words at the very least.

For many others, the connection between religion and what might have been termed 'secular' issues was much more than incidental. In the later conflict in the Highlands and Islands, over the Land Laws in the 1880s, the Church often found itself forced either to get involved or face the consequences of unpopularity. The grim example was the Church of Scotland, which had been all but deserted in the Highlands in 1843 partly as a result of Highland antagonism over the Church's lack of activity at the time of the Clearances.[40] When it came to the 1880s the religious input to the struggle was much more overt – the Land Laws campaigner Henry George saw the land campaign as 'essentially a religious movement'[41] – and the churchman had to ask himself if it was possible to turn a blind eye to the issue. The religious content of much of

[38] 'A sentence from the "Review of Reviews"', *FPM*, ii (9) (1898), p. 360.
[39] Ibid.
[40] E.g. Hunter, *Making of the Crofting Community*, p. 95.
[41] Wood, 'Transatlantic land reform', p. 97.

the crofters' language and rhetoric was deliberate and at times blatant; the membership card of the Highland Land Law Reform Association (later the Land League) gave prominent place to the text from Ecclesiastes v.9: 'The profit of the earth is for all', and the Land Law campaigner Donald MacCallum was just one of many who 'made extensive use of analogies and allegories based on the Bible'.[42] By forcing religion into what was essentially a socio-economic matter with political undertones, the anti-Land Law campaigners propelled churchmen into a secular battle which they may well have preferred to do without.

As the historian Iain Fraser Grigor has suggested, throughout the 1870s the social restiveness and change throughout the British Isles was mirrored in the Highlands. While established political and social norms were being called into question in the rest of the country, the Highlands were increasingly being opened up by improved communications such as the steam train, the steamboat and the telegraph. The 1870s saw a big rise in resistance to the landlords, with sixty writs served against crofters each year in Skye alone.[43] The situation was one of great flux in the Highlands and this actually increased in the following decade, when bad harvests combined with economic depression and poor fishing to make the crofters' situation even more miserable than it had been before.[44] This was to coincide with the most violent of the crofters' demonstrations, including the famous 'Battle of the Braes' in Skye, in which a party of Glasgow police lost out to a contingent of aroused crofters. It is hard to imagine how the Church could ignore a situation in which, in the words of D. W. Crowley, 'there were close similarities between the agitation of the Highland crofters and the questioning of the established order of society which was beginning to spread among the industrial workers at this time'.[45] It was a state of affairs which was a country-wide phenomenon:

> the Land War was only one aspect of growing dissatisfaction with the British social order in the late nineteenth century. Disillusion-ment with Gladstonian liberalism, the founding of the first socialist societies, and unrest among urban and rural workers were all part of the same socio-political ferment.[46]

---

[42] Meek, 'Land Question Answered From the Bible', pp. 84, 87.

[43] I. F. Grigor, *Mightier Than A Lord: The Highland Crofters' Struggle For the Land* (Stornoway, 1979), pp. 32–3. As well as improved communications, the Highlands were also experiencing the 'opening up' of minds through the process of education. The Bible was first widely available in Gaelic in 1801, and 1811 saw the formation of the Gaelic School Society with the 19th century witnessing a successful literacy campaign. It is inevitable that religion would play a part in any political struggle, given the fact that for many years the Bible and the New Testament were the only two Gaelic books available: Hunter, *Making of the Crofting Community*, p. 96.

[44] Smout, *Century of the Scottish People*, p. 71; Grigor, *Mightier Than A Lord*, p. 52.

[45] D. W. Crowley, 'The "Crofters' Party", 1885–1892', *Scot. Hist. Rev.*, xxxv (1956), p. 111.

[46] D. Meek, 'Gaelic poets of the land agitation', *Trans. of the Gaelic Soc. of Inverness*, xlix (1974–6), p. 316.

As will be shown later, however, although many ministers chose not to become involved, there were a significant number who were 'prepared to advocate the crofters' cause'.[47]

Although the Church's concern in Land Law agitation cannot be explored in depth at this time, it is clear that the Free Church became involved not only locally and spontaneously, but also nationally, in a formal and official manner. The Royal Commission of Inquiry into the Conditions of the Crofters and Cottars in the Highlands and Islands of Scotland, universally known as the Napier Commission, received a submission from the Highland Committee of the Free Church which was written by Robert Rainy and J. Calder Macphail in late 1883. Interestingly, what this report makes apparent is how proud Rainy was of the Free Church's role in minimising the disorder in the Highlands at that time. Describing the role of Free Church ministers and laymen, the report stated:

> the influence of the ministers, and, they might add, of the office-bearers and leading laymen of the Free Church, has not been used to embitter questions of this kind. On the contrary, the tendency undoubtedly has been to maintain peace and quietness, and to deprecate all violent and passionate measures ... Through the religious leaders of the people a public opinion which rejects, as disapproved by Christ, everything like 'the wild justice of revenge' has been remarkably maintained.[48]

Rainy's position is hardly surprising, though, given the fact that even Murdo Macaskill of Dingwall, portrayed by many as one of the principal leaders of the Highlanders in the Free Church,[49] described the 'agrarian disorders' which took place in Lewis in the late 1880s as having been 'stirred by Satan' to interfere with a local revival of religion.[50] The official Free Church submission to the Napier Commission continued:

> It is still well remembered in Sutherlandshire, how, at the times of the changes taking place there, wild talk and wild plans among the younger men were repressed by the resolute determination of the leading religious people to have nothing to do with any plans that proposed to avert suffering by sinning. Considering the lawless state of the Highlands four or five generations ago, the quiet which has

---

47 Meek, 'Land Question Answered From the Bible', p. 87.

48 *PDGAFCS*, 1884, *Report of the Committee for the Highlands and Islands*, pp. 25–6.

49 W. Ewing (ed.), *Annals of the Free Church of Scotland, 1843–1900* (Edinburgh, 1914), i, p. 214.

50 *PDGAFCS*, 1888, p. 100. In Macaskill's defence, it should be pointed out that he shared a platform in Greenock town hall with the Land Laws campaigner Henry George, and that he also worked closely with the landlord-turned-land-law-campaigner Munro-Ferguson of Novar: J. Macaskill, *A Highland Pulpit: Being Sermons of the Late Rev. Murdoch Macaskill* (Inverness, 1907), xvii–xviii.

generally obtained there could hardly have existed unless the minds of the people had been controlled by principles of duty and religion.[51]

Other Free Church documents echoed these sentiments.[52]

The position was complicated by the fact that alongside what might be called their natural deference to men in a divinely sanctioned position of supremacy, Free Church ministers harboured some feelings of indebtedness to those many landlords who had provided sites for Free Church buildings in the difficult years after the Disruption of 1843.[53] They also supported those landlords who were waging war on licensed premises and illicit drinking dens.[54] As late as 1887, Free Church ministers on the Isle of Skye were being censured severely for spending time with landlords; Donald Meek cites a Gaelic poem by Donald MacLeod of Waternish, Skye, which includes the lines,

> And as for Free Church ministers, they will not take our side;
> if they get people's possessions they are happy enough.
> What they seek especially is the company of the landlords;
> they would not wish there to be a poor person on the face of the earth.[55]

A not unrelated point was that to many Free Churchmen socio-political issues were simply not the most important matter with which they had to deal: 'The Church', said Gerald Crole, an Edinburgh advocate who had defended Land campaigners in Court, 'had something else to do than deal with questions of a purely social character.'[56] Believing as they did that Christ's kingdom was not of this world, social problems were seen as minor inconveniences on the road to Glory; the Church's reaction, therefore, was far from revolutionary.

Before concluding this section it is necessary to refer briefly to those Free Churchmen who did become socially involved. The roles of such Free Church ministers as John MacMillan of Lochbroom – who offered a 'perceptive analysis of the mechanics of Highland landlordism'[57] – and of Evan Gordon of Glasgow – 'In the Lowlands, there was no more ardent a supporter of the crofters' cause'[58] – have been well documented and often commented upon. But it is clear that it went deeper than the

---

51 *PDGAFCS*, 1884, *Highland Committee Report*, p. 26.

52 'Overture anent Highland Land Question', from the Free Synod of Glenelg, *Free Church of Scotland Assembly Papers*, No. I, 1888, p. 173; *PDGAFCS*, 1888, pp. 182–3, 186–7.

53 Despite the contemporary propaganda, it should be noted that there were only around 35 site refusals (not all in the Highlands) compared to 725 sites being granted: MacInnes, 'Evangelical Protestantism', p. 56.

54 H. J. Hanham, 'The problem of Highland discontent, 1880–1885', *Trans. of the Royal Hist. Soc.*, 5th ser., xix (1969), p. 45.

55 Meek, 'Gaelic poets', p. 359.

56 *PDGAFCS*, 1888, p. 181. As an advocate whose address was 1, Royal Circus, Edinburgh, 'social questions' were presumably not something which affected his daily bread.

57 Grigor, *Mightier Than A Lord*, p. 37.

58 Meek, 'Land Question Answered From the Bible', p. 88.

outspoken individual prepared to dedicate much of his life to the cause. As has been noted by I. M. M. MacPhail, it was not just ministers who became politicised by the Land War:

> Some of the 'Men' like Rory Bain MacLeod ... became earnest propagandists of Land Law reform, and many of the witnesses before the Napier Commission were Free Church elders whose eloquence and forthrightness carried conviction with their hearers.[59]

Even Rainy was willing to admit that there had been those who thought that 'the disposition to urge peace and submission at all hazards has been carried too far',[60] and it is evident that the Free Church's general failure to back up the more radical Land campaigners was regretted by many of its members.

Walter C. Smith was critical of the Crofters' Act in 1885, believing that there was little point in giving them fixity of tenure without giving them more land. There were, said Smith, 'almost none of our colonies where the poor crofter would not be better off than in the desolate rocky nooks and inhospitable islands in which he had been in late years shut up'.[61] He called the Bill a 'sin of omission', but said that it was an omission 'of so vital a kind as to render the bill ... altogether useless'.[62] The Free Assembly of 1888 witnessed a veritable deluge of Overtures from lower Church courts on the subject of the 'Highland Land Question', many of which came out in outright sympathy for the Crofters. The Free Presbytery of Caithness, for example, at their meeting at Reay on 1 May 1888, called for

> the adoption of measures for removing the causes of the prevailing distress, and the grievances which apparently have originated the unwonted display of want of respect for the law, with which the said population (the Crofters and Cottars in the Highlands and Islands) are at present accused.[63]

Meanwhile at their meeting of 28 March 1888, the Dingwall Free Presbytery implied that the Highlanders were not to be blamed, since the 'present state of poverty, and the memories of past injustice to which

---

[59] I. M. M. MacPhail, 'Prelude to the Crofters' War, 1870–1880', *Trans. of the Gaelic Soc. of Inverness*, xlix (1974–6), p. 161. The 'Men' were, in John MacInnes's words, 'a definitely recognised, but ecclesiastically unofficial order of evangelical laymen, who won public veneration by their eminence in godliness and supernatural endowments ... The "Men" were thus a brotherhood which constituted the spiritual elite of the Evangelical Highlands': J. MacInnes, 'The origin and early development of "The Men"', *RSCHS*, viii (1944), pp. 16–17. To use a much-quoted adage, they were called the 'Men' not to show that they were not women, but to show that they were not ministers.

[60] *PDGAFCS*, 1884, *Highland Committee Report*, p. 26.

[61] Ibid., 1885, p. 155.

[62] Ibid., p. 154.

[63] 'Overture anent Highland Land Question', from the Free Presbytery of Caithness, *Free Church of Scotland Assembly Papers, No. I*, 1888, p. 174.

that poverty is largely due, have a serious tendency to produce disregard of law and order'.[64] Even the Edinburgh Presbytery added its weight to this point, calling as it did for the restoration of regard for the law by the elimination of 'any grievance' of which the Highlanders saw fit to complain.[65] The Tongue Presbytery went further, launching what was, within the formal conventions of the language of an Overture, a quite sweeping attack on the system which they believed had got the Highlanders into the position which they now occupied:

> Whereas the state of the Highlands is at present very unsettled; whereas this situation arises from the impoverished condition of the people, who, in most cases, were deprived of the lands they formerly occupied, and are now without holdings sufficient for their maintenance in comfort, and this while much of the best land in the country is either lying waste and desolate, or consolidated into large holdings detrimental to the common weal.[66]

Not all Free Churchmen, to be sure, supported the crofters in their struggle. What these Overtures reveal, though, is a depth of feeling within the Free Church in support of the crofters which has been underestimated. Free Church ministers were hardly the most outspoken critics of the landlords, but within the limitations of social pressures and ecclesiastical convention – not to mention a powerful feeling that it was wrong to interfere with a divinely ordained social hierarchy – Free Churchmen were at times willing to comment bluntly on the state of Highland society.

What is important to bear in mind here is the prominence of this controversial issue within the Free Church at the same time as many other Church issues were coming under review. The Free Church was painfully divided over how to respond to the situation; and no churchman, particularly in the Highlands, could have been as sure of the old certainties in the wake of all this change in the external situation and bitter division in the Church. It is wrong to ignore the traumatic social upheavals in the nineteenth-century Highlands when considering the religious conflicts in that region; it was, indeed, a time of transition, with conflict all but inevitable and schism an ever-present prospect.

The Rise of Roman Catholicism

Yet another area where the conservative Free Churchman's world seemed to have been turned upside down was the appearance of an increasing Roman Catholic population in the southern urban areas. And

---

[64] 'Overture anent Highland Land Question', from the Free Presbytery of Dingwall: ibid., p. 176.

[65] 'Overture anent Highland Land Question', from the Free Presbytery of Edinburgh: ibid., p. 176.

[66] 'Overture anent Highland Land Question', from the Free Presbytery of Tongue: ibid., p. 178.

judging by the Free Presbyterians' ongoing fixation with the Roman Catholic Church over their hundred-year history,[67] it is arguable that the changing position of Roman Catholics in Scotland in the decades before 1893 had more of an impact on the Free Presbyterian Church than has been thought. Confronted as they were with so many changes in the world around them, the seemingly irresistible rise of 'Popery' must have seemed to be yet one more reason for standing firmly by their principles and speaking out for what they believed was right. Believing as they did that Protestant liberties were under very genuine threat from 'the real superhuman power which is lodged in the papacy',[68] and that it would require Divine intervention to prevent Scotland from falling into the hands of the Pope within twenty-five years,[69] the rise of the Roman Church in Scotland was obviously a matter of very immediate concern to the Free Presbyterians. While it was not a direct cause of the Second Disruption, the rise of Roman Catholicism in nineteenth-century Scotland was to have a profound and long-term impact in forming the Free Presbyterian psyche, and therefore these developments in Scottish Catholicism are worth examining in some detail.

The nineteenth century had witnessed an unprecedented level of Irish Roman Catholic migration to Britain, as the Industrial Revolution's demands for cheap labour continued to appear insatiable. Interestingly, the earliest Irish migrants to Scotland came into conflict with the Highlanders, who had expected the canal-building process in the south to provide them with much-needed employment.[70] The result was that some Highlanders chose to emigrate rather than face the Irish competition.[71] Irish migration was primarily an urban phenomenon, with Glasgow possessing a particularly magnetic appeal for the Irish. By 1822, there were 15,000 Roman Catholics in Glasgow compared to less than 500 a mere seventeen years earlier. By 1851, they comprised 7.2% of the Scottish population, and a staggering 18.2% of the population of Scotland's largest city, Glasgow.[72] By the time that the Roman Catholic Church restored the territorial hierarchy in Scotland in 1878, the Catholic population of Scotland had risen to around 330,000, with many of them (two out of three) living in the Glasgow archdiocese. Crucially, a great many of them were living in poverty – 40,000 lived in single-

---

67 This almost obsessive interest in the Roman Catholic Church was apparent from the earliest days of the Free Presbyterian Church. Every one of the first 12 editions of the *Free Presbyterian Magazine* contains references to the Roman Catholic Church, ranging from brief comments to elongated articles and including contributions from such anti-Catholic luminaries as Chiniquy and Barnardo.

68 'Cardinal Manning's fanatical zeal', *FPM*, i (5) (1896), p. 196.

69 'Pastor Chiniquy in Edinburgh', *FPM*, i (8) (1896), p. 316.

70 T. Gallagher, *Glasgow: The Uneasy Peace. Religious Tension in Modern Scotland* (Manchester, 1987), p. 11.

71 C. W. J. Withers, *Gaelic in Scotland, 1698–1981* (Edinburgh, 1984), pp. 108–9.

72 Gallagher, *Glasgow: Uneasy Peace*, p. 11; see also Bruce, *No Pope of Rome*, pp. 24–31.

roomed accommodation by 1881[73] – and as early as 1841 the Scottish Catholic community was considered to be sufficiently impoverished to qualify for a subsidy from the Oeuvre de la Propagation de la Foi, an organisation renowned for the careful stewardship of its financial resources.[74] The Catholic community tended to be found in the poorest living conditions, which in turn led to a communal feeling of hostility towards the dominant (Scottish and Protestant) culture which could be expressed in a resort to petty crime and drunkenness – a phenomenon common around the world among alienated immigrant populations.[75]

It has been shown by Anthony Ross that Catholic migration to Scotland in the years before the Famine of the 1840s was a fairly uncontroversial process, with immigrants in Galloway, for example, becoming assimilated easily into Scottish life. The difficulty arose, however, as the sheer scale of the Irish presence increased contemporaneously with the religious upheavals over the Disruption and the Oxford Movement, and the worries over revolution in Europe and increasing political radicalism at home.[76] As Tom Gallagher has pointed out, although conflict frequently did not take long to break out when the Irish Catholic immigrants were perceived to be an economic threat to the established potential work-force, the more serious and long-term source of friction was the religion of the Irish immigrants.

In a land where the influence of Westminster Calvinism was still strong, increasing Roman Catholicism was hardly going to be accepted without a murmur, and Graham Walker has demonstrated in his study of Protestantism in Glasgow that 'prejudicial notions of the Irish Catholics as priest-ridden, feckless, idle and criminally inclined wielded a tenacious grip on the indigenous population's outlook'.[77] As Anthony Ross has described, this preconception was not held only by people who were themselves religious or who were ignorant and uneducated. He argues that the Scottish people in general 'feared and distrusted the expanded Catholic community' and that this even applied 'among those with higher education'.[78] Part of the perceived problem was that the Catholic immigrants were believed to owe their loyalty not to their new state, nor indeed to their old one, but to the Roman Catholic Church. One Irish Presbyterian speaking to the Second Pan-Presbyterian Council, at Philadelphia in 1880, said that 'wherever they settle they bring with them their character and habits, and down deep in their heart

---

[73] B. Aspinwall, 'Popery in Scotland: image and reality, 1820–1920', *RSCHS*, xxii (1986), p. 235.

[74] R. MacDonald, 'The Catholic Gaidhealtachd', *Innes Rev.*, xxix (1978), pp. 62–4.

[75] Ross, 'Development of the Scottish Catholic community', p. 39.

[76] Gallagher, *Glasgow: Uneasy Peace*, pp. 33–4.

[77] G. Walker, '"There's not a team like the Glasgow Rangers": football and religious identity in Scotland', in Walker and Gallagher, *Sermons and Battle Hymns*, pp. 138–9.

[78] Ross, 'Development of the Scottish Catholic community', p. 37.

of hearts, their fealty to Rome'.[79] As E. R. Norman has demonstrated, the image of the Massacre of the Huguenots on St Bartholomew's Day was a familiar one in the Victorian era, adding to the 'numerous other tableaux on similar themes' which 'belonged to a tradition of anti-catholicism whose wide acceptance and long endurance, among all classes in society, secured it an important place in Victorian civilisation'. Norman also noted that even educated observers viewed Catholicism as superstitious, irrational, idolatrous, illiberal and unchanging,[80] while another recent writer has stressed the central place which the Virgin Mary had in the popular perception of Rome as 'alien and idolatrous'.[81] Meanwhile Foxe's *Book of Martyrs* was a very commonplace piece of literature which underwent a 'progressive corruption and vulgarisation'[82] throughout the eighteenth and nineteenth centuries, and which certainly contributed to the widespread anti-Catholic atmosphere. As John Wolffe recently observed, most nineteenth-century editions of Foxe were copiously illustrated with dramatic woodcuts in which the beatific expressions of the martyrs contrast strikingly with the violence and activity around them. The *Book of Martyrs* served to highlight the persecuting nature of Rome, while providing a sense of the spiritual legitimacy of Protestantism, born of heroism, suffering, and holy fervour.[83]

The Jesuit writer Herbert Thurston traced modern anti-Catholicism back to the Prayer Book of Edward VI, which he argued had 'begotten among many excellent people an attitude of hostility and suspicion, the fruitful soil in which no suggestion of papal corruption is too fantastic to take root and propagate itself'.[84]

Scotland in the later part of the nineteenth century, undergoing such great changes in many aspects of its social, cultural and religious life, was a fruitful soil for this kind of anti-Roman Catholicism. The library of the New College in Edinburgh still contains shelves filled with books from this period bearing the official label 'New College Library, Edinburgh,

---

79 Robert Knox, in J. B. Dales and R. M. Patterson (eds.), *Report of Proceedings of the Second General Council of the Presbyterian Alliance Convened at Philadelphia, September 1880* (Philadelphia, 1880), p. 424.
80 E. R. Norman, *Anti-Catholicism in Victorian England* (London, 1968), pp. 13–14. E. W. McFarland has pointed out that the Roman Catholic system was condemned as being unscriptural, and this was said to lead to three specified areas of fault: theological errors, superstition and cruelty: E. W. McFarland, *Protestants First: Orangeism in Nineteenth-Century Scotland* (Edinburgh, 1990), p. 5.
81 J. Singleton, 'The Virgin Mary and religious conflict in Victorian Britain', *Journal of Ecclesiastical History*, xliii (1) (1992), p. 23. As K. E. Skydsgaard has observed, 'There is probably no place where the difference between the two understandings of Christianity becomes so plain as in their differing conceptions of the Virgin Mary': quoted by David Wright in D. F. Wright (ed.), *Chosen By God: Mary in Evangelical Perspective* (London, 1989), p. 1.
82 W. Haller, *Foxe's Book of Martyrs and the Elect Nation* (London, 1963), p. 252.
83 J. Wolffe, *The Protestant Crusade in Great Britain, 1829–1860* (Oxford, 1991), p. 112.
84 H. Thurston, *No Popery: Chapters on Anti-Papal Prejudice* (London, 1930), p. vii.

Department of Romish Controversy', and there is no doubt that conservative Free Churchmen were to the fore in portraying what they perceived as the multifarious perversions of the Roman Church.[85] At a time of social and religious flux, when many previous certainties were becoming vague and open to new interpretations, the Roman Catholic Church – *semper eadem* – presented itself as an unchanging, albeit subtle, enemy beside which right and wrong could be unambiguously demarcated. And although many of the Scottish Presbyterian critics of the Roman faith were undoubtedly well read and well informed, much of what they wrote smacks of blind prejudice.

The *Free Presbyterian Magazine* of August 1896, for example, reported on a speech to the Women's Protestant Union in London by the famous philanthropist, Dr Thomas Barnardo. Barnardo was born in Ireland in 1845 and has been described by one recent biographer as a man who took 'every opportunity to attack Roman Catholicism', and who had a 'deep-rooted fear and mistrust ... towards Roman Catholics, amounting almost to paranoia'.[86] In this speech he drew his audience's attention to some statistics which indicated that in one given group of eight Catholic countries illiteracy was 59.6% in comparison to 4.15% in the given eight Protestant countries. Barnardo concluded with a survey of the situation in Ireland – 'a battlefield of the creeds for centuries' – and summed it up succinctly: 'Prosperity in the Protestant districts, rags and squalor amongst the Papists'.[87]

The Catholic Church was portrayed by conservative churchmen as a bible-burning,[88] 'cunning, powerful, and unscrupulous' enemy, whose 'priests of Antichrist' were 'sworn enemies of Jesus Christ'.[89] 'Imprisonment,

---

85 It should be noted, though, that while there were notable anti-Catholic campaigners, this was by no means the majority of Scottish churchmen. According to E. W. McFarland, the bitterness of inter-denominational rivalries 'left little energy for active "No Popery" in the churches'. She does say, though, that: 'Certainly one should not underestimate the strength of anti-Roman Catholicism which did exist, as expressed notably by James Begg and the Free Church's ultra-conservative wing': McFarland, *Protestants First*, pp. 131, 130. James Begg was notorious for his anti-Roman Catholic views to such an extent that one writer felt that his earlier successes in the field of social reform were eventually ignored: Bishop, 'Church and Society', p. 94, but how far Begg's views were shared by his fellow Free Churchmen is debateable: Bruce, *No Pope of Rome*, pp. 31–6.

86 G. Wagner, *Barnardo* (London, 1979), pp. 3, 216. Barnardo resigned from the National Society for the Prevention of Cruelty to Children because he believed it to be coming under too much Roman Catholic influence and he fought famous and controversial court cases to prevent children being returned to Roman Catholic homes: ibid., pp. 216, 219.

87 'Dr. Barnardo on Romanism', *FPM*, i (4) (1896), pp. 152–3. This is a plain example of what Elaine McFarland has classified as a kind of '"sociology" of religious affiliation', which identified socio-economic benefits as a consequence of Protestantism, with the opposite being the case with Roman Catholicism: McFarland, *Protestants First*, p. 6.

88 'The burning of Bibles', *FPM*, i (8) (1896).

89 J. Begg, *A Handbook of Popery; or, Text Book of Missions for the Conversion of Romanists: being Papal Rome Tested by Scripture, History, and its Recent Workings* (Edinburgh, 1852), pp. 9, 309.

tortures, or death in the most hideous forms' were alleged to take place within convents, of which it was said that 'when the priests have not fenced off the public out of earshot, cries of terror and pain have been repeatedly heard'.[90]

At the same time there was an intense Protestant hostility to the Jesuits, a hostility which had existed from the early days of Ignatius's Society of Jesus, but which seemed to reach a peak in the nineteenth century. A speaker at the National Convention of Protestants, held in Glasgow at the end of 1886, spoke of the

> subtleties, crafts, frauds, political and social intrigues, lyings, forgeries, violences, cold-blooded murders and massacres by which they attained their unhallowed ends. They did not shrink from any deed, even of the most horrible nature.[91]

The *Free Presbyterian Magazine* saw Jesuits hidden within the Church of England, concealing their true faith in order to do their insidious work, and it agreed wholeheartedly with the ex-priest Charles Chiniquy – whose 'large legacy of anti-Catholic hate literature ... is still being published around the world'[92] – who believed that

> the Jesuits, who ruled the Pope and the Church of Rome, were the shrewdest men the world had ever seen ... [and] it was one of the secret teachings of the Church of Rome that it was not a sin for a Roman Catholic to kill a Protestant.[93]

When a proposal was made in 1899 to change the Catholic Emancipation Act by formally removing certain prohibitions which affected the Jesuits, it was described by the Free Presbyterian organ as 'this latest plot against our welfare and liberties'. They addressed their readers in the following terms:

> It is the duty of every reader of this Magazine to pray and vote and contend against any such unpatriotic and suicidal step on the part of our legislators as the formal legalisation of this pestilent and notorious Order.[94]

What all this signifies, of course, is the very real fear that Papacy was going to 'win' the battle for the hearts and minds of the British people, a

---

90 'The suppression of convents: startling incident', *FPM*, i (9) (1897), p. 360. This article, like much of the Free Presbyterians' early anti-Roman material, was a reprint from *The Bulwark*.

91 A. H. Guinness, 'The Jesuits and social morality', in *The Papacy of Modern Times: Report of the National Convention of Protestants held in Glasgow, December, 1886* (Glasgow, 1887), p. 53. Interestingly, Guinness, like so many other Protestant critics of the Society of Jesus, was happy to use Roman Catholic anti-Jesuit material, in this case Pascal's *Provincial Letters*.

92 P. Laverdure, 'Creating an anti-Catholic crusader: Charles Chiniquy', *Journal of Religious History*, xv (1) (1988), p. 94.

93 'Pastor Chiniquy in Edinburgh', p. 316.

94 'The restoration of the Jesuits', *FPM*, iv (3) (1899), p. 120.

belief given greater exigency by the conviction that the Roman Catholic Church was very much more than a merely spiritual organisation.

Underlying the whole issue, in this period of uncertainty and the transformation of so many facets of life, was the firm conviction that the Roman Church posed a temporal, political threat to the British way of life. This was particularly so after Pius IX became Pope, and the Roman Catholic Church seemed to be adopting a more aggressive stance;[95] indeed, as Gerald Parsons has observed, between 1850 and 1851 'public opinion in Britain was much absorbed in an outburst of intense anti-Catholic feeling'.[96] As Elaine McFarland has pointed out, this more belligerent approach of the Papacy from the late 1860s onwards led to the adoption of a conspiracy theory. In her opinion, the view of a Papal Threat 'decisively shifted around mid-century from a millennial to a conspiracy emphasis, in accordance with political and ecclesiastical developments in the United Kingdom and on the Continent'.[97] Scottish Presbyterians – and many other Protestants of almost every hue – were convinced that there existed a Catholic plot to undermine the Protestant nature of the country. This view was still commonplace in the twentieth century, when it gave birth among Scottish Presbyterians to what S. J. Brown has called a sixteen-year 'campaign against the Scoto-Irish community in Scotland'.[98] In 1899, the *Free Presbyterian Magazine* said this of Franciscan monks: 'It must not be forgotten that these devotees of St Francis are in reality the sworn agents of a foreign power whose purposes of revenge against Britain have not slept for three centuries.'[99] As early as 1848, the venerated Free Church father, Robert Smith Candlish, described the advance of Romanism as 'the enemy coming in like a flood' and spoke at a public meeting against the establishment of diplomatic relations with the See of Rome in 1848.[100] And William Kidston, a Free Church elder speaking at the General Assembly in 1879, said that 'Popery is still at this moment the same, or rather worse, than she was during the deepest darkness of the Middle Ages ... both as a

95 According to E. E. Y. Hales, 'as Pope he forced himself upon the attention of Englishmen in his day by his "Papal Aggression" in restoring the Catholic Hierarchy to England, by issuing the Syllabus of Errors, by defining Papal Infallibility, by enraging both Gladstone and Exeter Hall, by reigning longer than any Pope had ever reigned, by recruiting an international army, by losing the most ancient sovereignty of Europe – the Papal State ... In an important sense Pio Nono was the central figure of the mid nineteenth century.' Hales concluded that, 'he earned for the Papacy much hatred in his own day. But ... he was, in short, the creator of the Modern Papacy': E. E. Y. Hales, *Pio Nono: A Study in European Politics and Religion in the Nineteenth Century* (London, 1954), pp. ix, xiii.

96 G. Parsons, 'Victorian Roman Catholicism: emancipation, expansion and achievement', in G. Parsons (ed.), *Religion in Victorian Britain*: vol. I (Manchester, 1988), p. 147.

97 McFarland, *Protestants First*, p. 8.

98 S. J. Brown, '"Outside the Covenant": the Scottish Presbyterian Churches and Irish immigration, 1922–1938', *Innes Rev.*, xlii (1) (1991), p. 20.

99 'The franchise in bad hands', *FPM*, iv (6) (1899), pp. 237–8.

100 W. Wilson and R. Rainy, *Memorials of Robert Smith Candlish, D.D.* (Edinburgh, 1880), p. 353.

religious and a political system.'[101] He concluded by linking the sacred and the secular: 'this supremacy will be at the expense of much in Britain ... First, scriptural truth; and second, what your forefathers died for, the inestimable blessings of civil and religious liberty.'[102]

James Begg, perhaps not surprisingly, felt much the same way when he wrote one of his anti-Roman works nearly three decades earlier, suggesting that it was a desire of the Roman Catholic Church that 'she should reconquer Britain, and thus overthrow the last and the strongest fortress of liberty and divine truth in the world'.[103] Charles Salmond, a Free Church minister who had studied at the University and the New College of Edinburgh, and also at Princeton, and who was the author of a prize-winning essay on 'Vaticanism',[104] felt that one of the most critical elements of the Roman Church was the fact that it was 'not merely a religion, but a political system'.[105] Two years later, the Free Presbytery of Edinburgh called for thorough instruction on the dangers of Romanism for all candidates for the ministry in order that they might educate their unsuspecting flock;[106] while in 1888, they were critical of the expected resumption of diplomatic relations with the Roman Catholic Church on the grounds that it 'would endanger the spiritual liberties of this country, and would ignore the whole teaching of history as to the malign influence of Romanist priestcraft on the prosperity of nations'.[107] Clearly, Scottish Presbyterians felt threatened by the Roman Catholic Church as an institution throughout the century, and increasingly so as the century wore on.

While Anti-Romanism had long been a powerful, if at times apparently unnecessary,[108] force in Scotland, in the nineteenth century the old fears of Romanism and 'Priestcraft' became more real to people as the numbers of Catholics increased. The anti-Catholic agitators tended to be concentrated in those towns where the economic rivalry had been most intense, for example in lower Clyde towns like Port Glasgow and Greenock.[109] And it was in the mid-nineteenth century that, in Gallagher's words, 'mainstream Scottish protestants took their own initiative in the crusade against religious error', with the formation of such groups as the Scottish Reformation Society (1850) and the Scottish

---

101 Kidston, in *PDGAFCS*, 1879, p. 233.

102 Ibid., p. 234.

103 Begg, *Handbook of Popery*, p. 299.

104 Ewing, *Annals of the Free Church of Scotland*, i, p. 309.

105 C. A. Salmond, 'Romish ascendancy versus British ascendancy', in *The Papacy of Modern Times: Report of the National Convention of Protestants held in Glasgow, December 1886* (Glasgow, 1887), p. 17.

106 'Overture anent dangers of Romanism', from the Free Presbytery of Edinburgh, *Free Church of Scotland Assembly Papers*, No. I, 1887, pp. 215–16.

107 'Overture anent diplomatic relations with the Vatican, etc.', from the Free Presbytery of Edinburgh: ibid., 1888, p. 182.

108 Gallagher refers to 'one nineteenth-century historian who claimed that in the 1790s, when Glasgow had no more than thirty-nine catholics, there were forty-three anti-catholic societies': Gallagher, *Glasgow: Uneasy Peace*, p. 9.

109 Ibid., p. 20.

Protestant Society (1854), and when men like James Begg began to be actively involved in the organised battle with Roman Catholicism.[110] Economic rivalry, of course, paled into insignificance for these men when they considered the great battle for hearts and minds which was perceived to commence in earnest about the time of the conversion of John Henry Newman to Rome in 1845.

Newman's defection to Rome, followed by a greatly overestimated number of other converts each year,[111] filled the minds of some Scottish Calvinists with horror.[112] Conversion did not only affect the Church of England, of course, and one of the more influential Scottish converts to Rome in the nineteenth century was James Burns, the brother of the China missionary William Burns and the Free Church Professor Islay Burns, who was converted to Roman Catholicism through the influence of the Oxford Movement, and who set up the Roman Catholic publishing house of Burns and Oates.[113] But the presence of men like Alexander Whyte, a deep and lifelong admirer of John Henry Newman, in positions of great influence in the Free Church of Scotland clearly reveals that there were two strains of response.[114] Some could go with

---

110 Ibid., p. 21.

111 This over-estimate went as high as 10,000 and has recently been repeated: A. C. Rhodes, *The Power of Rome in the Twentieth Century, the Vatican in the Age of Liberal Democracies* (London, 1983), p. 165. It seems certain, however, that conversion was much less significant in terms of numbers than that. Recent scholarship indicates that, 'as a source of growth conversion was of little significance in comparison with immigration from Catholic countries and the natural increase in England of Catholic immigrant communities': A. D. Gilbert, *Religion and Society in Industrial England: Church, Chapel and Social Change, 1740–1914* (London and New York, 1976), p. 45. And Owen Chadwick talks of only 'a small number of converts from other churches who knew themselves disapproved as converts by the main body of society': O. Chadwick, *The Victorian Church*, pt. 2 (2nd edn, London, 1972), p. 403. As Tom Gallagher points out, it should be borne in mind that Scotland was even less affected by conversion than was England; fear, however, does not need facts to be very real and the concentration of publicised conversion among the upper classes made such fears greater. One 1884 publication, e.g., listed no less than 13 two-columned pages of converts to the Roman Catholic faith from among 'the nobility and gentry': W. Gordon-Gorman, *Converts to Rome: A List of over Three Thousand Protestants who have become Catholics since the Commencement of the Nineteenth Century* (London, 1884), pp. 5–17.

112 Even American Protestants viewed these developments with something approaching bewilderment: in 1885 the *Presbyterian Review* commented that 'the remarkable swerve of Anglican Protestantism towards religious beliefs which it dismissed as superstitious in the sixteenth century, is one of the great intellectual paradoxes of our day': T. Croskery, 'Conversions to Romanism', *Presbyterian Rev.*, vi (22) (1885), p. 201.

113 J. J. Delaney and J. E. Tobin (eds.), *Dictionary of Catholic Biography* (London, 1962), pp. 187–8; R. S. Miller, 'Greatheart of China: a brief life of William Chalmers Burns, M.A.', in S. M. Houghton (ed.), *Five Pioneer Missionaries* (London, 1965); Croskery, 'Conversions to Romanism', p. 213; Aspinwall, 'Popery in Scotland', p. 250, note. Aspinwall incorrectly repeats that this man was W. C. Burns.

114 Whyte's great esteem for the Anglo-Catholic leader is well documented, and is perhaps best symbolised by his having not one but two portraits of Newman hanging in his study. Interestingly, another Free Churchman who admired Newman was Dr Horatius Bonar, who spoke of 'that nobility of spirit' and 'the singular fairness which he manifests towards his opponents': H. Bonar, *The Old Gospel: Not 'Another Gospel' but the Power of God Unto Salvation. A Reply to Dr. Kennedy's Pamphlet, 'Hyper-Evangelism'*

the ecumenical flow while others were kicking against the pricks. Either way, the Catholicisation of Britain – whether by immigration or, less significantly, by conversion – was not something which could lightly be ignored, and arguably it was one of the most profound changes with which Scottish ecclesiastical figures had to wrestle in the nineteenth century. With the more conservative it was an ever-present worry in their minds, and one which added to the background of doubt and fear with which they confronted those who sought to react to the changing world by changing the Church.

The Decline of Sabbatarianism

Another of the changes in nineteenth-century Scotland which required a rethinking of traditional Calvinist stances, and which has continued to be of ongoing interest to the Free Presbyterian Church, was the decline from its previously venerated position of 'the Sabbath Day'. John Wigley and others have suggested that Sabbatarianism was an import from England in the years after the death of John Knox in 1572,[115] and, as Willy Rordorf has observed, 'the seven-day week as we know it today has a complicated history behind it'.[116] Whenever it first arrived, however, there is no doubt that it was, by the end of the eighteenth century, in a position of some strength, reinforced by the pronouncements of the Westminster Confession of Faith on the subject.

Sabbatarianism was almost a badge of the Scottish Calvinist; as T. C. Smout expressed it:

> To natives and foreigners alike, the Scottish Victorian sabbath was the outward and visible sign of the Church's inward and spiritual sway. A universal stillness fell over Glasgow and Edinburgh (except in the unredeemed slums) at the time of the divine service, and pervaded small towns and villages from dawn to dusk ... On Sundays the churches held the country in thrall for Christ.[117]

William Ross's childhood duties had included being one of the 'Levites' in his own home, preparing their large living-room for the Sabbath

(Edinburgh, 1874), p. 24. This is in stark contrast to, e.g., Donald Macfarlane of the Free Presbyterian Church, who described Newman and his great friend Pusey as 'notorious hypocrites' and 'these treacherous men': D. Beaton, *Memoir, Diary and Remains of the Rev. Donald Macfarlane, Dingwall* (Inverness, 1929), pp. 42–3.

115 J. Wigley, *The Rise and Fall of the Victorian Sunday* (Manchester, 1980), p. 200.

116 W. Rordorf, *Sunday: The History of the Day of Rest in the Earliest Centuries of the Christian Church* (London, 1962), p. 9. For the origins of English Sabbatarianism, see K. L. Parker, *The English Sabbath: A Study of Doctrine and Discipline from the Reformation to the Civil War* (Cambridge, 1988). See also R. J. Bauckham, 'Sabbath and Sunday in the Protestant Tradition', in D. A. Carson (ed.), *From Sabbath to Lord's Day: A Biblical, Historical, and Theological Investigation* (Grand Rapids, MI, 1982).

117 Smout, *Century of the Scottish People*, pp. 182–3.

services held there,[118] while the young Neil Cameron took his Sabbatarianism so seriously that he spent a whole week during which his
'thoughts were swallowed with awful forebodings as to the coming
Sabbath' on account of the possibility that he might have to spend some
of it looking after a flock of lambs, believing as he did that 'a great deal
of what men call works of necessity and mercy are nothing of the
kind'.[119] The prominent early Free Presbyterian layman, John Hamilton
of Oban, was said to have 'shuddered at the sight' of a group of people
going for a drive on the Sabbath and

> another form of this deplorable sin which caused him much pain and
> grief, was that he saw some of the poor people putting clothes out to
> dry on the Sabbath day, and, should rain come, taking them in again.[120]

The very conservative view of the Sabbath held by Cameron and the
others who formed the Free Presbyterian Church did not change with
the changing times. These conservatives were, however, painfully aware
of the changes taking place all around them and repeatedly voiced their
bitter disagreement.

Their position was made very clear in the first issue of the *Free
Presbyterian Magazine*, in May 1896, when it was stated:

> We, as a nation, are clearly involved in the sin of sanctioned
> Sabbath-breaking. This should be a matter of serious consideration
> to all who love the Lord's day, the faithful observance of which
> secures a nation's prosperity, and a nation's enjoyment of the
> blessing of God. We regret the almost universal use of the word
> Sunday, which is of heathen origin. The Sabbath is a name that
> fully expresses the character of the day, and has the supreme
> sanction of the Lord of the Sabbath.[121]

To the mainly Free Church editors of the conservative journal *The
Signal*, the problem could be seen as one which started at the very top of
the legislative ladder, stating as they did in October 1883 that:

> It is deplorable to find our statesmen openly violating the Sabbath
> and carrying on their ordinary business for two or three hours on
> the Sabbath morning. A general and determined protest should be
> made to this daring opposition, both to divine and human law.[122]

This in turn was exacerbated by the conservative belief that Sabbath-
breaking was something which was, in the opinion of the Free
Presbytery of Sutherland and Caithness, 'in every form ... pre-eminently

118 Ross, *William Ross of Cowcaddens*, p. 8.
119 D. Beaton, *Memoir, Biographical Sketches, Letters, Lectures and Sermons (English and
    Gaelic) of the Revd Neil Cameron, Glasgow* (Inverness, 1932), pp. 23–4.
120 N. Cameron, 'The late Mr. John Hamilton, Oban', *FPM*, ii (10) (1898), p. 385.
121 'The opening of museums on Sabbath sanctioned by Parliament', *FPM*, i (1) (1896), p. 36.
122 'Parliamentary Sabbath breaking', *The Signal* (Oct. 1883), p. 168.

ruinous to the social and Christian well-being of individuals and communities'.[123] It was also, they believed, a sin which deserved, and indeed received, divine displeasure. The *Free Presbyterian Magazine* of August 1899 described an event which had taken place earlier that year in Rothesay, on the Island of Bute, which they took to be divine retribution for this sin. A boat had keeled over and sunk in Rothesay bay, with the loss of three lives:

> they were launched into eternity in the very act of desecrating the Lord's day ... The hand of God was stretched out, and three souls, red with the guilt of breaking the holy sabbath, were precipitated in a moment into what, to all appearance, was 'a lost eternity' ... The Lord will vindicate His law, which is holy, just, and good. He will do so by temporal and eternal judgements.[124]

The distance which Scotland had travelled away from the 'traditional Sabbath' (meaning exclusive and elongated religious activity) was brought home to Free Presbyterians and others alike at a meeting in 1896 in Glasgow, when it was revealed that

> there had been a great increase of tram cars and omnibuses on the Sabbath day. It was to be feared that the feeble and faltering utterances of many within the Church on this subject were due to the fact that so many in their congregations made use of them ... The number of shops open in the city on Sundays was 2,861 ... [and] the ice-cream shop was a great temptation to Sabbath School children, not only to keep them from the School but to spend the mission box pennies there, and thus demoralise the children.[125]

In 1886 the Sabbath Observance Committee of the Free Presbytery of Dundee made the following observation:

> the opening of shops for the sale of confections and grocery goods in all parts of the town is on the increase ... [and] during the summer months multitudes of our townspeople go to the country districts around, either on foot or by conveyances, and spend the sacred day in worldly recreation and amusement.[126]

There was no doubt in their minds what all this meant for the future well-being of Scotland and, for some at least, the price of lost employment was worth paying in an effort to fight for their interpretation of Scriptural teaching on the Sabbath.[127] Ten men from Ross-shire

123 'Overture anent Sabbath desecration', from the Free Presbytery of Sutherland and Caithness, *Free Church of Scotland Assembly Papers, No. I*, 1888, p. 217.
124 'A loud voice', *FPM*, iv (4) (1899), p. 159.
125 'Glasgow Sabbath Protection Association', *FPM*, i (7) (1896), p. 275.
126 'Report of Committee on Sabbath Observance', *PDGAFCS*, 1886, App. XXI, p. 10.
127 John Urquart of Greenock, who founded the Free Presbyterian congregation there, was dismissed by the MacBrayne's shipping company for his refusal to work on what

went further, being jailed for their protests against the Sunday run of a
train from Strome Ferry, and, as one letter to *The Scotsman* expressed it,

> if the crofters would be praised and rewarded for interfering to
> prevent the violation of the Sixth and Eighth Commandments, why
> should they be condemned and punished for interfering to prevent
> the breach of the Fourth Commandment, which is the law of the
> land, as well as the law of God?[128]

While some of the more well-known Sabbatarian figures in the South
may have been reluctant to go as far as law-breaking (*The Signal* referred
to the men's 'noble zeal – it may be said unwise zeal – on behalf of the
rest of the Lord's Day'), the ten's actions won wide approval, and when
an appeal was made to raise £500 on their behalf, the person to whom
the donations were to be sent was none other than the eminent Free
Church conservative leader, James Begg.[129] The great fear of the Free
Presbyterians and other like-minded Sabbatarians at this time of great
changes in the population's Sunday-habits was that the day was coming
when

> the sound of the church bell would be drowned by the echo of the
> hammer, the tramway, the omnibus and the cart; when the Bible
> would be supplanted by the newspaper and the magazine; when the
> votaries of pleasure would outnumber worshippers, and salutary
> thoughts of God, of eternity, and of the soul, would be checked by
> the cares of business, and by the pleasures and dissipations of the
> world.[130]

As the conservative voice of *The Signal* expressed it: 'A serious struggle is
evidently before us to maintain the rest of the holy Sabbath, and all
earnest men and ministers should engage in it at once.'[131]

The conservatives had little doubt as to the main source of the
'advancing tide of Sabbath desecration', laying the blame firmly at the
feet of the liberals within the Church:

> one cause of it is to be found in the growth of Rationalism which
> has taken place, to a very large extent, in the Established Church of
> Scotland, and of which there has been at least a too manifest
> beginning in the Free Church also ... with the consequent preaching of
> false doctrine by many ministers, and the withholding by many
> more of the precious doctrines of the Gospel, or the miserably
> imperfect exhibition of them ... Sabbath Desecration is a natural

---

he saw as the Lord's Day: 'The late Mr. John Urquart, Elder, Greenock', *FPM*, xxxix
(6) (1934), p. 263.

[128] Quoted in 'The Strome Ferry Case', *The Signal* (Oct. 1883), p. 162.

[129] 'The Strome Ferry prisoners', *The Signal* (Sep. 1883), p. 148.

[130] 'Glasgow Sabbath Protection Association', p. 276.

[131] 'Sabbath-breaking in Forfar', *The Signal* (Oct. 1883), p. 168.

fruit of this new religion, and is sure to prevail wherever it is embraced.[132]

The conservatives noted with considerable displeasure the decline of Sabbatarianism not only among 'the manifestly irreligious', but also among those 'whom it would be very uncharitable to include under that designation'.[133] For evidence of this they did not have to look beyond their own denomination, as the *Edinburgh Evening Dispatch* of Monday 4 June 1888 reported that a number of the members of the Free Church General Assembly had left Edinburgh by train on the previous Sunday. *The Signal* hoped that this was a case of the paper getting it wrong, but was not confident,

> seeing that there were in the Free Church General Assembly members who ... showed contempt for the Church's Confession of Faith, – one of them speaking at the same time most irreverently of the Holy Scriptures of the Old Testament, – we cannot dismiss this story of Sabbath profanation as absolutely incredible. It would not be more strange than what has taken place already, if, when the Report of the Sabbath Observance Committee brings the subject of the Sabbath before next year's General Assembly, the opinion should be avowed that the Sabbath was a mere Jewish institution with which we have nothing to do.[134]

Thus what John Wigley called the 'fall of the Victorian Sunday' is an extremely interesting phenomenon as, in some ways, it both provoked and reflected change. The more it was seen to be a moveable feast which could be interpreted as you pleased, the more the influence of the Calvinist Sabbath waned among those to whom its strictures were a painful chore. At the same time, it can be seen as just one more aspect of the general pressure that was being placed on traditional forms of organised religion, and to which the conservative lobby in the Free Church of Scotland felt they had to respond. The 'fall of the Victorian Sunday' was therefore accompanied by a widening of the gap between conservative and liberal, as it provided another stick with which each side could beat the other.

* * *

It can be seen then, that the nineteenth century was a time of great socio-economic and cultural change which churchmen could not avoid. Even the most conservative of Free Churchmen could hardly pretend that the changing world could be taken lightly – the century went on its way and you ignored it at your peril. Issues such as the growth of

---

132 'Sabbath desecration', *The Signal* (Sep. 1887), p. 258.
133 Ibid.
134 'Members of the Free Church Assembly alleged to have travelled on Sabbath', *The Signal* (Jul. 1888), p. 215.

Catholicism in Scotland, the paganised nature of the urban ghettos, the destruction of many of the old practices associated with the Sabbath, the ferment in the Highlands over landlords and Land Laws, and the great changes in population patterns in both Highland and Lowland Scotland, were all aspects of the nineteenth century which, although notionally unrelated to ecclesiastical affairs, came to have a considerable effect on churchmen. This effect could have come from a direct and deliberate response to those changes; or, on the other hand, it could have been a reaction by churchmen to someone else's response.

While none of these factors alone produced the Second Disruption, they were all in varying ways changing the world in which the men who were to form the Free Presbyterian Church lived and worked. Some, such as the rising power of the Roman Catholic Church and the decline of the traditional Scottish Sabbath, were to continue to engross the denomination that these men founded throughout its history. And arguably this wider background did much to give the pioneers of Free Presbyterianism their crusading zeal, their firm conviction of holding the moral and spiritual high ground, and, at times, their laager mentality. In many ways their self-perception as a small group of righteous men facing an alien and hostile world is a direct – if not inevitable – product of the times which moulded them.

In the years between 1860 and 1893, the Free Church of Scotland was becoming a divided communion. The very abundance of viewpoints is a clear indication that the Free Church was hardly free of conflict and dispute – something which will be explored at length in the next two chapters. Yet, on examining the world in which that Church's lot was cast, there seems to be a certain degree of inevitability about the appearance of disagreement. William Ross Taylor, the Free Church moderator in the historic year of 1900, reflected on the past century thus:

> men's ideas on many subjects have undergone a complete revolu-
> tion. We look at the world with new eyes. Theories and conclusions
> which science propounded in former days are being swept aside,
> for the new facts require wider conceptions ... Through national
> education and an informing newspaper press, the discoveries of the
> few become forthwith the possession of all; and everywhere the
> feeling of advance, of growing insight, of increasing mastery,
> pervades men's minds.[135]

The Free Presbyterians also noted that the world was changing, but this was something on which they cast a more jaundiced eye:

> We live in times of change. There are changes constantly taking
> place in almost every sphere of life. Some of them are for the

---

[135] Taylor, Moderator's Address, *PDGAFCS*, 1900, p. 3.

better; many of them are for the worse. But the Gospel changes not
... Intellect may substitute a new Gospel for the old, but the old
continues the same, and is ever new. A spurious gospel may
introduce a seeming paradise into the souls of men, but it is the
paradise of the opium-eater, that exists in his imagination for a
brief moment, and then departs him for ever, leaving a hell of
misery behind it.[136]

These contrasting responses to the reality of change speak volumes
about the Free Church in this era.

[136] 'The Gospel changes not', *FPM*, iv (4) (1899), p. 121.

CHAPTER TWO

The Free Church Response to Biblical Criticism and Darwinian Science

There is very little dispute that the second half of the nineteenth century placed great pressures on traditional Christian belief. As Alec Vidler expressed it: 'Beneath the surface of respectable religious conformity was a turmoil of doubt and uncertainty',[1] and it seems fair to say that this 'turmoil' affected virtually every denomination. The industrial revolution and its myriad side-effects, the increasing influence of biblical criticism, and the elevation to the status of scientific *sine qua non* of Darwinian evolution – all caused difficulty for conventional religious thinking. In many ways these revolutionary changes posed the same problems for the Roman Catholic Church, the Church of England, the Congregationalists, and the Established and Seceding Churches in Scotland as they did for the Free Church.

The Free Church had in its short history been racked by many disputes and divides of varying intensity, and if the epoch-making developments of the later nineteenth century were going to provoke conflict in any denomination, the Free Church was ripe for it. The developments detailed in the previous chapter had a fundamental effect on the modern world in general, and certainly on the shape of religious belief.

Some of these developments, though, produced conflict and debate without ever becoming fundamental areas of dispute. Alexander Whyte and James Begg for example, would never have agreed on their inter-pretation of the Roman Catholic Church and on how to react to that Church's phenomenal growth in the nineteenth century. That dispute illustrates the divide in the Free Church, but was not in itself a cause of it. Similarly, the editors of *The Signal* would never tire of bemoaning such issues as the decline of traditional Sabbatarianism among Free Church clergy, but each side seemed to be content to accept that there were more serious issues which divided them. Arguably, had these other major issues not existed, then the divisions over what a man thought of John Henry Newman, or whether a man could use a Sunday train to return home from the General Assembly, could have swelled, as it were, to fill the available space in the Free Church's energies. The conservatives in the Free Church undoubtedly felt strongly about a whole host of

---

[1] A. R. Vidler, *The Church in an Age of Revolution* (London, 1961), p. 112.

issues and, had they had the energy, would gladly have argued all these issues to a conclusion. However, much as they hated the Declaratory Act and similar attempts to reduce their belief to a definition of what were 'the fundamentals of the faith', the basic constraints of limited time and energy meant that they had themselves to admit a *de facto* division into what was 'fundamental' and what was not. Chapter 3 will deal with a vital divide in the Free Church which had little to do with theology – that between the Highland and Lowland portions of the Church – while Chapter 4 will concentrate on the issue which was the ultimate trigger for the Second Disruption of 1893: the process of modifying the Westminster Confession of Faith which culminated in the Declaratory Act of 1892. This chapter, though, will examine the divisions which emerged as the Church reacted to two of the most important areas of change in nineteenth-century Britain – biblical criticism and evolutionary science – and will commence with a broad survey of these changes.[2]

Academic and Intellectual Developments

In an age of change and development, almost every accepted religious theory was being tested in what Marcus Dods described as the 'crucible' of criticism. Men were being confronted with what the biographer of A. B. Davidson called 'the riddles to which the spirit of a new age was demanding a solution from every thinking man'.[3] In the memorable words of one Free Church moderator as he looked back over the developments of the nineteenth century:

> There has been no lack of scrutiny. Every question connected with the Faith has been placed under the microscope; everything sacred, whether book or doctrine, has been called on to show its credentials. Science, philosophy, criticism, history, have each been led forward to take part in the testing process.[4]

In the minds of conservative churchmen in general and of the Free Presbyterian founders in particular, the two great intellectual movements which did most to cast doubt on the veracity of 'the Old Paths' during the nineteenth century were biblical criticism and modern science. Side by side, sceptics and believers alike added fuel to the fire that the conservatives saw as burning up the 'faith once delivered to the Saints'. These seekers for truth had a wide variety of motives for the work that they did, but the conservatives could see but one – in the

[2] J. T. McNeil, Professor of Church History at Knox College, Toronto, Canada, wrote in 1925, 'The two profound thought influences of the nineteenth century can be suggested by two words: Criticism and Evolution': J. T. McNeil, *The Presbyterian Church in Canada, 1875–1925* (Toronto, 1925), p. 203.

[3] J. Strahan, *Andrew Bruce Davidson* (London, 1917), p. 102; Dods, *Recent Progress in Theology*, pp. 9–11.

[4] W. R. Taylor, Moderator's Address, *PDGAFCS*, 1900, 3.

words of Andrew Bonar: 'to wile ministers and people away from the great and glorious Gospel'.[5] This section will examine first the rise of biblical criticism, and then move on to look at the development of the various theories of the origins of the earth and of the human race. It will become evident in the following chapter that the Free Church did not make a unified response to these developments, and indeed the different responses produced a lasting bitterness which ultimately contributed to the fragmentation of the Free Church.

1. The triumph of biblical criticism – a brief summary

Biblical criticism had been in existence for many years before the nineteenth century made it a topic of everyday conversation. George Adam Smith (who would later be the subject of a Free Church heresy trial towards the end of the century for his advocacy of the critical method) argued in a lecture at Yale University that biblical criticism went back to the life of Christ: 'while we look to Christ as the chief authority for our Old Testament, we must never forget that He was also its first Critic'.[6] He did, however, acknowledge that modern criticism was of more recent vintage:

> The modern criticism of the Old Testament may be said to have begun in 1680. In that year a French priest called Simon drew attention to the fact that in the Book of Genesis the same event is often described in different words.[7]

A recent historian of British Old Testament criticism, Nigel Cameron, also mentions the early role of Simon, as well as Astruc in the 1750s and Geddes in the 1790s. For Cameron, however, the crucial figure was Spinoza, who in many ways foreshadowed the arguments of the eighteenth and nineteenth centuries.[8] Vital preparatory work was done in the eighteenth century, much of it the so-called Lower Criticism, but it was in the nineteenth century that the battle was joined with the greatest vigour and, arguably, with the greatest long-term results. As Cameron points out:

> The replacement of critical history for the doctrine of plenary inspiration as the fundamental principle governing the interpretation of Scripture was no less catastrophic in its implications for Christian thought than that of helio- or geo-centricity for the study of the heavens. It was not merely that certain data required reinterpretation;

---

[5] Quoted in G. N. M. Collins, *'Whose Faith Follow'* (Edinburgh, 1943), p. 59.

[6] G. A. Smith, *Modern Criticism and the Preaching of the Old Testament: Eight Lectures on the Lyman Beecher Foundation, Yale University, U.S.A.* (London, 1901), p. 11.

[7] Ibid., p. 33.

[8] N. M. de S. Cameron, *Biblical Higher Criticism and the Defence of Infallibilism in Nineteenth-Century Britain* (Lewiston, NY, 1987), p. 16.

the whole theoretical framework by which data were understood
had been overturned.[9]

The Free Church apologist, G. N. M. Collins, has called the Higher
Criticism 'a typical product of the times',[10] and in the opinion of John
Macleod, who sat through the Free Church heresy trials of Marcus Dods
and A. B. Bruce and who was to leave the Free Church at the Second
Disruption in 1893, 'the spirit of a new age was abroad'.[11] At the beginning
of the century, there were few churchmen in Britain who strayed far
from the accepted pale that the whole Bible was the inspired, inerrant
and infallible Word of God. The closing decades of the nineteenth
century, however, saw the start of what Barbara MacHaffie has called 'a
movement of considerable magnitude ... which aimed at popularizing
the methods and results of the higher criticism of the Old Testament'.[12]
By 1898 D. K. Paton would be speaking of seeing 'the Bread of Life, the
Word of God, systematically poisoned or adulterated' by what he called
'The Higher Criticism: the Greatest Apostasy of the Age', and he would be
hoping that 'the numbers will greatly multiply who join in this increasingly
serious "holy war" against the enemies of the Word of God'.[13]

At the commencement of the nineteenth century, there was very little
awareness in Britain of continental, especially German, biblical scholarship.
This was partly due to a suspicion of all things German, to the extent
that his biographer quotes Edward Bouverie Pusey as saying that in 1825
'only two persons in Oxford were said to know German, although German
introductions to the New Testament, if written in Latin, were read',[14] and
Cameron refers to what he terms an 'antipathy towards German thought
as a whole'.[15] As Gerald Parsons has argued, what was rare was not so
much awareness of German scholarship as sympathy for its more advanced
methods and conclusions.[16] Over the course of the century, this was to
change until the situation was all but reversed. By the closing years of the
nineteenth century, a more-or-less intimate knowledge of and admiration
for what Marcus Dods called 'the reputation of Germany for thorough
investigation and scientific work'[17] had become all but compulsory in the
Divinity halls of this country. It was a gradual and complex process, but to

9 Ibid., p. 4.
10 Collins, *'Whose Faith Follow'*, p. 59.
11 J. Macleod, *Scottish Theology in Relation to Church History Since the Reformation* (Edinburgh, 1943), p. 308.
12 B. Z. MacHaffie, '"Monument Facts and Higher Critical Fancies": archaeology and the popularization of Old Testament criticism in nineteenth-century Britain', *Church History*, 1 (3) (1981), p. 316.
13 D. K. Paton, *The Higher Criticism: The Greatest Apostasy of the Age, with Notable Examples and Criticisms of Several Scottish Theological Professors* (2nd edn, London, 1898), p. vi.
14 H. P. Liddon, *The Life of Edward Bouverie Pusey* (London, 1893), i, p. 72.
15 Cameron, *Biblical Higher Criticism*, p. 29.
16 G. Parsons, 'Biblical criticism in Victorian Britain: from controversy to acceptance?' in G. Parsons (ed.), *Religion in Victorian Britain* (Manchester and New York, 1988), ii, 241.
17 Dods, *Recent Progress in Theology*, p. 25.

a man like John Macleod, who watched it happen from within the Free
Church in the nineteenth century, it was essentially a fairly clear-cut one:

> [Scotland] had become, with the improved means of communication
> in the 19th century, much less isolated and self-contained than it was
> before. So the teaching of the German theological schools began to
> tell upon its younger ministry. Without well knowing at first what
> they were doing they borrowed to begin with from the Liberal Evan-
> gelicals and then from the Rationalistic schools of Germany the kind
> of theological ideas which found favour with them. These being on
> the whole so far Lutheran as distinct from Calvinistic, and unbelieving
> as distinct from Christian, were at war with the underlying principles
> on which the Orthodox Faith of the Reformed Churches builds.[18]

Macleod is doubtless not the least prejudiced commentator on these
affairs, having watched the 'recent progress in theology' with a less than
enthusiastic eye in the 1890s, but the influence of Germany upon biblical
criticism in Scotland is beyond dispute.[19]

German biblical criticism had virtually won all its battles by the time
that the battle was starting in earnest in Britain, and by the 1870s and
1880s many of the brightest and best theology students were travelling
to study in Germany. One of them was the brilliant young Free
Churchman, William Robertson Smith. The Free Church at this time
retained a reputation for being extremely orthodox; the Church into
which Robertson Smith dropped his critical bombshells was described by
a contemporary observer in these terms:

> other Churches had their Broad Schools, but in it there was hardly
> one man who had shown a disposition to leave the old paths; and
> although here and there there were scholars who knew that a storm
> was coming, they had not tried to disturb the prevailing peace.[20]

The Free Church was entirely unprepared for the kind of approach
advocated by Smith, and it was partly the shock of hearing the critical
method advocated by a Free Church professor which contributed to the
resultant conflict. Smith's widely publicised ecclesiastical prosecution[21]
did much to establish the place of higher critics in the public eye, both in

[18] Macleod, *Scottish Theology*, p. 309.
[19] It should be noted that Germany quite simply produced more biblical scholarship
than anywhere else. This was partly because of the much greater number of Protestant
theological institutions, and the resultant 'far greater amount of theological activity in
Germany as compared with Britain': Rogerson, *Bible and Criticism*, p. 69.
[20] N. L. Walker, *Chapters from the History of the Free Church of Scotland* (Edinburgh, 1895),
p. 272.
[21] The Smith controversy has been much discussed in recent years, but for the most
interesting near contemporary accounts, see J. S. Black and G. W. Chrystal, *The Life of
William Robertson Smith* (London, 1912); and Simpson, *Life of Principal Rainy*. See also
J. H. Brown, 'The Contribution of William Robertson Smith to Old Testament Scholarship, with Special Emphasis on Higher Criticism' (Duke University, Ph.D thesis, 1964).

Scotland and abroad. Both Charles A. Briggs and H. P. Smith, scholars tried for heresy over their Higher Critical views by the American Presbyterian Church,[22] corresponded with Smith, believing that 'his struggle ... [was] foreshadowing their own troubles',[23] and it has also been said that the debate within the Free Church over Smith was 'followed with eager interest through a large part of Protestant Christendom'.[24]

In Scotland the growth of biblical criticism was principally the result of the labours of two men, Andrew Bruce Davidson and William Robertson Smith, who were devout, gifted professors of the Free Church. Davidson was the assistant of and eventual successor to Professor John 'Rabbi' Duncan, the first Professor of Hebrew and Old Testament at the Free Church's New College, Edinburgh. Davidson began to gain a position of real influence in the College in the early 1860s, when so much seemed to be in the intellectual melting-pot. 'Rabbi' Duncan had been a revered figure at the College, famed far and wide for his style of imparting religious truths. John Kennedy of Dingwall said of one of Duncan's sermons that it was 'as if one of the Old Prophets had come from within the Veil to tell us what was going on there. Nothing more heavenly did I ever hear from human lips.'[25] Perhaps even more famous than his piety and erudition, however, was his astonishingly inept teaching style.[26] This was commented on by many students of varying theological shades. It was said that 'he taught his pupils everything but Hebrew',[27] and that he was 'hardly an effective teacher',[28] though his saintliness was universally admired. John Macleod summarised the phenomenon that was John Duncan:

> He was at once one of the most profound and versatile of scholars, one of the humblest of believers, and one of the most erratic and

[22] In some ways the Briggs Case and that of Robertson Smith were very similar, and in at least one respect the same criticism could be made of both men. The following was written in 1892 by Philip Schaff of Union Theological Seminary about Briggs, but could equally well have been said about Smith: 'Briggs was actually orthodox – even conservative ... but he stated his views on the authority and inspiration of the Scriptures and the higher criticism in such a defiant and exasperating tone against what he called 'bibliolatry', that ... [it] sounded like a manifesto of war and aroused at once a most determined opposition on the part of the conservative and orthodox press. Even some of his best friends deemed it unwise and uncalled for. It is this aggressive style and manner which brought on the fight': quoted in G. H. Shriver, *Philip Schaff: Christian Scholar and Ecumenical Prophet* (Macon, Georgia, 1987), p. 92. As the *British Weekly* put it at the time, 'It is impossible not to feel that Dr Briggs's own style and method have had much to do with this result, and that the question has been viewed as personal': *British Weekly*, 15 Jun. 1893, p. 115.

[23] R. R. Nelson, 'The Life and Thought of William Robertson Smith, 1846–1894' (Michigan University, Ph.D thesis, 1969).

[24] G. F. Barbour, *The Life of Alexander Whyte* (London, 1923), p. 202.

[25] Quoted in J. S. Sinclair (ed.), *Rich Gleanings After the Vintage from 'Rabbi' Duncan* (London, 1925), p. 8.

[26] A. Moody-Stuart, *Recollections of the Late John Duncan, LL.D.* (Edinburgh, 1872), pp. 84–5, 88–9; see also the remarks by Alexander Ross quoted in Brown, 'Disruption and the dream', p. 47.

[27] Black and Chrystal, *Life of William Robertson Smith*, p. 76.

[28] Simpson, *Life of Principal Rainy*, i, p. 91.

absentminded of men ... though he left his mark on many of his students by his words, he left next to nothing in writing.[29]

Several of the Free Church liberals who were to spend much of their careers undermining a great deal of what Duncan's admirers held dear remembered his contributions when they themselves were his students at the New College. Marcus Dods wrote, with hindsight, that

> if they had not learned from him a great deal of Hebrew they had learned, what was of greater value if less relevant, the reality of spiritual experience, and had gained glimpses into heavenly places such as nothing but genius could have opened to them.[30]

And, as a young student at the College in 1855, he wrote in a letter to his mother of the 'Rabbi': 'Dr Duncan is going through Job right now, and gives some most valuable notes, a good many queer stories, and a great quantity of minor matter difficult to carry across.'[31] A. T. Innes said of Duncan that

> at first appearance a mere scarecrow of erudition – he was soon recognized, even by us who had been passionate followers of Sir William Hamilton, as ruling an equal domain of learning, but with a more commanding intellectual sway. Yet he wrote no lectures; he published no books.[32]

For these and other reasons, then, it was felt that the time had come for a younger man to assume the mantle – as James Strahan elegantly expressed it:

> The Senatus had at last awakened to the fact that a Hebrew Professor might be expected not only to prelect as the spirit moved him, but to teach the elements of Hebrew. That was evidently beyond Dr Duncan's power. The metaphysician and saint had not the gifts of a teacher.[33]

It was A. B. Davidson to whom the Senate turned first to be Duncan's assistant in 1861 and then his replacement two years later, eventually earning his predecessor's affectionate nickname – 'the Rabbi' – as well as his job.[34] Thirty-four out of forty-six presbyteries recommended Davidson's name to the General Assembly of 1863, as did nine out of eleven synods. His appointment, which was proposed by probably the

---

[29] Macleod, *Scottish Theology*, p. 283.

[30] Dods, *Recent Progress in Theology*, pp. 4–5.

[31] M. Dods (Jnr) (ed.), *The Early Letters of Marcus Dods, D.D.* (London, 1910), p. 73.

[32] A. T. Innes, *Studies in Scottish History Chiefly Ecclesiastical* (London, 1892), p. 183.

[33] Strahan, *Andrew Bruce Davidson*, 82–3.

[34] *British Weekly*, Free Church Jubilee Supplement, 18 May 1893, p. 12; E. M. Mackenzie, *Rev. Murdo Mackenzie: A Memory* (Inverness, 1914), p. 8. His biographer commented, however, that 'no teacher was ever less Rabbinical than Davidson': Strahan, *Andrew Bruce Davidson*, p. 309.

most senior figure in the Free Church, Robert Smith Candlish, was carried by acclamation.[35] Considering the difference in their respective positions, the estimation in which Duncan held Davidson is nothing short of extraordinary. Candlish spoke of

> how thoroughly Mr Davidson had won the confidence and affection of the eminent man whose colleague it was proposed to make him. Beyond all question, the testimonial, couched in terms so warm, so cordial, and enthusiastic, which Dr Duncan had given Mr Davidson regarding his qualifications, was sufficient in itself, coming from a man who was undoubtedly entitled to speak upon such a subject, to carry conviction to the whole Church.[36]

Whatever Duncan would have thought of it all had he lived longer than seven years to see it, Davidson's appointment signalled an important phase in the advance of Higher Critical views in Scotland in general, and in the Free Church in particular. Robertson Smith's biographers remarked that it was Davidson who 'brought the first light into the dark age in Biblical Criticism and Biblical Theology in Scotland'.[37] On the other hand, to Neil Cameron, one of the Free Church students who joined the Free Presbyterians in 1893, he was the principal source of 'the poison that was soon to vitiate the theological scholarship of Scotland'.[38] To John Macleod, the effects and conclusions of Davidson's work were plain to see:

> Davidson's teaching, and even more than his positive teaching, his hints and suggestions, became the source of an alien infusion in Old Testament studies in Scotland. Robertson Smith caught the infection and spread the plague.[39]

For the conservatives within the Free Church, the contrast between the greatly revered Duncan and the greatly reviled Davidson, the purveyor of deadly poison, could hardly have been greater. On the other hand, Davidson saw himself as having a far-from-damaging role, saying in 1897 that his role had been merely 'to guide some whose feet were stumbling in the dark mountains'.[40] While there might be debate over Davidson's contribution to Bible scholarship, his influence on the young William Robertson Smith is beyond question.

The contemporary Norman L. Walker, for example, acknowledged that Smith did most to make the Critical movement 'visible', with his popular writings in such places as the *Encyclopedia Britannica* and his

---

35 *PDGAFCS*, 1863, 162 ff.; Wilson and Rainy, *Robert Smith Candlish*, p. 535.

36 *PDGAFCS*, 1863, 163.

37 Black and Chrystal, *Life of William Robertson Smith*, p. 76.

38 D. Beaton (ed.), *History of the Free Presbyterian Church of Scotland, 1893–1933* (Glasgow, 1933), p. 37. The author of much of the first section of this study (chaps. 1–3, 5, 6) was Neil Cameron.

39 Macleod, *Scottish Theology*, p. 288.

40 Quoted in H. Watt, *New College Edinburgh: A Centenary History* (Edinburgh, 1946), p. 90.

much publicised heresy trials in the late 1870s and early 1880s. Walker argued, however, that 'there were other men who had to do with its inception – Professor A. B. Davidson, for example, to whom Smith looked up as his master'.[41] Smith's role, perhaps, was to take his various mentors' ideas further than they had been taken before from within the pale of a Church which considered itself fairly rigidly Calvinist. In many ways he was also an alarm bell to those conservatives sufficiently complacent to think that their Church could resist such change. The conservative magazine *The Signal* commented wearily in 1883 that:

> The Robertson Smith case revealed, as all the world knows, a state of mind on the part of many of the ministers of the Church, as well as elders, on the doctrine of Scripture, that could not possibly have been credited had not the occasion called it forth.[42]

Having a man like Robertson Smith clutched to their ecclesiastical bosom was a sobering experience for some of the conservatives and probably a rather unpleasant one for both parties. As Norman Walker pointed out, writing in the following decade:

> As long as he remained in a College of the Free Church, he was hampered and burdened and embarrassed. He was the new wine seeking to be received into the old bottles. In the effort to reconcile the two there was a constant risk of explosions.[43]

In part this arose from a miscalculation on Smith's part – he genuinely believed that his Church would move along with the new opinions in much the same way as he had, and that German scholarship on Scripture would be as acceptable to others as it was to him. Smith believed, in a memorable phrase, that he could teach his Church the 'alphabet of criticism'.[44] He also believed that he could do so without damaging the Bible, and without compromising his own faith, which in his own words, *depended* upon the Bible:

> If I am asked why I receive Scripture as the Word of God and the only perfect rule of faith and life, I answer with all the Fathers of the Protestant Church, because the Bible is the only record of the redeeming love of God, because in the Bible alone I find God drawing near to men in Christ Jesus and declaring to us in Him His will for our salvation.[45]

---

[41] Walker, *Chapters from the History of the Free Church of Scotland*, p. 297.
[42] 'The coming struggle in the Free Church Assembly and its issues', *The Signal* (May 1883), pp. 65–6.
[43] Walker, *Chapters from the History of the Free Church of Scotland*, pp. 296–7.
[44] Rogerson, *Bible and Criticism*, p. 70.
[45] Quoted in A. C. Cheyne, 'Bible and Confession in Scotland: the background to the Robertson Smith Case', in W. Johnstone (ed.) *William Robertson Smith: Essays in Reassessment* (Sheffield, 1995), p. 39.

This miscalculation, and the response of others to it, was to have explosive consequences for the Free Church of Scotland.

By varied and complex routes, then, the doctrines of biblical higher criticism had 'arrived' in the Free Church of Scotland by the last quarter of the nineteenth century. At the same time, largely from outside ecclesiastical circles but with equally devastating results for the orthodox theological *status quo*, came the new scientific investigation of Origins, and it is to this that we now, more briefly, turn.

2. The scientific challenge to Scripture

Just as the nineteenth century witnessed great upheavals in social, economic, political and religious life and thought, it also was the period during which science made some of its most remarkable advances. Transport and housing, industrial and agricultural production, medicine and communication – all these and other areas were transformed by advances in scientific thought. So too in the understanding of the origins of man and of the earth, great leaps were made:

> the science based on Darwin's notion of a steady progression of more and more complex organisms as a result of natural selection has a legitimate claim to being the greatest intellectual and philosophical revolution in human history.[46]

Its relative importance in human history is not what is at issue here; what is important is that the adoption of evolutionary science was indeed a revolution.

Up to the beginning of the nineteenth century, two schools of geology provided competing explanations for the form and shape of the earth. These two schools, Neptunism and Vulcanism – the former stressing the importance of the force of water, and the latter placing its emphasis on the power of fire – were synthesised in the 1820s by geologists like William Buckland to form the theory of 'catastrophism'.[47] This view held that, over the centuries, the world had been racked by a series of devastating floods, of which only the last had affected man. This coincided comfortably with the Bible in many minds, and while it would be wrong to say that there was no opposition,[48] by the 1820s catastrophism was a widely accepted doctrine. Buckland had set out deliberately to reconcile religion and science – he is called a 'semi-deist' by the scientist J. R. Moore[49] – and

---

[46] R. E. Leakey and R. Lewin, *Origins: What New Discoveries Reveal about the Emergence of our Species and its Possible Future* (London, 1977), p. 21.

[47] Cameron, *Biblical Higher Criticism*, p. 292.

[48] See, e.g., L. E. Page, 'Diluvialism and its critics', in C. A. Russell (ed.), *Science and Religious Belief: A Selection of Recent Historical Studies* (London, 1973), pp. 214–15.

[49] J. R. Moore, *The Post-Darwinian Controversies: A Study of the Protestant Struggle to come to terms with Darwin in Great Britain and America, 1870–1900* (Cambridge and New York, 1979), p. 328.

Cameron argues that this was what contributed to the popularity of his ideas. The chief opposing theory eventually put into the lists against catastrophism was that of uniformity, of whom one of the strictest followers was Charles Lyell. Uniformists argued that geological events in the past had been caused by agents which could still be observed at work in the present. Lyell maintained that these agents had at all times in the past operated with the same force as they did now.[50] Lyell is often seen as the precursor of Darwinian Evolution, but it is probably fair to say that the catastrophists had also played a vital role in the development of the Darwinian theory. As Rudwick concludes:

> It is impossible to say, even with the advantage of hindsight, that either catastrophism or uniformitarianism was 'right', or even that one aided the progress of science more than the other. In fact ... there is no hard and fast line between catastrophism and uniformitarianism.[51]

The idea of evolution was far from being a novel one when it was expounded in its classic form by Charles Darwin in his most famous work, *The Origin of Species*, published in 1859.[52] It is probably fair to say, as J. S. Wilkie has done, that 'all its major theoretical positions had been advocated by one writer or another before it was printed'.[53] Men like Lamarck and Buffon, to name only two, had done vitally important work, but it is Darwin who earned, rightly, the credit for distilling the research, observation and data into a cogent – and accessible – summary. It has been rightly observed that

> it remained for the man himself to assemble all the data and to construct an unassailable theory ... his theory was not entirely new, but he presented it to the world at a time when the intellectual climate was at its most favourable.[54]

And J. S. Wilkie concluded his essay on 'the originality of Darwin' as follows:

> Viewing the historical development of the theory of evolution dispassionately we can now see that there really was a development, though a discontinuous one ... and anyone who likes to do so can say that Darwin only completed the building which others, under

[50] M. J. S. Rudwick, 'The principle of Uniformity', in Russell, *Science and Religious Belief*, p. 206.

[51] Ibid., pp. 206–7.

[52] C. Darwin, *The Origin of Species by Means of Natural Science; or, The Preservation of Favoured Races in the Struggle for Life* (London, 1859). And, as Donald Withrington has said, the Genesis account of creation had been under attack 'long before Darwin ... indeed, when Darwin's book was published, much of the ground of the "science vs. religion" debate had been well worked over in Scotland and, while Darwin provided a valuable and exciting extension to that debate, that indeed in Scotland was what it mainly was': Withrington, 'Ferment of Change', pp. 55–6.

[53] J. S. Wilkie, 'Buffon, Lamarck and Darwin: The originality of Darwin's Theory of Evolution', in Russell, *Science and Religious Belief*, p. 238.

[54] Leakey and Lewin, *Origins*, p. 25.

greater difficulties, had begun ... The fact remains that it was he who completed it.[55]

Darwin's theories in connection with natural selection gave the theory of evolution greatly increased credibility – they literally provided an explanation as to how evolution took place – but the controversy they aroused came not initially from churchmen or theologians, worried that he was destroying the Genesis record and with it the whole of the Old Testament, but from the scientific community. As James Moore and David Livingstone have both pointed out, to refer to the relationship between all churchmen and Darwinism as 'conflict' or 'warfare' is wide of the mark.[56] The responses of believers in God to these new challenges to the traditional interpretation of their Holy Text were many and varied, and these responses of churchmen to the challenges of science and higher criticism will now be examined.

The Free Church response to the changing world was multi-faceted, with probably no two Free Churchmen having identical world views. Having said that, it is possible to divide the Free Church reaction to higher criticism and evolutionary science into three broad bands. First, there were those who accepted the developments in Bible study and science as important steps towards man's understanding both of his world and of the divine revelation – seeing them as inevitable beneficial progressions on the journey from ignorance towards knowledge. The second group was made up of members of the Free Church who were implacably opposed to what they saw as a work of the Devil; these men rejected evolutionary science and all its implications while at the same time holding the direct, divine verbal inspiration of an inerrant and infallible Bible. And in between there was just about every other conceivable shade of opinion, which can best be summarised as 'the middle ground'. Some accepted evolution but not all of it; others rejected the Genesis account as a verbatim account of the origin of life but were reluctant to accept evolution as an alternative either; while there were some who compromised on both issues without ever being willing to place themselves in one camp or the other. It would perhaps be useful, then, to begin with a word about the complex nature of the divided Free Church.

A Word about Divisions

The belief that the Free Church experienced splits in 1893 and again in 1900 because two opposing camps had developed within it is not a new one. Douglas Murray in his Chalmers Lectures of 1991 was simply the

---

[55] Ibid., p. 281.
[56] Moore, *Post-Darwinian Controversies*, p. 20; D. N. Livingstone, *Darwin's Forgotten Defenders: The Encounter Between Evangelical Theology and Evolutionary Thought* (Grand Rapids and Edinburgh, 1987), p. 1.

latest in a long line of historians to express this view. In the later
nineteenth-century Free Church of Scotland, the presence of two
increasingly divergent points of view was becoming more and more
obvious, although what was actually happening was the fragmentation of
a denomination into many different groups. These groups identified
themselves, to varying degrees, with one or other of the 'two camps' for the
sake of convenience and the pragmatic considerations of ecclesiastical
politics and conflict.

Patrick Carnegie Simpson, Robert Rainy's friend and biographer, was
aware of the disappearance of unity within the Free Church and
suggested the date 1866 as the watershed. He explained that C. H.
Spurgeon, the distinguished Baptist preacher from the Metropolitan
Tabernacle in the centre of London, had described the Free Church
General Assembly of that year as 'so happily united that you have no
right hand and no left in that place'. Simpson's brief comment on this
speaks volumes: 'It was the last Assembly of the Free Church of Scotland
of which such a remark could be made.'[57] The fact that the divided
nature of their Church had become a fact of life is illustrated by the
following invitation card to a confidential meeting sent to opponents of
the proposed Declaratory Act of 1892, which states that it is 'addressed
to such as are understood to be in thorough sympathy with its objects,
and no others are entitled to be present ... no one will be admitted
without this passport'.[58] The divide in the Free Church must have
become a fairly deep one by the 1890s for the opposing sides to be
preventing each other from attending one another's meetings. As at the
Convocation in Edinburgh which preceded the Disruption of 1843,[59] this
was not the behaviour of men preparing to compromise; this was the
behaviour of men used to conflict and fully prepared for more.

The division, however, was by no means always cut and dried. In
reality, the Free Church was an extremely complex tangle of differing
stances complicated by tactical and often temporary alliances. Few men –
if, indeed, there were any – fitted neatly into one pigeon-hole and
remained in it without ever venturing out of it to express a divergent
point of view on one issue or another. As George Adam Smith commented in 1905, when looking back on Henry Drummond's position on
the Robertson Smith Case:

> Within as without the church courts discussion ran high and hot for
> three years. The old parties were broken up, and even groups of
> friends and fellow-workers divided sharply under the new tests. At
> first Drummond could not but share the general uncertainty. Many
> of his dearest friends and leaders were opposed to Professor

[57] Simpson, *Life of Principal Rainy*, i, p. 166.
[58] This card was sent to John Macleod, one of the Free Church divinity students who
    left the Church in May 1893 over the Declaratory Act (John Macleod Collection).
[59] Brown, *Annals of the Disruption*, pp. 49–51; Brown, 'Ten Years' Conflict', p. 19.

Smith's views; he himself was not equipped with the knowledge of the original languages of the Bible which would have enabled him to form conclusions of his own.[60]

James Begg was one of the most important figures in the Scottish Church's response to the social problems of the nineteenth century. He was one of the first churchmen to realise the extent of the challenge and one of the very few to propose national solutions. Yet Begg is certainly not a theological liberal in the Free Church and he was harshly criticised by many of his liberal opponents. But it must also be observed that Begg's advocacy of Saturday-night theatre concerts for the working classes, as an alternative to the traditional public drunkenness, attracted criticism from fellow conservatives on the grounds that it was a practice which, if not wrong in itself, might well lead to Sabbath desecration.[61] He was also criticised by William Ross, who, despite fitting more into what would have been the liberal wing of the Church, had an opinion of the theatre and the music hall which would not have looked much out of place in the seventeenth century: 'He hated the theatre and all its works and ways with a puritanic intensity, believing its influence to be mainly for evil.'[62] In this Ross, a theological liberal in so many ways, would have found himself in almost complete agreement with one of the most strict conservatives in the Free Church, Donald Macfarlane, whose opinion was expressed in one famous sermon as follows:

it gives pain to my heart – knowing the things of eternity and the preciousness of immortal souls – when I see and read of young boys and girls, and even their fathers and mothers, going to the dance and to the theatre at our very doors.[63]

Macfarlane said on another occasion:

One form of pleasure worship was theatrical plays, and ... the teachers of those performances and all who countenanced them would be (though not intentionally) the means of destroying the souls of the performers ... Those who taught theatrical performances to little children forbade them to come to Christ.[64]

Yet despite their differing views on theatres, Begg remained one of the great heroes of the Free Presbyterian Church for many years, and the man whose death was seen as opening the way to the triumph of

---

[60] G. A. Smith, *The Life of Henry Drummond* (London, 1905), p. 130.

[61] In the Free Church General Assembly of 1856, Archibald Bannatyne of Glasgow was very critical of Begg in this connection. He saw the concerts as 'tending to the desecration of the Sabbath; and would never have expected that any church, least of all that any ministers of the Free Protesting Church of Scotland, would have given countenance to such a means of preparation for desecration of the Sabbath': *PDGAFCS*, 1856, 109.

[62] Ross, *William Ross of Cowcaddens*, p. 90.

[63] Beaton, *Donald Macfarlane*, pp. 248–9.

[64] Ibid., pp. 185–6.

liberalism in the Free Church in the years preceding the Second Disruption.[65]

The divide in the Free Church, then, was not a simple one. In 1895, for example, the Free Assembly took a vote on whether or not Henry Drummond's pro-evolution *The Ascent of Man* was an acceptable piece of work from a Free Church professor. Despite the fact that Drummond was at the time suffering from his final illness – and the pressure to leave a respected and almost universally liked man in peace was intense – the Free Assembly actually had a vote on whether it would even discuss the issue, given the gravity of his illness. His old companion Marcus Dods was surprised at the way some men argued and voted, commenting that, 'Several voted on the other side whom one would not have expected to find there.'[66] The complexity was exacerbated by the fact that, as was inevitable, men's views underwent constant remodelling in response to the ever-changing world of ecclesiastical politics. The conservative Divinity student, Neil Cameron, for example, was frustrated when an expected ally in the fight against the Declaratory Act switched from a perceived position of passionate opposition to a more moderate stance. William Balfour of Edinburgh, who in 1892 described the Declaratory Act as 'a Jesuitical Act' and one which was 'palpably inconsistent' with the Free Church's position,[67] had by 1893 come to occupy the middle ground – Cameron actually talks of 'the "middle course" party'. When Cameron spoke publicly against that position Balfour became quite angry with his younger companion.[68] People clearly changed their minds for a variety of reasons, and from the letters of both Dods and Cameron

---

65 'Truth, conscience and consistency were clearly on the side of Dr Begg and his followers', Beaton, *History of the Free Presbyterian Church*, p. 15. Begg's work on social affairs, however, was ignored by his Free Presbyterian admirers.

66 M. Dods, *The Later Letters of Marcus Dods* (London, 1911), pp. 3–4. Despite this surprising discovery, the side of Dods and Drummond won the day on that particular occasion: *PDGAFCS*, 1895, 132. It is also worth noting that Dods's close friend and correspondent over a period of decades, William Robertson Nicoll, said to him of Drummond: 'I never could help feeling – that Drummond was a charlatan, in the sense that he was always trying tasks far beyond him ... he was as ill-read as a bishop.' Another Free Church-man from the liberal wing of the Church, James Denney – himself later a Free Church professor – said in a letter to Nicoll that Drummond had always aroused resentment among some people, stating 'what riled me, as it has done others, in his books was not so much anything that he said so much as what he did not say – the airy way in which he seemed to do without all that to common Christianity was indispensable ... Natural Law in the Spiritual World is not much better than an audacious series of paradoxes': T. H. Darlow, *William Robertson Nicoll: Life and Letters* (London, 1925), pp. 163, 155. A. B. Davidson was quoted as saying of Drummond's Natural Law: 'sometimes I think there is nothing in it ... sometimes I think there is something in it ... I feel sure that if there is anything in it, it is something bad': Strahan, *Andrew Bruce Davidson*, p. 271. It is quite wrong to assume that men who happened to vote the same way on particular issues agreed with each other all the time.

67 William Balfour, in *The Free Church Declaratory Act: A Criticism and Protest. Being the Speeches Delivered at a Public Meeting Held in Glasgow On Thursday, 18th February, 1892* (Glasgow, 1892), p. 6.

68 Neil Cameron to John Macleod, 7 Apr. 1893, John Macleod Collection, 2d.

it is evident that this was happening among both 'liberals' and 'conservatives'.

The divide was not hard and fast for another reason as well. Inevitably as they got older some men's opinions simply altered from what they had once been. 'Rabbi' Duncan developed from explicit atheism to become one of the Free Church's conservative heroes.[69] T. M. Lindsay, who was ordained Professor of Church History at the Free Church College, Glasgow, in 1872 is a classic example of a churchman who underwent an almost revolutionary change of views. As a student Lindsay was a conservative in virtually every respect, from politics and literature to philosophy and theology. 'His,' said the *United Free Church Magazine*, 'was a convinced and pronounced conservatism.' The change was as fundamental as it was surprising:

> It was a puzzle to his fellow-students to find Professor Lindsay a few years later an advocate of reform in almost all spheres of human activity. He advocated the right of women to an entrance into the University. He was identified with the movement which led to the Highland Crofters' Act. He stoutly defended the right of historical criticism within the church ... The process in his case was accomplished within half a dozen years, and it was thorough when completed.[70]

In some respects these changes were also present in the life of William Ross of the Cowcaddens who, for example, switched from being an opponent of the use of hymns in public worship to being an enthusiastic and practising advocate of the same. As a student he had been delighted at the passing of an anti-hymns motion and as the minister in Rothesay had moved for delay in their introduction, yet latterly he had become so supportive of hymns that at times he had four or five different hymn-books in use by his congregation at the same time. 'A man,' commented his son, 'is not built in a day!'[71] It might also be mentioned that while Ross was a social liberal, a Union-man, an advocate of Disestablishment and a keen supporter of the evangelising campaigns of Moody and Sankey, he was on the other hand a passionate critic of the Music Hall, sympathised with the conservative position on higher criticism and had a firm dislike for both the system and the ritual of episcopacy.[72]

It is significant that while the more advanced views of European criticism began to find acceptance in the Free Church, vital changes were also taking place in the key personnel of the Church. Some of the most senior and respected conservatives were dying, to be replaced in the positions

---

[69] According to A. Moody-Stuart, Duncan 'cast away the Bible; and this ground once lost, he sank down ... into material atheism': Moody-Stewart, *Recollections of the Late John Duncan*, p. 8. Duncan himself declared that he had had 'three years of dreary Atheism': D. Brown, *Life of the Late John Duncan, LL.D.* (2nd edn, Edinburgh, 1872), p. 49.

[70] *United Free Church Magazine*, Jan. 1906, p. 7.

[71] Ross, *William Ross of Cowcaddens*, pp. 26–7.

[72] Ibid., 27, 30–1, 33, 90, 148–9.

of influence by men of more liberal views. While such men as Alexander Whyte, Henry Drummond, James Denney, Marcus Dods and Robert Rainy rose to dominate the Free Church from their city pulpits and their college chairs, the conservative side was to lose such dominant figures as John 'Rabbi' Duncan, John Kennedy of Dingwall and James Begg.[73] Instead of rallying round some new champion, the conservative forces in the Free Church were, by their own admission, 'paralysed' and seemed unable to do more than mourn their passing with fine words.[74] John Duncan's virtual canonisation in the years after his death owed more to the fact that he was dead and unreplaced (as a senior conservative in a position of vital importance in New College, Edinburgh) than to any enormous practical contribution to the conservative cause during his lifetime.[75] The loss of Kennedy and Begg, however, was more serious.[76] In a letter of May 1891 to the future Free Presbyterian John Macleod, the conservative divinity student, Donald Munro, referred to Kennedy of Dingwall's passing:

> I've often been thinking today of the funeral I attended, exactly seven years this afternoon – the funeral of a greater man I'm not likely ever to attend. It's unnecessary for me to say that my mind often transferred today to Dingwall. These last seven years have truly been 'seven years of famine' and yet we are likely to 'see more abominations'.[77]

The Signal wrote 'with a heavy heart' of the death of James Begg, and commented that

---

73 These three major conservatives had the following dates: John Duncan (1796–1870); James Begg (1808–83); and John Kennedy (1819–84). Alexander Whyte became minister of the hugely influential congregation of Free St George's, Edinburgh, in 1870; Henry Drummond became Professor of Natural Science in the Free Church College, Glasgow, in 1884; James Denney was ordained in 1886, and became a Professor in 1897; Marcus Dods took the post of Professor of New Testament Exegesis at New College, Edinburgh, in 1889; and Robert Rainy was appointed Professor of Church History at New College in 1862, and became Principal of the same institution in 1874. In fact Rainy became a professor at New College on the very day that Whyte arrived there as a student.

74 Even the usually aggressive *Signal* said of Dr Kennedy's death: 'A Prince and a Great Man had fallen in Israel', and: 'meanwhile we may well cry, "Help Lord, for the godly ceaseth, for the faithful fail from among the children of men"': 'The late Dr Kennedy of Dingwall', *The Signal* (Jun. 1884), pp. 161–5.

75 As Black and Chrystal tartly put it: 'His fame among the present generation depends rather on the piety of posterity than on any tangible surviving performance of his own': Black and Chrystal, *Life of William Robertson Smith*, p. 73.

76 As late as the end of the century, some 16 years after his death, the Free Presbyterians were still quoting Kennedy's anti-unionist speeches from the 1870s; it can but be assumed that this was because there was nobody to equal or better Dr Kennedy. See, e.g., 'The late Dr. Kennedy on Union between the Free and U.P. Churches', *FPM*, iv (6) (1899), p. 214; and J. Kennedy, 'Speech on Union by the late Rev. Dr. John Kennedy, of Dingwall: at an anti-Union meeting at Inverness', *FPM*, iv (11) (1900), p. 409. Even Rainy acknowledged the great loss that Kennedy's death had brought, speaking of 'the vanishing from amongst them of a preaching power unequalled in the Highlands, and not commonly equalled anywhere': *PDGAFCS*, 1884, 132.

77 Donald Munro to John Macleod, 1 May 1891, John Macleod Collection, 1c.

it seems to some of us, yea, to many, as if a standard-bearer had
fallen – as if a trusted leader and commander-in-chief had gone,
and that not at a time when victory was secured, but when the
enemy was coming in like a flood ... there is no living man in
Scotland whose loss to the Church on earth would have been felt to
be so great as that of him whose decease we now mourn.[78]

Tears and pious regrets were never going to be enough to replace the
lost leaders though, and it would have taken a more powerful figure
than was available to hold back the tide of change promulgated by the
educated and eloquent liberal elite which was taking its place at the helm
of the Free Church.

This 'tide of change', of which higher criticism and evolutionary
science were two of the most obvious constituent parts, proved divisive
for the Free Church. It is interesting to note here that the divide in the
Free Church over higher criticism was frequently presented as being one
of age and experience against youthful ignorance. *The Signal*, for
example, listed eight prominent Free Churchmen whom it styled as
advocates of 'so-called toleration on the side of error' and referred to

the young men, the philo-Smithites, who cry 'Forward' at all haz-
ards ... 'Forward, at all hazards' will be the war cry of the young
Free Church under the leadership of Professors Bruce, Lindsay,
Salmond and Mr Ross Taylor.

It contrasted the 'ignorant cry of the young people of the Church' with
the 'grieved hearts and wounded consciences of multitudes who wish to
guard His house'.[79] The divided Free Church has been defined in many
ways, but this contemporary analysis of a kind of generational conflict
over higher criticism is fascinating. The writer continued, in the
following month's issue:

There is what may be called the young Free Church party ... [and]
what may be called the old Free Church party, the most prominent
representative of which is Dr Begg. The views of this party are
directly opposed to those of the former party.[80]

While this was clearly not quite the same generational conflict which
became such a fact of life in universities and other institutions in the
1960s and the 1970s – and which has been used as an explanation for
other religious conflicts[81]– it is an interesting indication that there was

---

78 'The late Dr. Begg', *The Signal* (Nov. 1883), p. 169. That entire issue of *The Signal* was
   devoted to the memory of Dr Begg. Even the *British Weekly*, writing some 5 years later
   in an honest and touching front-page tribute, could say of Begg: 'What made him
   great was that he had something of the old heroic strain, a kinship with those who
   loved not their lives to the death': *British Weekly*, 27 Apr. 1888, p. 481.
79 'Coming struggle in the Free Assembly', pp. 66, 68–9.
80 'What will the Assembly do?', *The Signal* (Jun. 1883), pp. 96–7.
81 It was argued in the 1960s, e.g., that the conflict over the Church attitude to American

more to the divided Free Church than might appear at first glance. The fact was that many of the men arguing so eloquently for change in the Church were much younger than those who sought only to hold what they already had and to avoid wandering any further off the 'old paths'. The Robertson Smith Case was almost a caricature of this with the young professor, aged only twenty-four on his appointment to the chair in 1870, backed up by such men as Marcus Dods (thirty-six in 1870), Alexander Whyte (thirty-three), James Candlish (thirty-five) and T. M. Lindsay (twenty-seven), pitted in the lists against what Ronald Nelson called a 'group of leaders in the Free Church, many of them old and revered, who were not prepared to accommodate their theology to the findings of higher criticism'.[82] In later years their respective ages became something of a stick with which each side would beat the other; it was also a reflection of the older ministers' fear that the young blood of the Free Church was becoming infected with the poison of heresy. This was, of course, the fundamental bone of contention which gave the conflict over the higher criticism its bitter edge; and it meant that one of the most crucial confrontations was over the Free Church's colleges.

The Position of the Colleges

Had the men who were propagating the new and advanced views been doing so in isolated parishes or in private discussions, the conservatives could have lived with it. The crux of the matter, though, was that the very men with whose opinions they disagreed so radically were frequently the holders of some of the most influential positions within the Free Church. This involved not only being in the pulpits of large congregations but, most importantly, being the occupants of chairs in the Free Church's divinity halls; men such as Dods, Drummond, Davidson and of course Robertson Smith, were all professors in Free Church colleges. Crucially, the character of the colleges was seen to be changing, and the change was overwhelmingly a move from conservative to liberal scholarship and theology.

The conservatives could perhaps have accepted the uncomfortable fact that for the time being, theological liberalism was on the rise; but what made this much worse was the fact that their opponents had a position from which they could control the future development of the Church, through its theological training. The conservative editors of *The*

---

slavery which surrounded the debates at the Lane Seminary, Cincinnati, in 1834 was a manifestation of the generation gap: the young men led by Theodore Dwight Weld, and the old men led by Lyman Beecher. Arguably, this analysis was itself very much a product of the times.

[82] Nelson, 'Life and Thought of William Robertson Smith', p. 121. Kenneth Latourette said of Smith: 'It was largely from the older men that the opposition came: for the most part the younger men were with him': K. Latourette, *Christianity in a Revolutionary Age* (New York, 1959), p. 413.

Signal had no doubts as to the long-term prospects, stating in 1888 that there could not

> be greater injury done to a church or a community, than to have men teaching in our Divinity Halls ... who seem to be continually oscillating between a lingering regard for the theology taught during many generations in Scotland by men who were owned by God and whose labours He blessed ... and a mongrel system of instruction largely tinged with Arminianism, and coated over with a scholarly and gentlemanly Rationalism which will not wound the sensibilities of the worldling or the sensualist, and which is altogether fitted to allow the sleeper to sleep the sleep of death.[83]

William Balfour of Edinburgh was another conservative Free Churchman who blamed what was being taught in the colleges for many of the Church's problems. Speaking of the alleged 'scruples' with which some young ministers viewed the Westminster Confession of Faith he said, at an anti-Declaratory Act meeting in Glasgow in 1892:

> This naturally raises the question – Is there anything about the teaching in our colleges now to account for the existence of these scruples and doubts among our aspirants to the ministry? There was more than ground to suspect that it was to the teaching of some of the professors in great measure that the doubts and scruples in the minds of our youth were to be traced.[84]

His solution to the problem was simple, and expressed in an equally forthright manner:

> That being the case, they did not need to frame an Act to meet their scruples, they needed to take action and rid the colleges of those men, who were flooding their church with men who were entertaining views other than those of the Confession of Faith.[85]

The *Free Presbyterian Magazine* held the same position as late as 1899. Commenting on the Free Assembly of that year it stated:

> any person of understanding knows that unless the Church loves the truth so much as to purge out heretical professors from her halls, there is little hope of the rising generation in pulpit or pew. Professors Davidson, Bruce, Dods, Smith, and others, are responsible for the dissemination of error among people as well as students, error of the most destructive and soul-ruining kind.[86]

The Signal groaned at the changed days when it had become true that

---

83 'Where are the Highlands drifting to?', *The Signal* (Jun. 1888), p. 171.
84 William Balfour, in *Free Church Declaratory Act: A Criticism and Protest*, p. 5.
85 Ibid.
86 'The Assemblies (Free Church)', *FPM*, iv (2) (1899), p. 50.

the popular characters in the colleges were men of a very different stamp from what they would have chosen themselves,[87] while, looking back in 1920 on the events which led to the Second Disruption of 1893, Neil Cameron summarised the process as follows:

> The Bible itself was attacked, and its infallibility and inerrancy scoffed at ... The infidels were placed in the Divinity Chairs of her colleges, so as to make sure that the future ministry within her pale would be all Higher Critics, if it would be possible to make them so. Of this I had a most painful experience in the New College, Edinburgh.[88]

Clearly, the position of the professors was a crucial one, and one well appreciated by all sections of the Free Church.

Cameron called the views of the professors 'this light which has proved to be truly darkness',[89] while *The Signal* provided for its conservative readership the following cheerless summary:

> It is a terrible thought, that parents who consult the true welfare of their sons, or of the community, instead of encouraging them to go forward to the ministry, tremble at the almost fatal ordeal through which young men have to pass on their way to the office of the holy ministry.[90]

The Signal, to be sure, was not the most unbiased paper in circulation, and for it to describe a young candidate's passage through a place like New College, Edinburgh, as an 'almost fatal ordeal' was stretching the point a little. It does indicate, though, the depth of feeling which was produced among the conservative sections of the Free Church at the thought of their future ministers acquiring the 'taint of rationalism' at the very places where they could in the past have sat at the feet of Cunningham, Chalmers, Candlish or Duncan.

This all emphasises the real fears of the conservatives; they disliked the new teaching in their colleges not merely because it was so different from what had always been taught there – and that was a serious enough charge – but because they believed that it would ultimately condemn those who accepted it to eternal damnation. This goes a long way to explain the aggression with which the conservatives fought what was to prove a losing battle. They were not fighting merely to assert their academic principles, or to score debating points, or even to prove that they were more well versed in the original languages of the Old Testament than their opponents. Ultimately they believed that their silence would condemn men and women, who might otherwise have been saved, to 'sleep the sleep of death' in a literal biblical Hell where

---

[87] 'Free Church students and orthodoxy', *The Signal* (Feb. 1888), p. 58.

[88] Beaton, *Neil Cameron*, p. 155.

[89] Cameron, in Beaton, *History of the Free Presbyterian Church*, p. 93.

[90] 'Effects of Free Church training for the Ministry', *The Signal* (Jun. 1888), pp. 183–4.

'the worm dieth not and the fire is not quenched'. It is easy to forget this when studying the debates of the time when theological and political games were played out on the floor of the Free Assembly, and when convention usually forced men to temper their language, but it is important to bear it in mind when considering the motivations of the various figures involved. Neil Cameron saw the difference between the two sides as a stark one indeed when he wrote:

> the amazing thing is that the large majority of her [the Free Church's] ministers and elders got so quickly out of the good old path and, as we shall see, even the minority who fought bravely till the day of acting instead of speaking had come, became so weak as to cave in to those who were abandoning not only the original creed and constitution of the Free Church, but also the gospel which the Lord had on several occasions blessed to the conversion of many sinners within her pale. That this was done for another gospel upon which the Holy Ghost pronounced a curse is amazing in the extreme.[91]

Cameron could not here resist the temptation to castigate those men who failed to join the Free Presbyterians at the Disruption of May, 1893, but even in what was a fairly polemic piece of party literature, the difference which the conservatives perceived between the old and the new was challengingly stated. It was, they believed, the difference between a gospel which enjoyed divine blessing and one which was under a divine curse.

It is probably fair to say that as well as a feeling of righteous indignation, the conservatives felt a degree of frustration in that they had been tactically out-manoeuvred by the liberals in getting the men they wanted into positions of power in the Free Church colleges. This was a vital part of the battle over higher criticism in the Free Church since, as we have seen, had the higher critics been in positions of little influence the issue would not have been such a bitterly contested one. 'The Professors' became figures of almost mythical proportions, whose potential to do evil at times seemed without limit, but part of the resentment at this was undoubtedly caused by disappointment that they had managed to get into the colleges in the first place. While some of the conservatives in the Free Church might have accepted that this was a sign of divine disapproval – Donald Macfarlane, for example, preaching that 'when the displeasure of God is shown to a people, unfaithful teachers are placed over their heads'[92] – at the same time they did their utmost to prevent it. They left no stone unturned in their attempts to prevent men whose pedigrees they doubted becoming professors; they harried them almost continually with accusations of heresy when they did succeed in getting a chair; and finally they began to call into question the validity of the

---

91 Cameron, in Beaton, *History of the Free Presbyterian Church*, p. 68.
92 Beaton, *Donald Macfarlane*, p. 206.

college system itself when it seemed that nothing could be done to limit the higher critical heresy that was being nurtured there.[93] In many ways the battle for the heart and soul of the Free Church was won and lost in the battle for control of what was being taught in her colleges; the party which won the colleges was going to dominate the Free Church's pulpits in the future. The burning problem for the conservatives within the Free Church was that while their *de jure* right to remove professors remained, the *de facto* situation was that their numerical disadvantage[94] meant that they were left with practically no chance of arresting the growing number of liberal professors. As their sense of grievance increased, conservatives felt it their duty to fight tooth and nail the liberalisation of the Free Church's Divinity Halls. The fact that this was a fight which was eventually lost goes a long way to explaining the Second Disruption of 1893.

Indeed, for those who left the Free Church at the Second Disruption of 1893, the presence of liberal and higher critical views in the colleges formed one of the fundamental justifications for doing what they did. The analogy of these allegedly false teachers being like Achan[95] was used in an editorial in the *Free Presbyterian Magazine* in April 1897. This stated that the lesson of Achan was 'the unspeakable danger of cherishing in the professing Church what is contrary to the Word of God, and the necessity of separation from every form of iniquity'.[96] It argued that there were men in the churches who had disobeyed the Word of God but

> instead of casting out such, they have given them the very highest honours in their power ... Achan is nowadays praised for the courage of his convictions and the liberality of his opinions, while Joshua and the elders are derided for the narrowness of their ideas, and the undue strictness of their adherence to the letter of the Word.[97]

The situation was one which clearly frustrated them, forcing them to do evil by countenancing evil, and from which they could see only one release:

> But if the Lord declared that He would not be with Israel any more if they did not destroy one hidden Achan, what will be His testimony in regard to modern professing churches which have numbers of Achans occupying the highest places of influence, and teaching others

---

[93] 'Where are the Highlands drifting to?' (Jun. 1888), p. 171.

[94] In the 1890 debate in which Dr Findlay of Larkhall said: 'Their colleges were the schools of the prophets, the nurseries of their future ministers. What was taught there would be reproduced in their pulpits; would, humanly speaking, mould the religious life of their Church', the conservatives were defeated in their attempt to censure Professor A. B. Bruce by 392 votes to 237, a majority of 155: *PDGAFCS*, 1890, 179.

[95] Achan was the Old Testament character – of Joshua VII – whose disobedient keeping of 'a goodly Babylonish garment' brought down divine punishment on Israel and who was ultimately destroyed in order to restore divine favour.

[96] 'Separation from an unsound Church viewed in the light of Scripture', *FPM*, i (12) (1897), p. 443.

[97] Ibid., p. 444.

to imbibe their opinions and follow their example? If the Lord is not with such bodies it is time for the true Israel to separate from them.[98]

The fact that the critics had gained positions of influence in the Free Church's colleges was plainly alienating those who would lead the Second Disruption in 1893. But before going on to look further at the positions of those who found themselves in opposition to the higher critics, it is important to examine the position of some of these much vilified men – the higher critics themselves.

The Liberal Response to Biblical Criticism

It is worth admitting at the very outset that the term 'response' in this context is in some ways a slight misnomer, given that the Free Church was itself one of the principal conduits which brought the principles of biblical criticism to the British population at large and to the Scottish population in particular. It was a continual source of shame to Free Church conservatives in the later nineteenth century that their Church played such an important role in propagating what one conservative termed 'vicious biblical criticism'.[99] Given its widely held reputation for rigid Calvinist orthodoxy, the Free Church contained a remarkable variety of views on the biblical criticism of the nineteenth century, with many of its most senior ministers and academics becoming enthusiastic recipients and later effective apostles of the new teaching. Conservatives in the Free Church were indignant over what they saw as 'poison' and 'error' being disseminated from their theological colleges and pulpits. In the late 1870s and the early 1880s they brought to heel one of the most brilliant and outspoken scholars which the Free Church had ever produced; in a long-running, highly public test of strength they forced William Robertson Smith out of his Aberdeen professorship, and ultimately out of the Free Church, over what they argued were heretical views. Very soon after that, though, the conservatives' power was on the wane. They had to look on while heresy trials collapsed time and time again, until the stage was reached, in April 1893, at which the conservative divinity student Neil Cameron could refer to remaining in the Free Church as being 'content to dwell in Sodom'.[100] This is a severe indictment of a Church which had once enjoyed the reputation of being one of the most conservative of churches in the Protestant world, with what S. J. Brown called its 'intense commitment to scholastic Calvinism, including the doctrines of election, limited atonement and man's total

98 Ibid.
99 'How far is the Church responsible for present scepticism?', *The Signal* (Sep. 1888), p. 267. The reference was to Marcus Dods.
100 Neil Cameron to John Macleod, 7 Apr. 1893, John Macleod Collection, 2d.

depravity'.[101] As has been seen, however, the world was changing and a significant part of the Free Church was changing with it.

After 1893, the Free Presbyterians had no doubt as to where the blame lay for the process by which 'one of the most evangelical churches in Christendom' became the place where 'the Higher Criticism which has done so much to throttle the spiritual life of Scotland showed itself first of all'.[102] In their own apologia for the first forty years of Free Presbyterian history, published in 1933, William Robertson Smith was the man to whom the 'credit' was given for raising the issue of biblical criticism. The story of William Robertson Smith is a long and over-familiar one, of which it can be said with T. H. Darlow 'we need not attempt to follow in detail these old, unhappy, far-off things, or to disentangle fights fought long ago from the intricate ecclesiastical procedure by which they were complicated'.[103] The attitude of the early Free Presbyterians to him is interesting and illuminating. There was acknowledgement of the young professor's brilliance, but the stance was generally one of regret that the entire situation had ever been allowed to arise:

> Dr Carnegie Simpson, the biographer of Principal Rainy, speaks of his [Smith] being driven from his chair as a tragedy – the real tragedy for the Free Church was the appointment of this young, brilliant scholar to such a chair ... A great flood of idle tears has been shed over the fate that overtook Professor Smith. His dismissal from his chair has been described as a blunder on the part of the General Assembly, but in the estimation of many the only blunder about it was that the dismissal did not take place sooner.[104]

The Robertson Smith case revealed the factions into which the Free Church was dividing on the issue of higher criticism. Smith had his passionate supporters – producing on at least one occasion in the General Assembly what Carnegie Simpson called 'an uproar of wild acclamation'[105] and what a Free Presbyterian historian called 'frenzied glee'.[106] On the other hand there were those conservatives, among them the men who were to form the Free Presbyterian Church, whose distaste for Smith was intense. And as in so many cases in the Free Church at this time, there were the men who found themselves sitting, often extremely precariously, on the fence.

The Smith case was undoubtedly vital in bringing the arguments of

101 Brown, *Thomas Chalmers*, p. 346.
102 Beaton, *History of the Free Presbyterian Church*, p. 50.
103 Darlow, *William Robertson Nicoll*, p. 39.
104 Ibid., pp. 51, 66.
105 Simpson, *Life of Principal Rainy*, i, p. 338.
106 Beaton, *History of the Free Presbyterian Church*, pp. 56–7. One writer in *The Signal* described the scene in 1877 'when Professor Lindsay of Glasgow stood on the back of one of the forms, and frantically waved his hat to express his joy and triumph over what was, in reality, the shame and dishonour of the Church': 'Where are the Highlands drifting to?', *The Signal* (Mar. 1888), p. 89.

higher criticism into the public eye in Scotland.[107] By the late 1880s, however, Smith was gone if not forgotten. Crucially for the Free Church, many of the young men who had supported him in his trial – some, no doubt, having cheered him with 'frenzied glee' – were now carrying on his torch. The men whom *The Signal* memorably dubbed the 'philo-Smithites' were able to take his ideas and popularise them, while at the same time successfully negotiating their way round or even through the minefield of conservative opinion. Of all the philo-Smithites, the one for whom the conservatives seemed to reserve a special place was Marcus Dods.[108] Other critics in the Free Church attracted attack from those who opposed them – A. B. Bruce and Henry Drummond being but two – but Dods seemed to irritate the conservatives most. He was an articulate and erudite spokesman for the critical position, and will here be treated as representative of the liberal Free Church position on higher criticism.

Dods, whose father was the eminent conservative minister Marcus Dods of Belford, the author of the revered work *On the Incarnation of the Eternal Word*,[109] aroused the ire of the conservatives as early as 1877 when one of his sermons was brought to the attention of the Free Presbytery of Glasgow. 'Revelation and Inspiration' was to become a famous sermon, including as it did the much quoted statement that:

> No careful student of Scripture can well deny that there are inaccuracies in the gospels and elsewhere – inaccuracies such as occur in ordinary writings through imperfect information or lapse of memory, sufficient entirely to explode the myth of infallibility.[110]

107 And, in the opinion of the conservatives, William Robertson Smith had a lot to answer for. *The Signal* made this abundantly clear in 1883: 'although in one sense ended [the case], has by no means ended in its painful results. It was the means of revealing a state of things in the Free Church on the question of Scripture, by many of the supporters of the discarded professor, which could not have been previously believed to exist, and by which the good name of the Free Church has been greatly injured': 'The present crisis in Scotland', *The Signal* (Feb. 1883), p. 18.

108 It almost goes without saying that Dods was also greatly admired within his Church. He was proposed for a Chair in New College at the age of 34, but 'magnanimously withdrew his name in favour of the candidature of a friend'. In 1875, he was nearly appointed to a Chair at Glasgow, but requested that the Church keep him where he was: S. J. Edwards (Jnr), 'Marcus Dods: With Special Reference to his Teaching Ministry' (Edinburgh University, Ph.D. thesis, 1960), pp. 396–7. When the Synods and Presbyteries of the Free Church were asked to propose a name to be the new Professor of New Testament Exegesis at New College in 1889, 5 Synods and 43 Presbyteries sent up the name of Dods, with 9 Presbyteries being sufficiently committed to him to send his name up alone. And despite conservative objections, he was elected by a clear overall majority: *PDGAFCS*, 1889, pp. 76, 88 and App. XXVI.

109 The name of Marcus Dods Senior was actually used in a debate on the floor of the General Assembly in May 1890. Robert Howie of Govan urged Dods Junior to bear in mind his father's theological position, a line of approach that earned cries of 'shame': *PDGAFCS*, 1890, p. 80. His son's position was 'refuted' by a series of quotations from one of his books, reproduced in a controversial pamphlet in 1890: *The Presently Controverted Opinions of Professor Marcus Dods, D.D. on The Inspiration of Holy Scripture, Refuted by the Rev. Marcus Dods, Belford, Northumberland, in 'Remarks on the Bible' (publ. 1828)* (Edinburgh and Glasgow, 1890).

110 Beaton, *History of the Free Presbyterian Church*, p. 69: quoting Dods.

This remark was a red rag to the conservative bulls, and is typical of the kind of thing that Dods was to say all through his Free Church career. Even his own admirers admitted that he had 'that kind of aloofness that makes him sometimes appear, to one who listens to him in the pulpit, as if he belonged to a different order of being from oneself'.[111] In much of his writing and preaching there seems to be some of the same reckless energy that characterised the brilliant but controversial work of Robertson Smith. Dods had no doubt that what he was doing was bringing the theology of the Free Church forward into the light of the nineteenth century; indeed he believed that it was something of which to be ashamed if theology had not progressed in the half century leading up to 1889:

> Nothing is to-day as it was fifty years ago ... If it were true that the-ology had made no growth during this auspicious season, this were a scandal, to be whispered in corners and bewailed in private, not to be trumpeted on the housetops.[112]

In this his inaugural lecture as Professor of New Testament Exegesis at New College, Edinburgh, he acknowledged that there were those

> men neither ignorant nor prejudiced who sincerely believe that there is great danger in present theological movements, or who suspect and fear that present tendencies will not contribute to the strengthening of Christ's kingdom.[113]

If he wanted to avoid wounding the sensibilities of such men, he scarcely showed much sign of it. His language was, if anything, even more shocking to the uninitiated than Robertson Smith's had been. In a sermon preached at St Giles's Cathedral in Edinburgh in September 1889 – only two months after his inaugural New College lecture – Dods's language was almost guaranteed to arouse intense passions on the part of the conservatives, with the phrase: 'we must not too hastily conclude that even a belief in Christ's divinity is essential to the true Christian',[114] producing reactions ranging from incredulity to downright horror.

Much of what could be called Dods's higher critical views, however, were no more than reiterations of what had been said in Germany for decades. What was so shocking to the conservatives in the Free Church was to hear them coming from the lips of a Free Church minister who was a D.D., and who became a New College professor. Dods himself admitted that what was being done was not new:

> the new method is known as historical criticism – sometimes since

---

[111] A. R. Simpson in *PDGAFCS*, 1889, p. 82. 'He was', said John O'Neil, 'always bold in speech, and his boldness got him into trouble': J. O'Neil, 'New Testament', in Wright and Badcock, *Disruption to Diversity*, p. 83.

[112] Dods, *Recent Progress in Theology*, p. 6.

[113] Ibid., p. 8.

[114] M. Dods, *What is a Christian?* (Edinburgh, 1889), p. 8.

Eichorn's time unhappily called 'higher criticism' – a method which is not really in itself new, but is now employed with much greater vigour and exactness than in the past ... this method is *inevitable*.[115]

Dods passionately believed in criticism, arguing that it was misrepresented and misunderstood as well as acknowledging that it was open to being abused. In the lecture quoted above, delivered in 1904 before Lake Forest College, Illinois, he stated of criticism that:

The popular suspicion or jealousy of it arises from a misunderstanding of its nature, its aims, its instruments. Sometimes it is even spoken of as antagonistic to Christianity. It is identified with certain of its manifestations, and is forthwith condemned. But the abuse of an instrument does not nullify or condemn its legitimate use.[116]

In this he was echoing his great clarion call for the further toleration of criticism which he delivered in his inaugural lecture before New College, Edinburgh, in 1889:

Of course, all criticism is not earnest and wise. There are frivolous and foolish critics, just as there are alas! frivolous and foolish men in all professions ... [but] if criticism and free discussion have opened the door to extravagances, it is they also that will eject them ... It is not only the Bible which is thrown into the crucible, but every theory concerned with the Bible is also sifted and tried. And to fear that, in the process, damage will accrue to the Bible, is to fear that what we have taken for gold may turn out to be only alloy. Free criticism and free discussion form the only path to the truth.[117]

This lecture was attended by an audience of sufficient size to cause it to be shifted to the Free Assembly Hall – so in a celebrated irony his ringing defence of criticism was delivered from the very same moderator's chair where Robertson Smith's teaching had been condemned less than ten years before.

Dods's refutation of the attacks on criticism was summarised in the Illinois lecture in the following analogy:

Criticism is not a hostile force hovering round the march of the Christian Church, picking off all loosely attached followers and

115 M. Dods, *The Bible: Its Origin and Nature* (Edinburgh, 1905), p. 167. Emphasis his. This was in a lecture entitled 'The Trustworthiness of the Gospels'.

116 Ibid., pp. 167–8.

117 M. Dods, *Recent Progress in Theology*, pp. 9–11. This is a fascinating echo of the words of the venerated Disruption Father Robert Smith Candlish; decades earlier he had written, 'The advocates of inspiration – even of verbal inspiration – have no objection whatever to cast the Bible unreservedly into the crucible of exegetical and antiquarian analysis; and they are not careful though the result should be, along with the explanation of many old puzzles, the raising of some new ones ... they accept the Scriptures upon deeper evidence than what the shifting discoveries or conjectures of the day can unsettle': R. S. Candlish, *Examination of Mr Maurice's Theological Essays* (London, 1854), p. 386.

galling the main body; it is rather the highly trained corps of scouts and skirmishers thrown out on all sides to ascertain in what direction it is safe and possible for the Church to advance.[118]

Indeed in an earlier lecture, Dods had seen the real enemy of the faith as being the traditional, non-critical view of Scripture. In his Illinois lecture of 1904 on 'Infallibility', Dods spoke about errors in the Bible and said that there were theologians who maintained the infallible accuracy of every single statement in it. Perhaps because he was in the United States, the examples he cited were A. A. Hodge and B. B. Warfield but their position was, give or take the occasional jot and tittle, exactly the position of Dods's ecclesiastical enemies at home.[119] In volume two of the *Presbyterian Review*, for example, it had been asserted by Hodge and Warfield that 'a proved error in Scripture contradicts not only our doctrine, but the Bible claims, and therefore its inspiration in making these claims',[120] and Dods pointed out that

> not a few less distinguished [than Hodge and Warfield] persons declare that their salvation depends on the absolute accuracy of every word from the first in Genesis to the last in Revelation ... and in some instances the recoil from a belief in the infallible accuracy of Scripture has had disastrous consequences. It is truly said that 'the man who binds up the cause of Christianity with the literal accuracy of the Bible is no friend of Christianity, for with the rejection of that comes the rejection of the Bible itself, and faith is shattered'.[121]

He cited the cases of Renan and Bradlaugh, both of whom lost their faith as a result of being tied to an interpretation of inerrancy which further study could no longer entertain, and he was highly critical of those who made such claims for literal inerrancy, stating that 'no doctrine more surely manufactures sceptics'.[122] He referred to the method with which he operated as 'the acid of criticism', a description which would doubtless have won the approval of men like Donald Beaton, John Macleod and Neil Cameron. But instead of seeing it as an acid which burned away everything with which it came into contact – a corrosive, destructive and painful process – he saw its function as to 'eat away every thing that has been interposed between the soul and Christ'.[123]

Dods's defence of criticism was a classic enunciation of the position of the so-called Believing Critics, and is symbolic of how large the gulf was between them and the conservatives. The point is that they not only

---

[118] Dods, *The Bible*, p. 168.

[119] By 1904, of course, most of his 'enemies' were not in his denomination; they had departed in one or other of the two schisms of 1893 and 1900 and now resided in the Free Presbyterian Church or in the Free Church (continuing).

[120] A. A. Hodge and B. B. Warfield, 'Inspiration', *Presbyterian Rev.*, ii (6) (1881), p. 245.

[121] Dods, *The Bible*, pp. 140–1.

[122] Ibid., p. 142.

[123] Dods, *Recent Progress in Theology*, p. 13.

fundamentally disagreed on the methods of criticism, but on the purpose of criticism and the basic validity of the critical approach. As Dods commented at the time of his 'trial' by the Free General Assembly in 1890, wearily if not bitterly, 'no theory of Scripture promulgated at present by me would be at all likely to find acceptance [from my opponents]'.[124] The conservatives, as will be seen, viewed biblical criticism within the Free Church as an attack on Christianity; Dods and those like him regarded it as a defence.

The problem was that the two sides had an ultimately incompatible interpretation of Scripture and what was involved in terms like 'inspired', 'inerrant' and 'infallible'. To men like those who departed the Free Church in 1893, the idea of admitting the existence of errors in the Bible – then or at any subsequent stage of their lives – was as inconceivable as declaring that the world was flat. To Dods, however, it was an absolutely essential part of the nineteenth-century counter-attack against the perceived ravages which science and criticism had wrought on religious belief. He believed that openly acknowledging the presence of errors or inaccuracies in the Bible stole much of the thunder from those whose attacks on the Christian faith were based solely on the apparent mistakes present throughout the sixty-six books of the Old and New Testaments. He called the attempts to deny Scriptural errors both 'disingenuous' and 'thoughtless', arguing that it really just produced new questions in the place of the original ones. But Dods, so often depicted as an ecclesiastical savage by his opponents, was in fact very understanding of what he considered to be the wrong approach and seemed to understand exactly the motivation behind what he called 'this wholesome Christian instinct':

> The reluctance to admit the existence of errors in Scripture is not surprising, and is even in a sense commendable. It arises from our natural instinct to reverence and exalt those who have been the organs of revelation, and in a manner mediators between God and us. Knowing how much we owe to them we cannot bear to ascribe to them any least degree of faultiness. When Peter and Paul disagree, we turn away from the quarrel, and refuse to draw the necessary inference that Peter did his best to mislead the Church on a matter of vital importance.[125]

To men who held to the view of the direct, dictated, verbal inspiration of every word of Scripture, admitting errors of any kind meant admitting errors at source, from the mouth of God himself. While this meant either denying the existence of the errors or else admitting that their original faith was fundamentally flawed, to men like Dods there was no such problem.

---

124 *PDGAFCS*, 1890: 'Special Report by College Committee with Reference to Certain Writings by Professors Dods and Bruce', p. 31.
125 Dods, *The Bible*, p. 145.

This was, in fact, a major reason why Dods was such a controversial figure in the nineteenth-century Free Church. He was perfectly at ease with the idea that there were errors in the Canon of Scripture. In 1900 he said:

> It is not my business to point out errors in Scripture, but to show that, notwithstanding the errors pointed out, Scripture infallibly accomplishes its purpose of presenting Christ to men ... only mischief comes of affirming the literal ignorance of Scripture, only good comes of maintaining its infallibility as a guide to Christ and God.[126]

He had raised this spectre as early as 1876 in the sermon cited above, and his position in the intervening years did not deviate much from the way he expressed himself when a visiting lecturer at Lake Forest College, Illinois, in 1904. Indeed virtually midway between these points lies Dods's inaugural lecture at the New College in 1889, which still burns with much of the energy which it must have possessed on its delivery. It was in the library of that College that Dods first appreciated that things were changing, when he realised that belief in the literal truth of what he believed to be an indefensible canon was no longer necessary. Dods quoted the words of Archdeacon Farrar:

> its science has been proved to be childish; its ethics are tainted with hatred and intolerance; its history and chronology are obsolete; its harmonistic methods are casuistical to dishonesty; its views about the inspiration of the vowel points, and the perfect accuracy of the text have been covered with confusion; its whole method of interpretation has been discredited and abandoned.[127]

While he recognised that these were 'strong words', he felt that they did not go too far in condemning the old theory of Scripture. This theory, which Free Church conservatives held so dear and considered to be essential, was a theory which he declared in ringing tones to have been one which

> has made the Bible an offence to many honest men, which is dishonouring to God, and which has turned enquirers into sceptics by the thousand, a theory which should be branded as heretical in every Christian church.[128]

---

[126] M. Dods, Letter to the *Dundee Advertiser*, 24 Oct. 1900.

[127] Farrar: quoted in Dods, *Recent Progress in Theology*, p. 30. Farrar himself was to come in for some criticism a few years later when the *Free Presbyterian Magazine* compared him to 'The Hollander who would busy himself destroying the sea wall that keeps his fields dry' on account of his 'amicably piloting a company of Romanists through Canterbury Cathedral'. Roman Catholicism never strayed far from the top of any Free Presbyterian list of movements to be feared: 'Insane Liberalism', *FPM*, ii (6) (1897), p. 236.

[128] Dods, *Recent Progress in Theology*, p. 30.

It is little wonder that the conservatives were enraged by this approach, given that Dods was not only denying the truth of the Old Paths but suggesting that these very paths had been driving men away from the Gospel and were in themselves heretical. The scene was set for a fairly explosive ecclesiastical showdown in which each side freely accused the other of heresy.

Dods's own opinion of the value of Scripture as a literal record of real events is worth sketching in briefly by way of contrast to those who opposed him. The conservatives in the Free Church, particularly those who left in 1893 to form the Free Presbyterian Church, held that the Bible was the Word of God, written by the hand of those whose names it bore. In their opinion, it contained not a single error from 'In the beginning ...' to '... Amen'.[129] Dods, on the other hand, found faults of varying magnitude in this theory. As he himself declared: 'not a few ... persons declare that their salvation depends on the absolute accuracy of every word from the first in Genesis to the last in Revelation. Happily their salvation depends on nothing of the kind.'[130] Of Genesis Dods said:

> No one can read the book without becoming aware that he is frequently presented with varying accounts of the same event. Thus we find two accounts of the Creation of man; two narratives of the Flood [etc.] ... this phenomenon gradually but surely conveys to the mind of the reader the impression, that he has before him not the free and continuous and single narrative of one author, but the work of a writer who is endeavouring to combine at least two narratives.[131]

Nothing terribly outrageous there by modern standards, certainly, but in the context of the nineteenth-century Free Church the presence of a statement like this in what was a 'Handbook for Bible Classes' must have been a stark warning to the conservatives that there was more to come from a man who would by 1890 have become, like A. B. Davidson before him, 'an idol of the students, and deservedly so'.[132] The Mosaic authorship, the unity of the narrative and the presence of divine verbal inspiration were all under attack. His precise interpretation of Genesis as against nineteenth-century science will be examined more closely shortly, but one statement will suffice to illustrate the general thread of his argument. In the introduction to the handbook cited above, Dods stated that:

129 See, e.g., 'The supreme need of the times', *FPM*, ii (5) (1897), p. 162.
130 Dods, *The Bible*, p. 140; see also M. Dods, *An Introduction to the New Testament* (London, 1892), pp. 235–47.
131 M. Dods, *The Book of Genesis: With Introduction and Notes* (Handbooks for Bible Classes Series, Edinburgh, 1882) [hereafter *Book of Genesis* (HBC)], p. x.
132 *PDGAFCS*, 1890, p. 76. The response to this statement by Dr Laird of Cupar was 'applause in the students' gallery'. Davidson, for his part, was admitted to be 'a born teacher, and the idol of his students' by none other than the Free Presbyterian father Donald Beaton: Beaton, *Neil Cameron*, p. 53.

There is no regard to scientific accuracy in the statement that God made the world in six days but the impression left is strictly true, that it was an easy matter, a mere week's work with God, to create the world. Science says this planet has been about one hundred million years getting into shape and reaching its present condition; and that the events spoken of in this chapter as occupying six days really occupied periods that must be reckoned by millions of years.[133]

Again this was what was being said by many at the time – indeed, there were plenty who were going much further – but to the men who were to part company with Dods and his Free Church in 1893, it must have seemed a glaringly heretical example of higher criticism.

Of the Old Testament in general Dods was on record as saying 'literal inherency cannot be claimed ... [there are] certain errors in chronology and other details', and he challenged the traditional theory of inerrancy when he said:

> If we are told in Samuel that the price paid for Araunah's threshing floor was fifty silver shekels, while in Chronicles we are told that it was six hundred gold shekels, does this prevent my perceiving that Christ reveals God and accepting that revelation?[134]

He went still further though, when he declared that the Old Testament did not only include errors but also what he termed 'immoralities'. This was a remark which aroused great anger among his conservative opponents but was a position which Dods was more than ready to defend, given that he made the remark as the Free Church's delegate at the Pan-Presbyterian Council on 5 July 1888 and the paper of which it was part had been printed and circulated in the *British Weekly* before it was delivered at the Council.[135] In his response to the official complaints to the General Assembly which this remark provoked, Dods was unrepentant and actually elucidated with characteristic clarity – even, it might be said, with a somewhat patronising note of sarcasm – what he had meant by the word 'immoralities':

> In speaking of 'immoralities' in Scripture, I do not mean that it records the immoral actions of persons whose lives are recorded as part of the history of Israel, for that was of course necessary, if it was to be a faithful record. But I mean that actions which are severely reprobated in the New Testament are allowed or commended, or even commanded, in the Old. Under this category fall such laws as 'An eye for an eye, and a tooth for a tooth', which our Lord explicitly repeals; the extirpation of tribes conquered in war; the

133 Dods, *Book of Genesis* (HBC), pp. xvii–xviii.
134 Dods, *The Bible*, pp. 135, 140.
135 'The Free Presbytery of Dundee and the Confession of Faith', *The Signal* (Aug. 1888), pp. 237–8.

occasional taking of young women into captivity; the permission of bigamy, and even of polygamy. It matters little what we call such things, but what I maintain is, that no true and sufficient theory of revelation is possible until such things are frankly recognized. We wrong Scripture by refusing to look at it as it is.[136]

As can be imagined, this remark of Dods's was one which the conservatives fastened on to with particular enthusiasm in their attempts to rid themselves of this turbulent priest.

When it came to the New Testament – he was, it should be remembered, Professor of New Testament Exegesis at New College, Edinburgh, from 1889 – Dods was equally certain that problems existed for those who claimed literal, word-by-word, inerrancy. In his 1904 lecture on 'Infallibility', delivered in Illinois, Dods asserted the following:

Restricting ourselves to the New Testament and to the Gospels, and to the universally admitted results of criticism, it has been put beyond all reasonable doubt that there exist irreconcilable discrepancies between the four accounts of some of our Lord's sayings and actions, and that it is impossible to determine, save on grounds of probability, which Gospel we should follow.[137]

He then proceeded to provide 'examples selected at random'. He cited the fact that none of the Gospel writers agreed on what had been written on the superscription on the cross during Christ's crucifixion, or in their accounts of Christ's post-resurrection appearances. According to Dods, the events surrounding the burial and resurrection of Jesus – absolutely central to the faith of the Free Church – were recounted in conflicting ways in different Gospels. 'The narrative of the events accompanying the resurrection, as it exists in Matthew,' he observed, 'is generally irreconcilable with that of the other Gospels.'[138] He pointed out that there were differences regarding the date of the Last Supper and Crucifixion, and that there were sayings which had a bearing on modern life which revealed 'very puzzling discrepancies':

For example, in Matt. xix. 9, we read, 'Whosoever shall put away his wife, except for fornication, and shall marry another, committeth adultery.' But in Luke this great law is given without any exception, 'Whosoever putteth away his wife, and marrieth another, committeth adultery.' Which of these two very diverse laws ought the Church to follow?[139]

He was also able, in the same lecture, to give examples of both Matthew

---

136 M. Dods, 'Remarks', in 'Appendix to the Special Report of the College Committee', *PDGAFCS*, 1890 (Report V–A), p. 31.
137 Dods, *The Bible*, pp. 135–6.
138 Ibid., p. 136.
139 Ibid., pp. 136–7.

and Mark ascribing Old Testament quotations to the wrong Prophet, while in his New College inaugural lecture a few years before he had spoken of 'the impossibility of harmonising the synoptical gospels', and that it would only be slightly exaggerating to

> say that we can now sit with each evangelist at his desk and read along with him the documents he employed and detect the motives which prompted him to omit this incident and give prominence to that, to leave one saying of Jesus where he found it, and shift another to a different connection.[140]

Dods, then, was a critic whose attack on the traditional view of Scripture was as sustained as it was devastating. What has to be borne in mind, though, is that Dods viewed himself as a Believing Critic. He spoke about the German higher critics with as much reverence and respect as the conservatives did about the Puritan fathers, because he believed that the critics had moved the study of the Bible forward and helped to protect the fundamentals of the faith. His words were often taken out of context, and, when cut off from the avowed faith which imbued them with life, they could indeed at times appear to be the words of a sceptical if not atheistic wolf in the sheep pen. The very method by which the Free Church handled matters of controversy lent itself to this process of misinterpretation, as presbyteries sent in with their complaints the words of Marcus Dods in little snippets. Divorced from the context of an intelligent mind struggling to accept – on his own terms – the questions which history and science were posing all men of religious persuasion, these words could be seen as distilled heresy.

But while they must in some ways stand on their own as one angle on this man's religious position, the statements of Dods the Critic must be seen alongside the words of Dods the Believer in order to grasp some of the complexities of Dods the Believing Critic. His inaugural lecture to his students at New College concludes with a remarkable paragraph, which is worth quoting at length in order to convey some of the essence of this much-reviled and much-revered professor:

> We may enter, then, on our study of the New Testament, assured that the accomplished criticism to which it has been subjected during the past generation has only added to its interest, and subtracted nothing from its power, that the fierce light which has beat upon it has only made it seem a more real and intelligible book, and that when stripped of the fictitious robes of honour which timorous and unworthy men have thrown over it, it stands out in its native majesty, and its real power is recognized ... The New Testament is a mine out of which the gold has not all been brought to the surface, nor all sifted and refined ... there remains much to be

---

[140] Dods, *Recent Progress in Theology*, pp. 31, 36.

done, and of a kind which will attract the energies and resources of the most ambitious mind. For the preacher of Christ this study is indispensable and invaluable. It is in the New Testament he can meet with Christ and learn His mind. It is there he can get rid of all that has overlaid the figure of the Lord, and see Him face to face. It is there that he can learn from the lips of Christ Himself the gospel he has to preach; and by living through the same scenes and breathing the same air with Him, come at length to understand His purposes and enter into His Spirit.[141]

The problem for the Free Church at this time was that many men would have listened to all that and pointed out that the road to Hell also was paved with good intentions.[142]

The Conservative Reaction to Biblical Criticism

1. The future Free Presbyterians

Not everyone in the Free Church was either a passionate supporter of the higher critics or a passionate opponent. There were, not surprisingly, men who fell somewhere between the two extremes, sensing a degree of virtue on both sides. But in the context of the Second Disruption of 1893, it is the contrast between these two extremes which is of most interest. Everyone who joined that exodus from the Free Church held firmly to the most conservative position on criticism, and, as will be seen, the increasing influence of the higher criticism was one of their principal retrospective justifications for taking the step which they took.

The *Free Presbyterian Magazine* in 1896 went so far as to suggest that there was no point in the Free Church attempting to preach the Gospel as long as it had higher critics in positions of influence. It accused the Church of rank hypocrisy over a plan by the Free Presbytery of Edinburgh to organise a ten-day evangelistic campaign, saying:

> Before they attempt to evangelise others, let them evangelise themselves. Let the heads and chiefs of the Church repent of their manifold backslidings since 1863, or earlier, when they ... perfected their fall by giving place in the Church to those who rob Christ of His glory and destroy the foundation of all evangelistic work. It is vain to affect zeal for the salvation of souls, while those who insult the majesty of Christ sit in the high places of the Church.[143]

The language here has a distinctly Old Testament ring to it, with talk of 'heads and chiefs' repenting of 'manifold backslidings'. And the term

---

[141] Ibid., pp. 36–7.
[142] An excellent summary of the controversial aspect of Dods's career is found in chap. 3 of S. J. Edwards's thesis: Edwards, 'Marcus Dods', pp. 108–80.
[143] 'More labour in the fire', *FPM*, i (5) (1896), p. 195.

'high places' has connotations – possibly subconscious on the part of the writer – of the high places which the Israelites had been wont to set up to worship false Gods in Old Testament times; the consequences for Israel were generally severe divine judgements. Clearly, the Free Presbyterians believed that one divine judgement had already come upon the Free Church in the withdrawal of God's favour on its preaching, rendering their attempts at evangelism 'vain'.

Marcus Dods and other critics had argued over the previous two decades that the divinity of Christ and the other central precepts of the Christian faith were not tied to the literal inerrancy of Scripture or, for example, to the Old Testament being written by the men whose names it bore.[144] The Free Presbyterians, however, saw things very differently:

> there is no Christ to save souls in Edinburgh but the Christ who has staked His infallibility on the Mosaic account of the fall, or Isaiah's true and proper authorship of the whole book which bears his name, and as long as Professors Henry Drummond and George Adam Smith are calmly allowed to give Christ the lie in these respects, it is perfectly in vain for the Free Church to play at evangelistic work in Edinburgh or elsewhere.[145]

This, again, was very strong language for the Free Presbyterians to use. To suggest that the very presence of men with higher critical views in college chairs rendered the Church's attempts at spreading the Gospel null and void was an extraordinary charge.

It is another manifestation of the 'Achan' analogy which appeared in the magazine the following year, to which some reference has been made already. Again it has the scent of a subtle change of their position after the event. The logical conclusion to be drawn from the above statement is that the Free Church was equally incapable of preaching the Gospel when other critics sat 'in the high places of the Church'. Therefore the Church had been just as flawed, it had been just as 'vain ... to play at evangelistic work' before the Free Presbyterians came out. It has to be stressed that the position apparently advanced in this article was the result of a retrospective judgement on their part, as there was never any suggestion before May 1893 that the mere presence of higher critics in the Church rendered the Church's evangelising efforts in vain. Quite the contrary, since all the students, as well as Macfarlane and Macdonald, had continued to preach – presumably, they felt, with divine sanction – in the Free Church up to 1893 when Dods, Bruce, Drummond, Smith *et al.* were either in formal 'high places' or were well on

---

[144] Dods, as has been noted above, declared that 'not a few ... persons declare that their salvation depends on the absolute accuracy of every word from the first in Genesis to the last in Revelation. Happily their salvation depends on nothing of the kind': Dods, *The Bible*, p. 140. See also Dods, *Introduction to the New Testament*, pp. 235–47.
[145] Ibid., p. 195.

their way up to them. Neil Cameron, in fact, preached what he considered to be Gospel sermons while actually a student of Marcus Dods at New College, Edinburgh,[146] but does not seem to have considered that they were made any less effective on account of the Church having men like Dods clutched to its bosom. Despite this he is on record as saying, in January 1898, 'Allow the truth of God to be doubted and carved by ungodly men at their pleasure, and you cannot be guiltless in church fellowship with such.'[147] This was not an admission of guilt on the part of those men who had cohabited with the higher critics up to May 1893, but was a critique of those who had remained in the Free Church after that date. Willing – albeit unhappily – to live with the higher criticism while members of the Free Church, the Free Presbyterians were willing – and happy – to use it as another stick with which to beat their old Church when they had left.

There was, though, some measure of predictability about it, as there was an instinctive need to look back and justify what had been a controversial – and bitterly opposed – separation. Having taken a step which had caused them a great deal of personal trauma and difficulty, the Free Presbyterians can perhaps be excused for demonising the Church from which they had fled in 1893. In doing this they considered many developments in the Free Church after they had left, and most especially after the Union with the United Presbyterians in 1900. Cameron's New Year's Day lecture of 1926[148] looked at a wide spectrum of activities in the other Churches but reserved a special place for the distance the United Free Church had gone 'in denying the infallibility and inerrancy of the Scriptures of the Old and New Testaments'. He quoted from a report read to the General Assembly of the United Free Church, entitled 'How Do We Regard the Bible?', and the impact on Free Presbyterian listeners can be well imagined when they heard statements like:

> Do we hold that every word of the Bible is true? No, we do not. Do we accept the views of the Bible on scientific questions? No, we do not. Do we approve of all the moral sentiments expressed in the Bible? No, certainly not. Do we regard the Bible as infallible history? No. Do we agree with all the opinions of St Paul? No, we do not ...

---

146 'When he came to study theology in the New College he was deeply pained with some of the teaching of the Professors – Dr Davidson and Dr Dods particularly': Beaton, *Neil Cameron*, p. 53.

147 N. Cameron, 'Jude 3.', *FPM*, ii (9) (1898), p. 335.

148 The New Year's Day lecture was a tradition instituted early in the history of the Free Presbyterian Church – in July 1898 – by which the service of thanksgiving on the first day of the year (or the second should the first day happen to be a Sabbath) should see the ministers preaching 'on the Church's principles'. This usually took the form of an apologia of their actions in 1893, outlining the process by which the Free Church declined from a position of divine favour to being a Church from which departure became necessary. The tradition has continued, virtually unbroken, to the present day. See Beaton, *History of the Free Presbyterian Church*, p. 130.

> Further, we know that large parts of the early books of the Old Testament are not history at all in the modern sense ... Possibly the amount of Scripture which is thus living, and which actually operates in the lives of some Christians, might turn out to be little more than a tenth of the whole.[149]

His conclusion was a calculated and brilliant *coup de grâce*:

> But enough of this blasphemy. Any body of men who could in the name of a Christian Church homologate the above statements about the Bible has ceased to have the least claim to be denominated Christians. Was it not fully time for us to have fled from such in 1893? Is not this blasphemy against God and His Word the strongest proof imaginable that we did what was right then?[150]

Time and again, the Free Presbyterian founders were able to look back on the higher criticism and portray it as an unspeakable evil from which they had to flee, like Lot from Sodom. Cameron, it will be remembered, had described those who stayed in the Free Church as 'content to dwell in Sodom'. Like Lot in Sodom, though, questions might well be asked, such as: 'What were they doing there in the first place?' and 'Why did it take them so long to leave?' The doctrines of the higher critics were there in the 'high places' of the Church long before the Declaratory Act had even been thought about, and these doctrines seem to have taken on a more important role in the Second Disruption with the benefit of hindsight than they actually had in 1893. Indeed, Donald Macfarlane's biography of his old friend and fellow founding father of the Free Presbyterian Church, Donald Macdonald, published in 1903,[151] does not mention higher criticism or anything related to it even once. If the Free Presbyterians were as horrified at the presence of 'Achans' in 'high places' as they said in statements made after May 1893, perhaps their Disruption would have taken place some years before.

The crucial point in their defence is that they believed that the higher critics' attack on the Bible paved the way for the later formalisation and legalisation of the liberal position in the Declaratory Act. It was when this Act was passed and subsequently ratified that they believed the time had come to take the step of separation. Neil Cameron, for one, made this clear in at least two of his New Year's Day lectures, stating in 1920 that 'all the changes they had made were now to be bound on the neck of the Free Church'[152] by the Declaratory Act, and in 1926 that it was the attack on the Bible which resulted in the later attack which

---

[149] N. Cameron, 'New Year's Day Lecture, 1926', in Beaton, *Neil Cameron*, pp. 179–80.

[150] Ibid., p. 180.

[151] D. Macfarlane, *Memoir and Remains of the Rev. Donald Macdonald, Sheildaig, Ross-shire* (Dingwall, 1903).

[152] Cameron, 'New Year's Day Lecture, 1926', p. 156.

was launched against the Confession of Faith, and particularly against the doctrines of election; the fall of his posterity in Adam; the doctrine of the atonement as set forth in the Confession; and the doctrine of the necessity of regeneration by the Holy Ghost through the Word of God.[153]

Here the ideas of the higher critics were seen as the vital precursor to the ultimately unbearable attacks which were to follow on what were seen as 'fundamentals'. Ironically, the initial attack on the Bible was not seen at the time as something which could not be endured; but when this was institutionalised in the form of the Declaratory Act, which tied them formally to doctrines they could not accept, the Free Presbyterians could stay no longer.[154] It was, moreover, a convenient way of associating something which could easily be portrayed as evil – the higher criticism – with the labyrinthine complexities of the Declaratory Act – something which was not so easy to portray as stemming from 'the dragon'. The higher criticism, it seems, had its uses even for the most conservative of conservative Free Churchmen.

There is no doubt that the men who later became Free Presbyterians felt extremely strongly about the issue, although, as has been suggested, they seemed to consider it a more fundamental and fatal flaw in the Free Church after they had left it than when they were still within its communion. It would be extremely unfair, though, to say that the Free Presbyterians' opposition to higher criticism was formulated solely as a retrospective justification for what some of their adversaries called the sin of schism. Nearly all their writings and sermons burn with a passion which goes beyond mere point-scoring in an ecclesiastical tiff. Neil Cameron, for example, referred to the men responsible for making 'the absolute infallibility and inerrancy of the Bible, as being the Word of God ... become a thing of the past' as 'traitors to God and men', while referring to the changes which were taking place in the Free Church as 'this flood which Satan was casting out of his mouth in order to carry her [the Free Church] away completely'.[155] Donald Beaton, his friend and colleague over a period of decades, said of Cameron's time as a student at New College, Edinburgh:

No one admired scholarship more than he when it was used in the interests of truth, but he unsparingly denounced it when it was used to undermine the eternal truth of God ... When he came to study theology in the New College he was deeply pained with some of the teaching of the Professors – Dr Davidson and Dr Dods particularly.[156]

153 Ibid., pp. 172–3.
154 It should be noted, of course, that defence of the Westminster Confession of Faith and of the inerrancy of Scripture were not inevitably linked. There were many people in the United States, e.g., who resolutely defended inerrancy while being at the same time critics of the Westminster Confession of Faith and the Calvinism which it championed.
155 Beaton, *Neil Cameron*, p. 20.
156 Ibid., p. 53.

Davidson and Dods were two of the principal enemies of all that the conservatives held dear, but although they were both seen as men who did immense damage, Beaton did see a distinction:

> [Davidson's] great gifts were used in administering the higher critical poison in small doses. It was done cautiously, but none the less effectively, and one of the first effects of it was seen in the teaching of Professor Robertson Smith, the most brilliant of Davidson's students. Dr Dods was not quite so cautious; he poured out glassfuls where Davidson administered drops, but both in the Old Testament and in the New Testament studies the deadly poison was instilled into the minds of students until even Dods himself had to confess that he was a backslider and had given up prayer.[157]

Cameron faced the higher critical views at first hand while at New College but he also saw that the prevailing wind in the Free Presbytery of Edinburgh was not blowing in favour of those who held his position. At a meeting of that Presbytery around 1890, he witnessed an attempt by the Synod of Glenelg and Presbytery of Chanonry to serve a libel against Dr Dods being frustrated by a tactical manoeuvre on the part of the liberals in the Edinburgh Presbytery, led by Robert Rainy. Cameron's opinion of this outcome was clear:

> the libel was shelved and the heretic was allowed to go on uncurbed instilling his poison into the minds of the future ministry of the Church. I felt pained at heart when I saw such trickery used in a court of the Church which was considered Christian. It would be bad enough in a court of Jesuits, as it savoured much of their casuistry. I saw that discipline was a thing of the past in the Free Church.[158]

As early as the third issue of the *Free Presbyterian Magazine*, the Rev. Alexander Macrae, one of the first ministers in the new denomination after the Second Disruption, was quoted in a sermon talking about those men who chose to attack the Bible. Preaching from Matthew iii.12 on God purging His threshing-floor with a fan, Macrae stated that the floor was a metaphor for the Church, and that

> the floor is much polluted by the too many unscriptural views of truth that are given out. The floor was wonderfully purged in Scotland through the instrumentality of the excellent reformers whom God raised up; but now there is an imaginary enlightenment that looks with contempt upon the attainments of the Reformation ... doctrines are authoritatively sanctioned that are subversive of the doctrines of the Word of God. They 'wrest the Scriptures to their own destruction'.[159]

---

[157] Ibid., pp. 53–4.
[158] Ibid., p. 48.
[159] A. Macrae, 'Matthew iii.12.', *FPM*, i (3) (1896), p. 93.

To call the background to the rise of higher criticism in Scotland an 'imaginary enlightenment' is a classic example of the Free Presbyterian position, bearing in mind the fact that Neil Cameron was to call the higher criticism 'this light which has proved to be truly darkness',[160] and 'this sacrilege', and called the critics 'these infidels'.[161]

The conservatives in the Free Church, and particularly those who left at the Second Disruption, simply could not conceive of the notion of the 'believing critic' – the two words were incompatible and made no sense when put together, unless the definition of criticism was very different from the one men like Marcus Dods or William Robertson Smith would have used. While Dods and Smith and the others saw themselves as men of God, the conservatives in their Church saw them as servants of the Devil, and indeed Donald Beaton referred to Dods's work as 'unbelieving scholarship'.[162] In a New Year's Day lecture at St Jude's, Glasgow, in 1926 Neil Cameron made it abundantly clear where he considered the source of 'believing criticism' to be:

> The Church of Scotland Free began first in her Colleges to deny the inspiration of certain parts of the Bible about twenty years prior to our separation from her communion. Efforts were made to stem this tide of rationalism and infidelity. But the tide flowed into the Church with a force and velocity that caused intense anguish of heart to all lovers of God's Word, and it became clearer every year that, should the Lord allow her to drift down with the flood which the dragon poured out of his mouth to carry her away, she would become a complete wreck. While she lay on the lee-shore, and very near dangerous rocks, the 'doctrines' of the Word were attacked.[163]

This was very strong language indeed, especially when used about the doctrines held by some of the most esteemed men in the Free Church at that time and, if General Assembly votes are to be believed, by a majority of her communion as well. By the time the majority of the Free Church began voting for doctrines which 'the dragon poured out of his mouth', men like Neil Cameron found it easy to justify separation.

This is a point which is well worth stressing; the men who became Free Presbyterians did not oppose the critics on the grounds of a gentle academic disagreement over the placing of emphasis, but rather opposed them as the very servants of Satan. Neil Cameron in 1898 stated that:

> No works are more wicked in the sight of God, than those which lead immortal souls away from worshipping God, as he has

---

160 Cameron in Beaton, *History of the Free Presbyterian Church*, p. 93.
161 N. Cameron, 'New Year's Day Lecture, 1920', in Beaton, *Neil Cameron*, p. 155. His text on this occasion was 1 Samuel vii.12.
162 Beaton, *History of the Free Presbyterian Church*, p. 93.
163 Cameron, 'New Year's Day Lecture, 1926', p. 172.

appointed in His Word. Satan's aims are to get this nation to disbe-
lieve the truth of God, to pull down that which our Godly fathers
built upon Christ, the rock, and to set up idolatrous worship.[164]

It was the attitude to the Bible which they believed divided them from
the men who called themselves critics. To reject one word of the Old
Testament, which they believed Christ himself had accepted in its
entirety, was tantamount to rejecting Christ himself. In the words of
Alex Macrae again:

> The chaff went away; but the wheat remained. That is exactly the
> case till now. Many will not listen to the faithful declarations of the
> Word of God, 'The time will come when they will not endure sound
> doctrine; but after their own lusts shall they heap to themselves
> teachers, having itching ears, and they shall turn away their ears
> from the truth, and shall be turned into fables' ... infinitely better it
> is to have the company of a few despised disciples who receive the
> words of Christ as the 'words of eternal life', than be associated with
> thousands who regard His doctrines as 'an hard saying'. He will,
> therefore, purge His floor with the fan of His Word.[165]

They had little doubt that the division in the Free Assembly over the
sanctity of every word of the Bible would be repeated at the great final
division into the wheat and the chaff. This was no divide between north
and south, between the academic and the self-taught, between the
believing critic and the plenary literalist; this, believed the conservatives,
was the divide between the Elect and the Damned.

The integrity of Scripture was such a central tenet of the Free Church
conservatives that the idea of interfering with it filled them not only with
anger but also with horror. Alex Macrae's sermons, like those of most
Free Presbyterian ministers, were heavily peppered with quotations from
Scripture. In some sections of his sermons, every second line holds a
portion of Scripture, appealing to the Bible to make and prove virtually
every point. It is this love of, reverence for, and familiarity with the Bible
that must be borne in mind when considering the Free Presbyterian
opposition to the higher critics. Macrae gave a solemn and heart-felt
warning to those who tried to denigrate what he termed the 'fan' of
God's Word:

> How many attempt to rend it to pieces! But it shall rend terribly the
> consciences of many eternally; for the worm shall not die, neither
> shall the fire be quenched ... how sadly deluded those are who
> endeavour to interpret it in a way to suit their own carnal tastes!
> The Scriptures, however shall not be changed, 'Till heaven and
> earth pass, one jot or one tittle shall in no wise pass from the law till

164 Cameron, 'Jude 3.', p. 333.
165 Macrae, 'Matthew iii.12.', p. 96.

all be fulfilled.' Some Churches think they can make any alterations they like on this fan. Can anything be more dishonouring to God than a deliberate denial on the part of any individual or Church, of the integrity and inerrancy of His Word? ... No individual or Church, or any power whatever, can take the fan out of Christ's hand, 'Strong is Thy hand, and high is Thy right hand.'[166]

Macrae and the other conservatives were literalist up to 'one jot or one tittle', and they believed that any who rejected this view were storing up damnation for themselves.

Although such issues as Sabbatarianism, the use of hymns in public worship or different attitudes to the Roman Catholic Church were argued over from a Scriptural perspective, such arguments involved different interpretations of the Bible's teaching. Men could legitimately differ in their interpretations, and even the Westminster Confession of Faith admitted that 'synods ... err'.[167] But the inspiration of the Bible was different. To a Highland Calvinist, raised on the infallibility and absolute verbal inerrancy of every biblical pronouncement – scientific, historical, legal and doctrinal – the calling into question of parts of the Bible was like telling him it was no longer necessary to retain his own vital organs in order to sustain life. Brought up on the Bible, in all probability first learning to read from the Bible – indeed for many Gaelic speakers their only reading material would have been the Gaelic Bible – venerating 'the Books' each morning and evening as they were brought out for the twice-daily family worship,[168] it is little wonder that such perceived attacks on that central part of their religious identity were unacceptable to the men who left the Free Church in 1893.[169]

---

[166] Ibid., p. 95.

[167] *The Westminster Confession of Faith* (Edinburgh, 1877), chap. 31, section 4.

[168] Rev. John Munro of Halkirk, e.g., had the duty of reading the Bible aloud at family worship from the age of 9; and it was said of James MacDonald of Halkirk that he knew his Bible so well that, despite being unable to read a word, he could recite it exactly as if he were reading, and that if he heard anyone misquoting a passage of Scripture he would correct them: A. Auld, *Ministers and Men in the Far North* (Wick, 1896), pp. 77–8, 165. One school teacher from Skye commented that there were many schools in the Highlands and Islands where 45 minutes every morning were dedicated to religious instruction and that in no school in the region was less than half-an-hour spent on it. 'Surely,' commented the writer, 'those teachers who devote one-seventh of every school day to the teaching of a subject not recognised by H. M. Inspector and on which no grant is paid, are nobly doing their duty': 'Letter to the editor', *The Signal* (Jun. 1888), p. 192.

[169] The central role of the Bible in the Highlands has been stressed by many observers who seem to be well qualified to make such judgements. James Hunter has said that 'its importance to the nineteenth century crofting community can hardly be over-estimated': Hunter, *Making of the Crofting Community*, p. 98; John MacInnes called the Highlanders 'a Bible-loving and church-going people': J. MacInnes, *The Evangelical Movement in the Highlands of Scotland* (Aberdeen, 1951), p. 7; while Donald Meek spoke of 'the elevation of the Bible to a position of pre-eminence among Highlanders. It was the Book of Books, which came to be known as An Fhìrinn ['The Truth'] and the message it contained presented a challenge to falsehood and error': D. E. Meek, 'The Bible and social change in the nineteenth-century Highlands', in D. F. Wright (ed.), *The Bible in Scottish Literature* (Edinburgh, 1988), p. 188.

It might be argued that the pivotal position of the Bible in the Highlands was due in part to its special place in what was still a largely oral culture. It is easy to understand that the few books which had any place at all in such a culture[170] might take on a disproportionate importance.[171] It is also possible to argue that the very nature of Highland religion channelled popular devotion exclusively towards the Bible. In an attempt to keep away from what was seen as the stultifying darkness of the Roman Catholic Church and its perceived ally, the Scottish Episcopal Church,[172] popular veneration which was directed towards anything like church buildings or vestments or even the bread and wine of the Lord's Supper had to be discouraged; every innovation in worship was seen as a step back to Rome, and communion seasons were deliberately infrequent.[173] The Disruption of 1843 had made clear the transient nature of other outward signs of Christianity – church, manse and glebe – underlining the fact that ultimately all the Highlander had in an external religious sense was his Bible. Talking of the writers of the Bible, Alex Macrae of Kames said in a sermon preached in 1897:

> They spake as the spirit gave them utterance. They were influenced and infallibly guided by Him, so that His inspiration equally extends to every word in the Scriptures of the Old and New Testaments; for no part of Scriptures can be more inspired than another. The Church of Christ in this age is specially called to emphasise this fundamental doctrine of truth.[174]

---

[170] D. J. MacLeod said that 'the output of gaelic books built up from an average of about one-and-a-half per year at the end of the eighteenth century to an average of five by the end of the next': D. J. MacLeod, 'Gaelic prose', *Trans. of the Gaelic Soc. of Inverness*, xlix (1974–6), p. 202.

[171] Anthony Ross reveals that his own Highland Free Presbyterian grandmother would never allow books to be thrown away; 'even worn-out school-books were left to natural decay in a sort of terminal library'. Books, he said, 'were regarded with a kind of reverence as though something of the religious significance of The Book was shared by other books': A. Ross, *The Root of the Matter: Boyhood, Manhood and God* (Edinburgh, 1989), p. 25.

[172] Conservatives said of the Scottish Episcopal Church: 'if we may not go so far as to say it is nothing else than Popery without the Pope, we think we are well warranted in saying it comes very near to it': 'The Scottish Episcopal Church', *The Signal* (Oct. 1887), p. 315. Their opinion of the Roman Catholic Church was even clearer; Neil Cameron described the Reformation as a process in which men 'emerged out of darkness so intense that it might be felt into the glorious light of God's Word': Cameron in Beaton, *History of the Free Presbyterian Church*, p. 22.

[173] Cameron, writing of innovations in worship, said that Knox and Calvin 'knew by painful experience while under the thraldom of the papacy the dreadful effects of human inventions on the souls of men. This made them leave a warning behind them as to the fatal effects of these innovations ... but the Free Church turned her back upon this light, and was making strides towards the very darkness from which God delivered Scotland in the sixteenth century': Cameron, in Beaton, *History of the Free Presbyterian Church*, p. 22. Interesting comments on the infrequency of communion seasons can be found in G. B. Burnett, *The Holy Communion in the Reformed Church of Scotland* (Edinburgh and London, 1960), pp. 16–17, 124–5, 210–13, 297–301.

[174] A. Macrae, 'John xvi.8.', *FPM*, ii (3) (1897), p. 95.

This was a ringing declaration of what was to the Free Presbyterians an absolutely non-negotiable posture, echoing Donald Macfarlane's remark that 'every grain of the seed of the kingdom, as contained in the Scriptures of the Old and New Testaments, is incorruptible seed'.[175] If every word was equally inspired, then it followed that there was a solemn duty to defend every word in the Bible – 'None of His words are meaningless', said the Rev. John Macleod of Ullapool in a sermon printed in the *Free Presbyterian Magazine* in late 1897. Every word was indispensable and to be treated with respect because they each represented a thought of God. In the words of Macleod:

> They convey His thoughts, and these thoughts are a great deep. Their greatness exceeds search. High as the Heavens are above the earth, so are God's thoughts above our thoughts. They are His. We are but creatures and He the Creator. So in length, depth, breadth and height they are measureless.[176]

Again, like Macrae, he actually used the words of Scripture in preaching almost all the time – here working in at least five quotations or near-quotations from the Bible into what was only six lines of a sermon. It was almost as if he felt that his own vocabulary alone was unworthy, and felt that the Bible should be used in its own defence. Macleod also warned against being over-familiar with the Bible:

> the danger of inattention to their sense owing to familiarity with their sound is a very real danger, and one to be at all hazards avoided. To skim over the surface of God's word is to give it unworthy treatment. This is not what it deserves at our hand. He has in great condescension and grace sent it to us. Let us then give it its own place, and own it as His by meditating on it, and seeking to enquire into those thoughts of His that He would have us learn.[177]

If it was considered to be 'unworthy' to 'skim over the surface', it can be imagined how heinous the crime of suggesting errors in the Bible was in their eyes.

The idea that taking issue with parts of the Bible was tantamount to a criticism of Christ himself was explicitly stated in the *Free Presbyterian Magazine*. As part of a long-running series of articles entitled 'Some Features of Present-Day Preaching', it was said:

> The preaching of our day is largely under the influence of the so-called higher criticism. When preachers and others treat the Old Testament Scriptures as of purely human composition, and not of divine authorship, they go far to deny the divinity of Christ. He

---

[175] D. Macfarlane, 'Luke xiii.18,19.', *FPM*, iv (2) (1899), p. 59.
[176] J. Macleod, 'Psalms li.7.', *FPM*, ii (7) (1897), p. 244.
[177] Ibid., p. 244.

referred to the Old Testament as the infallible Word of God, and to insinuate that He erred in this, is practically to deny that He is God.[178]

This was again a back-handed swipe at men like Marcus Dods who, despite all their protestations to the contrary, were considered to be weak on this cardinal doctrine. Neil Cameron preached on the centrality of the Bible in a sermon printed the following month. He believed that as long as the Church kept 'lies without [outside] her ground, and the truth in its entirety emblazoned on her standards, she is terrible as an army with banners'. He looked at the saintly men and women who had made up the Church of God in times past, and believed that their example was the only one to follow:

> The saints having His Word as a lamp to their feet and a light to their path listened to the voice of God in that word, and refused to be led away by the delusions of Satan. The Bible contained their whole faith regarding spiritual and eternal realities and the purpose of God towards a guilty and perishing world. The word that proceeded from His mouth was of more value to them than thousands of gold and silver.[179]

The clear implication was that to toy with something of such extraordinary value was not only sinful, but defiant of all logic, and that the arguments of the 'so-called higher critics' were simply 'the delusions of Satan'. To Donald Macfarlane, the Word of God was the starting-point of his – and all – religion, believing as he did that it was both the 'seed' (a reference to the parable of the 'grain of mustard seed' of Luke xiii.18) and the 'granary' wherein the seed was stored. He was quoted in 1899 as saying: 'the Lord has taken good care to preserve the seed, and the granary in which that seed is stored up is the Word of God, the Scriptures of the Old and New Testaments'.[180] He went on to show that although this great store had been under attack in previous years, yet its awesome power continued unabated:

> It is indeed a marvellous thing ... that we have indeed the whole truth preserved in the midst of all the attacks which have been made upon the Bible, that we have not only the seed but the granary also. We have the Bible, my friends, and the Bible has been used as a means by God to bring into His kingdom many a soul without the instrumentality of ministers or any man whatever. If you have the blessed Bible, though you should not have either minister or elder, the Lord may bless it to your soul ... and make you a new creature in

---

178 'Some features of present-day preaching', *FPM*, ii (8) (1897), p. 282.
179 Cameron, 'Jude 3.', p. 327.
180 Macfarlane, 'Luke xiii.18,19.', p. 59.

Christ Jesus, make you a true child of God, a true subject of the kingdom.[181]

With the Bible occupying such a central part of both faith and life, it is indeed little wonder that these men resisted the work of the higher critics with such energy. The two groups were approaching a problem from diametrically opposed positions, and it would be a mistake to conclude that their differences could have been swept under the carpet.

It can be seen, then, that men like Donald Macfarlane and those who acted with him in the Second Disruption sincerely believed that in propagating the higher criticism the Free Church was engaging in grave error; moreover, they believed that this was an error which would have divine consequences. Macfarlane likened the work of the critics to the time in Old Testament Judah when the good work of King Hezekiah had been undermined and overthrown by his son Manasseh, leading to the loss of the book of the law in the temple. When this happened, it was argued, the temple worship went astray:

> It is a fearful thing when the law of God is lost in the Church ... In a sense the Bible is lost in our days. People may say we have the Bible ... they might say the same thing in Josiah's [Mannaseh's reforming successor] day. The law was in the temple, but at the same time it was lost there. It was lost under the rubble that was heaped over it. It is hid from the eyes of many in our time, but the Lord be praised, not from the eyes of all. You may ask who have lost it? The Higher Critics have. Those also have lost it who misinterpret its teaching about man's fall, and his hopeless ruin in an undone eternity and other fundamental doctrines.[182]

Here is another indication of the Free Presbyterians' Old Testament-tinged world view, as the rise of higher criticism in the Free Church is candidly equated with one of the Old Testament's most celebrated cases of backsliding. Such backsliding had not only brought the wrath of God down on Israel, but had also produced a reformation – this lecture was aptly entitled 'Josiah's Reformation' – and eventual redemption.

Macfarlane expressly believed that Britain would go the way of Israel and Judah if it continued to turn its back on God – 'Unless we as a nation return to the law of the Lord, as sure as the kingdom of Israel and Judah fell, we shall fall'[183] – but more than that, he clearly saw the Free Presbyterian Church as on an even closer parallel with Old Testament times. The Free Church had been raised up, Israel-like, but had succumbed, again like the biblical Israel, to error and sin for which it was punished. The result was that the Free Presbyterians would have to

---

[181] Ibid., p. 59.
[182] D. Macfarlane, 'Notes of lecture delivered at Portree on 14th March, 1898', *FPM*, ii (12) (1898), p. 452.
[183] Ibid., p. 454.

enter the wilderness for a time. His belief was firm that their actions in 1893 were correct, as he stated in ringing tones in a sermon published in the very first issue of the *Free Presbyterian Magazine*:

> is it not a fact that another disruption was pressed upon us in 1893 by the errors introduced into the church? – a disruption for which there were graver reasons than those which caused the disruption in 1843. The tabernacle of the testimony left the camp, and we followed it in order to have the Lord's presence with us, and that 'the truth as it is in Jesus' might be continued in our land, kept pure and entire, and perpetuated to coming generations.[184]

There can be little doubt that the Free Presbyterian Church's founding fathers viewed the higher criticism as a development which denigrated the Bible, and brought nothing but shame to the Free Church: shame which was shared by all those who did not separate themselves from its polluted communion.

This crucial point is worth repeating; the Bible was of such importance to all those who left in 1893 that the perceived attacks upon it by the higher critics were sufficient justification for separation. Macfarlane felt departure from the Bible in the Free Church to be such a weight that at one time he professed, remarkably, that he would have rather died, but it was a weight which had to be borne: 'we take upon ourselves the burden of Christ's cause, and we cannot but take that burden upon us, because God laid it on our shoulders, and we dare not throw it off until He takes it off Himself'.[185] They may have exaggerated the impact of the higher critics for reasons of Church politics, but it would be wrong to underestimate their devotion to Scripture. The Bible meant almost everything to these men, and their whole attitude to the higher critics was shaped by that Bible-centred perspective. In the Free Assembly of 1872 Dr Alexander Duff, the revered missionary to India, said this of the Highlanders in the Free Church:

> to their praise be it said that to them not the most charming of human compositions can be within any appreciable distance or measure half so precious as the Book of Books – the Book of God – the altogether peerless, matchless Bible.[186]

To Donald Macdonald, the oldest of those ministers and students who

---

[184] D. Macfarlane, 'Exodus xxxiii.14.', *FPM*, i (1) (1896), p. 8. Rhetoric of this kind is a good example of one of the uses to which Highlanders put the Bible; as Donald Meek said, 'The Bible provided a model by which Highland history could be interpreted, and it offered a guide by which devout Highlanders could respond to the changing society to which they belonged ... The patriarchal narratives not only provided comfort for those who may have felt that they were venturing into the unknown, but they also reinforced a sense of the sovereignty of God in the affairs of men': Meek, 'Bible and social change', pp. 180, 185–6.

[185] D. Macfarlane, 'Micah iv.1,2.', in Beaton, *Donald Macfarlane*, p. 241.

[186] *PDGAFCS*, 1872, p. 309.

left at the Second Disruption in 1893, the Bible was central because he saw it as containing the whole message of the gospel. In a sermon preached at Dingwall on 2 August 1896, he said:

> Christ is to be found in His own Word. Do you search the Scriptures for Christ? ... Many found Christ in His Word. The Bible is sweet to God's people, because they find Christ and His blessings there.[187]

In this he was only expressing what all his Free Presbyterian companions said themselves at different times. It is worth concluding this summary with the words of Donald Macfarlane once again, when he said:

> Ah, my friends, let us prize this Book – the Bible. There is great enmity against the Bible in our day, but it is the powerful means by which the kingdom of Satan is destroyed and the kingdom of Christ is advanced; and hence the enmity and hatred of Satan to the blessed Word of God. If he had his way there would not be a Bible in the world, and as he is a spirit he cannot destroy the Bible, so he uses as his instruments men who can handle material things, and he keeps the Bible from the people, or tears it in pieces, or destroys it in every way he can. Satan is afraid of the Bible. Ah, then, my friends, if you got any good from the Bible, take good care of it.[188]

2. The other Conservatives

When it came to the Second Disruption in May 1893 only a tiny minority of the Free Church conservative section actually chose to leave. It would be wrong, however, to assume that those conservatives who remained in the Free Church did so because they approved all that was going on in the Church. On the contrary, many of the conservatives who remained after 1893 were most vociferous on the issue of higher criticism.

The battle was carried to the higher critics by a succession of influential conservatives, in the pages of pamphlets and books, in virtually every copy of *The Signal*, in Presbyteries, Synods and public meetings, and, often despairingly, on the floor of the Free General Assembly itself. The fact that the bitter battle for the heart and soul of the Free Church was fought mainly by men who later became their ecclesiastical rivals was glossed over by the Free Presbyterians in later years. By then it was in their interests to portray those who had not joined the Second Disruption as weak and vacillating, if not downright evil.

The Signal was a conservative monthly journal which was chiefly concerned with fighting the innovations that were being introduced into

---

[187] D. Macdonald, 'Luke vii.37–38.', *FPM*, ii (1) (1897), p. 5.
[188] Macfarlane, 'Micah iv.1,2.', pp. 260–1.

the worship of the Free Church, but given that its subtitle was 'A magazine devoted to the maintenance of sound doctrine and pure worship', it also had a considerable amount of comment to make on the subject of the advance of higher critical views in the Church. This was increasingly so as the 1880s drew to a close, and the higher critics began to gain the ascendancy in the higher courts of the Church. As early as 1882, though, the attitude which *The Signal* was going to take to the higher critics was clear. The following letter was printed, ostensibly from 'A Free Churchman':

> Sir, I have been hearing that Professors and others have been publishing books which bring the Bible into doubt and ridicule. How long are we to suffer such men to trouble us, and pay them for it? I pray that God might raise a storm against them, and hurl them from their positions.[189]

The issue here was one which took the Free Church back to its much-vaunted roots, to the Disruption of 1843. As *The Signal* commented in August 1883: 'The men of the Disruption have left us with a noble inheritance, and it will be a sin and a shame if we, their successors, are prepared tamely to stand aside and allow it to be filched from us.'[190] The Free Church conservatives had seen much of what they did not approve over the previous few years, and despite their 'victory' in the Robertson Smith Case, they did not look to the future with much confidence that the heritage of Chalmers and Candlish was in safe hands.[191]

To find influential agreement with this analysis of the situation, the conservatives had only to look south and listen to the words of the celebrated Baptist preacher, Charles Haddon Spurgeon. Spurgeon was something of a hero for Scottish Presbyterians, despite his baptist views, and he was widely quoted both during his lifetime and long after his death.[192] *The*

---

[189] 'Infidelity in the Church', *The Signal* (Jul. 1882), p. 9.

[190] 'Free Church Defence Association', *The Signal* (Aug. 1883), p. 128.

[191] It should be borne in mind, though, that recent research has indicated the presence of some signs of 'higher criticism' in the minds of the Disruption Fathers. Richard A. Riesen argued that biblical criticism was nurtured in the Free Church partly as a result of the attitude of the Free Church Fathers. In his words: 'a closer look will reveal, however, not only a surprising variety of opinion on issues of fundamental importance, but also more than might be expected of the kind of argument that is either critical in itself or tends to invite critical analysis': R. A. Riesen, '"Higher Criticism" in the Free Church Fathers', *RSCHS*, xx (1980), pp. 123–4.

[192] John Macleod, one of the leaders of the Second Disruption, came from a house where Spurgeon was held in high esteem. His mother was a subscriber to *The Metropolitan Tabernacle Pulpit* and Macleod often had the task of reading her the weekly offering from Spurgeon on a Sabbath afternoon. When he left home to go to school in Aberdeen, aged 13, he took with him 'a well-worn volume of The New Park Street Pulpit series': G. N. M. Collins, *John Macleod, D.D.* (Edinburgh, 1951), p. 17. The *Free Presbyterian Magazine* also made use of the famous Baptist: see, e.g., 'The late Mr. Spurgeon and the Free Church', *FPM*, ii (5) (1897), pp. 196–7. See also A. Auld, *Life of John Kennedy, D.D.* (London, 1887), pp. 71–2; Mackenzie, *Rev. Murdo Mackenzie*, p. 78; and Barbour, *Life of Alexander Whyte*, pp. 41, 45, 265, 290, etc. On the other hand, Marcus Dods was so

Signal frequently used portions from his paper, *The Sword and Trowel*, when the Englishman's conservative evaluation of the ecclesiastical situation happened to strike the correct chord. In September 1882, Spurgeon commented on the Free Church professor, A. B. Bruce, saying of the type of theological training which he was giving:

> Alas, alas for the pulpits of the immediate future, if this is the kind of logic your students are to learn while in training for pastors! We look back no further than to the times of Chalmers and Candlish, whose careers have so lately closed. We think we hear their prayers for your Presbyteries. Oh that God would hear and answer them.[193]

What aroused Spurgeon's wrath, and that of the admiring editors of *The Signal* who used his comments, was that although Bruce was a professor of apologetics, to them he appeared to concede too much to the enemies of the faith. As products of a school of thought which had been brought up to concede absolutely nothing to rationalist arguments – indeed, which considered the word 'rationalist' to be pejorative in the extreme – this was a grave mistake, if not an example of downright iniquity. Spurgeon seemed to have had some difficulty in understanding the motivation of a man who was being paid to help students defend their faith, yet who 'takes occasion to assail the rudiments of that study which they were placed in this institution to learn, and he was selected to teach'.[194] The Bruce approach, that of conceding some ground in order to defend the crucial area more efficiently, was seen by Spurgeon as being suicidal. The note of outrage was obvious when *The Signal*, using the words of Spurgeon, declared:

> he would concede every position to the gainsayers ... charlatans, wise in their own conceit. While they pay fulsome complements to the purity of Jesus Christ, they dislike His doctrines and decline to be His disciples.[195]

The conservatives in the Free Church saw rationalism as something which was to be fought every step of the way, with *The Signal* commenting in October 1883 that:

> Rationalism is, radically, the denial of the supernatural ... recognition of the Divine and supernatural is the life-blood of Christianity;

harshly critical of Spurgeon on his death in 1892 that it prompted Dods's friend William Robertson Nicoll to write to him in the following terms: 'Your paragraph about Spurgeon really vexed me – and it is the only thing you have ever said, or written, or done, that did vex me or that I thought not worthy of your magnanimity. It also amazed me, for never yet did I hear anyone speaking of Spurgeon in that way': Darlow, *William Robertson Nicoll*, p. 103.
193 C. H. Spurgeon: quoted in 'Mr. Spurgeon on Professor Bruce', *The Signal* (Sep. 1882), p. 12.
194 Ibid., p. 11.
195 Ibid.

this belief in the Divine Word, in a God-man, in a Divine Saviour, in Divine Grace. This is the rock against which unbelief dashes its waves from generation to generation.[196]

To James Balfour, a conservative Edinburgh elder, the rise of what he would have seen as rationalism within the Free Church was a 'great crisis':

as serious a crisis as had occurred perhaps since the Disruption, and he thought he would be a strange man who did not feel awed by it ... the air of the country, and the theological literature of the coun- try, was full of the wildest ideas about inspiration and the loosest thoughts about the atonement.[197]

The divided nature of the Free Church was clearly illustrated during that debate, over the election of Marcus Dods to be the New College professor of New Testament exegesis. Even during these few remarks of James Balfour there were cries of 'Oh, Oh', 'No, No' and 'Hear, Hear', epitomising – within the conventions of what was acceptable behaviour in the Assembly – the wide divergence of opinion within the Church. What is interesting is the appearance yet again of references to the Disruption, as it illustrates the fact that for many of the conservatives, their affection for the Bible and the old doctrines was bound up with their loyalty to the Free Church as they perceived it. One could not easily change one's attitude to one without changing the others also.

The worry for these conservatives was that although the Bible might survive the crisis, the Free Church as they knew it might well fail to do so. As James Balfour expressed it in 1889:

He had no fear for the Bible, the Bible had stood many a shake before that ... but he had a great fear for the Free Church ... to which he had been so long attached, and which he loved so warmly ... He would regret deeply if the Church were to proclaim to the whole of Christendom that they had imbibed what were commonly known as the Broad Church views.[198]

It involved much the same dichotomy as that which affected the Free Presbyterian understanding of the higher critical position. Balfour considered it a crisis when men like Dods suggested that there were errors in the Bible or that the doctrine of inspiration as they had understood it might not be correct. To Dods, on the other hand, the real crisis was that people like Balfour did not understand what he was seeking to do. The Free Church conservatives held to the position of 'all or nothing' – much as some conservative Anglo-Catholics in the Church

---

[196] 'Rationalism and moderatism', *The Signal* (Oct. 1883), p. 163.
[197] *PDGAFCS*, 1889, pp. 86–7.
[198] Ibid., p. 87.

of England had done earlier in the century – believing that without an inerrant Bible, they had nothing on which to pin their faith. It was articulated by Robert Howie of Govan the following year, when he said, again before the Free Assembly, 'the main question was about Holy Scripture, for if they had not an infallible *book*, where were they to get their doctrines and duties?'[199] In this he was doing no more than echoing the stance which had been taken by James Balfour a year before when, in an archetypal statement of the very position which Dods was doing his best to render obsolete, he stated:

> though he was not a trained theologian, he trusted that by the grace of God he was a Christian, and that he knew something of the pre-ciousness of the Bible. He believed in its inspiration from the first chapter of Genesis to the last chapter of Revelation, and if any doubt should ever be imparted to his mind on anything in and between these two chapters, it would very much shake his peace in life and his hope in death.[200]

It is illustrative of how deep the gulf was between the two sides in the Free Church when one side was roundly condemning what the other was openly declaring from the housetops.

What this illustrates again is the critical significance which men placed upon these issues, seeing them as being absolutely vital. Marcus Dods was described by one writer in 1890 as being the 'chief apologist' for what he termed 'Vivisection in Theology'. This writer, Dr Kerr of Glasgow, argued that the rationalism of a man such as Dods was one of the perennial enemies of the true faith.[201] This was not a view which saw the disagreement over higher critical views as being merely one of degree – it was a rudimentary separation into good and evil. Kerr, although himself a Reformed Presbyterian, had great interest in the Free Church and he believed Dods to be 'the leader, at present, in what is, without doubt, a very deliberate and persistent assault on some of the primary grounds of the Christian faith'.[202] This was the battle between Christianity and its enemies at its most stark, and one which Kerr regarded with some worry, believing that:

---

199 *PDGAFCS*, 1890, p. 79. Emphasis his.

200 *PDGAFCS*, 1889, p. 87. An interesting comparison can be made with the response of the Anglican Bishop Lee of Manchester to the critical position: 'the very foundations of our faith, the very basis of our hopes, the very nearest and dearest of our consolations are taken from us when one line of the Sacred Volume on which we base everything is declared to be unfaithful or untrustworthy': quoted in B. M. G. Reardon, *Religious Thought in the Victorian Age: A Survey from Coleridge to Gore* (London, 1980), p. 343.

201 J. Kerr, *Vivisection in Theology, and its Chief Apologist, Prof. Dods, D.D.* (Glasgow, 1890), pp. 3, 5.

202 Ibid., p. 5. James Kerr D.D. was a Reformed Presbyterian minister who preached in Glasgow and Greenock. As well as higher criticism, he also spoke out against music in worship. See also J. Kerr, *The Higher Criticism: Disastrous Results. Professors Smith, Dods and Denney* (Glasgow, 1903).

If Professor Dods stood alone, the situation would not be so ominous of evil. But the number and activity of those who sympathise with him and the circumstances in connection with his elevation by the General Assembly to the chair of Exegetical Theology [*sic*], are fitted to arouse the apprehensions of every lover of the Word of God in the land.[203]

Thomas Murray of Midmar, a conservative Free Churchman of the most persevering kind, believed that the critics' undermining of the traditional doctrine of inspiration could have only one conclusion: 'This teaching would level the word of God to that of the teaching of man. It is, therefore, infidel in its essence.'[204] He believed that there was a deliberate agenda behind the singling out of certain books for critical attention:

An ominous feature in the writings and the preaching of our Broad School is, that the most evangelical books, both of the Old and New Testaments, seem to be singled out as special subjects of their rationalistic exegesis. I refer especially to Isaiah and John's Gospel.[205]

This, argued Murray, was no coincidence, given that affection for these books, especially John's Gospel, was virtually what would have been termed a 'mark of grace', a sign of religious orthodoxy. As he said of the fourth Gospel:

It very naturally breathes more of the spirit of Christ and of the aroma of heaven than any other book in the sacred canon. The natural consequence of this is, that the more spiritually minded the believer is, the more highly he appreciates and values this book, and *vice versa*.[206]

To imply in this way that the critics were less than spiritually minded was a charge of immense magnitude, given the oft-quoted belief that 'to be carnally minded is death, but to be spiritually minded is life and peace'. This phrase – originating in the Epistle to the Romans viii.6 – would have been very familiar to a Free Churchman, having no doubt been hearing it from an early age in sermons, in public prayer, from

---

203 Ibid., p. 5.
204 T. Murray, *Heretical Declamation in the Free Church Brought to the Test of Argument* (Edinburgh, 1890), p. 27. Murray was of such stubborn bent that when his speech at the 1889 Assembly was curtailed by 'interruptions and signs of impatience ... [and] some laughter' (*PDGAFCS*, 1889, pp. 146–7), his response was to publish the full text of his speech as a riposte to those 'who are for ever speaking, and seem unwilling that a silent member should do anything but remain silent and listen to their endless talk': Murray, *Heretical Declamation*, p. 3.
205 Ibid., p. 32.
206 Ibid. Emphasis his. Arguably, Murray is here choosing one part of Scripture as more important than another; something which contrasts with the Free Presbyterian stance of every word being equally hallowed, with each and every one conveying a thought of God.

'The Men' at fellowship meetings, and at family worship. The subtle technique here was to juxtapose the higher critics with the 'spiritually minded'. To take this to its logical conclusion was tantamount to saying that a disrespect for Isaiah or the Gospel of John was a sign of spiritual death. Although frequently reluctant to say this openly of men like Dods (in contrast to the Free Presbyterians, who had no such qualms), there is little doubt that this was what the majority of the conservatives thought of the higher critics.

In 1886, for example, *The Signal* chose to take the opportunity to look back on the Robertson Smith Case, and in particular to look at the influence on that famous ex-Free Churchman of the views of Wellhausen. To the conservative Free Churchman, Wellhausen's views were anathema. *The Signal* said that it would illustrate some of his views and then concluded:

> The grossness of Wellhausen's Rationalism will in this way be made fully apparent; and readers ... will be able to judge for themselves how nearly it approaches to absolute infidelity, how entirely it precludes the possibility, for those who accept it, of maintaining the greatest and most essential doctrines of Christianity, and, especially, how entirely it sets aside the Inspiration and Divine Authority of the Holy Scriptures.[207]

The serious consequences of all this were summed up in a series of rhetorical questions 'without [Inspiration and the Divine Authority of the Bible] ... what remains to us of doctrine? what remains to us of faith? what remains to us of hope?'[208] The point is that *The Signal* was preaching to the converted and the vast majority of the Free Church conservatives would have agreed with this analysis.

The higher critics within the Free Church were certainly respected at some level by their opponents – even a man like James Balfour of Edinburgh 'cordially concurred in ... [Dods's] Christianity and in his learning',[209] while at the Free Assembly of 1890, Robert Howie

> wished that time had permitted him to say all the kind things he would like to have said about Dr Dods personally, and about the benefit he had received from Dr Dods writings ... [he was] one for whom he had such a high regard, and who had rendered so many eminent services both in the defence and the exposition of the Word of God.[210]

Some of this was undoubtedly rhetoric, but the fact remains that the critics themselves were men of some standing not only with their

---

207 'The rationalism of Wellhausen and Robertson Smith', *The Signal* (Mar. 1886), p. 65.
208 Ibid., p. 65.
209 *PDGAFCS*, 1889, p. 87.
210 *PDGAFCS*, 1890, pp. 77–8.

supporters, but even with their ecclesiastical antagonists. It was their views which the conservatives hated and which they fought with such energy. The conservatives had only a limited personal hostility towards the higher critics, but considered their views to be absolutely unacceptable. They could conceive of the critics being wrong whilst remaining capable of rendering 'eminent services' to the faith; their views, however could not be tolerated, being 'utterly inconsistent' with true Christianity. Two such divergent groupings existing within the Church made unity on a long-term basis seem almost impossible.

Part of the irony of this stage of Free Church history is that many of the men who were loudest in their condemnation of what they saw as declension in the Church were acquiescent when it came to the Declaratory Act of 1892 and the Union with the United Presbyterian Church in 1900. And hardly any of the men who viewed the higher criticism as a great threat to the Church in their public pronouncements joined the Second Disruption in 1893. Murdo Macaskill of Dingwall, though he did not join the Free Presbyterians in 1893, could easily have been writing in the *Free Presbyterian Magazine* when he said in 1889 of the critics:

> they will go on misrepresenting one truth after another until the whole circle of *Revealed Truth is buried under the rubbish heap of their critical jargon* unless the Church of God will timeously assert her authority.[211]

As a man who was content to remain in the Free Church up to 1900 and thereafter join Dods, Bruce, Smith and the rest in the United Free Church,[212] Macaskill's statements about higher criticism make very interesting reading. In the same report as quoted above, Macaskill said the following on the subject of the election of Marcus Dods to the professorship at New College:

> And what is to become of our Church if its future ministry is to be trained in such a school as this? The outlook is most serious ... *Dr Marcus Dods does not stand alone*. Of the ministers who voted him to the chair, close upon a hundred are said to have left our Divinity Halls since 1880. This shows how the current flows, and will continue to flow, with greater rapidity still, if the Church is to remain quiescent and let things take their course.[213]

If the Free Presbyterians can be accused of changing their tone, if not

---

[211] M. Macaskill, *Report of a Committee of the Presbytery of Dingwall Appointed to Consider the Appointment of Dr Dods* ... (Edinburgh, 1889), p. 10. Emphasis his.

[212] In the words of Ewing: 'In the first Union Controversy he was a follower of Dr Begg. His views, however, underwent a change, and he entered into the Union of 1900 with the bulk of his congregation': Ewing, *Annals of the Free Church of Scotland*, i, p. 215. His ecclesiastical adversary Marcus Dods was the Moderator of the United Free General Assembly in 1904, and became Principal of New College in 1907.

[213] Macaskill, *Report of a Committee of the Presbytery of Dingwall*, p. 10. Emphasis his.

their actual tune, after the event, then Macaskill must stand accused on at least the same charge. A man who was happy to cohabit with the most radical of the Free Church critics after 1900 was saying in 1889 to his Dingwall Presbytery that 'a most solemn crisis has come, not only in the history of our Church, but also in that of a pure evangel in Scotland', and that 'to shelve the question is to deepen the dissatisfaction ... and aim the deadliest blow at the future usefulness and prosperity of the Free Church'.[214] What had to be done was clear to Macaskill, at least in 1889:

> In the face of all this, Moderator, is there not a loud, a most urgent call, upon all who love the truth, who prize their Bibles, who glory in the sin-atoning Cross of Christ to arise, as one man, and solemnly vow, in dependence on divine grace, that this Church of ours must be purged from this soul-ruining leaven.[215]

Macaskill was one of the sternest critics of the critics, pursuing Dods to the Presbytery of Edinburgh with a libel in 1890 on account of 'the dangerous and compromising character of the views promulgated by Professor Dods'.[216] And it was he who suggested contemptuously that the critics had much to learn about the Bible, given that many of the Highland lay people were more familiar with it than they were:

> our people ... know their Bible – aye, much better than many of the critics – for it is the daily food of their souls, their daily companion and counsellor, and they will not believe either that it teaches 'immorality', or is a congeries of 'mistakes', 'inaccuracies' and 'irreconcilable statements'.[217]

This is again very close to defining the higher critics as being 'carnally minded', enemies of the 'little flock' of Christ. Yet having failed to purge the Free Church of the 'soul-ruining leaven', Macaskill was able to come to terms with this failure and seems to have been content to remain in close ecclesiastical affiliation with the very men whom he accused of 'publishing and promulgating ... doctrines and opinions which contradict or are opposed to the Holy Scriptures and the doctrines and

---

[214] Ibid., p. 2.

[215] Ibid., p. 12.

[216] 'Petition to the [Free] Presbytery [of Edinburgh] from Mr M. Macaskill and Mr W. Sinclair', *Free Church of Scotland Assembly Papers, No. II*, Case of Prof Dods, D.D. (Edinburgh, 1890), p. 5.

[217] Macaskill, *Report of a Committee of the Presbytery of Dingwall*, p. 5. This opinion had been expressed in the pages of *The Signal* some two years earlier: 'We would enjoy seeing Professor [James] Candlish ... subjected to an examination on the doctrines of the Bible by some old men, and indeed by old women, in different parts of the Highlands': 'Where are the Highlands drifting to?' (Jun. 1888), p. 171. The Rev. J. A. MacCaskill, Onich, said at a meeting to protest against the Declaratory Act in Oban in 1892: 'old men and women in the Highland glens could state more explicitly the way of Salvation than the theologians of the Declaratory Act': *Free Church Declaratory Act of 1891: Report of Speeches Delivered at a Public Meeting held in the Free Church Mission Hall, Oban, Against this Act, on Wednesday, 13th April, 1892* (Oban, 1892), p. 20.

Confession of Faith of the Free Church of Scotland'.[218] Macaskill, it
seems, was able to reconcile himself to it gradually and ultimately accept
that he could peacefully coexist in a Church alongside the likes of
Marcus Dods, A. B. Bruce and George Adam Smith. He was a figure on
whom the Free Presbyterians heaped a great deal of criticism for not
joining them in 1893, but he was one of the most indefatigable of the
critics' critics in the years before the Union of 1900.

As this brief summary has shown, the men who left the Free Church at
the Second Disruption in 1893 did not have unique views when it came
to the higher criticism. Indeed, many of their ecclesiastical rivals were
the men who did most in the battle against the 'heresy' of criticism. And
while the men who refused to join them in 1893 have been all but
expunged from an honourable place in the Free Presbyterians' own view
of history, there is no doubt that it was they who did most to fight the
critics from within. Taken as a bloc, though, the conservative opponents
of higher criticism, irrespective of what way they went in May 1893, were
a formidable body whose battles on the way to an ultimate bitter defeat
did a great deal to make the cracks in the Free Church widen into
schism. Their stance could hardly have been more opposed to the
position of the higher critics, and goes a long way to explaining why the
Free Church ultimately split in the closing decade of the century. But
before moving on to look at the parallel divisions which emerged over
Darwinian Science, it is worth taking a very brief look at the position of
those who were not committed to either side in the bitter dispute over
the higher critical views.

The Middle Ground

It would be quite wrong to assume, merely because there was such a
fundamental divide in the Free Church between those who thought
higher criticism was a positive and necessary phenomenon and those
who thought it was an evil influence, that therefore everyone in the
Church fell into one or other of these two camps. Although the disputes
in the General Assembly invariably concluded with a vote between two
motions, forcing men to stand up and be counted on one side or the
other, it is clear that many viewed criticism with ambivalence.

Of all these people, perhaps the clearest example would be Robert
Rainy, seen by the men who took part in the Second Disruption as a
friend of the critics and as the ultimate architect of the Declaratory Act.
Despite that, however, Rainy's position on criticism was by no means as
cut and dried as at first might be assumed. He read some of the early
German critics during his ministry at the High Church, Edinburgh
(1854–62), and some of his ambivalence was revealed when he spoke of

[218] Libel served on Marcus Dods, 23 Oct. 1890, *Free Church of Scotland Assembly Papers, No.
II*, Case of Professor Dods, D.D. (Edinburgh, 1890), p. 7.

an interesting phenomenon. Very remote from mere infidelity, men with a great deal of earnestness and real respect for the historical religion of the Jews and of the Apostles as a truly divine revelation whose excellence they will enthusiastically illustrate, and yet men who apply the freest criticism to all the records, hold that perhaps no book of the Old Testament existed in its present shape until long after Solomon, thoroughly give up the historical existence of Adam and Eve, consider Abraham, Isaac and Jacob as three different versions of the misty traditional personage, etc. ... I have little doubt that we shall have a fight for the sacred record in which ... we shall have to meet them on their own ground and show the intrinsic untenableness of their theory on any supposition.[219]

His position, however, evolved over the years. He wanted to permit 'believing criticism' in the Church, but he was not an unhesitating supporter of all the positions of criticism. As such he is a useful symbol of the fact that the Free Church was not on this issue divided merely into 'two camps', and will here serve as a representative for all those who shared his views.

Rainy's ability to steer a course between a rock and a hard place was one of the qualities that made him famous, and on the issue of the higher criticism this was precisely what he tried to do.[220] In the first great test of this position, during the Robertson Smith Case, he was widely seen as being willing to sacrifice Smith in order to allow Smith's position, albeit in a more subtle form, breathing space inside the Free Church. For this he attracted odium – Smith himself called Rainy a 'Jesuit',[221] and, most memorably, a 'slimy cold blooded reptile'[222] – but according to Rainy's biographer, the Free Church minister Patrick Carnegie Simpson, 'He was sacrificing position and influence with a great section of the public and of the Church ... [for] the securing of critical liberty within the evangelical and orthodox Free Church of Scotland.'[223] He stood between the keenest supporters on both sides, and, while unable to keep anyone entirely happy, managed to secure a plausible compromise. The cost was the loss of Robertson Smith, a brilliant mind, but at the time it seemed unavoidable, Rainy himself describing Smith as 'an impossibility'.[224] In the later controversies on the subject of criticism Rainy

---

219 Simpson, *Life of Principal Rainy*, i, pp. 136–7.
220 His critics did not see this in a positive light. 'When dealing with two very different parties and tendencies', said *The Signal* of Robert Rainy, '[he] *seems to make it his aim, as far as possible, to stand well with both*. This may seem to the world to manifest a very Christian-like and charitable spirit, but unfortunately it is far from favourable to the cause of truth': 'Dr Rainy's sermon at opening of Assembly', *The Signal* (Sep. 1888), p. 297. Their emphasis.
221 Simpson, *Life of Principal Rainy*, i, p. 396, note. This was in private conversation with Simpson.
222 Quoted in Rogerson, *Bible and Criticism*, p. 60.
223 Simpson, *Life of Principal Rainy*, i, pp. 396, 398.
224 Ibid., i, p. 400.

remained largely on the middle ground also, determined to allow higher criticism to be conducted without acknowledging its more advanced conclusions.

Rainy recognised that some of what Marcus Dods had said was distressing to the more orthodox-minded, but he still believed that Dods was the best man for the vacant New College position when this came up in 1889. Rainy was in Australia at the time of the 1889 Assembly, but he wrote to Dr Adam:

> I doubt whether any man could with more power protect in the minds of students the essential positions ... But, for many reasons, that might well turn out to be an impossible proposal; nor could I myself contemplate it without some sense of risk.[225]

He suspected that the election of Dods could pose problems, and the later heresy trials and pamphlet battles over Dods's opinions confirmed his suspicion. But although Rainy tended to the more orthodox view on the absence of mistakes from the Scriptures, albeit 'under difficulties',[226] he was not ready to condemn those who in all conscience disagreed with that stance. He thought it was an issue which had to be discussed further, and that Church members had no right to 'turn one another out of doors in connection with it'.[227]

His 'Report of Sub-Committee on Papers relative to Work of Dr. Bruce on the Kingdom of God', produced in the first half of 1890, was one of the clearest examples of the delicate balancing act which Rainy had to pursue in his attempt to steer between the two sides in the bitterly divided Free Church. In it he sketched briefly the difficulties of criticism:

> It is a difficult and a delicate matter to fix what limits can fairly be set in such discussions. There is room for a good deal of wise toleration ... there is a difficulty in combining two points of view so as to do justice to each other ... there is a difficulty even when the point of view of the believer in inspiration is frankly adopted ... In the present state of discussion allowance must be made for these difficulties.[228]

There is obviously a very thin line between what one man would call 'making allowance' and what another would call 'Jesuitry', but Rainy was clearly doing his best in a very tricky situation. His position was given in the following statement: 'the Church does not suspend her faith in the canonical character of the Gospels, and ministers and professors do not suspend their faith in it while they take part in critical discussions'.[229]

[225] Ibid., ii, pp. 109–10.
[226] *PDGAFCS*, 1890, p. 113.
[227] Ibid., p. 115.
[228] 'Special Report by College Committee with reference to certain writings of Professors Dods and Bruce', App. IV, *PDGAFCS*, 1890, Report V, pp. 33–4.
[229] Ibid., p. 36.

and later in the same document he stated that the duty of the higher critic within the Church was plain:

> It is desirable that a believing critic, in works addressed to the general public (which includes the believing Church) should make his own position clear. If he thinks it needful in such works to make frequent reference to critical doubts, he should explain the principles on which he is to be understood. Otherwise it will appear to many readers that ... if a doubt be suggested as open on some point, every other point may not become doubtful in the same manner.[230]

The latter was of course the precise position of the 'all or nothing' conservatives within the Free Church and elsewhere, of which Rainy could have read a clear statement in James Balfour's speech in the previous year's *Proceedings*. It is useful to conclude this brief summary of the stance of the most important occupant of the 'middle ground' with his own definitive pronouncement on what he felt the Church's position should be towards the critics within her communion. On the meaning of the election of Marcus Dods, Rainy said this:

> it did not mean, it could not mean, that the Free Church generally was prepared to adopt Dr Dods' view or to sanction it, but he thought that it must probably mean that there was a feeling that, on these questions which occupied so peculiar a position in God's providence just now, the Free Church thought it wisest to entertain what might be said earnestly, seriously, by honest and believing men, and was not at present disposed to boycott anybody, so long as they believed that he was a believing man, holding the principles of her Church, and earnestly dealing with the word of God.[231]

The battle lines over higher criticism were being drawn, but on this issue, as on so many others, not everyone was on one side or the other. The other area of change in the nineteenth century which provoked division in the Church was that of science, and it is to this area that this chapter will now, more briefly, turn.

The Free Church Response to Darwinian Science

Belief or otherwise in the absolute accuracy of the first chapters of Genesis was symbolic of the whole conflict over biblical inerrancy in the nineteenth-century Free Church. And again the issue was one that generated a fairly wide range of views, from enthusiastic embrace to uncompromising rejection, with a character like Hugh Miller standing, somewhat incongruously, somewhere in between.

[230] Ibid.
[231] *PDGAFCS*, 1890, p. 115.

The impact which science had had on traditional belief was summarised memorably by Sir John William Dawson in 1889 when he surveyed the previous decades and commented:

As children we listened with awe and wonder to the story ... A little later, though the idea that all the fossil remains embedded in the rocks are memorials of the deluge had passed away from the minds of the better informed, we ... felt that the antediluvian age had become a reality. But later still all this seemed to pass away like a dream. Under the guidance of Lyell we learned that even the caves and gravels must be of greater age than the historical deluge, and that the remains of men and animals contained in them must have belonged to far-off aeons, antedating perhaps even the biblical creation of man; while the historical deluge, if it ever occurred, must have been an affair so small and local that it had left no traces on the rocks of the earth. At the same time biblical critics were busy with the narrative itself, showing that it could be decomposed into different documents, that it bore traces of a very recent origin, that it was unhistorical, and to be relegated to the same category with the fairy tales of our infancy.[232]

This could not be ignored by any religious community, and the Free Church was no exception. The debate over Darwinian science revealed elemental disagreement within the Church, which went beyond arguments over the nuances of science to the very heart of the Christian faith. It was, moreover, another of the decisive issues in forcing the Second Disruption.[233]

---

[232] J. W. Dawson, 'The Deluge: biblical and geological', *Contemporary Rev.*, lvi (Dec. 1889), p. 884. Dawson was renowned as a geologist and educationalist who had 'distinctly conservative' views on the relations of theology and geology: T. G. Bonney, 'Sir John William Dawson (1820–1899)', *Dictionary of National Biography*, Supplement, vol. II (London, 1901), p. 120. On his death in 1899, the *Free Presbyterian Magazine* quoted the following tribute from *The Bulwark*: 'Almost alone, but with ability ... he has consistently defended the belief that the geological history of the world is summed up with literal accuracy in the first chapter of Genesis. Though his voice may not be heard again in support of the full inspiration of the Scriptures, his writings endorsed by a worthy life remain as strong defences': 'Death of Sir William Dawson', *FPM*, iv (9) (1899), p. 320.

[233] It should be emphasised that although the Free Church was the scene of a battle over evolution, this was not always the case when science and religion differed: 'recent scholarship has shown the warfare metaphor to be neither useful nor tenable in describing the relationship between science and religion': D. C. Lindberg and R. L. Numbers, 'Beyond war and peace: a reappraisal of the encounter between Christianity and science', *Church History*, lv (3) (1986), p. 340. J. H. Brooke has observed that the division cannot simply be analysed as science against religion; and he has warned that since 'both are rooted in human concerns and human endeavour, it would be a profound mistake to treat them as if they were entities in themselves – as if they could be completely abstracted from the social contexts in which ... [they] took their distinctive forms': J. H. Brooke, *Science and Religion: Some Historical Perspectives* (Cambridge, 1991), pp. 8–10.

The Liberal Response to Darwinian Science

It is one indication of the importance with which the Free Church viewed the impact of science that there are twenty-five heavily laden shelves in the New College Library given over to the subject of 'the Bible and Science', with most of the books dating from the late nineteenth century. It was undoubtedly an area to which the Church gave a great deal of thought, and many of her most famous sons were heavily involved in this. If it is symbolic that Marcus Dods chose to discuss biblical criticism in his inaugural address at New College in 1889, then it is no less so that Robert Rainy chose for his inaugural address in 1874 the topic of 'Evolution and Theology'.[234] At that time, the topic of evolution had been vexing churchmen of all hues for at least a decade, and the declaration of a major Free Church figure like Rainy on the subject was awaited with considerable interest.

Rainy himself sketched in the background to his lecture when he told his audience:

Ecclesiastical and religious questions are working everywhere, forcing their significance upon the most reluctant minds by means of the effects which they prove able to produce. And among the questions which are most loudly agitated, are those which concern the foundations of the faith ... I do not know whether there are more unbelievers now than there were a generation back; but the unbelief is at all events more earnestly and confidently proposed.[235]

He singled out the problems surrounding the relation of science to revelation for particular attention, and while he acknowledged that science was 'often in its right in keeping its own path', said that there were times when its conclusions were not as complete or reliable as might be thought. But on the subject of evolution he argued that it was not necessary for the two worlds – religion and science – to be in conflict. As he put it very near the start of his address:

As far as Theism and Christianity are concerned, Evolution is, or is supposed to be, objectionable, when it is asserted in opposition to Divine interposition, and as the substitute for that. But then it may be maintained that the Theist and the Christian object unreasonably; that they have no interest or right to interfere with the discussion, which ought to be left to scientific treatment – and are not justified in imputing an irreligious position to the Evolutionist.[236]

Since most of their opponents spent most of their time imputing that exact position to the proponents of evolution, it must indeed have been

---

[234] R. Rainy, *Evolution and Theology* (Edinburgh, 1874).
[235] Ibid., pp. 3–4.
[236] Ibid., p. 6.

rather surprising to hear these sentiments being expressed by the man who had just been elected unanimously to the principalship of New College.[237]

Rainy could openly acknowledge the presence of evolution taking place all around them – he was happy to admit that 'Evolution has its own rights' and that:

> Evolution is continually going on before our eyes in the perpetual marvel of the reproduction of animal and vegetable life. It would be absurd to suppose that one can draw an arbitrary line, and say that so much of Evolution and no more shall be admitted into our thoughts of the history of things – that so much and no more shall be held to comport with the character and matters of God.[238]

Rainy was not fond of 'drawing lines' – his speech to the General Assembly in 1890 made this evident when in response to those who were asking where to draw the line when it came to biblical criticism he stated: 'God's way was not always to give them mathematical lines.'[239] But he did go as far as to say that even if in the future evolution was proved to be the result of 'the gradual action of permanent forces', the Christian's position would not be affected. If any of the 'inexplicable beginnings' in the natural world, which the Christian now used as evidence of the divine force, should be proved to be just part of a gradual process, argued Rainy, then

> the essential argument remains just the same, if, in any of these cases, that which seemed to us to be a divine beginning should turn out to be only a step in a process of nature which can be traced further back. All that justifies the faith in God remains, only it is now divided or distributed ... He [the Christian] knows there is many a process going on around him, each wonderful, and each bespeaking a divine power working and ruling.[240]

He admitted that there were many atheists who held evolutionary views, but he refused to condemn men for the mere possession of these views. He did, however, recognise the many conflicts which existed between the twin topics of his address, particularly when it came to evolutionary explanations of the origin of man – this, he said, 'comes inevitably into conflict with revealed truth as to the peculiarity of man in his constitution, responsibilities and destiny'.[241]

---

[237] Rainy succeeded the Disruption Father Robert Candlish into that position, having had it 'bequeathed' to him on Candlish's deathbed, the old man's final words to Rainy being: 'I leave the College and the Assembly to your care – goodbye': Simpson, *Life of Principal Rainy*, i, p. 284.

[238] Rainy, *Evolution and Theology*, p. 7.

[239] *PDGAFCS*, 1890, p. 115.

[240] Rainy, *Evolution and Theology*, pp. 9–10.

[241] Ibid., p. 15.

Rainy was not one who recoiled from the theories of evolution. He calmly assessed their claims and returned to the fray, confident that there was a place – an indispensable place – for both science and religion. His position is perhaps best summarised as a careful acceptance of the claims of science, and is summed up in his own words:

> Let us frankly assert God's supernatural interposition, let us assert divine power, divine revelation, up to the full measure which Scripture claims. And yet let us remember here also that the study of natural causes, of moral and intellectual principles, of social forces, to the effect of asserting some natural process in the closest connection with the divine influence, may have its own place ... God, in preparing and establishing the order of grace, which He set in motion supernaturally by wonders and mighty works, did yet seat it in the heart of the natural order, and made the one take up the other into itself.[242]

According to his biographer, the fact that Rainy seemed to be so comfortable with the two apparently irreconcilable beliefs 'reassured many minds'.[243] The views of some other notable Free Churchmen were to have precisely the opposite effect.

Perhaps unsurprisingly, one of these men was Marcus Dods, no stranger to controversy and no silent partner when he felt that something contentious needed to be said.[244] His commentary on the book of Genesis did not keep his reader in doubt for long as to the author's stance on Genesis; the opening lines of the book were in their own way as blunt a launch as 'In the beginning God created the heaven and the earth.' Dods's words were as follows:

> If any one is in search of accurate information regarding the age of this earth, or its relation to the sun, moon and stars, or regarding the order in which plants and animals have appeared upon it, he is referred to recent textbooks in astronomy, geology, and palaeotology. No one for a moment dreams of referring a serious student of these subjects to the Bible as a source of information. It is not the object of the writers of Scripture to impart physical instruction or to enlarge the bounds of scientific knowledge.[245]

Coming from a Free Church minister who was about to be elected to a

---

242 Ibid., pp. 20–1.

243 Simpson, *Life of Principal Rainy*, i, p. 285.

244 Dods did not always retain a terribly high regard for those with whom he disagreed. He said of one Assembly debate on the subject of science that all it did was illustrate 'how utterly incompetent the Church is to enter on such matters. The things that were said made one shiver and faint with hopelessness ... had I been permitted [I] would have explained some things that seemed much in need of explanation': Dods to Henry Drummond: Dods, *Later Letters*, p. 3.

245 M. Dods, *The Book of Genesis* (Expositor's Bible Series, London, 1888) [hereafter *Book of Genesis* (EBS)], p. 1.

professorship at New College, Edinburgh, this was hardly what the conservative literalists would have wanted to hear. They could have encountered his views even earlier had they read his 'Handbooks for Bible Classes' volume on Genesis. That was published in 1882, and in it he said much the same thing, although on that occasion he did not even wait until page one. Instead he made his point in the introduction:

> Its object is not to teach physical science and anticipate the investigations for which natural human faculty is sufficient ... We do not need an inspired record to tell us that the sun is set to rule the day and the moon to rule the night – at no period of the world's history did men need this information.[246]

Dods had no hesitation about nailing his colours to the mast in this way, and in this respect it is entirely consistent with his attitude towards higher criticism which is given in some detail above. He referred to 'the universal light shed by the great modern doctrine of Evolution',[247] and he did not see evolution as being in any way an attack on, or inconsistent with, Christianity. He saw the role of Genesis as being not that of a scientific text-book but as a means – indeed, he believed, the only means – of finding the connection between the world and God. As he put it himself, 'its object is the higher one of determining the connection of nature with God',[248] or,

> if we are to understand what is here written we must burst the trammels of our own modes of thought and read these chapters not as a chronological, astronomical, geological, biological statement, but as a moral or spiritual conception.[249]

Dods was happy to write books about Genesis and probably knew as much about that particular part of the Bible as most of the conservatives, but he was entirely unwilling to tie himself to an interpretation of the book which he believed flew in the face of all the discoveries which God had, in His grace, permitted men to make in the nineteenth century. What comes across overwhelmingly from Dods's treatment of Genesis is that he had the greatest respect for the book, which he passionately believed contained essential instruction for Christians. Moreover he unquestionably rated its account of the origins of life as far superior to other ancient versions, Genesis having 'a singular freedom from those errors which disfigure all other primitive accounts of the creation of the world'.[250]

Dods was, however, a resolute adversary of those who tried to compromise both science and Scripture in order to reconcile the two. He

---

[246] Dods, *Book of Genesis* (HBC), p. xvii.
[247] Dods, *Recent Progress in Theology*, p. 17.
[248] Dods, *Book of Genesis* (EBS), p. 1; *Book of Genesis* (HBC), p. xviii.
[249] Dods, *Book of Genesis* (EBS), pp. 2–3.
[250] Ibid., p. 3.

said that there could be no dispute that the account of the creation given in Genesis simply did not fit in with scientific discoveries. And he believed that it was damaging to the Bible to try to thrust the two together:

> All attempts to force its statements into such accord are futile and mischievous. They are futile because they do not convince independent inquirers ... and they are mischievous because they unduly prolong the strife between Scripture and science, putting the question on a false issue. And above all, they are to be condemned because they do violence to Scripture, foster a style of interpretation by which the text is forced to say whatever the interpreter desires, and prevent us from recognising the real nature of these sacred writings.[251]

In particular Dods was out to debunk the so-called 'day-age' theory which some compromisers, including the venerated Hugh Miller, were broaching. To many people for whom the theory of evolution was a devastating attack on their faith, this compromise, which seemed to allow the conclusions of science without discarding the Genesis version of events, was a heaven-sent avenue of escape. But to Dods the critic such half-measures had no place in his apologetics as he aggressively pointed out in the later of his two books on Genesis:

> The Bible needs no defence such as false constructions of its language bring to its aid. They are its worst friends who distort its words that they may yield a meaning more in accordance with scientific truth. If, for example, the word 'day' in these chapters, does not mean a period of twenty-four hours, the interpretation of Scripture is hopeless.[252]

Interestingly, Dods's views here appear to have undergone something of a development during the 1880s, since in 1882 he was of the opinion that the above method had 'a very great deal' to be said for it. He himself seems to have been quite content that the writer of Genesis was making no attempt to portray scientific information accurately, since that was not his remit. However, although the world was not, in Dods's opinion, constructed in six days, 'the impression left is strictly true, that it was an easy matter, a mere week's work with God, to create the world'.[253] Although he believed in 1882 that the 'day-age' theory involved 'some violence' being done to the sacred text (which must have seemed rather ironic to those men who considered Dods to be one of the most destructive of the Free Church critics) he was able to say this:

> No doubt many able men, whose judgement in such matters cannot be lightly set aside, have been satisfied with one or other of the

251 Ibid., p. 4.
252 Ibid.
253 Dods, *Book of Genesis* (HBC), p. xvii.

various schemes of reconciliation which have been promulgated. Hugh Miller, e.g., considered that the two accounts were in substantial agreement ... A few years ago it was almost heresy to say that the word day means period – now it is almost heresy to hold that when the writer says 'day' he means 'day'. It is the advance of scientific knowledge which has brought about this change.[254]

Dods did not take this position himself, but seems to have accepted – at least in 1882 – that it was an understandable and reasonable one. To him the way to read and interpret the opening passages of Genesis was clear:

It seems fair, therefore, to read the narrative as a child reads it, and accept the words in their plain and obvious meaning. And if the man of science objects and says to me that this chapter thus interpreted gives a false view of creation, I reply that it does not give a false view of the Creator – that it conveys a perfectly true and accurate impression regarding the points on which it was meant to convey instruction. It was not meant to be a revelation of nature, but a revelation of God, and the ideas regarding God which it conveys are just and weighty.[255]

What this conveys with great clarity once again is Dods's declared position as a believing critic. What many of his ecclesiastical opponents saw as a scurrilous attack on the Holy Bible was what Dods himself saw as nothing more than an attempt to adopt a reasonable and sustainable defensive posture *vis-à-vis* the Bible. And given his reputation as a higher critic whose position on inspiration was considered to be inadequate to say the least, the brief summarising comment on Genesis Chapter One which he made in 1882 speaks volumes: 'Free as this chapter is from all pedantic accuracy, no part of the Bible bears more evident marks of inspiration.'[256] Dods was happy to accept evolution, because he did not see it as being in any way incompatible with the Word of God. He was to have a profound effect on many men within the Free Church, but of all the men whom he influenced, few were to have a more controversial impact on the debate over the Bible and Science than Henry Drummond.

Henry Drummond was perhaps the Free Church's most outspoken champion of evolutionary science, and if Dods is often seen as the representative critic of the 1880s and 1890s, then Drummond is the representative evolutionist. He had the nerve to say openly and repeatedly what many other people were saying quietly, and he accepted the consequences. To many of the conservatives, he symbolised all that

254 Ibid., pp. xx–xxi.
255 Ibid., p. xxi.
256 Ibid.

was wrong in the Free Church, with his advocacy of the New Theology and his acceptance of Darwinian evolution as the method by which God created the World. He himself outlined the impact which Marcus Dods had had on him when he said: 'I can claim Dr Dods not only as a friend and as an elder brother, but as the greatest influence in many directions that has ever come across my life.'[257] One of his biographers, George Adam Smith, who later was himself the subject of a heresy trial for his critical views on Scripture, added that two of the directions in which this influence manifested itself were 'Biblical criticism and the application of the hypothesis of evolution to the interpretation of religion'.[258]

Part of the reason for the controversial nature of Drummond's life and work was the fact that he held a very influential position in the Free Church. First as lecturer and then, after no little controversy, as the first Professor of Natural Science at the Glasgow Free Church College (appointed on 31 May 1884), he had an unprecedented chance to disseminate his views. It should be said that the principle of having a science course as part of the theological curriculum for Free Church students had been established as early as 1845, the motion being proposed by Cunningham and being strongly supported by men like Thomas Chalmers and Hugh Miller,[259] but it could hardly have been predicted that such a controversial future lay ahead. By the 1880s, science had become a battleground on which many of the conservatives' most dearly-held principles were threatened with destruction.

As a man who in 1881 described the Robertson Smith verdict as 'suicidal policy' and 'a very serious blow to the Church',[260] Drummond's position on evolution should perhaps not be surprising. His view of the scientific value of the Bible was very close to that of Dods, saying as he did in February 1886 that the Bible was 'absolutely free of natural science':

> The critics find there history, poetry, moral philosophy, theology, lives and letters, mystical, devotional and didactic pieces; but science there is none. Natural objects are, of course, repeatedly referred to ... but neither in the intention of any of the innumerable authors nor in the execution of their work is there any direct trace of scientific training ... there was no science then. Scientific questions were not even asked then. To have given men science would not only have been an anachronism, but a source of mystification and confusion all along the line.[261]

---

257 Smith, *Life of Henry Drummond*, p. 132.
258 Ibid., pp. 132–3.
259 C. Lennox, *Henry Drummond: A Biographical Sketch* (London, 1901), p. 49. See also *PDGAFCS*, 1845 (Second Meeting, Inverness), p. 109.
260 Smith, *Life of Henry Drummond*, pp. 130–1.
261 H. Drummond, 'Mr. Gladstone and Genesis: Articles by T. H. Huxley and Henry Drummond', *Nineteenth Century*, xix (1886), p. 206: quoted in Smith, *Life of Henry Drummond*, p. 239.

The idea that the Bible had to be looked at in a new light, and that the opening passages of Genesis did not explain scientifically the origins of the world, seems to have been something which Drummond could assimilate without a great deal of difficulty. He actually compared the Genesis record to a nursery rhyme by the Scottish author, George MacDonald, telling a child where he came from – 'Where did you get those eyes so blue? Out of the sky as I came through.' – and commented that although the poem contained not 'a word of literal truth' it conveyed exactly the message which was intended. Much the same, he argued, could be said of Genesis:

> Genesis is a presentation of one or two great elementary truths to the childhood of the world. It can only be read aright in the spirit in which it was written, with its original purpose in view, and its original audience ... a scientific theory of the universe formed no part of the original writer's intention. Dating from the childhood of the world, written for children, and for that child-spirit in man which remains unchanged by time, it takes colour and shape accordingly. Its object is purely religious, the point being, not how certain things were made, but that God made them. It is not dedicated to science, but to the soul. It is a sublime theology.[262]

He acknowledged without hesitation the triumph of evolution, saying in his classic and controversial work, *The Ascent of Man*, that:

> While many of the details of the theory of Evolution are in the crucible of criticism, and while the field of modern science changes with such rapidity ... it is fair to add that no one of these changes, nor all of them together, have touched the general theory itself, except to establish its strength, its value and its universality ... Evolution has done for Time what Astronomy has done for Space.[263]

In an address to the students of Amherst College, he had made his position crystal-clear:

> I have always believed that man has descended from the animal creation. There seems to me to be a great body of evidence to prove that man has come up step by step through the ages that have passed, and that he has in him, this moment, some of the relics of that old life which he used to live ... the muscle for wagging a tail ... the muscle for erecting the ear.[264]

---

262 Drummond, 'Gladstone and Genesis', in Smith, *Life of Henry Drummond*, pp. 241–2.

263 H. Drummond, *The Lowell Lectures on the Ascent of Man* (London, 1894), pp. 9–10. Interestingly, Drummond here uses a phrase, 'crucible of criticism', which Dods used with reference to the Bible: Dods, *Recent Progress in Theology*, pp. 9–11.

264 H. Drummond, 'Temptations (an address to the students of Amherst College)', *British Weekly*, 22 Jun. 1893, p. 130.

He was not the only Free Church professor to see evolution as the orthodox scientific position. James Inverach, Professor of Apologetics and Exegesis at the Aberdeen Free Church College, observed in a review of the above book in 1894 that, 'Now ... Evolution holds the field, and everyone is more or less an Evolutionist.'[265] A. B. Bruce stated in his 1897 Gifford lecture series that 'As to the animal nature of man, there is now comparatively little controversy. It is generally admitted that the human body has been evolved.'[266]

Henry Drummond saw evolution as being not an attack on religion but as something which had actually done religion a favour. His views on this issue were made clear in January 1892 in an address to the Theological Society of the Glasgow Free Church College, in which he pointed out that science could benefit the development of doctrine:

> In several well-known instances it has already imposed upon religion the useful task of remodelling its doctrines; and in each case the gain has been in the direction of greater inwardness, greater naturalness, greater spirituality ... As it destroys, it fulfils – the very discoveries which begat its doubt become, when rearranged and incorporated by religion, the materials for a firmer faith.[267]

In order to make it clear what kind of example he had in mind, Drummond spelt it out:

> For instance, the grossness and externalness of the old theory of a Six Days' Creation was once a serious stumbling block to science. Students of nature were unaccustomed to find nature working in ways so abrupt; facts proving the slow development of the world had accumulated; the Divine-fiat hypothesis was challenged, and finally abandoned. And then out of these very facts grew the new and beautiful theory that Creation was not a stupendous and catastrophic operation performed from without, but a silent process working from within. So, having destroyed the old conception, science itself contributed the new – a conception which it could not only intelligently accept, but which for religion also left everything more worthy of worship than before.[268]

This is what underlines the fundamental difference between Drummond and the conservatives. He could talk about 'remodelling doctrines' or the 'grossness' of an old doctrine in a way which would have made a conservative blanch. To him science was not a threat, but

---

265 J. Inverach, 'Professor Drummond's new book', *British Weekly*, 24 May 1894, p. 65.
266 A. B. Bruce, *The Providential Order of the World* (London, 1897), p. 30.
267 H. Drummond, *The New Evangelism and Other Papers* (London, 1899), p. 69.
268 Ibid. In the first of the Lowell Lectures in 1893, Drummond had declared that evolution was 'seen to be little more than the story of creation as told by those who know it best': H. Drummond, 'The evolution of Man: being the First Lowell Lecture delivered at Boston, April 4th, 1893', *British Weekly*, 20 Apr. 1893, p. 409.

was a tool to aid the process of change and development in Scottish theology. Of the Bible and science, he said: 'Let science and religion go each in its own path, and they will not disturb each other. The contest is dying out. The new view of the Bible has made further apologetics almost superfluous.'[269] This was said in 1892, and, while to a man like Drummond this may well have been an accurate summary of the situation as he saw it, all men could not see things in this light. Many conservatives were being driven to the point of despair by what they saw as the 'attacks' of science, and would not have been reassured by Drummond's assurances that they had nothing to fear. Part of the problem of the Free Church at this time was that the liberal, critically minded, wing of the Church had little empathy with those who opposed them. They saw themselves as being on the side of progress – Drummond called his New Evangelism 'the Gospel for the Age'[270] – and could not accept their opponents' view that what they were doing was disastrous compromise with the greatest devil-inspired attack that the Christian religion had ever confronted. One close and life-long friend of Drummond commented: 'you might as well have beaten a spirit with a stick as prosecuted Drummond for heresy'.[271] George Adam Smith was correct when he summed up Drummond's spiritual journey:

> These [older orthodox] positions had been the intellectual basis of the Christian faith for centuries. To question them seemed to many to be treason, to abandon them madness. But Drummond was forced from them by his study of facts in the departments of natural science and of Biblical criticism and Biblical theology. And upon the new positions to which he was led he has evidently found a basis for his faith more stable than ever the older was ever imagined to be – richer mines of Christian experience and truth, better vantage grounds for preaching the Gospel of Christ, and loftier summits with infinitely wider prospects of the power of God, and of the destiny of man.[272]

That not everyone in the Free Church took such a sympathetic stance on the supporters of evolution will now be made clear.

The Conservative Reaction to Darwinian Science

As mentioned above, there appears to have been a basic lack of understanding of the feelings of their more conservative brethren on the part of the Free Church liberals. But there is similarly little doubt that the conservatives in turn had little conception of the notion of a 'believing

[269] Lennox, *Henry Drummond*, p. 153.
[270] Drummond, *New Evangelism*, p. 4.
[271] Lennox, *Henry Drummond*, p. 162: quoting Dr John Watson.
[272] Smith, *Life of Henry Drummond*, pp. 243–4.

critic' or a 'believing evolutionist'. Much of the writing of Dods, Rainy and Drummond, to name but the three cited above, is of a most reverent and respectful tone, pointing out that the Bible simply did not need to be treated in the way it had been up to that point. Drummond maintained, for example, that the need for apologetics was all but gone, and that 'science has made religion a thousand times more thinkable and certain'.[273] To the conservatives, however, 'infidel science' was a serious threat to the faith, and had to be resisted tooth and nail. The Bible was 'the same yesterday, and today, and forever', and to find one fault with it was to undermine the whole. Science was seen as a determined and co-ordinated assault on the vitals of the Christian religion.

The principle on which the conservatives in the Free Church resisted the advance of evolutionary thought was in essence a very simple one, and as such had a great deal of appeal. The feeling was that the damage which was being done to the credibility of the first chapters of Genesis was having a serious negative impact on the rest of the Christian faith. It was not a feeling which was confined to the Free Church, nor indeed to Scotland; Sir John William Dawson wrote in 1889 that

> Christianity founds itself, its founder himself being witness, on the early chapters of Genesis, as history and prophecy, and the treatment which these ancient and inspired records have met with in modern times at the hand of destructive criticism is doing its worst in aid of the anti-Christian tendencies of our time.[274]

This belief that to undermine Genesis was to undermine Christ himself was fundamental to the whole conservative reaction. It was also closely tied to the controversy over biblical criticism – the English High Churchman, H. P. Liddon, for example, said that criticism ruled out the 'infallibility, moral no less than intellectual, of Jesus Christ our Lord'[275] – and this seemed to be the prevailing feeling among Free Churchmen on the subject of evolutionary science as well. As the ecclesiastical historian, Alec Vidler, said of the impact of Darwin's *Origin of Species*:

> The whole scheme of Christian belief, which was based on the supposition that man had all at once been created with a fully-formed capacity for communion with God, a capacity that the human race had lost through the disobedience of the first human pair, was thrown into disarray ... the doctrines of redemption and atonement stood in jeopardy too.[276]

The attack on Genesis, then, was widely seen as part of a broader assault on the Christian faith.

---

273 Lennox, *Henry Drummond*, p. 153.
274 Dawson, 'Deluge', p. 899.
275 Liddon: quoted in Cameron, *Biblical Higher Criticism*, p. 6.
276 Vidler, *Church in an Age of Revolution*, p. 117.

For many conservative critics of evolutionary science, the answer to the questions of science was to be found wholly in the Bible. They did not allow the slightest compromise with science where that seemed to contradict Scripture, and they were unashamed of their reliance on what Henry Drummond compared to a nursery rhyme, what James Denney, another Free Church professor, called a 'myth',[277] and what Dr W. Ross Taylor, speaking from the Free Assembly moderator's chair, called 'poetry'.[278] Principal Robert Candlish, the venerated Free Church father, acknowledged that there were problems with the Bible but he did not let that worry him unduly:

> I put it as a problem – which only the Omniscient can solve – how a revelation which is to range over centuries of comparative ignorance on matters of secular and mundane science – and is necessarily, according to its plan, to mix up these matters freely with its higher themes – is to be so constructed and so recorded that it shall not anticipate human discoveries, and yet shall be in entire harmony with them, as in course of time they emerge. I maintain that this precise problem is found actually solved, in point of fact, in the Bible.[279]

D. K. Paton, a Presbyterian writer who compared men like Dods and Denney to 'wild beasts', dismissed the idea of the existence of scientific errors in the Bible with some aplomb:

> while there are confessedly portions of these Scriptures we cannot as yet understand or fully explain, we do not doubt their truthfulness, and are sure that every seeming obscurity will in due time be entirely removed. As in the material universe we are permitted to know much, and all that may be essential to our chief good, we yet find that man, even the greatest philosopher and scientist, has to confess that he at best only touched the mere surface of things.[280]

Professor John Duncan, another of the revered fathers of the Free Church, was just as confident in his rejection of Darwin's theory, asking:

> why have we no fossil link? There are no existing species which shade into each other by insensible degrees. And development could not have gone on as by leaps. So far as scientific evidence has as yet gone, I consider species to be distinct creations. I deny that

---

[277] Denney called the Genesis account of Creation 'the myth, in which the beginnings of human life, lying beyond human research, are represented to itself by the child-mind of the race': quoted in Paton, *Higher Criticism*, p. 198.

[278] Taylor said of Genesis: 'The whole trouble had arisen from the mistaken assumption that the opening chapter in Genesis was meant to be an authoritative account of the method and order of the creative work, instead of being, what it is, an inspired and rejoicing recognition of God as the one creator of all': Taylor, Moderator's Address, *PDGAFCS*, 1900, p. 4.

[279] Quoted in Paton, *Higher Criticism*, pp. 50–1.

[280] Ibid., pp. 51–2.

there is any scientific evidence for Evolution. And I think we should have something better than a guess or a conjecture in a matter so weighty.[281]

For the men who departed the Free Church at the Second Disruption in 1893, the issue was an equally uncomplicated one. In a critique of A. B. Bruce's Gifford Lectures of 1897, the *Free Presbyterian Magazine* produced a ringing declaration of support for and belief in the doctrine of creation. Bruce had suggested that the debate was not a terribly important one, to which the Free Presbyterians responded with some warmth:

> We are quite convinced that the issue has 'a serious aspect' for believers in the authority of the Scriptures both of the Old and New Testaments. Our author insinuates that it is doubtful whether the Scriptures teach or imply any particular theory as to man's origin. This insinuation could only be made by one who has determined to go in for evolution at all hazards. It is written in Gen. i.27 – 'So God created man in his own image, in the image of God created he him; male and female created he them.' Nothing could be clearer from these words than that man was directly created by God, and that in His own image.[282]

To the Free Presbyterians, the whole issue was here rendered even more fundamental by their tying together – as in almost every other time they spoke on either science or criticism – of the Old and the New Testaments. Their position was quite simply that if one fell, so too did the other; the Genesis account was science which had had the ultimate ratification:

> There is no evolutionary process here, in respect of body or soul. The Lord Jesus also sets His seal to this account. 'From the beginning of the creation God made them male and female.' – (Mark x.6) The issue is certainly a serious one for the evolutionist. He must refuse to accept the testimony of Christ or give up his favourite theory. By cleaving to the latter ... [there cannot be] faith in the God of the Bible, who is the only living and true God, nor faith in Jesus Christ – in His Divine person, authority, and infallibility.[283]

---

[281] Quoted in ibid., p. 210. Archaeology was also used in the battle against higher criticism, most memorably in books like A. H. Sayce, *The 'Higher Criticism' and the Verdict of the Monuments* (London, 1893). As B. Z. MacHaffie observed, 'The argument from the monuments, a nineteenth century media event, was the most significant obstacle to the popularization of the Higher Criticism of the Old Testament ... The conclusions of the critics, sound and profitable as many of them were, were no match for the dictum that "archaeology proves the Bible"': MacHaffie, 'Monument Facts and Higher Critical Fancies', p. 319.

[282] 'Professor Bruce's new book: "The Providential Order"', *FPM*, ii (9) (1898), p. 340.

[283] Ibid., pp. 340–1.

There could hardly have been a more unclouded denunciation of the idea of a 'believing evolutionist'. To the Free Presbyterians, belief in God and belief in evolution were completely incompatible – acceptance of evolution was in their eyes indistinguishable from rejection of the God of the Bible. A. B. Bruce had called evolution 'simply God's method of communicating to man the light of reason and the sense of duty',[284] but the Free Presbyterians viewed it in a very different light: 'To us it appears an absurd God-dishonouring theory, the product of irreverent imagination, destitute of any foundation in fact, and contrary to the clearest testimony of the Word of God.'[285] Indeed, in the following month's edition of the *Free Presbyterian Magazine*, they stated their position with unambiguous clarity; Bruce's views, they said, were 'of a remarkably extreme type, and to us it appears no better than atheism'.[286]

Commenting in 1900 on Dr Ross Taylor's Moderator's Address – which was briefly cited above – the Free Presbyterians produced a classic statement of their position regarding evolution. As so often, the rigours of debate forced the writer to make unequivocal statements and the passage of time has not dulled the vigour and the anger with which they burn. Describing Taylor as 'entangled in no ordinary degree in the meshes of the net of modern science', the writer says this of evolution:

> there is no warrant for this theory in the Bible; there is everything to nullify it. There is no warrant for it from history, reason, or observation. It is simply a piece of imagination that has captivated the understandings of men who want to be done with the God of the Bible. The God of the Bible is too mighty and overwhelming a personality for them.[287]

There is no word here of believing criticism or of evolution removing the need for Christian apologetics; this is an aggressive refutation both of the theory of evolution and of the concept of the compatibility of evolution and the biblical record. Evolution, according to the Free Presbyterians, was merely an attempt to supersede God:

> The whole theory of evolution is just an attempt to fashion the operations of God after the manner of men, and to set up a deity that is no better than an enlarged man. But the erection of this deity involves, as far as human belief is concerned, the dethronement of the God and Father of our Lord Jesus Christ.[288]

Far from retiring from the field of apologetics, the Free Presbyterians saw the need for a new belligerent approach which aggressively confronted

---

[284] Bruce, *Providential Order of the World*, pp. 47–8.
[285] 'Bruce's new book', p. 342.
[286] 'Professor Bruce's new book: "The Providential Order" (Second Notice)', *FPM*, ii (10) (1898), p. 374.
[287] 'Free Church Moderator's Address', *FPM*, v (2) (1900), p. 43.
[288] Ibid.

evolution and attempted to arrest its progress. While recent scholarship has suggested that the warfare metaphor is unsuitable for describing much of the contact between evolutionary science and religion, in the case of the early Free Presbyterians, it is a metaphor which is hard to avoid.

Again, it can be seen here that there was a very deep and rudimentary misunderstanding between the two sides. While the evolutionists saw themselves as fighting to protect religion from the ravages of science, their conservative opponents saw them as the very men who were doing much of the damage. Of A. B. Bruce, the Free Presbyterians made the following comment:

> Our author, whilst very tender to everything which favours the extremist evolutionism, is always ready to give a blow to the Scriptural doctrine of creation. He tries to disparage the doctrine that God created all things at the beginning by the word of His power.[289]

Of Henry Drummond, their conclusion on his untimely death in 1897 was that he 'was an apostle of error, against whom the right ways of the Lord need to be vindicated'.[290] Drummond was something of an enigma to the Free Presbyterians:

> On the one part he extols Christ as the guide and glorifier of human life, on the other he traduces Moses, who wrote the story of the world's creation by the inspiration of the spirit of Christ, as a mere fabulist, not worth mention by a man of science. These things are puzzling to the plain man.[291]

But, although Drummond was harder to categorise than some of the other evolutionists would have been, the *Free Presbyterian Magazine* felt that they had him evaluated:

> the 'Ascent' [*The Ascent of Man*] is an attempt to popularise the Darwin theory of evolution, and to show what a rich theory it is, able to account for all the phenomena of mind and matter ... Whatever poetry and originality there may be in his utterances, so far as his evolutionary philosophy is concerned he is, we think, a mere fountain-head of Atheism.[292]

In the opinion of many conservatives, evolutionism and atheism were synonymous.

A central part of the conservatives' difficulty with evolution was that they believed it to undermine the doctrine of the Fall of man. The Atoning death of Christ, his blameless life which preceded it and the sin of man which made it necessary were all believed to be dependent on

---

[289] 'Bruce's new book (Second Notice)', pp. 374–5.
[290] 'Professor Drummond's theology', *FPM*, i (12) (1897), p. 456.
[291] Ibid.
[292] Ibid., pp. 456–7.

the doctrine of the Fall, and the subsequent imputation of Adam's sin on to all the men that descended from him. If the story of the Garden of Eden were false, it was argued, so too must be all the rest of the basis of the Christian faith.[293] The Free Presbyterian position was elegantly summarised in 1900:

> Evolution ... gives no place to the Fall: there therefore cannot have been the loss of the divine image, or the transgression of the divine law. Sin upon this theory does not exist; what is called 'sin' is only a circumstance in the upward progress; it entails no guilt upon the sinner. The glorious scheme of Redemption from sin and the curse is completely invalidated: it has no meaning whatsoever; there is no need or scope for any such thing.[294]

When A. B. Bruce spoke about the presence of 'primitive man' existing for tens of thousands of years before history began, the conservatives saw this as a direct contradiction of some of the most fundamental tenets of the faith. The *Free Presbyterian Magazine* was strikingly clear once again in defining the implications of this belief:

> The Scriptures tell us, in language of unmistakeable clearness, and without dubiety, that God created man at the beginning, male and female, in the fully developed powers of mind and body. Adam and Eve are acknowledged throughout the Scriptures as the parents of our whole race. To introduce, therefore, primitive pre-historic man is to subvert the doctrine of man as taught in the Word of God. If this Word is wrong on this fundamental matter it cannot be right on anything else.[295]

This is another striking instance of the conservatives openly declaring a position which the believing critics and evolutionists thought was untenable.

While the 'all-or-nothing' approach was one which men like Dods rejected out of hand, to the Free Presbyterians it was unthinkable to believe anything else. The theory of evolution, they argued, was an attack on their religion:

> The doctrines of sin and salvation are subverted by this theory. We are told in the Scriptures that 'by one man sin entered into the world' and 'that in Adam all die', so that the whole race was bound up with Adam to stand or fall with him. Further, the Lord Jesus Christ is spoken of as the second Adam, the head and representative of a

---

293 It might also be said that if the story of the Garden of Eden were true, and if the doctrine of the Fall were correct, then much of the basis for Enlightenment ideas about human progress and perfectibility was under strain. For men of religion and men of reason alike, the Fall had become a battleground.

294 'Free Church Moderator's Address', pp. 43–4.

295 'Bruce's new book (Second Notice)', p. 376.

spiritual seed. It is evident, therefore, that the Scriptures must be accepted or rejected as to their doctrine of man, and they who reject that doctrine also reject the whole system of divine truth concerning sin and salvation.[296]

It is clear that to many conservatives, the theory of evolution was not an issue over which Christians could agree to disagree. Like criticism, holding the more liberal view point was in their eyes synonymous with a thorough renunciation of all the most basic principles of biblical Christianity, and for an evolutionist to claim to be a believer simply did not make sense.

Marcus Dods, unsurprisingly, was another Free Church professor whose evolutionary views brought criticism from the conservatives in the Church. As early as 1882, his earlier work on Genesis, in the 'Handbooks for Bible Classes' series, was attracting the attention of conservative critics in *The Signal*. They wrote in December 1882 of its 'unsatisfactory and, as we think, dangerous characteristics',[297] and concluded that, 'a hasty perusal of it has filled us with sadness ... in several respects its publication is deeply to be deplored. It is about the last book we would think of placing in the hands of our young people.'[298] Six years later, in May 1888, they had turned their attention to Dods's later work on Genesis, or rather to the review thereof in the *Free Church Monthly*. According to *The Signal*,

> It would have been better had the book been left unnoticed than it should, through this Free Church public organ, have been virtually recommended to the favourable consideration of her ministers, students and people.[299]

As has been seen already, this book was a rather controversial offering from a man who was seldom less than controversial himself, but it should be said that its manner of delivery was mild and often reverent. *The Signal*, however, was not swayed by Dods's approach:

> When a man is anxious to administer a dose of poison to a friend, he does not produce the article and enter into a controversy as to its reliable and wholesome qualities in order to induce him to receive it ... the quieter, the more unaggressive and candid-like he appears, the more likely he is to attain his end. We cannot, therefore, see anything specially deserving of admiration in the man who has recourse to the quiet and uncontroversial method, when endeavouring to insinuate, what we regard as erroneous and dangerous views of truth into the minds of men.[300]

296 Ibid.
297 'Genesis, by Marcus Dods, D.D.', *The Signal* (Dec. 1882), p. 4.
298 Ibid.
299 '"The Free Church Monthly" and Dr. Marcus Dods', *The Signal* (May 1888), pp. 146–7.
300 Ibid., p. 148.

Their critique of the review of Dods's work was concluded with this observation:

> For this author [Dods], therefore, while he continues a minister of the Free Church, to assert, maintain, and defend doctrines at variance with those of the Confession, whatever may be the spirit in which he does it, is deserving of a very different epithet from that of 'candour', and must excite a very different feeling from that of admiration in the mind of every candid reader.[301]

The fact was, though, whether the conservative opponents of evolution liked it or not, there were many men in influential positions in the Free Church who agreed more or less wholeheartedly with Marcus Dods's position.

The following month, *The Signal* turned its attention to the book itself, and made it clear just where the Free Church conservative stood on the evolutionary interpretation of Genesis. Dods's description of the state of man before the Fall is described as

> a gross parody upon Scripture, which it would not surprise us to find in the work of some blatant atheist; but here it is, in what purports to be a series of lectures on Genesis by a Free Church minister, on which the editor of the Expositor's Bible [William Robertson Nicoll], who is also a Free Church minister, puts his imprimatur!![302]

As editor of the liberal *British Weekly*, Robertson Nicoll was never going to be a favourite of the conservatives in the Church,[303] and this was merely another example of what they saw as the liberals working in concert to foist their pernicious convictions upon the Church at large. As far as Dods's analysis of the scientific content in Genesis was concerned, *The Signal* was no less scathing. It stated of Genesis:

> It was not written merely for those to whom it was first delivered, as this author seems to believe, but as part of the rule which God has been pleased to give to direct men, the most scientific and the most unlettered, how to fulfil the end of their being. And, if so, though it does not profess to teach science, there cannot possibly be found in it any allusion whatever which conflicts in the slightest degree with the discoveries which true science, when it shall have completed its

---

301 Ibid., p. 149.
302 'The Expositor's Bible: *The Book of Genesis*, by Marcus Dods, D.D.', *The Signal* (Jun. 1888), p. 179.
303 'I will mention one or two matters of my special aversion. One is your devotion to the "new learning", namely, which busies itself in picking holes in the Bible, which saws Isaiah asunder, cuts up Daniel, breaks Moses in pieces, and fathers Deuteronomy on a pious forger who flourished in the days of Josiah. For some sinister reason, you have given your heart and your pen to this bad cause, and are always ready to splinter a lance on its behalf': 'Open letter to the editor of the "British Weekly"', *FPM*, ii (9) (1898), pp. 342–3.

researches, will bring to light. To suppose otherwise, as this author does, is to deny that the Author of creation is the Author of this book which gives us an account of his work.[304]

This was an unclouded proclamation of the conservative stance on science, and it could hardly have been in more direct conflict with the position of men like Dods, Drummond, Bruce, Denney, and even Rainy. The claim of absolute biblical infallibility was believed by liberals like these to be not only indefensible but even unscriptural. To the conservatives in the Free Church on the other hand, the matter was clear-cut; either you believed the Bible in all its intricacies or you did not. If the Bible and science were indeed telling different stories, it was not the Bible that was at fault:

> The whole question here of course turns upon this, whither we are to accept the accuracy of Scripture or of science; and if we do, as every Christian does, accept the former as a divine revelation, there is no room for any possible inaccuracy in its information, so that we must reject the information of science with all its boastful accuracy, in so far as it conflicts with Scripture ... The information given in the Bible might, and no doubt did, strangely and unaccountably conflict with the cosmogonies of early times, as it may conflict in many things with the findings of great scientists in our days; but amid the rude ignorance of the past and the learned ignorance of the present, as a revelation from heaven, it claims the unquestioning faith of peasant and sage, in the perfect accuracy of all its allusions to science, which will one day be fully verified.[305]

The Free Church conservatives acknowledged, however, that it was not just within their own Church that evolution had taken hold. Commenting on Darwin's death in 1883, *The Signal* stated that:

> Not a few pulpits of ministers of the British Church sensational school resounded with the praises of Darwin at the time of his death, and hailed him as a Christian. This sycophancy in the churches and in the supposedly 'Christian' press does greatly more damage than the attacks of avowed sceptics. No men are more to be despised than false prophets.[306]

Again, *The Signal* clearly countenanced no compromise with the men of science on religious matters:

> It will be found that the Darwinian principles cannot by any ingenuity be fitted into Christianity, that they are suggested chiefly

---

304 'The Rev. Dr. Marcus Dods on Genesis and at the Pan-Presbyterian Council', *The Signal* (Jul. 1888), p. 241.
305 Ibid., p. 242.
306 'Darwin and Darwinism', *The Signal* (Feb. 1883), p. 29.

for the reason of explaining the universe apart from God, and that they supersede, if they do not absolutely exclude, a revelation.[307]

This is essentially the same position taken up by the bulk of conservative opinion in the Free Church, and again they stressed that to undermine Genesis was to do more than merely undermine one part of Christian belief:

> Darwinian principles ... destroy necessarily one of the fundamental positions of the Christian faith, viz., the universal corruption of human nature, and its degradation from the position it occupied in creation. If this position be condemned, the whole Scriptural account of the work of Redemption is invalidated. Yet numbers of weak sensational men avow their Darwinism and Christianity.[308]

This theme was reiterated later when it was stated in 1884 that the story of the universal Flood as detailed in Genesis (on which Dods and Drummond, to name but two, both cast doubt) was also essential for the Christian faith:

> if the Biblical doctrine of the fall does not involve the most terrible catastrophe known to mortals in the spiritual sphere, then that word, among others, becomes to us meaningless, and the whole doctrine of redemption an inscrutable mystery.[309]

What seemed to frustrate them most was their belief that the evolutionary doctrine before which so much of traditional Christianity was crumbling was itself no more than unsubstantiated speculations which would not stand the test of time. As *The Signal* expressed it in 1883: 'Darwinism has not now, and never will have, any place in real science. It is still, as always, a mere theory or dream, unsupported by observations in all departments of science.'[310] With divisions as fundamental as this present as early as 1882, the Free Church faced a worrying future. Given their lack of expertise, it was perhaps predictable that they would not agree on the scientific credibility of evolution;[311] but to disagree so deeply on the theological implications signalled that there were exceedingly troublesome times ahead.

---

[307] Ibid., p. 30.
[308] Ibid.
[309] 'The Chair of Natural Science in Glasgow Free Church College and Mr. H. Drummond', *The Signal* (Feb. 1884), p. 41.
[310] 'Darwin and Darwinism', p. 30.
[311] Dods wrote to Drummond on 1 June 1895 on the subject of the Free Assembly's recent discussion of Drummond's *The Ascent of Man*, and said: 'All the other speeches proved Rainy's position by themselves illustrating how utterly incompetent the Church is to enter on such matters': Dods, *Later Letters*, p. 3.

The Middle Ground

As was the case with the divide in the Free Church over the higher criticism, it would be quite inaccurate to portray the division over evolution as one simply between men who accepted Darwinian evolution completely and those who rejected every nuance of the new science out of hand. In fact, as in so many issues which affected the Church at this crucial period in its history, there were many who did not wholeheartedly take up a position in either of the two opposing camps. And of all the men in the Free Church who took this stance, there are probably none more interesting than Hugh Miller. Space does not allow a detailed examination of the 'Middle Ground', but as a solitary example, Hugh Miller is a useful and arresting figure.

Miller, the great journalist whose influence on the Disruption of 1843 could hardly have been greater,[312] was also an important figure in what was one of the monumental intellectual battles of the nineteenth century: the question of the origin of life and the struggle between evolution and creation. His conservative views at the time of the Disruption should not be taken as a symbol of this man's viewpoint on other issues, and as his biographer has pointed out, he was an 'enigmatic and often baffling man'. Despite his sentimental Scottish nationalism, his firm Presbyterianism, his pious Christianity and his ability to conduct exhaustive and meticulous scientific experiments and observations, he was on the other hand a supporter of the Union with England, a backer of Roman Catholic emancipation and secular education, and a man with a great deal of mysticism in his psyche, who believed that he saw ghosts and phantoms.[313] He was a man who disagreed strongly with socialism and Chartism, but whose advice to the Highlanders at the time of the Clearances was to turn to violence, given that 'Government will yield nothing to justice, but a great deal to fear.'[314]

It is thus not surprising that he cannot be categorised easily as an uncomplicated anti-evolutionist. Certainly, Hugh Miller was an enemy of evolutionism and a great deal of what he saw as the 'infidel' science which he believed it to represent. But as one of his earlier biographers commented, Miller made acceptable among Christians many ideas which had previously been seen as being incompatible with Christian faith. His popularisation of the idea that the six days in Genesis represented six ages was perhaps the clearest illustration of this, but the notion of the Genesis Flood being a local event and the earth being much older than the Mosaic account allowed are also examples.[315] His position has been summarised by Donald Withrington:

---

312 For recent biographies of this complex figure, see Rosie, *Hugh Miller*; and M. Shortland (ed.), *Hugh Miller's Memoir: From Stonemason to Geologist* (Edinburgh, 1995), pp. 1–86.
313 Ibid., p. 16.
314 W. M. Mackenzie, *Hugh Miller: A Critical Study* (London, 1905), p. 191.
315 Ibid., p. 126; Rosie, *Hugh Miller*, p. 73.

Miller aimed to prove that there was no necessary opposition between the implications of recent advances in man's geological understanding and the Biblical account of the Creation. For Miller, what recent scientific research demonstrated was nothing more nor less than a hitherto unrevealed design in geological evolution; but that still depended, of course, on there being a great designer.[316]

As a result of his position, Miller was a controversial figure at the time, provoking fairly heated responses from people on both sides of the scientific divide. As MacKenzie commented in 1905 'the unread and unstudious, orthodox, people up and down Scotland, even when friendly to Miller, were ever in a state of dread anticipation as to what new heresy might burst from his pen'.[317] Miller's great self-appointed role was to find a reconciliation between his two passions, geological science and Calvinist Christianity, and it was almost unavoidable that this would never keep all the people on either side happy. David Livingstone's recent work on evolution and evangelicalism points out that Miller was a quite novel figure in the attempt to harmonise the two apparently conflicting records. Miller was 'pointedly different' from such earlier harmonisers as Thomas Chalmers:

comparing himself to the Christian geographer who practised his subject in a day when a round earth was dismissed as unscriptural and to the Christian astronomer working at a time when the notion of a heliocentric universe was heresy, Miller said that his only reply as a Christian geologist to the learned opposition of any theologian was frankly to question the validity of their handling of Scripture. Ecclesiastic authority could not outweigh scientific experience.[318]

As such, Miller had nothing but contempt for those religious men who saw 'every scientific advance as an assault on the mysteries of Christianity and the work of the Devil'.[319] He reserved particular bile for his old enemies the Anglo-Catholics, whom he saw as obscurantist opponents of all advances in science. Rosie quotes Miller:

The medieval miasma, originated in the bogs and fens of Oxford, has been blown aslant over the face of the country and not only religious but scientific truth is to experience, it would seem, the influence of its poisonous blights and rotting mildew.[320]

Miller, then, while never conceding an inch on the presence of a Creator God as the prime mover in all scientific development, was willing to compromise on some of the more literal interpretations of the early parts

[316] Withrington, 'Ferment of Change', p. 55.
[317] Mackenzie, *Hugh Miller*, p. 129.
[318] Livingstone, *Darwin's Forgotten Defenders*, pp. 12–13.
[319] Rosie, *Hugh Miller*, p. 73.
[320] Ibid., p. 167.

of Genesis. He resisted all his days the anti-religious tendency of nineteenth-century science, but tried to do so in as modern and open-minded a way as he possibly could. For this he attracted attack from conservatives – Thomas Davies saying in 1860 that 'it should be the duty of every Christian pen to denounce, in unmeasured terms, his attacks upon the Bible, and his frenzied attempt to blast the truth of the Mosaic narrative of creation'.[321] Ultimately, though, his struggle and eventual tragic death by his own hand can be more fairly summed up in these words:

> Hugh Miller was a tragic intellectual hero. He volunteered to cover God's retreat, to hold off as long as he was able the encroaching armies of scientific materialism. Miller was the last man in Scotland who, until even his Atlas-muscles failed, held together the ancient sky in which science, philosophy and theology were stars in the same firmament.[322]

A conservative he was without doubt, but one which it would be unwise to attempt to include carelessly with the other conservative opponents of evolution. Given his obvious willingness to advance at least some of the way to meet nineteenth-century science head-on, his more rightful place lies somewhere between the two camps.

* * *

While the issue which was to be the direct and immediate cause of the Second Disruption was the Declaratory Act of 1892, there is clear evidence that a great deal of the discontent which contributed to that division had been caused by the attitude of the Free Church to the twin questions of biblical criticism and evolutionary science. As this chapter has shown, the divide over these matters in the late nineteenth-century Free Church could hardly have been wider, and as such they played a integral role in preparing the ground for the Second Disruption of 1893.

Having said that, it is also clear that the Free Church did not divide itself simply into two parties on these two issues. What emerges from a study of this period is that Free Church members were in fact embracing many divergent viewpoints. In this chapter that complex reaction, inside a geographically divided Church and over a period of several years, has been simplified for the sake of argument into two fundamentally opposed 'armed camps' with a disgruntled middle ground trying to live with both sides. The tragedy for the Free Church was that although the middle ground contained figures of such immense and varied talents as Robert Rainy and Hugh Miller, it was not strong enough to persuade the bitterly divided factions to compromise for the sake of unity.

---

321 T. Davies, *Answer to Hugh Miller and Theoretic Geologists* (New York, 1860): quoted in Mackenzie, *Hugh Miller*, pp. 131–2.
322 N. Ascherson, in Rosie, *Hugh Miller*, pp. 10–11.

The reason for this failure is also evident, given the sheer scale of the divide between the opposite ends of the Free Church spectrum on these two issues. The statements of a man like Marcus Dods on the literal integrity of Scripture could hardly have been further from those of a Donald Macfarlane or a John Macleod, despite the fact that all claimed loyalty to the Free Church of the Disruption and all were professedly trying to do God's work in their own way. Dods would have considered himself to be as much a 'believer' as he was a 'critic' but despite the evidence for this, to the men who left at the Second Disruption of 1893 (and, indeed, to many who did not), the phrase 'believing critic' was a palpable nonsense.

Dods is still spoken about in terms of the utmost obloquy in Free Presbyterian New Year's Day Lectures, and the idea that he might have been a sincere Christian trying in his own way to respond to the desperate challenges being thrown at the faith is quite simply not entertained. Questioning one jot or one tittle of the Bible was taken as being commensurate with rejecting a whole series of cardinal doctrines, ranging from the Fall to the Divinity of Christ, and as such was seen as being absolutely incompatible with membership of a Christian Church. The Free Presbyterians felt they had no Scriptural warrant for compromise with men whom they considered to be making shipwreck of the faith, and perhaps the real question to be asked is why they chose to remain until 1893 within the pale of a Church which was doing so much to honour men with whose view of Scripture they could hardly have disagreed more strongly.

Having looked at these two vital areas of division in the Free Church, it is now time to turn to another issue which illustrates the depth of the divide. This issue went to the very core of the Church, and was in itself a major factor in the Second Disruption: the Highland–Lowland divide in the Free Church.

CHAPTER THREE

The Highland–Lowland Divide in the Free Church

During the fifty years between 1843 and 1893, there was a growing division between the Highland and Lowland congregations of the Free Church. It was a divide between two different cultures, two languages, two value-systems, two economic realities and, more than anything else, two different forms of Christianity. It was a divide which by the close of the nineteenth century took the form of a bitterly divided Church.

Free Churchmen in the South could disagree with each other over Disestablishment, the timing of Church Union or the revision of the Westminster Confession of Faith, and yet retain a broad respect for one another as members of the same communion. Towards the Highlands, however, the attitude of many Free Churchmen was, underneath a superficial gloss of affection and respect, one of patronising superiority. Highlanders have been accused of dividing the Free Church by their Luddite refusal to move with the times. Certainly their attitude towards the Church in the South contributed to the eventual breach, and this will be explored in due course. But we must begin with the attitudes and outlook of the powerful liberal Lowland elite which dominated the Free Church by the latter part of the nineteenth century, and ask whether their attitude of superiority to a 'different' form of religion did not play an equally important part in the growing Highland–Lowland divide.

The Nature of Highland Religion

This is a subject which has been covered in some depth over the years,[1] and the 'distinctive nature of Highland religion' cannot be examined at any length here. William Garden Blaikie commented that: 'the Highland

---

[1] For contemporary accounts see, e.g., J. Kennedy, *The Days of the Fathers in Ross-shire* (Edinburgh, 1861); Auld, *Ministers and Men*; Auld, *Life of John Kennedy*; K. Macdonald, *Social and Religious Life in the Highlands* (Edinburgh, 1902); A. T. Innes, 'The religion of the Highlands', *British and Foreign Evangelical Rev.*, xxi (Jul. 1872), p. 413, etc. More recent delineations of the distinctions are found in such works as MacInnes, *Evangelical Movement in the Highlands of Scotland*; MacInnes, 'Origin and early development of "The Men"'; J. Macleod, *By-Paths of Highland Church History* (Edinburgh, 1965); J. MacInnes, 'Religion in Gaelic society', *Trans. of the Gaelic Soc. of Inverness*, lii (1980–2); MacInnes, 'Evangelical Protestantism'; K. R. Ross, 'Calvinists in controversy: John Kennedy, Horatius Bonar and the Moody Mission of 1873–74', *Scottish Bulletin of Evangelical Theology*, ix (1) (1991); K. R. Ross, *Church and Creed* (Edinburgh, 1988), pp. 238–48.

type of religion has peculiarities of its own, very intense, very decided, very unchanging',[2] while Thomas McLauchlan, the great Free Church Highland Committee Convener, was more explicit:

the ecclesiastical history of the highlands has never been written. From the planting of Christianity in the land it had features peculiar to itself, and differing from those which characterised the Lowlands. In every period of its history, – even at this day, – the Christianity of the Highlands was and is characterised by peculiarities of its own; and to have its history fairly before us would require that it should be written separately. Scottish church history hitherto has just been that of the Scottish Lowlands.[3]

J. R. Fleming's Church history of Scotland echoed McLauchlan, saying that 'No account of theological tendencies in the Scottish Church can be complete without some reference to the peculiar quality and trend of Highland religion,'[4] which he summarised as containing, among other things, the following:

the Sabbath is revered as the outward sign of inward rest, the Bible as enshrining the Spirit in a sacrosanct letter, the Calvinistic Creed as an Ark of the Covenant conserving treasure too precious to be handled.[5]

John Kennedy, one of the most celebrated apologists for this distinctive Highland piety, observed in 1875 that the Highlands were largely united by 'the general harmony of religious views, the prevailing poverty, and the peculiar language spoken throughout the Highlands'.[6] Thomas Murray of Midmar delineated the difference in 1890, saying that the Highlanders were 'nearer to the truth' and that this was proved by the fact that

in calling ministers, their chief concern is about the man's genuine piety. It is not a litterateur they want, but an able feeder of their souls with heavenly food, and who speaks because he believes. They would not listen to some ministers who are applauded in the Lowlands.[7]

Major Macleod of Eskbank, a Free Church elder, declared that the Highlanders 'look with suspicion upon all Southerners coming there, whether on holiday or on a deputation'[8] and the Disruption hero Hugh

---

[2] Blaikie, *After Fifty Years*, p. 88.

[3] T. McLauchlan, *Celtic Gleanings; or, Notices of the History and Literature of the Scottish Gael* (Edinburgh, 1857), pp. 166–7.

[4] J. R. Fleming, *A History of the Church in Scotland, 1875–1929* (Edinburgh, 1933), p. 241.

[5] Ibid.

[6] J. Kennedy, *The Distinctive Principles and Present Position and Duty of the Free Church* (Edinburgh, 1875), p. 29.

[7] Murray, *Heretical Declamation*, pp. 44–5.

[8] *PDGAFCS*, 1884, p. 135.

Miller commented on the distinct (and old-fashioned) nature of High-land religion as early as 1854.[9] When the Free Presbyterian Father, Donald Macdonald, was in the Glasgow Free Church College in the 1860s it was said that he was

> sound in the faith ... as the Highland students then in general were. From their knowledge of the Bible, the Shorter Catechism, and the Confession of Faith, the Highland students knew most points in theology previous to their entering the Divinity Hall.[10]

By the 1890s the stage had been reached where it could be said that

> The adherents of the Free Church in the Highlands had, for a considerable time, felt themselves out of line with the great body of their fellow adherents, as represented by the General Assembly, in regard to the allowance of modes of teaching and of worship, at variance with the long established usages of the Church. The want of harmony, thus resulting, showed itself, not only in divided councils in the Courts of the Church, but in free criticism of the action of public men, by private members of the Church ... and in a growing feeling of restlessness, on the part of individuals, on account of the responsibility that was thought to attach itself to continued association in the same religious body with those from whom they differed.[11]

The Highlands and the Lowlands

It was not simply in religion that this divide was apparent. For centuries the Highlands and the Lowlands, despite nominal connection by law and 'nationhood', had been living almost as two separate countries. There was a *de facto* border across Scotland which separated two very different ways of life, and the Church historians Drummond and Bulloch underlined the starkness of the divide:

> Divided by the Highland line, Scotland had always been a peculiarly unbalanced country with one half providing the population, resources, and energy and the other contributing, if the facts be squarely faced, little to the national life beyond romance and rebellion.[12]

During the nineteenth century the Highlands, partly due to their topog-raphy, partly due to their history and partly due to economic and social realities, became increasingly isolated, psychologically if not practically,

---

9 H. Miller, *My Schools and Schoolmasters* (Edinburgh, 1854), pp. 31–2.
10 Macfarlane, *Donald Macdonald*, p. 25.
11 *Narrative and Engagement Adopted at a Meeting of Ministers and Elders in Inverness* (Inverness, 1893), p. 3.
12 A. L. Drummond and J. Bulloch, *The Church in Late Victorian Scotland, 1874–1900* (Edinburgh, 1978), p. 195.

from the industrialised and often over-populated Central Belt in the South.[13] While the population of the Highlands had declined, the Central Belt had enjoyed a massive and continuous growth. And as Callum Brown points out, the widening divide between the two covered more than just population statistics, sobering though these were. The Lowlands underwent a period of increasing social and economic prosperity, while the Highlands became more and more tethered to an out-dated and static social system, with the Crofters' Act merely tying them to this 'unchanging economic structure'.[14] The Highlands were being left behind by the South, and it was a separation which neither side particularly regretted.

In some senses this had been true from the early Middle Ages. Jane Dawson has observed that it was a long and intricate process which linked the Western Isles to the Highlands in the first place and that,

> paradoxically, only after the full incorporation of the Isles into Scotland and Britain could the complex geographical, cultural and linguistic differences be reduced to the simplistic concepts of 'Highland' and 'Lowland'.[15]

Scottish historian Christopher Smout argues that almost as soon as the inhabitants of Scotland had ceased to consider themselves 'in terms of Pict, Scot, Gallovidian, Angle, Briton and Norseman', they separated into 'the hardly less formidable divisions of Highlanders and Lowlanders which had not been envisaged before'.[16] Smout argues that by the fourteenth century the Highlanders emerged for the first time as a people with their own self-conscious identity, one on which the Lowlands looked with some apprehension.[17]

The Aberdeen chronicler John of Fordun called the Highlanders 'a savage and untamed nation' as early as 1380, and this was by no means an unusual stance to take:

> This passage, with its hostility expressed in tones of mingled fear and contempt, is already a mature example of the attitude towards Highland Gaelic society that was to persist in the Lowlands for nearly six centuries. Every medieval writer after Fordun makes the division – to John Major it was the 'wild Scots' and the 'householding Scots', for many of his successors simply the 'Irish'

---

[13] C. W. J. Withers, *Gaelic Scotland: The Transformation of a Culture Region* (London and New York, 1988), pp. 64–72.

[14] Brown, *Social History of Religion in Scotland*, p. 128.

[15] J. E. A. Dawson, 'The origin of "The Road to the Isles": trade, communications and Campbell power in early modern Scotland', in R. Mason and N. Macdougall (eds.), *People and Power in Scotland: Essays in Honour of T. C. Smout* (Edinburgh, 1992), p. 76.

[16] T. C. Smout, *A History of the Scottish People, 1560–1830* (London, 1969), p. 21.

[17] Withers, too, sees the 14th century as crucial: 'neither the terms themselves ('Highland' and 'Lowland') nor the division within Scottish culture and geography they denote had any meaning before the end of the fourteenth century': Withers, *Gaelic Scotland*, pp. 3, 5.

and the 'Scots' ... this deep rift became obvious in the late four-teenth century in a way it had never been before.[18]

Fordun was probably the first writer to make the key linguistic distinction between the population of Northern and Southern Scotland:

The manners and customs of the Scots vary with the diversity of their speech. For two languages are spoken amongst them, the Scottish (Gaelic) and the Teutonic (Scots English); the latter of which is the language of those who occupy the seaboard and the plains, while the race of Scottish speech inhabits the Highlands and outlying Islands.[19]

By 1881, this distinction had crystallised to such an extent that W. F. Skene could comment that

the boundary line which separated the Highlands from the Low-lands, and is known as the Highland Line, was in the main an imaginary line separating the Gaelic-speaking people from those using the Teutonic dialect [sic].[20]

As Gaelic increasingly retreated into a diminishing – albeit still enormous[21] – area called the Gaidhealtachd, the division between the Highlands and Lowlands took on the linguistic and racial nuances which it has had ever since. According to Jane Dawson:

the firm association of geography and culture created a simplistic division into Highland and Lowland and ensured that previous distinctions between the Western Isles and the Highlands were submerged within a common cultural identity. The new region was regarded as a single entity which was linguistically, socially and culturally distinct from the rest of Scotland. From a Lowland pers-pective, the Highlands were increasingly regarded as inaccessible, alien and hostile. Such an attitude could only intensify after 1603 when the Scottish monarch moved South. The 'Highland problem' had been created.[22]

---

18 Smout, *History of the Scottish People*, pp. 39–40.
19 Quoted in C. W. J. Withers, 'The Scottish Highlands outlined: cartographic evidence for the position of the Highland–Lowland boundary', *Scot. Geog. Magazine*, xcviii (3) (1982), p. 143.
20 Quoted in Withers, *Gaelic in Scotland*, p. 77.
21 This is something which it is very easy to forget when talking about a minority religion and language. As Thomas McLauchlan declared at the 1874 Free Assembly: 'I have found it sometimes difficult to convey an adequate sense of it to some friends in talking on the subject. They seem not ready to take in that the Highlands are a large integral part of Scotland, extending to about one half of its territorial surface, and that the inhabitants of this portion of the country are real live Scotsmen, in fact, the original Scots, from whom the country took its name': *PDGAFCS*, 1874, p. 130.
22 Dawson, 'Origin of "The Road to the Isles"', p. 97. It should be noted, however, that the *Gaidhealtachd* included some parts of the Lowlands as well as the Highlands –

As the Highlands came to be identified with the Gaidhealtachd, so both the region and its religion saw their fate inextricably tethered to that of a language whose history, according to one recent study, has essentially been one of decay.[23] Robert Auty has said that 'languages are intimately bound up with human societies, in particular national societies, and cannot be studied in isolation from the history of those societies'.[24] The fate of Highland religion and particularly the attitude towards it of Lowland intellectuals closely paralleled that of the Gaelic language. With the whole ethos of the Gaidhealtachd under attack, their religion could hardly hope to escape. Language and religion became inexorably linked, with prejudice towards the one often accompanied by hostility towards the other. In an earlier conflict the persecuted Highland Celtic religion had been Roman Catholicism.[25] But by the nineteenth century, rigorous Westminster Calvinism, and the Gaelic language were tied together. If one went, they all went.

The Attitude to the Gaelic Language

As Charles Withers has demonstrated, the modern history of the Gaelic language is fundamentally one of retreat. From the early modern period onwards, 'both the Gaelic language and its speakers were to be equated with backwardness and incivility'.[26] English rapidly advanced to become

areas which, as Withers has elegantly expressed it, 'although semantically embraced in the term *Gaidhealtachd*, do not geographically so correspond': Withers, *Gaelic in Scotland*, p. 6; Withers, *Gaelic Scotland*, p. 3. One prominent example is the Clyde port of Greenock, which in the late 18th century had so many Highlanders resident that 'one could walk from one side of the town to the other without hearing anything but Gaelic spoken': C. W. J. Withers, 'Kirk, club and culture change: Gaelic chapels, Highland societies and the urban Gaelic subculture in eighteenth-century Scotland', *Social History*, x (1985), pp. 177–8. Even as late as 1872, it was said that three-quarters of the population of the town were either Highlanders or their descendants, and that one 'could not move many yards in the streets without hearing a blash of the Gaelic': R. M. Smith, *The History of Greenock* (Greenock, 1921), p. 297. Greenock was also one of the first Lowland towns to have a Free Presbyterian congregation: 'Late Mr. John Urquart, Elder, Greenock', p. 259.

[23] 'The story of Gaelic in Scotland is largely one of decline': Withers, *Gaelic in Scotland*, p. 16. See also V. E. Durkacz, *The Decline of the Celtic Languages: A Study of Linguistic and Cultural Conflict in Scotland, Wales and Ireland from the Reformation to the Twentieth Century* (Edinburgh, 1983).

[24] Quoted in H. Seton-Watson, *Language and National Consciousness* (London, 1981), p. 2.

[25] 'After 1560 the Highlands, excepting Argyll, retained their allegiance to Catholicism. Hence their language and culture, together with their religion, were redefined as alien and hostile by anglicised, lowland Scots. In this way Gaelic became identified in lowland minds with popery, barbarity and rebellion, and a period of persecution directed at the Gaelic language began': Durkacz, *Decline of the Celtic Languages*, p. 4.

[26] Withers, 'Scottish Highlands outlined', p. 143. It should be emphasised here that not all visitors came away from the Highlands with such impressions. Thomas Wilkinson, a Quaker and a friend of William Wordsworth, said of his 1787 Highland tour that the inhabitants were 'an amiable, intelligent, polished and hospitable people', and of Highland ministers he said that they 'seem, many of them, enlightened men': G. B. Burnett, *The Story of Quakerism in Scotland* (London, 1952), pp. 161–2. The *London Daily Chronicle* was one English paper which was actually impressed by Highland

the language of gentility, of status, and as the medium of progress and the yardstick of cultural acceptability ... there has been a particularly long-standing antipathy towards the language and its culture.[27]

Those Scots who spoke what one Free Churchman called 'the language of the homes, the hearts, and the religion of nearly 300,000 of the people of this country',[28] became perceived as being part of an alien civilisation which was not merely different but inferior; the prevailing Lowland view being, in the words of Charles Withers again, 'suspicion and even hatred'.[29] According to one Highland apologist, those Highlanders driven south at the time of the Clearances had to face the fact that there 'their language and simple manners rendered them objects of derision and ridicule'.[30]

Gaelic was perceived as an obstacle to advancement, the infamous Gartmore Manuscript of 1747 stating that the Highlanders' 'want of our language evidently prevents their making improvements in the affairs of common life, and in other knowledge, as it is the means to acquire them'.[31] Crucially, this conviction was shared by prominent Free Churchmen. For example, Alexander Duff said that the Gaelic language,

> though powerful for lyric and other poetry, and also for popular address, contained no works that could possibly meet the objectives of a higher or comprehensive education. Hence those who sought that found it in English colleges, and returned as teachers and preachers to distribute the treasures of knowledge acquired through English among the Gaelic people.[32]

In some senses Duff was correct; a survey of Gaelic writing of the eighteenth and nineteenth centuries reveals a distinct lack of works on philosophy, technology, science or history, and an abundance – it might be said an overabundance – of works of a religious nature.[33] What this

customs. Commenting on a long Gaelic service in one London church, the *Chronicle* said: 'The whole scene was one of simplicity, and in that lay its impressiveness ... [there] was an organ, but it was silent ... There is melody enough in the Gaelic': quoted in Mackenzie, *Rev. Murdo Mackenzie*, pp. 61–2.

27 Withers, *Gaelic in Scotland*, p. 1.

28 Thomas McLauchlan, *PDGAFCS*, 1874, p. 130. And, as he pointed out, 'the great mass belonged to the Free Church'.

29 Withers, *Gaelic in Scotland*, p. 102.

30 D. MacLeod, *Gloomy Memories in the Highlands of Scotland* (Glasgow, 1892), xv.

31 'An Inquiry into the Causes which facilitate the Rise and Progress of Rebellions and Insurrections in the Highlands of Scotland, etc.', in E. Burt, *Letters from a Gentleman in the North of Scotland to his Friend in London* (London, 1754; 5th edn, London, 1818), ii, p. 363.

32 G. Smith, *The Life of Dr Alexander Duff, D.D., LL.D.* (4th edn, London, 1900), p. 95. See also A. A. Miller, *Alexander Duff of India* (Edinburgh, 1992). Duff held similar views about other non-English languages: see C. P. Williams, 'British religion and the wider world: mission and Empire, 1800–1940', in S. Gilley and W. Sheils (eds.), *A History of Religion in Britain* (Oxford, 1994), pp. 386–7.

33 M. Ferguson and A. Matheson, *Scottish Gaelic Union Catalogue* (Edinburgh, 1984), cited by I. Maxwell, 'Alexander Duff and the Theological and Philosophical Background to the

led to in practice, though, was an attitude of mind which played down the worth of Gaelic and, in the words of Ian Maxwell, 'assumes that if the language of lower status must be taught, it can only be as a peraedeutic to English, the language of modernity'.[34] Robert Rainy held this view explicitly, stating in evidence to the Napier Commission that:

> it is perfectly certain that the more ... [the Highlanders'] minds are stirred, and their intelligence awakened through their own language, the more will their desire be whetted to pass the limits which the Gaelic language imposes, and to open their way to the larger resources which are obtainable only through the English. All this is familiar to our experience as a Church.[35]

Men like Duff and Rainy went beyond their public statements and viewed Gaelic, albeit subconsciously, as a mark of inferiority. Duff, like a man escaping the ghetto and seeking to deny his origins, had forsaken the Gaelic language by his adult years.[36] Rainy was vehemently accused of holding the Highlanders in contempt over their stance on the Union controversy.[37]

The attitude to Gaelic is not merely an incidental one when it comes to looking at the divide in the Free Church between the Highlands and the Lowlands. It has to be stressed that Gaelic was overwhelmingly the language of both the preachers and the congregations who stood out against the 'New Evangelism' of the young, liberal and Lowland Free Church. The Free Church divinity student Donald Munro's letters to his friend John Macleod, for example, demonstrate the degree to which the Highlanders laid stress on the Gaelic language as the medium in which to pass on the Gospel. One letter almost seemed to imply that the influence of 'pious men' and 'pure gaelic'[38] were equally important, a feeling which is evident when he said 'Highland ministers can't dispense with Classics, but they assuredly need Gaelic.'[39] The Highlanders had a special veneration for the Scriptures in their own tongue, having waited a long time to get them,[40] and Donald Meek has shown that Highlanders would frequently become literate purely in order to read the Bible once they had undergone a religious conversion experience.[41] The Highlanders, however,

---

General Assembly's Mission in Calcutta to 1840' (Edinburgh University, Ph.D. thesis, 1995), chap. 1.

34 Maxwell, 'Alexander Duff', p. 23.
35 Rainy: quoted in Withers, *Gaelic in Scotland*, p. 175.
36 Maxwell, 'Alexander Duff', pp. 2, 23.
37 'The Gaelic record of the Free Church', *The Signal* (Nov. 1888), p. 338.
38 Donald Munro to John Macleod, 30 Jan. 1890, *John Macleod Collection*, 1b.
39 Ibid. See also Withers, *Gaelic Scotland*, p. 338.
40 As Donald Meek has pointed out, the Welsh Bible appeared in 1588, an Irish Classical Gaelic New Testament was available in 1602, the King James Version of the Bible appeared in English in 1611, and yet there was no Gaelic Bible until as late as 1801. The translation of the Bible into Gaelic took place 200 years after the Reformation and took 40 years to complete: D. E. Meek, 'The Gaelic Bible', in D. F. Wright (ed.), *The Bible in Scottish Life and Literature* (Edinburgh, 1988), pp. 10, 21.
41 D. Meek, 'Evangelical missionaries in the early nineteenth-century Highlands', *Scottish*

were far from certain that this reverence was something shared by the 'Southron'. Donald Munro, indeed, went further, arguing to John Macleod that 'Dr [Marcus] Dods is anxious that it [Gaelic] should die out. He thinks – thinks truly – that his seed won't grow so quickly in Gaelic ground.'[42] It is difficult to ascertain whether or not Marcus Dods actually held this view, although given his attitude to certain aspects of the religion of the Gaelic-speaking Highlander, Munro's suspicion is understandable.

Free Church conservatives viewed Gaelic not only as a particularly suitable language for the propagation of the Gospel but also as resistant to the 'poison' of the higher critics and the New Theology. For this reason, the necessity of learning the language became urgent for a young divinity student with conservative sympathies. Donald Munro stressed this when writing to his friend:

> Edinburgh has its attractions but I'm very sorry that you did not stay in Lochaber, for the sake of the Gaelic. Perhaps, however, after the bustle of the Assembly you may retire to some Highland glen where you can drink in the language of Ossian ... In order to derive some benefit from the trip, it will be necessary for you to pick up some Gaelic.[43]

Gaelic was a crucial point of departure between the two sections of the Free Church in the nineteenth century, and almost became a badge which could be used to identify 'who was on the Lord's side'. Time and again there is evidence of the Gaelic language, Highland religion and resistance to theological change being closely, if not irrevocably, tied together.

Rainy's biographer, Patrick Carnegie Simpson, admitted that one of the reasons for the Principal's failure to win the Highlanders over was his inability to speak their language. Rainy himself was the first to acknowledge the fact: 'to reach the hearts and minds of the people, it is necessary to speak to them in the tongue they best understand'.[44] Many of his opponents would doubtless have argued that his problem in the Highlands was that the Highlanders understood him too well, but whatever the truth or otherwise of that, there is little doubt that Rainy's inability to speak the language of the Highlands caused him problems: his own sister considered it an 'irretrievable pity' while the Principal himself came to regret it in later life.[45] In this respect it should be borne in mind that to some Highlanders a minister's inability to speak Gaelic

---

Studies, xxviii (1987), p. 14. Other books were available in Gaelic before the Bible, however, such as Joseph Alleine's *Alarm to the Unconverted*, translated into Gaelic by the Rev. John Smith in 1781, and causing a revival in 1786 in the parish of Kilbrandon and Kilchattan: MacInnes, *Evangelical Movement in the Highlands of Scotland*, pp. 161–2.

42 Donald Munro to John Macleod, 30 Jan. 1890, *John Macleod Collection*, 1b.

43 Ibid., 1 May 1891, *John Macleod Collection*, 1c.

44 Simpson, *Life of Principal Rainy*, i, p. 455: quoting Rainy's first report as convener of the Highland Committee.

45 Ibid., i, p. 455.

was a sign that he was not of the desired theological tendency. One Free Church minister, Kenneth Macdonald of Applecross, remarked that 'there was another class of ministers who were regarded by the Highlanders as Moderates, but who did not belong to that party at all'.[46] Given the magnitude of the charge, Macdonald's revelation of who these men were speaks volumes about the attitude of the Highlanders:

> They were men who failed to make themselves acceptable to the people because their knowledge of their language was defective. Their Gaelic was acquired, and therefore their preaching appeared to the pure Celt to be awkward and uninteresting at best compared with that of those who were familiar with the language.[47]

Macdonald, although himself a Highlander by birth,[48] was not in sympathy with the Highland conservatives – he described some of them as 'more Calvinistic than Calvin'[49] – but although his account is more than a little partisan, it serves the purpose of communicating something of the essence of the Highland commitment to the Gaelic language.

Thomas McLauchlan, the much-venerated and long-serving Convener of the Free Church Highland Committee, stated in 1880 that the Church was in a predicament since many of its most able young ministers who could speak Gaelic were choosing to settle in the South: 'it is a serious loss for the Highlands to have several of their best-equipped Gaelic-speaking students drawn away to places where their most important talent is utterly useless'.[50] William Ross, a close personal friend of McLauchlan and a tireless secretary to the Highland Committee while a student at New College, Edinburgh,[51] had said the previous year that 'two things were said to be necessary to preserve the people of the Highlands to the Free Church and the Free Church to the Highlands, and these two things were grace and Gaelic'.[52] Ross did not specify which of the two was the more important, but it is clear that in some eyes, the two were on an almost equal footing. Thomas McLauchlan had acknowledged in 1875 that Gaelic was of vital importance in his own preaching:

> for a Highland minister, Gaelic is more important than Greek. I know it is so at least to me, and that I could convey but little instruction to my flock by means of the most eloquent and classic addresses in the Greek or Latin tongues, while by means of the Gaelic I am able to preach to them the full gospel of the grace of God.[53]

---

46 Macdonald, *Social and Religious Life*, p. 82.
47 Ibid.
48 Ewing, *Annals of the Free Church of Scotland*, i, p. 223. He was, in fact, born in Applecross.
49 Macdonald, *Social and Religious Life*, p. 5.
50 *PDGAFCS*, 1880, p. 163.
51 Ross, *William Ross of Cowcaddens*, p. 17.
52 *PDGAFCS*, 1879, p. 206.
53 *PDGAFCS*, 1875, p. 192.

John Kennedy of Dingwall was another who revered the Gaelic language, saying in the 1875 Free Assembly debate on the proposed Celtic Chair at the University of Edinburgh that he would have liked to make a point by delivering his speech in Gaelic 'just because the majority could not understand me, I might succeed, better than by any intelligible speech I could deliver, in making felt the need for a Celtic chair'.[54] Kennedy's support for the Celtic Chair was because, as he humorously added, his 'Highland blood' was quickened by 'anything Celtic, be it chair, or be it stool'. It went deeper than that, though, as this much-denigrated language had a particularly important role for Kennedy:

> I like to see the language prized, in which I prefer to speak to God. As a Highland minister I feel thankful for all that would extend my acquaintance with the language in which I more frequently preach the gospel. And it is the duty of the Church, which licences so many to preach in Gaelic, to aid in securing to them the means of becoming acquainted with that, by the use of which alone they can perform the work to which they have been set apart.[55]

The language which was seen as barbaric and uncouth by some, was thought to be best fitted to communicate the gospel truths by others.[56]

The 'Irish' Factor

Alongside the loss of prestige suffered by Gaelic went an increasing separation of the language from a sense of Scottishness. Gaelic had at various times since the fourteenth century been known as 'Irish', 'Ersch' or 'Erse',[57] and this linking of the Highland and the Irish language was of central importance to the attitudes of Lowland Free Churchmen in the nineteenth century. While the two languages had much in common, and indeed were arguably branches of the same tongue, one early twentieth-century commentator was in no mood to accept an 'Irish' designation:

---

[54] Ibid., p. 197.
[55] Ibid.
[56] While there was a great appreciation of the Gaelic language as having in some ways a special place, this was not an uncritical pro-Gaelic stance. The Free Presbyterians never hesitated to criticise methods of promoting the language which they felt to be unscriptural, such as the use of 'vain songs and dancing': Beaton, *Donald Macfarlane*, p. 46. On the other hand, there were supporters of the Gaelic language who saw the contribution of the clergy as being of a poor standard if not downright detrimental. Malcolm MacFarlane, in a paper presented to the Gaelic Society of Glasgow, said that 'The standard of preaching in the Gaelic language in Scotland is that of the illiterate, and few clerics can write a passable Gaelic article for publication ... To their minds anything is good enough for Gaelic preaching': M. MacFarlane, 'The Gaelic language and the people who speak it', in *The Old Highlands: Papers Read Before the Gaelic Society of Glasgow, 1895–1906* (Glasgow, 1908), p. 302.
[57] Withers, *Gaelic in Scotland*, pp. 23, 112; Withers, 'Kirk, club and culture change', pp. 181–2; Withers, *Gaelic Scotland*, pp. 4, 5.

'Irish' refers to the soil and not to the speech. It was the English-speaking man who began to call 'Gaelic' 'Irish,' and this he did in Scotland as well as in Ireland. There is no reason why we should accept and continue his mistake of calling the Gaelic language by a name which is not its proper one.[58]

The bigotry which seemed to apply only to Irish Roman Catholics could also be transposed to the Highlander.[59]

What emerges from even a cursory study of racism in this period is that there was a real willingness to place the Irish and the Scottish Gael in the same position. As S. J. Brown has observed, a belief in the inferiority of the '"Irish" or "Celtic" race' informed much anti-Catholicism in the twentieth century.[60] But perhaps what has not been widely recognised is that this easy interchange of the two terms – 'Irish' and 'Celtic' – contributed to the systematic denigration of the Scottish Gael in the nineteenth century.[61] The Convener of the Free Church Highland Committee, Thomas McLauchlan, talked in 1871 of 'the Irish Celt ... [and] his brother Celt of Scotland',[62] and Kenneth Macdonald, Free Church minister at Applecross, said that the 'Highlanders like the Irish are naturally poetical and musical'.[63] Dr John 'Rabbi' Duncan was another Free Churchman who, while admitting that there were distinctions, was willing to bracket the Highland and the Irish Gael together.[64] Dr Thomas Guthrie, an old Disruption ally of Duncan who did a great deal of philanthropic work for, among others, homeless children,[65] was more than willing to abuse both Scottish and Irish Celt alike. In a speech of welcome in the early 1850s to the American anti-slavery campaigner Harriet Beecher Stowe, he was quoted as saying the following: 'Take an indolent Celt, let him go to America, he becomes active, – take a wild Irishman, he becomes civilized, – a blind bigoted Papist, his eyes are opened, and he turns his back on Rome.'[66] Arguably,

---

[58] MacFarlane, 'Gaelic language', pp. 284–6.

[59] Christopher Smout speaks of the Highland crofter being 'transmogrified sometimes into a comical "Sandy" to parallel the Irish "Paddy": Smout, *Century of the Scottish People*, p. 10.

[60] Brown, 'Outside the Covenant', p. 21. In the words of Steve Bruce, 'Anti-Catholicism was essentially anti-Irish': Bruce, *No Pope of Rome*, p. 25.

[61] This has continued into the 1980s, with Hugh Trevor-Roper, in a famously provocative article, referring to the Highlanders as 'simply the overflow of Ireland', and calling the Highlands 'racially and culturally ... a colony of Ireland': H. Trevor-Roper, 'The invention of tradition: the Highland tradition of Scotland', in E. Hobsbawm and T. Ranger (eds.), *The Invention of Tradition* (Cambridge, 1983), p. 15.

[62] *PDGAFCS*, 1871, p. 40.

[63] Macdonald, *Social and Religious Life*, p. 197.

[64] W. Knight (ed.), *Colloquia Peripatetica: Notes of Conversations with John Duncan* (Edinburgh, 1879), p. 117. They did, he said, 'express their feelings differently ... with the Gael, pathos; with the Irishman, humour'.

[65] Ewing, *Annals of the Free Church of Scotland*, i, p. 179. Guthrie, however, was not remembered with great favour by the conservatives; according to the Free Presbyterians, he was 'never a favourite with the more stable orthodox people in the Church': 'The Union debate in the Free Assembly', *FPM*, v (3) (1900), p. 110.

[66] Guthrie: quoted in MacLeod, *Gloomy Memories*, pp. 84–5. His speech made a considerable

most of the 'blind bigotry' was coming from Guthrie himself, a fact to which the Highland apologist Donald MacLeod succinctly alluded: 'all this unfounded foulsome calumny which he poured out against Highland and Irish Celts is as incompatible with Christianity as is falsehood with truth'.[67] It is, perhaps, significant that during the academic year 1825–6, Thomas Guthrie had attended the lectures of none other than Robert Knox, a man who, as will be seen, probably did more than any other to popularise racist notions in this period.[68]

Taylor Innes, while not a dispenser of 'foulsome calumny' on this subject, was content to say that 'there is something unprotestant in the Highland mind',[69] and that there were similarities between 'the Protestant Celt and his brother who remains a Catholic'.[70] John Watson, a product of New College, Edinburgh, who, as 'Ian Maclaren', became one of the most popular authors of the nineteenth century,[71] made the remark that 'Whether Calvinism or Catholicism be the more congenial creed for the Celtic nature may be a subject of debate.'[72] These statements were not going any further than those of the arch-racist Robert Knox in his classic work on the races of mankind; with reference to D'Aubigné's theories about the geographical distribution of the Reformation, Knox said:

> Let him look to the map, and he will find there that, with a slight exception ... the Celtic race universally rejected the Reformation of Luther; the Saxon race as universally adopted it. There need be no mystery in stating so simple a fact.[73]

Knox went further than religion, though, clearly believing that the Highlanders and the Irish were of one race. He spoke of 'the pitiable state of the Irish' and then immediately went on to ask:

---

impression on Mrs Stowe – she said that it 'rivalled the efforts of Daniel Webster': O. Smeaton, *Thomas Guthrie* (Edinburgh, 1900), p. 104, and in response 'her eye kindled, and her whole face beamed': T. Guthrie, *Autobiography of Thomas Guthrie and Memoir by his sons, the Revd David K. Guthrie, and Charles J. Guthrie, M.A.* (London, 1874–5), ii, p. 365.

67 MacLeod, *Gloomy Memories*, p. 85.

68 Guthrie, *Autobiography of Thomas Guthrie*, i, p. 279; Smeaton, *Thomas Guthrie*, p. 21.

69 Innes, 'Religion of the Highlands', p. 439.

70 Ibid., p. 438. Innes, to be fair, also pointed out where the two diverged. He also saw the Highland veneration of 'The Men' as 'forming a Hagiology curiously parallel to that set up at the opposite pole of Christianity': A. T. Innes, *Chapters of Reminiscence* (London, 1913), p. 10.

71 John Watson's books sold in huge quantities on both sides of the Atlantic: I. Maclaren, *Beside the Bonnie Briar Bush* (London, 1895) sold over 250,000 copies in Britain and almost 500,000 copies in the United States. His admirers included Queen Victoria and William Gladstone: W. F. Gray, 'John Watson (1850–1907)', *Dictionary of National Biography*, 2nd Supplement, vol. III (London, 1912), pp. 605–7; W. R. Nicoll, 'Ian Maclaren', *Life of Rev. John Watson, D.D.* (London, 1908), pp. 168, 170.

72 I. Maclaren, *St. Jude's* (London, n.d.), p. 25.

73 R. Knox, *The Races of Men: A Philosophical Enquiry into the Influence of Race over the Destinies of Nations* (2nd edn, London, 1862), pp. 3–4.

Is the Caledonian Celt better off than the Hibernian? Is he more industrious? more orderly, cleanly [*sic*], temperate? has he accumulated wealth? does he look forward to tomorrow? Though a seeming Protestant, can you compare his religious formula with the Saxon?[74]

The intended answer to that series of rhetorical questions is obvious, but in case his reader missed the point, Knox spelled it out: 'the Celtic natives of Ireland, Wales and Caledonia ... must be classed together ... They are one; the same fate, whatever it be, awaits all'.[75] Patrick Carnegie Simpson – biographer of Robert Rainy and student of Marcus Dods – had no doubt when it came to his own racial definitions, making the distinction between the Gaels and the 'more strictly Scottish sections of the Church'.[76] In case of confusion, help was at hand: 'It is well to distinguish these terms. The Gaels are the Celts of the Scottish Highlands, of Ireland, and of the Gaelic-speaking population of the Isle of Man. All Gaels are Celts, but not all Celts are Gaels.'[77] He also echoed the words of his friend Taylor Innes and, indeed, of Robert Knox, saying that 'the Celtic nature is less Protestant than its creed',[78] and argued that there was a force which affected both the Irish and the Scottish Celt: 'that setting of things awry which pursues [the] Celtic story – it is in Irish politics as well as in Scottish ecclesiastical history'.[79] Subtly, but definitely, the Highlander and the Irishman were being placed in the same leaking boat.

Much of the British attitude to the Irish, both in Britain and in Ireland, has been explained in terms of the English (and the Scots) considering themselves superior to an alien race with an alien religion. Given the conspicuous willingness to see the terms Highland Celt and Irish Celt as synonymous, it seems reasonable to come to some similar conclusions regarding the Highlanders. It is possible to consider the attack on the Gaelic language, the destruction of traditional Highland relationships before, during, and after the Clearances, and the assault on the distinctive Highland religion in the Free Church as all being informed by the same racist assumptions of Lowland 'Teutonic' superiority as those which lay behind anti-Irish prejudice. And just as the Clearances, the assault on Gaelic and the Land Laws were only actively resisted by a minority; so, too, the attacks on Highland religion by the Free Church Lowland elite in the later nineteenth century only met with limited resistance. The Free Presbyterian Fathers, although they did not know it, were in some ways part of a racially motivated

[74] Ibid., p. 69.
[75] Ibid., p. 78.
[76] Simpson, *Life of Principal Rainy*, i, p. 429.
[77] Ibid.
[78] Ibid., p. 451.
[79] Ibid., p. 439.

conflict which had been waged in the Highlands and in Ireland for centuries. Before proceeding further, though, it is necessary to delineate the context from which such a situation emerged.

The Influence of Race Theory: (1) Science

The mid-to-late nineteenth century was a time when racism was rife in the British Isles, having been given the spurious camouflage of pseudo-science. One of the foremost proponents of 'scientific racism' was a Scot: Burke and Hare's old client Robert Knox. Knox was an influential Fellow of the Edinburgh College of Surgeons and 'a highly-esteemed lecturer in anatomy' at the University, where by Session 1828–9 he had 504 students, and lectured for three hours a day.[80] At the zenith of his popularity he had two-thirds of the Edinburgh medical school listening to his lectures,[81] and in the words of Susan Collinson:

> his lectures ... were enormously popular, and were attended not only by medical students and doctors, but by lawyers, judges and members of the professional and upper classes and many others who wished to improve their knowledge.[82]

Indeed, in the mid-1820s his students involved several men who would later rise to prominence in the Free Church; Thomas Guthrie, William Cunningham and Sir George Sinclair.[83] For his involvement in the grisly affair of Burke and Hare, Knox was forced to quit his home in Edinburgh after having been burnt in effigy by the Edinburgh mob, and was ultimately ruined both professionally and financially. It is as 'The Anatomist' that he is most popularly remembered,[84] but it is as a racist that his legacy is more important.[85] His direct influence was through his students at Edinburgh:

> Previous to his time little or nothing was heard about race in the medical schools: he changed all this by his Saturday lectures and Race became as familiar as household words to his students through

---

80 G. T. Bettany, 'Robert Knox (1791–1862)', in *Dictionary of National Biography*, xxxi (London, 1892), pp. 331–3.

81 E. Richards, 'The "Moral Anatomy" of Robert Knox: the interplay between biological and social thought in Victorian scientific naturalism', *Journal of the History of Biology*, xxii (3) (1989), p. 381, note 21.

82 S. Collinson, 'Robert Knox's anatomy of race', *History Today*, xl (Dec. 1990), p. 46.

83 Guthrie, *Autobiography of Thomas Guthrie*, i, p. 279, note.

84 E.g. the titles of both Rae's and Lonsdale's biographies: H. Lonsdale, *A Sketch of the Life and Writings of Robert Knox the Anatomist* (London, 1870), and I. Rae, *Knox the Anatomist* (Edinburgh and London, 1964); A. S. Currie, 'Robert Knox, anatomist, scientist and martyr', *Proceedings of the Royal Society of Medicine*, xxvi (1933), p. 39; J. Bridie, *The Anatomist* (London, 1931) was still being studied in Scottish secondary schools in the 1980s, and was still being performed on the Edinburgh Festival Fringe in 1992.

85 E.g. M. D. Biddiss, 'The politics of anatomy: Dr Robert Knox and Victorian racism', *Proceedings of the Royal Society of Medicine*, lxix (1976), p. 245.

whom some of his novel ideas became disseminated far and wide both at home and abroad.[86]

Philip Curtin went so far as to call him 'the real founder of racism' and 'one of the key figures in the general Western movement towards a dogmatic pseudo-scientific racism'.[87]

His infamous 1850 work, *The Races of Men*, is accepted as 'one of the most articulate and lucid statements of racism ever to appear',[88] and while it is mainly studied because of its stance on the differences between the White and the Coloured races, it also contains important references to the Celt. Knox believed that conflict between the Anglo-Saxon peoples and the Celts was not only inevitable but also imminent in the mid-nineteenth century. He believed, moreover, that the common Celtic characteristics – such as 'furious fanaticism' and 'a hatred for order'[89] – were shown up in their religion. This was usually Catholicism, but even non-Catholic Celts were not much of an improvement in Knox's judgement:

> the reformed Celts have never joined the churches 'as by law established'. It is the Saxon who accepts of his religion from the lawyers; the Celt will not. Accordingly, the Welsh and Caledonian Celt are strictly evangelical.[90]

Knox did not believe that the Celts were entirely without virtue; since he was allegedly the purveyor of 'racism with substantial traces of benevolence',[91] it would be surprising if he could not have found something generous to say about them. Knox was, however, unwilling to proceed beyond a few platitudes about the Celts being inventive and imaginative, and the vast bulk of his references were absolutely negative. Given what has been said already about the popularity of the views of a man like Knox, it should come as no surprise that some of this negative picture should influence prominent liberal Free Churchmen. Among the Celtic traits which Knox identified were 'mental slavery', being 'without self-reliance', 'irascible', 'uncertain, treacherous', and he believed that the Celt was 'a despiser of the peaceful arts, of labour, of order, and of the law, it is fortunate for mankind that the Celtic race is ... broken up into fragments'.[92] With this in mind, it is little wonder that many influential minds in the nineteenth century harboured negative opinions of the Celts.

[86] M. Banton, *Race Relations* (London, 1967), p. 30: quoting Knox's biographer, Henry Lonsdale. Lonsdale's is a superior work to the later one by Isobel Rae, which chooses to concentrate on the Burke and Hare Affair to the detriment of an analysis of Knox's life as a whole.

[87] P. D. Curtin, *The Image of Africa: British Ideas and Action, 1780–1850* (Madison, 1964), p. 377.

[88] Banton, *Race Relations*, pp. 28–9.

[89] Knox, *Races of Men*, p. 26.

[90] Ibid., p. 327.

[91] Biddiss: quoted in Richards, 'Moral Anatomy', p. 375.

[92] Knox, *Races of Men*, pp. 18, 320, 322.

What frustrated Knox was that although the notion of the Celts being a separate race was as clear as daylight to him, he believed that this 'fact' had been deliberately suppressed; it is worthwhile here to quote Knox at some length:

> The obvious differences in the races of men attracted my attention ... from my earliest years. In my native country Britain, there have been, from the earliest recorded times, at least two distinct races of men ... To me the Caledonian Celt of Scotland appears a race as distinct from the Lowland Saxon of the same country, as any two races can possibly be: as Negro from American; Hottentot from Caffre; Esquimaux from Saxon. But statesmen, historians, theologians, have not only refused to acknowledge the importance of this fact; they have gone further; they have denied its existence and purposely falsified history: the fact has been carefully excluded from the high educational institutions of the country.[93]

Knox believed that it was the Caledonian Celtic race which perished at Culloden, a battle at which, he said, there was 'scarcely a Scottish man, properly speaking, in the Stuart army', and at which the 'Caledonian Celtic race, not Scotland, fell ... never more to rise'.[94] In some ways this parallels the views which equated the Highlanders with the Irish; at the very least it parallels the views which sought to portray the Highlander as being in some way un-Scottish, as being 'outside and below' in terms not just of prestige but of Scottish identity – a view which, as will be seen, found considerable echo in the opinions of the Lowland Free Church.

Another posture taken by Knox was that the Scottish Celt was incapable of self-improvement. He firmly believed that the Celt remained a Celt in every circumstance, his actions and outlooks formed not by environment but by innate racial characteristics; the Caledonian Celt, said Knox:

> still lingers in diminished numbers, but unaltered, on the wild shores of his lochs and friths [*sic*], scraping a miserable subsistence from the narrow patch of soil left him by the stern climate of his native land. Transplant him to another climate, a brighter sky, a greater field, free him from the trammels of artificial life, the harassed routine of European civilization; carry him to Canada, *he is still the same*; mysterious fact.[95]

Knox was later to repeat and expand this analysis of the Celt, saying that

[93] Ibid., pp. 12, 14.
[94] Ibid., p. 15. As Murray Pittock has observed, despite the fact that the Jacobite army at Culloden was a mixture of Highlanders and Lowlanders and included English, French and Irish soldiers, 'a Highland battle Culloden became. It remains so in the popular imagination to this day': M. G. H. Pittock, *The Invention of Scotland: The Stuart Myth and the Scottish Identity, 1638 to the Present* (London and New York, 1991), p. 64.
[95] Ibid., p. 18. Emphasis his.

neither 'time nor circumstances have altered him from the remotest period', and talking of

> the character which I now know to be common to all the Celtic race, wherever found, give him what name you will ... under every circumstance he is the same, unaltered and unalterable. Civilization but modifies, education effects little; his religious formula is the result of his race; his morals, actions, feelings, greatnesses and littlenesses, flow distinctly and surely from his physical structure; that structure which seems not to have altered since the commencement of recorded time.[96]

The slur here cast on the Highlanders is an important one in that it can be seen to have informed much of the criticism heaped upon them in the years leading up to the Second Disruption of 1893. As will be seen, the charge that the Highlanders were either unable or unwilling to change with the times was a favourite approach of the Lowland liberals. While it would be harsh to call them racists, there is clear evidence that, perhaps subconsciously, they were here imbibing and responding to the racist views of men like Robert Knox.

Although unsophisticated and almost risible as they might be by modern standards of scholarship, Knox's views certainly helped produce what L. P. Curtis has called a racist 'consensus' which

> amounted to an assumption or a conviction that the 'native Irish' were alien in race and inferior in culture to the Anglo-Saxons ... [this] derived a great deal of force from theories about race and national character which were steadily gaining in popularity during the Victorian period.[97]

Curtis has stressed the vital role played by Scots in the formation of racially stereotyped views of the Irish Celt, and has gone as far as to say that: 'there were few parts of the British Isles where anti-Irish prejudice had worked its way [further] into the marrow of society than in the Scottish Lowlands'.[98] He concludes that Scottish artists, scientists and pseudo-scientists had a much more important part to play in shaping negative English perceptions of the Irish than had been realised.[99] Given that there was, as has been seen, a gradual but definite blurring of the distinction between the Scottish and the Irish Gael, this is vital evidence in producing a picture of the intellectual *Zeitgeist* in which the Lowland Free Church formed its views of the Highlanders. The Scot Daniel Mackintosh read a paper before the Anthropological Society of London

---

[96] Ibid., p. 318.

[97] L. P. Curtis, *Anglo-Saxons and Celts: A Study of Anti-Irish Prejudice in Victorian England* (Bridgeport, Conn., 1968), p. 5.

[98] L. P. Curtis, *Apes and Angels: The Irishman in Victorian Caricature* (Newton Abbot, 1971), p. 97.

[99] Ibid., p. 98.

in 1865, in which he gave characteristics of 'the Gaelic type' which, as will be seen, eerily echo some of the later pronouncements by leading lights in the Free Church. He said the Celt was

> deficient in depth of reasoning power, headstrong and excitable ... [with a] tendency to oppose; strong in love and hate; at one time lively, soon after sad; vivid in imagination; extremely sociable, with a propensity for crowding together ... [and] veneration for authority.[100]

At the same time newer developments in evolutionary thought provided a 'scientific' basis for there being clear-cut racial differences between Anglo-Saxon and Celt.[101]

It would be quite wrong to assume that pseudo-scientific theorising of this type was confined solely to academics in ivory towers. A magazine like the *Edinburgh Review*, a copy of which was taken by the New College Library, contained various articles which denigrated not only the Irish Celts but also the Highlanders. In 1846 a commentary on the Irish Poor Law in the *Edinburgh Review* observed that 'the people of Ireland and Great Britain are among the most dissimilar in Europe. They differ in race, in religion, in civilization, and in wealth',[102] and in a quite astonishing review of the Duke of Argyll's *Scotland As It Is and As It Was*, the same journal revealed that

> in the Western Highlands and Islands, indeed, the Duke of Argyll sees something like a return to barbarism, which reminds him of that tendency to revert to an older type in animal structures pointed out by Darwin.[103]

It also described the Anglicisation of the Highlands in the years before the Forty-Five as 'civilization ... steadily advancing on the strongholds of barbarism'.[104] According to Peter Womack, 'barbarous ferocity' was assumed to be the natural product of the Highlanders' geographical and social situation, giving rise to what he called, 'the image of the highland past as an endless pageant of bloodshed'.[105]

Sir Walter Scott, writing in an anonymous article of 1816 which was republished under his name in 1893, observed that English knowledge of the Highlands was very limited, at least until 1745:

> The more intelligent, when they thought of them by any chance, considered them as complete barbarians; the mass of the people

---

[100] Ibid., pp. 17–18.
[101] Ibid., p. 21.
[102] 'Proposals for extending the Irish Poor-Law', *Edinburgh Rev.*, lxxxiv (170) (1846), p. 267.
[103] 'Review of *Scotland As It Is and As It Was, by the Duke of Argyll*', *Edinburgh Rev.* (338) (Apr. 1887), p. 546.
[104] Ibid., p. 551.
[105] P. Womack, *Improvement and Romance: Constructing the Myth of the Highlands* (London, 1989), pp. 34–6.

cared no more about them than the merchants of New York about the Indians who dwell beyond the Alleghany mountains.[106]

Jonathan Swift, for all his sophistication and wit, expressed surprise on finding two Highland gentlemen with whom he had dined to be 'persons of ordinary decorum and civility'.[107] Dr Johnson was another English gentleman who was surprised by what he found in the Highlands, writing that he had arrived too late to find what he expected: 'a people of peculiar appearance, and a system of antiquated life ... ferocity of temper ... military ardour ... dignity of independence ... [and] reverence for their chiefs'.[108] At the time of the great famine of the later 1840s, the Highlanders were perceived as being 'dirty, lazy, untameable beings'.[109] Sir Walter Scott was 'forcibly struck' by how closely, in their manners and customs, the Highlanders resembled the mountain tribes of Afghanistan – themselves old adversaries of the British Empire.[110] Scott spoke of the Highlanders' 'insatiable thirst for revenge',[111] observing that

they resembled these Oriental mountaineers in their feuds ... in their laws, in their modes of conducting war, in their arms, and, in some respects, even in their dress ... their simplicity of manners exactly correspond. Their superstitions are the same, or nearly so.[112]

He argued that the two cultures were at 'the same state of society and civilization',[113] which was hardly intended as a compliment.[114]

---

[106] W. Scott, *Manners, Customs and History of the Highlanders of Scotland* (Glasgow and London, 1893), p. 14. Some research reveals that the original article, a review of a book called *Culloden Papers*, appeared anonymously in the *Quarterly Review*: 'Culloden Papers', *Quarterly Rev.*, xiii (28) (1816), pp. 283–333. Footnotes will, however, refer to the later publication.

[107] Scott, *Manners, Customs and History of the Highlanders of Scotland*, p. 14.

[108] Quoted in Burt, *Letters from a Gentleman*, p. 87.

[109] MacLeod, *Gloomy Memories*, p. xi.

[110] Among those who fought for the British Empire in Afghanistan were, of course, Scots: D. M. Henderson, 'The Scottish soldier abroad: the sociology of acclimatization', in G. G. Simpson (ed.), *The Scottish Soldier Abroad, 1247–1967* (Edinburgh, 1992), p. 129. Edinburgh Castle Esplanade celebrates their heroics in that particular field and, as Sydney and Olive Checkland have observed: the 'Thin Red Line' of the British Army was composed of Highlanders': Checkland and Checkland, *Industry and Ethos*, p. 157.

[111] This was a trait on which Burt also commented. He wrote that the Highlander was 'most mischievous when much offended, and will hardly ever forgive a provocation': Burt, *Letters from a Gentleman*, pp. 27–8.

[112] Scott, *Manners, Customs and History of the Highlanders of Scotland*, pp. 22, 25, 27.

[113] Ibid., p. 27.

[114] The great Scots missionary David Livingstone, himself a Gael by birth, was another writer who compared the Highlanders to foreign peoples with whom the Empire was in conflict. He spoke of the descendants of the warrior tribesmen who had fought the redcoats at Culloden being 'transformed' by the Gospel and education to become lawyers, doctors, ministers and teachers – and argued that the same thing could happen in Southern Africa to 'the sons and daughters of the Tswana and Kololo and of the Xhosa who were even then fighting the redcoats'. What made Livingstone different from many 19th-century observers was that he believed these African tribes to be capable of advancement: A. C. Ross, *Livingstone: The Scot and the Doctor* (Glasgow, 1990), p. 9.

Furthermore, as Charles Withers has indicated, various publications linked the Gaelic language to barbarism. The anonymous *Highland Complaint* of 1737, for example, noted that:

Our poor People are from the Cradles train'd up in Barbarity and Ignorance. Their very Language is an everlasting Bar against all Instructions ... the Barbarous Customs and Fashions they have from their forefathers.[115]

The Gartmore Manuscript, written in 1747, argued that the Highlanders' use of the Irish tongue prevented them from acquiring the means to improvement,[116] while, as late as the 1820s, the writer L. A. Necker de Saussure, in his *Travels in Scotland*, called the Highlanders 'semi-barbarians'.[117] The *Scottish Review* of 1883 said that the Gael had a mentality of which the result was 'an unwillingness, and partial incapacity, to enter the arena of civilization'.[118] Further, Peter Womack has argued that English-speaking culture

identifies the Highlander, in the first instance, with the traditional stereotypes of the social reject. In particular, the Highlander is textualised as the fool, as the rogue, and as the beggar ... [and] as people originally and irreducibly different from ourselves.[119]

Martial language is much in evidence in the religious debates which took place in the Free Church between Highlands and Lowlands,[120] and the repeated characterisation of the Highlanders as a warlike and uncivilised people must have contributed to this.[121] The Highlander might well have been perceived as a noble savage, but before someone is thought of as a 'noble savage' that person must be thought of as 'savage'. The Highlands had been warlike at one time, of course, but in the prevailing view of many educated and influential people the Highlands

---

[115] Withers, *Gaelic in Scotland*, p. 103.

[116] Ibid., p. 106.

[117] Ibid., p. 111.

[118] Ibid., p. 113.

[119] Womack, *Improvement and Romance*, pp. 6, 20.

[120] Patrick Carnegie Simpson spoke of the 'ramparts of the Grampians': Simpson, *Life of Principal Rainy*, i, p. 448, and this was echoed by the conservatives themselves: 'Where are the Highlands drifting to?' (Jun. 1888), p. 172. 'Highland Host', a much-used epithet, has distinct military overtones – for the origins of the phrase, see J. R. Elder, *The Highland Host of 1678* (Glasgow, 1914); and ecclesiastical innovations were described as an invasion of the Highlands 'by Southern Heretics': 'Gaelic record of the Free Church', p. 341. This will be examined in some more detail later in the chapter.

[121] In the eyes of those who held these views, the problem of Highland violence was solved by recruiting Highlanders to serve in the British Army as what Alan MacInnes has called 'cannon-fodder for the British Empire': MacInnes, 'Evangelical Protestantism', p. 44. Peter Womack has described Highland recruitment as 'a triumph on most of its several grounds', in that it produced quality regiments, removed some alienated Highlanders, provided career prospects and offered some 'cultural consolation' for otherwise disaffected clansmen: Womack, *Improvement and Romance*, p. 31.

remained a bastion of barbarism, containing an inferior race.[122] This has
scarcely been recognised before, but is a critical factor in explaining the
attitude of the Lowland Free Church to their supposed brethren in the
Highlands; given what was being said about the Highlands in general,
Highland objections to ecclesiastical innovations could then be explained
away as further examples of feral and boorish conduct.

The Influence of Race Theory: (2) History

Along with the so-called 'scientific' racism, historiography also played a
part. By the later part of the nineteenth century, the 'harsh, imperious'
ambience of Knox's racism was to be found in the work of those who
wrote English history. By then most of Britain's leading historians were
advocates of what has been called Anglo-Saxonism: stressing the over-
riding importance of Race, believing that all that was good in English
history was as a result of Teutonic origins.[123] As L. P. Curtis put it:

> The most important article in this creed was the notion that the
> Anglo-Saxon people or race, as clearly distinguished from all other
> races in the world, had a peculiar genius for governing themselves –
> and others – by means of a constitutional and legal system that
> combined the highest degree of efficiency with liberty and justice.[124]

Curtis has argued that the zenith of Anglo-Saxonism occurred between 1860
and the mid-1890s – the very years during which the Highland–Lowland
divide in the Free Church widened to become an unbridgeable gulf –

---

122 The 19th century, however, was also the time when the Highlander was most frequently
portrayed in a sentimental way. The year 1822 saw Edinburgh becoming 'tartanised'
for the state visit of George IV, producing what John Prebble called a 'bogus tartan
caricature of itself': J. Prebble, *The King's Jaunt: George IV in Scotland, August 1822.
'One and Twenty Daft Days'* (London, 1988), p. 364; Trevor-Roper, 'Invention of
tradition', pp. 29–31; indeed Murray Pittock points out that after the 1745 Jacobite
Rising 'tartan became a fashionable statement of opposition to the government' in
London: Pittock, *Invention of Scotland*, p. 64. Charles Withers has spoken of the fact
that 'in the nineteenth century ... the Highlander was often depicted as a romantic
figure, a noble savage, whose language was the last vestige of a primitivism to be both
marvelled at and pitied': Withers, *Gaelic in Scotland*, p. 113; and Grant Jarvie said that
'A culture was destroyed after Culloden, and yet, precisely because of this, its symbols
became available not only to a nascent European romantic movement, of which
Walter Scott was a part, but also to Scottish cultural identity in general ... The literati
had relatively few problems locating a sentimental Scottish nationalism north of the
Highland line': G. Jarvie, 'Culture, social development and the Scottish Highland
Gatherings', in D. McCrone, S. Kendrick and P. Shaw (eds.), *The Making of Scotland:
Nation, Culture and Social Change* (Edinburgh, 1989), p. 198. As Christopher Smout
observed: 'Romance ... had its abode only in the Highlands, the land of the mountain
and the flood ... glamorous, shrouded in the historic mists and poetry of Scott's *Lord
of the Isles* and studded with forests and moors': Smout, *Century of the Scottish People*, p.
10. The whole issue has recently been discussed by Charles Withers: C. W. J. Withers,
'The historical creation of the Scottish Highlands', in I. Donnachie and C. Whatley
(eds.), *The Manufacture of Scottish History* (Edinburgh, 1992).
123 T. F. Gosset, *Race: The History of an Idea in America* (Dallas, 1973), p. 98.
124 Curtis, *Anglo-Saxons and Celts*, pp. 6–7.

and that although it was 'unsystematic, illogical, unhistorical, and, at times, downright incoherent ... it had a powerful emotional appeal'.[125]

It should be stressed that the men putting forward these ideas were not Jonahs crying to an unheeding Nineveh. The foremost exponents of this type of historiography were William Stubbs, Edward Freeman and John Richard Green: men whose influence went far beyond academia. Green's *Short History of the English People* (1874), for example, was what would now be called a best-seller:

> [it] had a success such as few books on a serious subject have had in English literature. The first edition was exhausted immediately; five fresh issues were called for in 1875, and one or two issues have marked every subsequent year.[126]

William Stubbs was appointed Regius Professor of History at Oxford University in 1866; of his *Constitutional History of England in its Origins*, Professor T. F. Tout said that it remained unsuperseded for forty years after its publication.[127] The enormous respect with which Stubbs was held as a historian at the time is reflected in the fact that he was a member of the Academies of Berlin, Munich and Copenhagen, a corresponding member of the Academie des Sciences Morales et Politiques of the French Institut, and held honorary doctorates from the Universities of Heidelburg, Cambridge, Dublin, Oxford and Edinburgh.[128] His obituary in the *English Historical Review* suggested that fellow historians would have awarded him a laurel wreath and said that his place among historians would be high: 'I fancy that those who fix it high among the highest will be those who by their own labours have best earned the right to judge.'[129] Edward Freeman, another of the foremost Anglo-Saxonists and a man renowned for his 'hatred of the Celts',[130] succeeded Stubbs as Regius Professor of History at Oxford in 1884 on the recommendation of none other than William Gladstone.[131] He also received the plaudits of an awed academic community, being awarded honorary degrees by both Oxford (1870) and Cambridge (1874) and accepting his honorary LL.D. from Edinburgh University in 1884.[132] Clearly, then, the men who did most to propagate the dogma of Anglo-Saxonism were not working in obscurity; rather they were the most eminent historians of their generation.

[125] Ibid., pp. 31, 12.

[126] M. Creighton, 'John Richard Green (1837–1883)', *Dictionary of National Biography*, xxiii (London, 1890), p. 48.

[127] T. F. Tout, 'William Stubbs (1825–1901)', *Dictionary of National Biography*, 2nd Supplement, vol. III (London, 1912), p. 447.

[128] Ibid., p. 450.

[129] F. W. Maitland, 'William Stubbs, Bishop of Oxford', *Eng. Hist. Rev.*, xvi (1901), pp. 418, 426.

[130] Gosset, *Race*, p. 100.

[131] J. Bryce, 'Edward Augustus Freeman', *Eng. Hist. Rev.*, vii (1892), p. 497.

[132] W. Hunt, 'Edward Augustus Freeman (1823–1892)', *Dictionary of National Biography*, Supplement, vol II. (London, 1901), pp. 248–9.

Along with all its other half-baked assumptions and bigoted prejudices,
Anglo-Saxonism, almost inevitably, laid great emphasis upon 'the dichotomy
of Saxon and Celt'.[133] Freeman was described as 'intensely English and
Teutonic', something which went to the extent of his having a 'preference
for words of Teutonic origin'.[134] The review of Bishop William Stubbs's
Constitutional History of England in the *Edinburgh Review* for 1879 is an
uncritical celebration of the ethnocentric triumphalism of the so-called
Oxford School of Anglo-Saxonists. Let two quotations from Stubbs, repeated
enthusiastically on behalf of the *Edinburgh Review*'s readers, suffice:

> The Anglo-Saxon race has now and again paused in its advance. It has
> appeared to stumble and stagnate ... [but] simply it has bowed its head
> till the wave has spent its force. When the onset of opposing elements
> has exhausted itself, the English nationality is seen not merely to be
> surviving, but to have absorbed the rival energies which had
> attempted to override it. Dane and Norman, Celt, and Flemming.[135]

The Teutonic origins could not be allowed to go uncredited, of course,
and Stubbs added that the germs of English institutions 'may be traced
to a purely Germanic source. Thence we derive language, laws and
customs'.[136] By the end of the review the *Edinburgh Review* was informing
its readers that it would be 'a bold critic who would venture to assail
Canon Stubbs' facts'.[137] The very presence of this review in a journal like
the *Edinburgh Review* says much about the prevalence of such views
among the Scottish Lowland intelligentsia.

There is no doubt that Anglo-Saxonism was an influential creed in the
nineteenth century. J. A. Mangan cites the case of one nineteenth-
century Headmaster of Winchester College, who 'regarded the Anglo-
Saxon race as the rightful leaders of the world',[138] and he concludes that
such views were commonplace. It was also a creed of which the Celts
were themselves aware, and one of its most powerful critiques from a
Celtic perspective came from none other than Thomas McLauchlan,
longtime Convener of the Free Church Highland Committee. As early as
1857, in a lecture delivered on popular demand from the staff and
students of New College, Edinburgh, he felt constrained to make the
following comment:

> Reviews, newspapers, popular lectures, all teem with the incomparable
> excellencies of the Anglo-Saxon; and the Celt, who is favoured with this

---

133 Gosset, *Race*, p. 74.
134 Bryce, 'Edward Augustus Freeman', pp. 501, 507.
135 'Review of *The Constitutional History of England in its Origins, by William Stubbs*', *Edinburgh Rev.* (307) (Jul. 1879), pp. 1–2.
136 Ibid., p. 2.
137 Ibid., p. 35.
138 J. A. Mangan, *The Games Ethic and Imperialism: Aspects of the Diffusion of an Ideal*
   (Harmondsworth, 1986), p. 33. The man was Montague Rendall, later Chairman of
   the Imperial Studies Committee of the Royal Colonial Institute.

peculiar self-laudation very much at his expense, while perhaps moved with a measure of indignation, is almost stunned into acquiescence with what he finds is a very general and popular belief.[139]

McLauchlan complained of his Anglo-Saxon 'neighbours' 'from whom, of late years, we have been called to listen to such loud claims of superiority over their Celtic brethren',[140] and provided his listeners with an amusing yet clinically accurate summary of the whole racist historiography of the Anglo-Saxonists:

> It is indeed a very popular belief that there is some peculiar excellence about the Anglo-Saxon character. To be an Anglo-Saxon is, in the eyes of many, to be a being of a superior order altogether ... It would appear as if everything great and good in this land of ours was due to its Anglo-Saxon connections![141]

Expressed like that, Anglo-Saxonism does indeed sound like a quaint notion, good only for jokes at its own expense. The truth was more sinister, of course, as beneath the veneer of apparently harmless myopic stupidity, lay a popular but harsh ethnocentricity which condoned the severest anti-Celtic racism. Its potency lay in its popularity, for as J. A. Mangan concluded, 'buttressed by mythology, insensitivity and stupidity, by the end of Victoria's reign this belief in Anglo-Saxon superiority was firmly established'.[142]

As McLauchlan himself realised at the time, the danger lay not so much in the theory itself as in its ramifications. Arguably there is no real harm in feeling superior to another human being so long as that feeling is not acted upon to the detriment of the other party. Arguably it would have done the Celts little harm had the Anglo-Saxons thought them inferior but left it at that; the problem was succinctly summarised by McLauchlan, who declared that

> men might be allowed to indulge in their own ideas on the subject, were it not that those ideas are far from harmless. It cannot be doubted that certain views on the subject of ethnological distinctions, have entered into the treatment which the Celtic race has received both in Britain and Ireland.[143]

---

[139] McLauchlan, *Celtic Gleanings*, p. 10. The lectures had been given in response to a letter from the staff and students of New College, 'anxious to see some steps being taken for the purpose of awakening an interest in our Celtic History and Literature': ibid., p. v.

[140] Ibid., p. 10.

[141] Ibid., p. 11. Commenting on the supposed innate superiority of the Anglo-Saxon race, McLauchlan said to the author, J. W. Donaldson, 'I should have thought that their wretched mismanagement of the Crimean War would have been quite enough to drive that delusion from men's heads': W. K. Leask, *Dr. Thomas McLauchlan* (Edinburgh and London, 1905), p. 261.

[142] Mangan, *Games Ethic and Imperialism*, p. 114.

[143] McLauchlan, *Celtic Gleanings*, p. 15.

He was, moreover, explicit as to what he meant when he spoke of 'treatment'; he had no doubt that arguments based on racial theories about the distinctions between the races were 'made use of to defend a system leading to the rapid extirpation or extradition of the native population [of the Scottish Highlands]'.[144] Donald MacLeod's critique of the Clearances hinted at the same point, when he said that his purpose was not to 'dilate ... upon the antiquity and character of the Celtic race' but to

> expose the cruelty and injustice to which they have been subjected by the aristocracy of Great Britain, and tolerated by the Government, seemingly with the avowed intention to extirpate them root and branch from the land of their birth and home of their forefathers.[145]

Alongside this, which MacLeod saw as part of the English desire to 'subdue the Celts',[146] went the English attempt to malign the Celts through the use of history:

> that Scotland might be left defenceless from the attacks of England's hired historians, to defame her in her government and chivalry, in her patriotism, her customs, her science and literature, and to make everything that was great and good, English.[147]

This is a fairly conspicuous reference to Anglo-Saxonism, and Thomas McLauchlan had no doubt as to what lay behind it: 'It is vain to attempt concealing that there are parties, and parties possessed of leading influence in many portions of the country, who cherish the belief that it would be well to be rid of [the Celtic race].'[148]

It is difficult to calculate how deeply ideas like this would have been held by the Lowland Free Church intellectuals; as Norman Gash has observed, there are 'the implicit fundamental attitudes which condition everything but are often unconscious or taken for granted, and therefore rarely discussed and recorded'.[149] But it has to be said that racial theories such as these would have provided a very convenient vindication of an instinctive prejudice. It was most useful that Highland opposition could be explained away on the grounds that the Highlanders were 'different', that they were, in the phraseology of one of Robert Rainy's biographers, David Gibb Mitchell, 'apart, unique – a nation within a nation'.[150] Matthew Arnold discovered in the 1860s that there was 'a deep-seated antipathy towards the Celtic peoples of Wales, Scotland, and Ireland',[151] and the fact that

---

144 Ibid.
145 MacLeod, *Gloomy Memories*, p. i.
146 Ibid., p. vi.
147 Ibid., p. vii.
148 McLauchlan, *Celtic Gleanings*, p. 15.
149 Quoted in Curtis, *Anglo-Saxons and Celts*, pp. 3–4.
150 D. G. Mitchell, *The Life of Robert Rainy* (Glasgow, n.d.), p. 160.
151 Curtis, *Anglo-Saxons and Celts*, p. 42.

the Victorians who gave the greatest impetus to the dichotomy of
Saxon and Celt were some of the most eminent historians in the
country ... [who] wrote regularly for the established periodicals with
which educated Englishmen and women satisfied their intellectual
appetite[152]

has to have played a part in this. It can hardly be stressed enough that
these views were being put forward by some of the brightest and most
progressive minds in Britain. That these views had an impact on the
progressive men in the Lowland Free Church seems to be almost a
certainty, and for evidence it is necessary to look no further than their
own words.

The Influence of Race on Lowland Attitudes

1. 'Highland remoteness'

One much-repeated generalisation about the Highlanders was that their
views reflected the geographical remoteness of their situation. A. T.
Innes – one of the Free Church's finest legal minds and a close friend of
such prominent Church liberals as Robert Rainy and Alexander Whyte –
stressed the introspective nature of the religious Highlander and the
relative lack of emphasis in Highland preaching on 'external walk and
conversation'.[153] He suggested that one reason for this might have been
'the peculiarities of the circumstances of the Scotch Highlander – his
remoteness from commerce and public business, and his being shut out
from his countrymen by difference of language as well as local
distance'.[154] Innes further maintained that the religious Highlanders
would 'deal, or try to deal, with the facts and events of their own inner
life apart from the history and changes going on around them'.[155]
Patrick Carnegie Simpson, writing some twenty-seven years later in his
biography of Robert Rainy, referred to those Highlanders who left the
Free Church over the 1892 Declaratory Act as 'an impressionable and
uninformed people'.[156]

   In the Free Assembly of 1872, Alexander Duff, who probably knew more
about the people of India than he did about the Highlanders,[157] asserted:

[152] Ibid., p. 74.
[153] Innes, 'Religion of the Highlands', p. 423. 'It was,' said Innes, 'a religion character-
      ised by great inwardness and tenderness, both of them enveloped in a brooding
      melancholy – the same racial melancholy – no doubt, of which Matthew Arnold tells us
      that in Ossian "all Europe felt the power"': Innes, *Chapters of Reminiscence*, pp. 9–10.
[154] Ibid., p. 425.
[155] Ibid., p. 429.
[156] Simpson, *Life of Principal Rainy*, ii, 129.
[157] Smith, *Life of Dr Alexander Duff*, p. 8. His biographer said that Duff's 'genius was
      Celtic by nature and by training', and his religious conversion was partly triggered by
      the effect of a vivid nightmare based on the – admittedly nightmarish – Gaelic poem
      Latha Bhreitheanais, or '*The Day of Judgement*', by Dugald Buchanan: ibid., p. 9.

the present untoward state of things [divisions] might in part be attributed to the isolation of the great bulk of the Gaelic-speaking population, not merely in the stormy Hebrides, but in the remoter glens of the mainland. There were still great numbers of them who would not read or speak English, or listen intelligently to an English discourse ... there was no Gaelic newspaper from which they could glean items of ordinary intelligence, and no religious and secular periodicals from which they might be able to judge aright of the real merits of the controverted topics of the day.[158]

Another Free Church minister and a biographer of Rainy, David Gibb Mitchell, described the Highlanders as

a people shut off from the crowd of cities, with a different tongue, traditions of their own, and customs peculiar to themselves. They live in the lonely glens among the silent mountains. They see few strangers, and only meet each other at times.[159]

These men were not uninformed about Highland religion. Instead of ignorance, what their comments reveal is a misunderstanding of the Highland situation in all its complexity, and one which was to have long-term results.

2. 'Highland tendency to follow leaders'

Permeating the whole debate was the assumption – sometimes implicit but more often stated directly – that the Highlanders were not only remote and ill-informed but that they were also prone to following leaders unhesitatingly. This was a common aspersion cast in the Celts' direction by their critics: Robert Knox argued that the Celts were in 'a mental slavery' and described them as a race 'without self-reliance; without self-confidence'. He also told the Celt that 'without a leader, you feel that you are lost'.[160] Francis Leiber taught that the Celts were 'easily swayed by mass appeals',[161] while one eighteenth-century writer, widely read in the nineteenth century, observed of the Highlanders that they

esteem it the most sublime degree of virtue to love their chief, and pay him blind obedience, although it be in opposition to the government, the laws of the kingdom, or even to the law of God. He is their idol; and as they profess to know no king but him ... so will they say they ought to do whatever he commands them without inquiry.[162]

---

[158] *PDGAFCS*, 1872, p. 308.
[159] Mitchell, *Life of Robert Rainy*, p. 159.
[160] Knox, *Races of Men*, pp. 18, 327.
[161] Gosset, *Race*, p. 94.
[162] Burt, *Letters from a Gentleman*, pp. 2–3. Burt's letters were written in the mid-1720s

Even Thomas McLauchlan's biographer, W. K. Leask, was of the opinion that 'the Celtic race is prone to follow leaders and not institutions'.[163] Whenever the 'Highland Host'[164] chose to become bellicose on one issue or another their opponents repeatedly produced the argument that the Highlanders were being led astray, as was their wont, by some malevolent outside force. More often than not this force was not identified.

Norman Walker, a Free Church minister who at various times edited the *Free Church Missionary Record*, the *Family Treasury*, and the *Presbyterian*,[165] was another influential critic. Referring to the Declaratory Act of 1892 and the resultant Second Disruption, Walker maintained that the Highlanders had been led astray and deceived. Although the Act was 'one of the most innocent that the church had ever been called upon to adopt',[166] yet the Highlanders had been misled by leaders who should have known better: the Act, he said, 'was expounded in ways which ... resulted in a secession'.[167] He argued that it was not so much the Declaratory Act itself which caused the Second Disruption as the way in which it was explained to the Highlanders. The Act, he said, was an innocent piece of well-meaning legislation 'but a different account of it was given in the Highlands, and the result has been the most out-standing secession from the Free Church which has taken place since the Disruption'.[168] Despite the fact that debate over confessional revision had taken the form of a long-running and rather sophisticated exchange of views, Walker claimed that the Highlands took part in 'the most outstanding secession from the Free Church since the Disruption' as a result of being fed, and readily digesting, a spurious version of the truth. He continued:

> It is exceedingly unlikely that any number of them had the words of the Act really in their hands ... It is not to be wondered at that so many of them lost faith in the Free Church. But it is evident that the Highlands have been imposed upon and deceived and we may

but were not published until 1754; they were republished in 1755 and 1759 and enjoyed 'several reprints during the nineteenth century': A. J. Youngson, *Beyond the Highland Line. Three Journals of Travel in Eighteenth-Century Scotland: Burt, Pennant, Thornton* (London, 1974), p. 39. Sir Walter Scott used the book of letters for his own writing on the Highlanders, saying of it that it 'has been lately reprinted; and as it contains the observations of an impartial, and, on the whole, an unprejudiced stranger, it is a good record of highland manners at the commencement of the 18th century': 'Culloden Papers', p. 294, note.

163 Leask, *Dr. Thomas McLauchlan*, 168.

164 This was itself a somewhat disparaging phrase; it was called a 'reproachful epithet' by Thomas Murray: Murray, *Heretical Declamation*, p. 44, and it was seen as a sign of the low tidemark of Highland treatment at the hands of the Lowlanders in the Free Church by James Sime: *PDGAFCS*, 1883, p. 96.

165 Ewing, *Annals of the Free Church of Scotland*, i, p. 350.

166 Walker, *Chapters from the History of the Free Church of Scotland*, p. 145.

167 Ibid., p. 140.

168 Ibid.

hope that when the truth is known, they will return, in their
entirety, to their allegiance.[169]

When he argued that 'a gross perversion of the Act ... was no doubt
accepted in all simplicity',[170] he was perpetuating the notion that the
guileless and unthinking Highlanders were simply doing as they were
told by their unscrupulous leaders. Not that it was really their fault,
conceded Walker, as they displayed a 'tendency to move in masses ... the
habit of following leaders [is] a remnant of the old feeling of loyalty to
the chiefs'. Indeed, he had even managed to discover that, 'individuality
is less common in the Highlands than in the Lowlands'.[171] Statements
such as this would be remarkable if it were not for the fact that they were
so common.

If Walker had read the article by Taylor Innes in the *British and
Foreign Evangelical Review* of 1872 he would have found there even more
so-called 'evidence' for this viewpoint. Although it is perhaps going too
far to call Innes a racist, there is no doubt that what he and the others
were saying was itself the product of a period which can safely be called
the pinnacle of 'acceptable', 'intellectual' racism.[172] In the article Innes
stated, with all the innocent assuredness of a student of mid-Victorian
ethnography, that:

> The Celtic nature has an extraordinary attraction to powerful
> personalities ... the men who 'followed Prince Charlie' must always
> have someone to follow; and when they follow they do it loyally and
> unquestioningly.[173]

---

[169] Ibid., p. 146. In 1900, Walker alleged that the Free Presbyterian Church possessed
only one scholar (John R. Mackay), and suggested again that the Denomination
would die out, with its members rejoining the Free Church or going into the Establishment: *British Weekly*, 14 Feb. 1900, p. 405. See also 'The latest opinion of Free
Presbyterianism', *FPM*, iv (11) (1900), p. 401. J. R. Mackay eventually received a D.D.
from St Andrews University, while John Macleod, another early Free Presbyterian,
received his D.D. from Aberdeen.

[170] Walker, *Chapters from the History of the Free Church of Scotland*, p. 146.

[171] Ibid., p. 132.

[172] It might be helpful to consider racism as part of, in George Rudé's words, the 'inherent
ideology' of Lowland Scotland: Rudé, cited in Withers, *Gaelic Scotland*, pp. 330 ff. And it
is worth mentioning that during this period Lowland Scotland was portrayed as being
an Anglo-Saxon region; Robert Knox, e.g., considered himself to be an Anglo-Saxon.

[173] Innes, 'Religion of the Highlands', p. 435. The contention that they were following
leaders in much the same way as they had followed Charles Edward Stuart would
have been anathema to the Highlanders who joined the Free Presbyterians. In the
very first sermon published in the first number of the *Free Presbyterian Magazine* Macfarlane
made it clear which leader they believed themselves to be following: 'It was Christ
then that was with the church, and led her in the wilderness. Oh, what a leader! Let
us follow Him. There are many who are followers of men, and not of Jesus Christ,
who is the King of His church as well as her Prophet and Priest. Such cry, "There are
no leaders." But the church of God is never without a leader. Jesus Christ, the glorious
head of His church ... may, according to His sovereign will, make use of the weakest
instruments to promote His glory and advance His cause and kingdom in the world':
Macfarlane, 'Exodus xxxiii.14.', p. 14.

This, a view which he expressed more than once,[174] is a clear echo of the sentiments of Robert Knox, and indeed Innes himself spoke of the Highlanders' 'natural and racial submissiveness'.[175] He argued that the only decision that the religious Highlander felt himself obliged to make was which man he was going to follow:

> Having made up his mind who is, on the whole, in the right, he is relieved of the (to him) most irksome duty of considering each new situation as it comes up on its merit – relieved from it in the most gratifying of all ways, by the necessity of going in enthusiastically for the man or men who have been found to be champions of the right ... In private, parochial and social religious life it is the same. Their whole literature bears witness to it.[176]

'The process of independent thought,' Innes informed his reader, '... is far less popular among serious minds in the North than it is with the corresponding class in the South.'[177] John MacInnes commented in 1951 that 'we may accept his racial psychology for what it is worth', but did not go any further than that, clearly not seeing it as being a major issue.[178] Indeed, when taken individually, statements like these from Taylor Innes might be explained away as aberrations, or simply as the products of frustration over ecclesiastical opposition from men of perceived lower intellect. But when they are put alongside one another they add up to evidence that the racist ideology of the nineteenth century was being used by the Free Church's Lowland intelligentsia when it suited them. Race became the key whenever the Highlanders acted in a way which the Lowlanders in the Free Church could not explain.

David Gibb Mitchell, for example, made much the same point as Walker and Innes when he informed his readers of 'the simple, backward, but righteous and rugged people ... [who] were a great race and lacked the brighter spirits of the towns to quicken and lead them on ... they required a leader to follow'.[179] Even William Ross, not hostile to the religion of the Highlands and himself a frequent visitor to that part of the country, believed that a great deal of the trouble associated with the Second Disruption and the Union of 1900 was as a result of the actions of leaders like Kennedy and Begg, who were greatly respected in the Highlands. He argued (as did Robert Rainy) that they split up communities which would otherwise have remained united by sowing distrust in the hearts of their presumably gullible supporters. Begg and Kennedy were the

---

174 'The men who followed Prince Charlie must always have someone to follow': Innes, *Chapters of Reminiscence*, p. 10.
175 Ibid., p. 11.
176 Innes, 'Religion of the Highlands', p. 436.
177 Ibid., p. 433.
178 MacInnes, *Evangelical Movement*, p. 211.
179 Mitchell, *Life of Robert Rainy*, p. 160.

founders of a school which had done untold harm to the cause of evangelical religion in Scotland. They had sown seeds of suspicion in the minds of their followers; they had followed a policy of suspicion, as though they had deemed their fellow-workers concealed enemies rather than true friends.[180]

Once again there was no acknowledgement of the possibility that the Highlanders had given any thought of their own to the great ecclesiastical issues at stake; there was no consideration that the Highlanders might have become suspicious of men like Dods or Rainy or Drummond without having these seeds sown by manipulative leaders who would be followed at all costs. Instead the myth that it was all down to 'leaders' was repeated one more time.

Alexander Duff had no doubt that the Highlanders were being blindly led. He argued in 1872 that

Those therefore who were removed far away from the great thoroughfares of traffic and tourists were very much at the mercy of stragglers and wanderers, who, by sundry arts and winning ways, might succeed in conciliating and gaining their confidence. In this way exaggerated rumours and distorted reports of divers proceedings in the South were apt to reach them and find currency, without the means of immediate correction.[181]

As he believed that the Highland Gaels and the ancient Galatians were of common stock, so Duff saw considerable similarities between the situation in the Highlands and that among the Galatians at the time of Paul's Epistle:

in it [Paul's Epistle to the Galatians] would be found some apposite strokes and touches that hit off, with a precision that was very remarkable, certain distinguishing peculiarities in the Celtic character, that could not fail even now to be distinctly recognized and forcibly felt by members of the Celtic family.[182]

Two months later, Taylor Innes delineated what exactly these were:

The old Galati, who 'would have plucked out their own eyes and given them' to the apostle who brought them the new blessedness, were like their modern namesakes in this passionate attachment, as much as in the changeableness which is a necessary result of trust in men rather than in principles.[183]

Duff also contributed what he felt linked the two groups, arguing that the ancient Galatians, too,

[180] Ross, *William Ross of Cowcaddens*, pp. 296–7.
[181] *PDGAFCS*, 1872, p. 308.
[182] Ibid., pp. 308–9.
[183] Innes, 'Religion of the Highlands', p. 436.

had been early disturbed by 'troublers', who raised questions that interfered with the purity and simplicity of the gospel of grace and salvation ... at present many of the earnest, simple-minded people were puzzled and distressed by accounts and representations which reached them, often through untrustworthy channels, of dissentions and divisive courses among brethren in the south.[184]

The bizarre, almost laughable, nature of this approach should not be allowed to dull its sharp edge. Highland resistance to proposed innovation in the beliefs or practice of the Church was here being explained and trivialised in terms of the Highland racial characteristic of being 'simple-minded'.

Patrick Carnegie Simpson was one more Free Churchman who believed that the Highlanders were easily led. He argued that the Second Disruption of 1893 was the result of the 'incredible' and 'most violent language' being used by people who 'had led their people to the brink of secession and then, at the last moment, themselves drew back'.[185] He had nothing but obloquy for what he described as

the violent and virulent language used by the men – sometimes even amid the sacredness of a communion season ... which incited an impressionable and uninformed people to shake the dust of the Free Church off their feet if this 'vile Act' were passed.[186]

Again, there was no consideration even of the possibility that some of those who left the Free Church might have done so out of principle and after careful consideration. Kenneth Macdonald, the Free Church minister at Applecross and no friend of the Free Presbyterians, argued that many people joined the Second Disruption precisely because they had been misled from the pulpit:

we find that assertions of the wildest kind make impressions on some minds with whom the clearest reasoning in sober language go for nothing. Our Highland people are very credulous and very excitable, and consequently they are easily alarmed and roused by religious questions whether they understand them or not.[187]

This is a quite staggering stance from a man who was not only himself a Highland minister but who was Highland born. Macdonald argued that, in the future, the Highlanders would not be so easily duped as they had been in 1893:

The schoolmaster is now abroad, and it is to be hoped that the rising generation will not be so easily imposed upon by priestcraft as their

184 *PDGAFCS*, 1872, p. 309.
185 Simpson, *Life of Principal Rainy*, ii, p. 129.
186 Ibid.
187 Macdonald, *Social and Religious Life*, p. 247.

grandmothers were. I have no doubt the day is coming when native intelligence will be more fully developed, and when our Highland people in general will resist all attempts to befool them.[188]

In this he is echoing the views of Principal Rainy himself. It was Rainy's decided view that, over the Union question of the 1860s, the Highlanders had been led into unnatural and unfamiliar territory by strong external influences. This process, which Rainy characterised as 'fanaticising the Highlands', was described by his biographer, Carnegie Simpson: 'Dr Begg did not create the division between the Highlands and the church of the South. That division, I repeat, is racial. But Dr Begg fomented faction within it. He inflamed it.'[189] Rainy saw this process as one which had been going on for years, and laid the blame not on the Highlanders themselves – if they did not think, they could hardly accept blame – but on unnamed malevolent forces. In 1903 he expressed it very clearly when he said:

> for years there was assiduously instilled into the minds of these people the impression that the church which they loved was turning away from the principles for the sake of which they loved it ... how for years and years distrust and animosity and all sorts of unquiet impressions and tendencies were instilled into the minds of a trustful and affectionate people.[190]

This perhaps has more of the tone of a regretful (and elderly) father making retrospective excuses for a wayward son who has been keeping bad company. It is the underlying attitude, the revealed patronising racial assumption of Highland naïvety, which is important as it had such an effect on Church affairs during this period.

It might be argued that by apportioning blame not to those simple-minded, loyal Highlanders who chose to quit the Free Church but to their unscrupulous and anonymous leaders, Rainy was endeavouring to open the door to the reunion of the splintered Free Church. There is further evidence of this in May 1894, when in response to Dr Henderson's *Report of the Special Committee of Commission on Cases in the Highlands (The Secessions in the Highlands)*, Rainy stated that

> in regard to the two ministers who had taken part in these secessions, he did not feel any strong disposition to complain of them either, although he very much regretted their step. He believed that both of them had been laid hold of, and exploded, as it were,

---

[188] Ibid., pp. 247–8.

[189] Simpson, *Life of Principal Rainy*, i, p. 440.

[190] Ibid., ii, p. 276: quoting Rainy. He also spoke of 'a school of men ... who saw it to be their duty – a melancholy duty surely – to inspire ... with suspicion and hostility towards the Church to which they belonged ... a people not indisposed to receive with confidence the asservations of religious men': Rainy, in Leask, *Dr. Thomas McLauchlan*, p. 11.

into space by forces with the origination of which they had nothing to do, and for the effects of which they had no special responsibility.[191]

Those two seceding Highland ministers, Macfarlane and Macdonald, were not the first Highland leaders to be themselves led, according to the Lowland liberal argument. P. C. Simpson had argued that even John Kennedy of Dingwall, for whom he had considerable personal esteem for a variety of reasons,[192] was himself under a nefarious influence. Despite his undoubted virtues, Kennedy was

> impressionable and impulsive, and a man who could be led by natures more commonplace than his own. Dr Begg, a far less spiritual and less noble but a far more forceful man, could lead him and use him.[193]

This had been already stated almost exactly by Kenneth Macdonald of Applecross, who said that Kennedy was 'impulsive and credulous to a high degree ... easily led by a man of Dr Begg's plausibility and pretensions'.[194]

William Rose of Poolewe was one Highlander who had become conscious of what he called this 'more or less common assumption in the south – viz., that it is our ignorance that is to account for our attitude',[195] and he bitterly refuted the oft-repeated claim that the Highlanders were led through the inappropriate use of the pulpit.[196] 'You did not,' he observed to their Lowland critics, 'ascribe to ignorance our adherence to the principles of the Free Church at the Disruption.'[197]

3. 'Highland resistance to change'

One more area of consistent Lowland criticism of the 'religion of the Highlands' is perhaps even more important in the context of the Second Disruption of 1893. This is the allegation that the Highlanders resisted ecclesiastical changes for the simple reason that they were changes. Like other anti-Highland prejudices, this view must be seen against the background of the racist thought outlined above. The Frenchman Ernest Renan had said in the 1850s that the Celts were likely to display a 'refusal to accept modern civilization' and that they 'lacked a sense of reality'.[198] Mackintosh's paper before the Anthropological Society of

---

191 *PDGAFCS*, 1894, p. 53.
192 These ranged from Kennedy's 'quite remarkable personal charm' and the fact that he was 'an extraordinary preacher' to his being 'an authority on English cricket': Simpson, *Life of Principal Rainy*, i, p. 443.
193 Ibid.
194 Macdonald, *Social and Religious Life*, p. 169.
195 *PDGAFCS*, 1872, p. 312.
196 E.g. in Walker, *Chapters from the History of the Free Church of Scotland*, pp. 146–7.
197 *PDGAFCS*, 1872, p. 312.
198 Curtis, *Anglo-Saxons and Celts*, pp. 39–40.

London in 1865, which has been quoted already, had attributed to the Celt a deficiency in 'depth of reasoning power ... [and a] tendency to oppose'.[199] Robert Knox also believed the Celt to be incapable of change, calling them 'nature's antiquaries', and alleging that 'even in the clear and broad sunshine of the day, they dream of the past'.[200] Patrick Carnegie Simpson's lengthy analysis of reasons for Highland opposition to ecclesiastical innovation provided a remarkable indication of the mind-set of that section of the Church to which he belonged.

Simpson referred to the changes which were taking place within the pale of the Free Church, listing biblical criticism, the evangelism of Moody and Sankey, and the introduction of hymns and organs into public worship. He then went on to appraise the reasons for the negative Highland response:

> Behind the ramparts of the Grampians and in the distant Hebrides a people of different race and different tongue heard of all these changes from afar. They were constitutionally prejudiced against all changes, for their lives, physically and intellectually, knew little variety and, in many things, traditional usage had become to them sacred. Besides, they had been poisoned in their minds with suspicion and hostility against all changes promoted by the Church in the south. Moreover, these movements were extraordinarily rapid; and the whole environment of these people made their thoughts move slowly, because their character was moulded, not by the novelties of the outer world and amid the excitement of the hour, but by undisturbed introspections on an eternal world within, and under the solemn influences of the slow-moving round of nature and the unaltering hills and the overarching sky and the great sea. Their whole mental being became thus something that was set. And being set, how easily was it found set against such changes as these that touched things so near and sacred. They fastened – naturally, inevitably – on the familiar things these movements were taking away or losing. And with wounded hearts, as men who were being robbed of the very treasure of their homes, they stood on the defensive. Of course, the result was that they confounded essentials and non-essentials: in a time of transition, only education delivers from that.[201]

In many respects this analysis reveals much more about Simpson's attitude than it does about Highland religion, moving as it does from racial to psychological to sociological explanations for the fact that the Highlanders did not think like him. In one paragraph Simpson succeeded in including almost every single one of the assumptions of

199 Curtis, *Apes and Angels*, p. 18.
200 Knox, *Races of Men*, p. 322.
201 Simpson, *Life of Principal Rainy*, i, pp. 448–9.

anti-Celtic racism. As one of the leading intellectual lights of the late nineteenth-century Free Church, Simpson cannot be dismissed either as ignorant or insignificant. He was a clever and influential man, and as such his racism is not only consequential but censurable.

Simpson argued in conclusion that the Highlanders' defensiveness tended to become extremist, as they responded to the shifting tides of opinion in the South by becoming even more stringent advocates of plenary inspiration of every word of Scripture, of the Divine Decrees, of the darker side of religion – they 'let the gloom of a stern and exacting religion settle deeper, like the mist on their mountains'.[202] As Simpson concluded:

> the problem of the Highlands within a progressive Church passing through the transitions of the nineteenth century takes on the shades of pathos ... It was inevitable in the sense that the breach must come some day between a section of the Church that lived its life in the progressive movement of the thought of the nineteenth century and a section that took an attitude to this wholly of isolation and opposition.[203]

Given the attitude of men like Simpson, the real reason for the inevitability of the eventual breach might well lie elsewhere.

Patrick Carnegie Simpson was not the only prominent Free Church liberal to respond in this manner to the Highland attitude towards religious change. Norman Walker believed that an area like the Highlands was 'in especial danger during a transition period', with prudence and open-mindedness being needed more there than in any other part of the country,[204] while David Gibb Mitchell said this of the Highlanders: 'They are sternly religious, and wish no progress. Give them the Bible and the old doctrines, and nothing need advance.'[205] A. T. Innes, in turn, laid stress on the introspective and melancholy aspects of the Highlander's character which he believed contributed to the overwhelming influence of what he styled as 'dogma'. The love of dogma and orthodoxy, argued Innes, was 'inherent in the Celtic nature,' and he was careful to point out what he meant by 'orthodox', explaining that orthodoxy was not necessarily 'truth'. Rather, it was 'the tendency to reverence and submission which gives to dogma its over-bearing power in this region'.[206] Nobody, it seemed, resisted change because they had considered each proposed change on its merits and then rejected them.

---

[202] Ibid., i, p. 450.
[203] Ibid., i, p. 451. Simpson used race theory to contrast those in the 'progressive' section of the Church with those who were opposed to them; it is crucial to remember that race theory was itself the darling of 'progressive' and 'avant-garde' thinkers, and it was very convenient that the theories of the 'progressives' could be used to denigrate those people who happened to oppose them on other issues.
[204] Walker, *Chapters from the History of the Free Church of Scotland*, p. 148.
[205] Mitchell, *Life of Robert Rainy*, p. 159.
[206] Ibid., p. 432.

4. The legacy of Race Theory

At almost every point of departure between the Highland and Lowland viewpoint in the late nineteenth-century Free Church, the disparity was explained in terms of the Highlanders being, in Simpson's words, 'a people impressionable, not always informed, and already, by racial differences of temper and habit, inclined to look strangely and even suspiciously across the Grampians'.[207] As Christopher Smout and others have said, the racial basis for the confrontation between Highlands and Lowlands had appeared at least as early as the fourteenth century, and it has already been demonstrated that a vast racial gulf between the Anglo-Saxon and the Gael was being stressed by science and history alike. The idea that the Highlanders might have carefully and logically thought through their position was never admitted, at least publicly. Disagreement was seen as a reflection of the racial gulf that they believed to exist between the two regions, with Taylor Innes talking of the 'difference of language, and the difference of race which that indicates ... with the development of religious feeling in marked contrast on several points with that of the Scotch Lowlands'.[208] His friend and ally P. C. Simpson was blunter still:

> Between the Celtic or, rather, Gaelic and the more strictly Scottish sections of the Church is a difference of race ... such a natural racial divergence is, from its very nature, exposed to the poison of a spirit of suspicion and hostility; and when this is introduced, a painful alienation follows. This is what happened in the Highlands of the Free Church during a certain period of her history.[209]

To Patrick Carnegie Simpson, radical and far-reaching changes in the Free Church's stance on several vital issues had nothing to do with the 'painful alienation' which occurred; it was, he believed, caused by the fact that the Free Church was made up of two distinct races within Scotland. Crucially, in the opinion of Simpson, one of these races was not 'strictly Scottish'.

Again, it would perhaps be a rather imprecise use of modern language to call these men 'racists'; Kenneth Macdonald himself said that 'education and environments' had more to do with shaping people than what he called 'constitutional peculiarity'.[210] What requires to be emphasised again, however, is that they were accepting as their underlying assumptions many theories which were undoubtedly racist. In this respect they were still more innocent victims of mid-Victorian racism. This is perfectly illustrated by the fact that Thomas McLauchlan, a convener of the Free Church Highland Committee for nearly thirty

---

207 Simpson, *Life of Principal Rainy*, i, p. 441.
208 Innes, 'Religion of the Highlands', p. 414.
209 Simpson, *Life of Principal Rainy*, i, p. 430.
210 Macdonald, *Social and Religious Life*, p. 13.

years, could be quoted as saying 'the Highlander possesses all the peculiarities of the Celtic race ... his temperament is ardent and impulsive, different in many respects from his Teutonic brethren'.[211] This is the same Thomas McLauchlan who spoke about 'the fallacy and absurdity of the whole doctrine of race', and who urged a return to 'the sounder doctrine, that "God made of one blood all the nations of the earth"'.[212] Despite that, he could argue that

> there are forms of thought that are peculiarly Saxon, and there are forms of thought that are peculiarly Celtic. These often remain unchanged, even when the races intermingle or pass into each other. The forms of thought which belong to the dominant race in it will always distinguish a nation.[213]

Even the best-selling author 'Ian Maclaren', the Free Church College graduate John Watson, made the remark that 'there is nothing so different as Scottish and Highland blood'.[214]

This language of race theory was all-pervasive, with John Laidlaw, Professor of Systematics at New College, Edinburgh, being criticised in the Free Assembly of 1887 for using the term 'Anglo-Saxon'; according to his critic, 'when ... [he] next preached that sermon he should speak of the predominance in the civilized world of the 'Anglo-Celtic' race'.[215] Despite his own protestations to the contrary, Kenneth Macdonald's language betrayed the acceptance of racist assumptions on a subconscious level at the very least. Exactly like McLauchlan, while paying lip-service to what he called 'the truth that "God has made of one blood all nations of men"', Macdonald was still able to discover that 'the Celtic people' had 'certain peculiarities of temperament'. In a marvellous example of a double-edged statement he observed:

> They [the Celts] have the reputation of being an impulsive, impressible, a credulous and violent race. And yet they are not more so than other nations who have passed through the same experience ... If they are still behind the age in some respects, it must be by the want of the advantages by which others have progressed.[216]

In Macdonald's defence it might be pointed out that he at least held out the possibility of the Gael advancing, given the correct circumstances, but there was little doubt that for the time being the Gael was perilously close to the bottom of the heap.

---

211 Quoted in Blaikie, *After Fifty Years*, p. 88.
212 McLauchlan, *Celtic Gleanings*, pp. 14–15.
213 Ibid., p. 23.
214 Maclaren, *Beside the Bonnie Briar Bush*, p. 45. In another passage he described one character as being 'of the pure Highland breed, kindest of friends, fiercest of foes': ibid., p. 119.
215 *PDGAFCS*, 1887, p. 181.
216 Macdonald, *Social and Religious Life*, p. 13.

Although it can be argued that misunderstanding was what lay at the root, the Highland–Lowland division in the Free Church went much deeper than that misunderstanding. Simpson's *Life of Principal Rainy* is a vital source as, in revealing what Robert Rainy and Patrick Carnegie Simpson and others thought about the central issues, it is a useful indication of the stance of a whole influential cadre within the Free Church over a period of decades. Their view of the Highlands is often portrayed as the same affectionate paternalism which many other Free Churchmen sought to exude. The reality was somewhat different, with Simpson, in looking at Rainy's performance in the years following the Robertson Smith crisis, observing that

> Principal Rainy's career had, from this time forward, a permanent problem which it is necessary carefully to describe in order to understand his whole subsequent life ... The problem was the Highlands.[217]

Rainy and Simpson were both well aware that they had a 'problem' in the Highlands – a problem which Simpson himself acknowledged had led to the situation where 'Principal Rainy – "Black Rainy" – was denounced as a traitor to the truth.'[218] At one stage Rainy was even compared to the Pope, with one writer saying that

> he has long played as Pope in the Free Church; all must bow to his rule and sway. His word is law ... his practices and cunning policies, all leading to the advancement of Popery, has stamped on the Free Church 'the number and name' of the beast.[219]

As the Highlanders themselves recognised, the problem with Rainy was that he appeared on the wrong side of the divide too often for it to be mere coincidence

> Dr. Rainy's great abilities and extensive influence cannot be questioned, but it is too true that these have been exercised in connection with all the public questions which have agitated the Church, in opposition to the Highlanders and their most trusted leaders.[220]

---

[217] Simpson, *Life of Principal Rainy*, i, pp. 428–9.

[218] Ibid., ii, p. 129.

[219] *Private Gillies Collection*, p. 8. One writer, recalling a Free Church manse in the early decades of the 20th century, said this: 'I was raised and nourished on the iniquity, the grasping worldliness and the vindictive chicanery of the Reverend Principal Robert Rainy of the Free Church College; a man in whose devious heart there glimmered not a spark of Christian brotherhood and charity ... I must plead guilty if I describe Principal Rainy as a trimmer, lax in doctrine and principle, a subverser of constitutions, and an opportunist "skilled in the science of exigencies"; for I picked up these epithets when I was at my most impressionable': A. Phillips, *My Uncle George: The Respectful Recollections of a Backslider in a Highland Manse* (London, 1984), pp. 35–6.

[220] 'Gaelic record of the Free Church', p. 339.

For all Rainy's claims that he loved the Highlanders, and the claims of Mitchell that the Highlanders loved Rainy, the fact is that the Highlands were a problem for Rainy's leadership which would not go away. Far from seeing the Highlands romantically, as a constituency filled with loyal and Godly Free Churchmen, to those proposing radical change in the Church the Highlanders were a 'problem' wrapped in what David Gibb Mitchell memorably called 'their mantle of prejudice'.[221] It was a problem to which they frequently reacted with patronising and racist tones.

Robert Rainy and Kenneth Macdonald, David Mitchell and Norman Walker, Taylor Innes and Carnegie Simpson were all 'good New College Men'.[222] They were by most standards highly educated, urbane and erudite men. They were no fools. But holding the views that they did, and influenced by current racist thought as they were, these men were incapable of correctly assessing Highland opposition to religious change. As has been shown, they simply could not see it as being anything else but the prejudiced and ill-informed response of a fundamentally reactionary and obscurantist culture.

The Highland Attitude

It would be quite wrong, though, to give the impression that all the impetus for the divide in the Free Church came from one direction only. The Highlanders themselves were well aware of the distinction between 'the religion of the Highlands' and that south of the Grampians and were not afraid to talk about it. There is ample evidence to suggest that the Highlanders looked askance at the religion of the Lowland Free Church, considering themselves in many respects to be a separate and indeed superior denomination. Many religious communities in the Highlands displayed a degree of doctrinal and intellectual rigidity which must have forced the cracks in the Free Church to open wider. To a Lowland representative of what Carnegie Simpson called the 'progressive movement', this must often have seemed to confirm many of his racial assumptions. Highlanders often viewed the Free Church in the Lowlands as a source of iniquity and error, with the southern university cities seen as fountain-heads of the 'new theology'. It is worth examining the evidence which suggests that the prejudice cut both ways – that Highlanders frequently considered themselves to be superior to the Lowlanders when it came to religion.

This comes out very clearly in some of the correspondence of those ministers and students who either joined in the Second Disruption of 1893 or at least heartily sympathised with it. The Free Church divinity student, Donald Munro, writing to his friend and fellow-divinity student,

---

221 Mitchell, *Life of Robert Rainy*, p. 161.
222 Dr James Strahan's excellent biography of A. B. Davidson is dedicated 'to the goodly fellowship of all New College men'.

John Macleod (later Principal of the Free Church College, Edinburgh), was anxious to underline the difficulties and dangers which the South held for the Highland student. Macleod faced the possibility of leaving Edinburgh and going even further south to Cambridge, and it was a prospect which Munro viewed with some alarm:

> I'm not a bit surprised that the professors should be anxious to have their best men sent South. This is the case with professors in all Universities – they are anxious to uphold the reputation of the College ... It is true that one would extend his classical knowledge by going to one of the Southern Universities, but that is only one side of the business. I'm afraid the loss endured on the one hand would conceal the gain got on the other. The lack of congenial society and many other things would necessarily tell on one. It would be sure to spoil the fine edges. And of course there are many in Cambridge and Oxford that Prof. Ramsay would naturally call 'fine fellows', but I can't believe that you would find many of them congenial companions. Though men might not influence one for evil, in the ordinary sense of the word, their company might have a withering effect on one all the same.[223]

It was a problem to which Munro surmised that he had the ideal solution:

> I'm not sure that a Summer in Lochaber, where one can (enjoy) a pure atmosphere, and drink in pure Gaelic and come under the influence of pious men, would be quite as good – and even a much better – preparation for the ministry than a session at Cambridge ... We are told that Abraham journeyed constantly going South; but I hope you won't follow him in this particular case. I should like better to see you reverse the order and to go 'Reaching to' the north.[224]

The Highlanders, then, were well aware of the gulf which existed between the two cultures, and this letter shows something of the depth of feeling which was present.

It is difficult to decide whether they were justified in quite this level of alarm, but the fact is that the Highlanders were jealously proud of their religious heritage and were terrified at the prospect of seeing it being undermined by the worldliness of the South, a worldliness which they saw as having an ever-increasing influence where it was least warranted – in Church affairs. Part of the problem was that there was a level of

---

[223] Donald Munro to John Macleod, 30 Jan. 1890, *John Macleod Collection*, 1b. Donald Munro sympathised with much of what those who formed the Free Presbyterian Church said. In 1893, however, he decided to remain in the Free Church and he was one of the 27 Free Church ministers who remained out of the Union of 1900. His friendship with John Macleod continued long after Macleod's eventual decision to join him in the Free Church, and Macleod was later to write Munro's biography.

[224] Ibid.

misunderstanding from the Highlanders which was compounded by the fact that there was a distinct lack of mixing of the two communities. Many observers commented on this, with it being elegantly summed up in 1887 by James Stalker of Glasgow when he said: 'the ministers of the South are not enough in the Highlands, and the Highland ministers are not often enough in the pulpits of the South'.[225] Arguably, had the Highlanders listened to what their perceived enemies were saying, dialogue might have been possible, and one side could even have learned from the other. Stalker told the Free Church General Assembly that more Southern ministers should follow in the footsteps of the ex-moderator, Dr Somerville, and visit the Highlands. Those

> who know how to combine with the fruits of the newest culture that pectoral theology, which is the only key to the heart of the Highlands, should follow in Dr Somerville's track; and I am sure they would bring home at least as much as they left behind from contact with the religious depth and contagious fire of the Highland mind.[226]

Even Alexander Whyte provided some surprises for a cynical Highland congregation:

> the people were afraid that he was tarred with the innovation principles of the South, for they look with suspicion on all Southerners coming there whether on holidays or on a deputation. But when they heard him, their first test was to ascertain whether he had the boldness to rebuke sin, and on this point it was said – Oh, he spares nobody. Whoever was in fault, whether rich or poor, got the same sentence.[227]

It is quite possible, of course, that Alexander Whyte was adapting his message to make it sound like what his audience wanted to hear – he would be neither the first nor the last minister to do that. But what is important is that there was a distinct lack of ecclesiastical intercourse between the two regions, and this unfamiliarity contributed to the Highland feeling of defensiveness.[228]

Some were, however, willing to go much further than mere defensiveness. John Kennedy's celebrated Highland apologia, *The Days of the Fathers in Ross-shire*, may be viewed as a Highland claim to be better in religious terms than their Southern neighbours. Kennedy himself accepted that it was a work which was open to this interpretation, admitting in the preface to the book's second edition of 1861:

---

225 *PDGAFCS*, 1887, p. 179.
226 Ibid.
227 MacLeod of Eskbank, in *PDGAFCS*, 1884, p. 135.
228 As Major MacLeod of Eskbank commented in 1886: 'some Highlanders thought their ways and affairs could not be understood by Lowlanders': *PDGAFCS*, 1886, p. 175.

I expected that its Highland tone, and its seemingly anti-Lowland spirit, would have excited prejudice in some minds against it. Its thorough Highlandism I neither tried, nor was I able, to prevent. I was very often translating from Gaelic as I wrote, and I could not quite hide the tartan under the English mantle.[229]

Kenneth Ross has suggested that Kennedy's primary ecclesiastical loyalty was not to the Free Church but to the distinctive religion of the region in which he lived and laboured, and where his position as a great leader was seldom in doubt.[230] Ross argued that he could with some accuracy be accused of 'a lack of sympathy with religious life in the Lowlands as a whole'.[231]

Ross draws attention to a fascinating debate between Kennedy and Horatius Bonar, over the Moody and Sankey mission of 1873, during which many remarks were made which give significant indications of how *The Days of the Fathers in Ross-shire* was interpreted by its Lowland readers. Bonar accused Kennedy of being incapable of 'appreciating the religion of 'the "Southron"' and said that Kennedy was suspicious of any man who did not have the same characteristics as the 'Men' in the North: 'the biographer of these men will naturally look suspiciously upon the men of the South, who have not the peculiarities of the North, and question the depth of any movement going on under them'.[232] Bonar did not believe that Kennedy had any 'confidence in the piety or theology of the Lowlands', and said that any reader of Kennedy would be left in no doubt that the real Gospel was not preached in the Lowlands.[233] As Bonar put it towards the close of his argument: 'What an untrustworthy race we "Southrons" are! All we do seems evil in the eyes of the North!'[234] Kennedy denied vehemently that his attack on the 'hyper-evangelism' of Moody and Sankey was motivated by any feeling of superiority of Highland religion over Lowland religion; indeed he accused Bonar in turn of such feelings – 'What he intends to say is, that in the South they have the right, and that in the North we have the wrong, standard.'[235] What the debate indicates, however, is how the writings of Kennedy were being construed in the Lowlands, even by a man who would have agreed with Kennedy's stance on many issues.[236]

---

229 Kennedy, *Days of the Fathers*, p. xi.
230 One opponent mockingly referred to Kennedy as 'the great Rabbi and leader of the "Highland Host!"': R. Young, *Hyper-Criticism: An Answer to Dr. Kennedy's 'Hyper-Evangelism'* (Edinburgh, n.d.), p. 1.
231 Ross, 'Calvinists in Controversy', p. 60.
232 Bonar, *Old Gospel*, pp. 13, 16.
233 Ibid., pp. 22, 26–7.
234 Ibid., p. 65.
235 J. Kennedy, *A Reply to Dr. Bonar's Defence of Hyper-Evangelism* (Edinburgh, 1875), p. 20.
236 Bonar, like some other ecclesiastical conservatives, was a political conservative who took a dim view of political democracy and social reform: Smith, *Passive Obedience and Prophetic Protest*, p. 204. He was, however, instrumental in the introduction of hymns into the public worship of the Grange Free Church in Edinburgh, an issue which aroused enormous controversy and which provoked bitter division, culminating in

The strident tone of some of the 'thorough Highlandism' of *The Days of the Fathers in Ross-shire* must have been, at least partly, a result of the pressure being placed on traditional Highland forms of piety and interpretations of religion by Lowland Free Church liberals. In *The Days of the Fathers in Ross-shire*, Kennedy acknowledged that the religious state of Ross-shire of which he spoke had raised some eyebrows: 'There are not wanting some who suspect the healthfulness of the religious spirit which was thus so extensively excited.' He was, moreover, not slow to point out from which direction this suspicion was emanating;

> As there are certain peculiarities which distinguish it [religion in the North] from the type assumed by the religious feeling in the Lowlands, the Southrons have been anxious to make out that the difference is owing to some defect or excess that may be charged against the north.[237]

He believed that the Lowlanders had an unhealthy disregard for Highland religion, and that

> all the peculiarities of the type of religion prevalent in the Highlands are traced to one source; and would be designated by those who are unfriendly the gloominess, the bigotry, and the closetism of Highland Christians, the undue influence of 'the men', and the extreme paucity of communicants.[238]

In the Preface to the second edition of his work, Kennedy was quite clear that he felt it necessary to come to the defence of the Highlander and that he cared not a jot if that were to prove offensive to some. He even went so far as to state that he would have been disappointed had the book not been found offensive by 'a certain class of readers' since

> I was acting ... on the defensive. It was not my vocation to be searching for Highland faults; I was engaged in warding off Lowland blows ... The fault-finding had been done, *usque ad nauseam*, by others.[239]

Kennedy clearly resented the idea of Godly Highlanders coming under attack from Lowland critics – 'the hosts across the Spey who are marshalled against [them]'[240] – whom he regarded as their moral and spiritual inferiors.[241]

the famous resignation from the eldership of Hugh Martin. See, e.g., 'The story of the Grange Free Church: a tragedy', *The Signal* (May 1884), pp. 152–9.
237 Kennedy, *Days of the Fathers*, p. 115.
238 Ibid., pp. 116–17.
239 Ibid., p. xi.
240 Ibid., p. 130.
241 It should be stated, though, that not all of the critics of *The Days of the Fathers in Ross-shire* were Lowlanders. Norman MacLeod, a native of Stoer in the parish of Assynt and one of the celebrated 'North Country Separatists', was one of the book's sternest critics. Among other things, he described it as an 'unfortunate and misguided publication'

In many respects that is the crux of the matter. Their own belief in the superiority of the Highland brand of religiosity was characterised by the inability of the Highland apologists to see a critique of Highland religion as anything else but an attack on 'true' religion. Some critics, surmised Kennedy, used the attack on some of the quainter Highland practices as 'an expression of their enmity against vital religion', and resented these practices because 'they are offensive to them, merely because they are more palpable signs of the reality of communion with God'.[242] To Kennedy and others like him, criticism of their religion was taken as the opposite of what 'the Men' referred to in their Question Meetings as 'A Mark of Grace'; it was instead a mark of someone who had taken at least the first steps on an extremely retrograde path. As Thomas Murray put it:

> As to the reproach of being 'heresy hunters', it is more Christian and honourable than being heretics. The applying of such epithets in such a sacred cause speaks little for the character of the maligner or his cause.[243]

Even a gentle criticism of the Highlands was interpreted as being unacceptable by many – when John McNeil talked in the 1899 assembly of being unaware of 'any special grace in bad singing', and when he said that 'you should not be conceited as if nobody can be Highlanders but yourselves', the response verged on the hysterical and contained not a little petulance.[244] Highland religion was under attack from Southern sources; but the Highlanders themselves exacerbated an awkward situation by losing their composure.

Kennedy said that such attacks came 'under cover of superior enlightenment',[245] while Donald Macfarlane's famous sermon on Exodus xxxiii.14, which by analogy compared the Free Presbyterians to the Children of Israel being led by God out of Egypt, said of the 'false teachers occupying high positions in the visible church in this age' that

> It is said that it is because of the great learning of these men they have adopted their new theology. They may have a learning of a sort. But we read in Scripture of some who were 'ever learning and never able to come to the knowledge of the truth'. But that the views which they promulgate are an evidence of their learning none

containing 'sadly glaring and self-unsuspected errors' on the part of Kennedy, whom he accused of 'desperate blindness and presumption', 'sore ignorance', and 'ignorant freedom on topics quite beyond ... [his] present ken and count': N. MacLeod, 'A letter addressed to the Rev. John Kennedy, author of *The Days of the Fathers in Ross-shire*, by a New Zealander', in Macleod, *By-Paths of Highland Church History*, pp. 152–5.

242 Kennedy, *Days of the Fathers*, pp. xii–xiii.

243 Murray, *Heretical Declamation*, p. 44.

244 *PDGAFCS*, 1899, p. 115. One speaker even threatened to walk out if McNeil 'was going to make use of the platform of the Assembly to insult the religion that was dear to many of them'.

245 Kennedy, *Days of the Fathers*, p. xiii.

can believe but those who are ignorant of the history of the church. There are no errors introduced now but that a schoolboy may know as well as they by reading Dr Owen and other great writers, who discussed and refuted them by the Word of God in their own day.[246]

This is not so much an obscurantist anti-intellectualism as a firmly held belief that for someone to attack the 'old paths' was a sign not just of a lack of piety but of plain stupidity, which even a young schoolboy (assumed as a matter of course to be well versed in the Puritan Divines) could identify. It was a theme to which the Free Presbyterians returned in 1899, when in a stirring editorial on the unchanging nature of the gospel, the following remarks were made:

> The wisest philosopher, the most accomplished man of letters, the most acute scientist, the most masterful politician, and the most eloquent ecclesiastic, all require to know the same Gospel of salvation in their souls as the poorest, weakest, and silliest creatures of the race ... Many in our day believe that if a man has learning, intellectual ability, and moral behaviour that he needs nothing more of a salvation. No greater delusion of this could take possession of the heart of man no matter how cultured.[247]

In some ways it was inverse intellectual snobbery; for all their learning, the Lowland intellectuals lacked the 'one thing needful'. The Highlander seemed to look at the Lowlands' religion and utter the prayer of the Pharisee in all sincerity, thanking God that he was not as other (Southern) men were. For all its sincerity, though, it revealed a very definite feeling of superiority which in turn made its contribution to the widening gulf between these two sections of the nineteenth-century Free Church.

Kennedy's attitude to the Church of the 'Southron' went even further, though. Something of the bellicose stance which he took towards the southern critiques can be divined in the preface to the fourth edition of *The Days of the Fathers*, written by him in 1866. There he used the analogy of his book being a weapon. In a colourful section he admitted that the book was a gun which could have done with a new lock, stock and barrel, but that nevertheless

> believing that it was charged with truth before, and having no desire to change or to reserve my ammunition; and many hard blows, which were meant to shatter, having failed to disable it, it is now for the fourth time loaded, and is ready to go off.[248]

---

246 Macfarlane, 'Exodus xxxiii.14.', p. 15. The view of the Second Disruption as an exodus from a land of bondage is an ironic and antonymic echo of J. H. Leckie's description of the United Presbyterian Church, in the wake of its 1879 Declaratory Act, as 'a pioneer of the modern movement out of Calvinistic bondage': J. H. Leckie, *Secession Memories: The United Presbyterian Contribution to the Scottish Church* (Edinburgh, 1926), p. 219. One man's freedom is often another man's bondage.
247 'Gospel changes not', p. 123.
248 Kennedy, *Days of the Fathers*, p. xix.

The military language used in the debate has been commented on briefly already, but is worth mentioning again. What it reveals is significant; a willingness to use warlike vocabulary frequently predates actual warfare, and the more bellicose the language, the more lasting any divide usually becomes. Conservatives looked on the Grampian Mountains as providing a barrier against the progress of doctrines with which they disagreed, and made the following historical comparison:

> as long ago the mountains formed a rampart that prevented the further progress northward of the Roman invader, so we trust the threefold cord ... of doctrine, of national religion, and of scriptural worship, will not be easily broken in Highland hearts and in Highland homes, and that the wave of sensationalism, and doctrinal error, and innovation in the worship of God, which has set in of late in so threatening a way, will have spent its force without submerging the religion of Christ as it has hitherto existed among us.[249]

Later in the same year *The Signal* was more explicit still, arguing that, as long as great leaders remained in the North,

> the Highlands could not be invaded without challenge by Southern Heretics or their abettors, with their doctrines, practices, or views ... If they could discredit Dr. Kennedy, and raise a false prejudice against his memory and writings, they would necessarily reduce the influence of the party to which he attached himself, and of which he was an honoured leader. Hence his memory is set up as the mark at which the enemy flings his arrows dipped in the bitterness of gall. The hand of Joab the son of Zeruiah is in the matter.[250]

Kennedy himself had said that taking a firm stance was to risk being designated a 'bigot', but that that was precisely what was needed: 'No Christian,' said Kennedy, 'can be true and faithful now-a-days on whose brow the world shall not brand the name of bigot. But let him bear it. It is a mark of honour, though intended to be a mark of shame.'[251] He believed that there was a current need for 'the men whom the world calls bigots', saying that the time was coming when they could 'follow the cause of truth only amidst the scoffs of unbelievers and the shafts of persecutors'. He saw a need to find some common ground on which the conservatives could 'stand, "shoulder to shoulder", in defence of the Crown rights of Jesus'.[252] And in a remarkable rallying call, which is reminiscent of the Islamic Jihad, he said this:

> let no lover of the truth – let none whose eye ever rested on the hope of the gospel – turn crave-hearted back from the trial. To fall

[249] 'Where are the Highlands drifting to?' (Jun. 1888), p. 172.
[250] 'Gaelic record of the Free Church', 341.
[251] J. Kennedy, '"Bigot": a name and a nickname', in Auld, *Life of John Kennedy*, p. 320.
[252] Kennedy, *Distinctive Principles*, pp. 30–1.

in the cause of truth is but to rise in the kingdom of glory. To be trampled under foot till crushed dead by the heel of persecution is but to have the prison broken open, that the ransomed spirit may pass from bondage to a throne.[253]

This is of course very good propaganda from a man who was one of the most renowned orators of his generation, and doubtless it comes from a long tradition of tying present causes to old images of martyrdom. But the language, taken along with the other examples, is a vivid illustration of the depth and width of the divide in the Free Church. Language like this, moreover, could only have heightened the siege mentality of the Highland conservatives.

The 'loaded weapon' which Kennedy had pointed at the Lowland critics, however, contained more than simply a determination to resist the changing tides from within the Free Church. Kennedy's desire to keep the 'religion of the Highlands' intact from the pernicious influences emanating from beyond the Tweed went so far as the threat of forming a separate Church which he described as a 'Caledonian Church'. The *Free Presbyterian Magazine* quoted in 1897 from a letter of Mrs C. R. Auld, the wife of the Rev. Alexander Auld,[254] in which she recounted a conversation between Dr Kennedy and an unnamed friend. There Kennedy was quoted as follows:

> The other party is revolutionising the Church bit by bit. Do you know I am contemplating a Caledonian Church? ... I believe that the Lord has a remnant in our land who will not brook a creed framed to suit and to shelter men of Arminian and Rationalistic opinions, a remnant that will separate, and as I think the separating party will be found especially in the districts lying north and west of the Caledonian Canal, I am naming it prospectively the Caledonian Church.[255]

Kennedy believed that a crisis was inevitable, although he was not sure whether he would live to see it, and that large-scale Highland Secession, maintaining the Claim of Right of the 1843 Free Church, would be the required response. 'I would be very far,' said Kennedy, 'in the present circumstances, from regarding an additional Church, such as would be thus occasioned, to any extent a calamity.'[256]

To a degree, this was no more than the continuation of a long-term tradition of Highland secessionism, memorably styled 'conditional loyalty' by the expert writer on Highland Evangelicalism, John Macinnes.[257] This

253 Kennedy, 'Bigot', p. 322.
254 Alexander Auld was the author of the famous Highland apology *Ministers and Men of the Far North*, as well as a biography of John Kennedy. Beaton quotes Mrs Auld from a letter of 10 November 1894, which appeared in the *Northern Chronicle*.
255 Kennedy: quoted in a letter of 10 November 1894, sent by Mrs Auld to the *Northern Chronicle*: 'Dr. Kennedy and separation from the Free Church', *FPM*, ii (5) (1897), p. 180.
256 Kennedy, *Distinctive Principles*, p. 30.
257 MacInnes, 'Origin and early development of "The Men"', p. 32.

readiness of the Highlander to walk away from a minister or church with which he was dissatisfied – producing separation on at times an endemic scale – was yet another characteristic which emphasised the gulf between the two sections of the Free Church. In 1890, when the Free Church General Assembly was debating their response to some of the allegedly heretical statements and writings of Professor Marcus Dods, this was again brought to the fore. Murdo Macaskill of Dingwall – Dr Kennedy's successor in that pulpit – presented himself as a messenger from the Highlands, and moreover as one who had been libelled by those in the South. He had, he said,

> in his possession papers of a libellous and almost blasphemous description posted from the south of the Grampians; and he said to himself on receiving these – 'If these be the production of men who favour these views, God helping me, I will fight the battle.'[258]

After enthusiastic applause Macaskill continued by pointing out that the Highlanders had remained loyal to the Free Church despite what many in that region had perceived to be backsliding, or at least 'not in accordance with the Constitution of this Church'. This, he cautioned, would not continue:

> Pass your motions and shield your professors ... but let this House in any way denigrate the Holy Word of God, and you may bid good-bye as a Free Church to your influence in the Highlands ... though they might be weak in comparison with their predecessors – they had still men in the Highlands, in the ministry of the Free Church, that would know what it was to fight a keener battle than any that had yet been fought before they would surrender the position that had descended to them in regard to the preaching of the Gospel and the revelation of the Holy Word of God.[259]

He concluded with a thinly veiled warning about the production of a divided Church when, amid loud hisses and cries of 'withdraw', he warned the supporters of Dods – and the proposer of the principal pro-Dods motion at that Assembly, Dr Adam of Glasgow, in particular – that

> there were many here today who knew the circumstances as well as he [Macaskill] did, and he knew this, that if any one of them gave a vote in this House for any of these motions derogatory to Scripture and the dignity of the Lord Jesus Christ, Dr Adam had better find a nook for them somewhere south of the Grampians ... for their usefulness north of them would just end with their vote.[260]

---

[258] Quoted in *PDGAFCS*, 1890, p. 93.
[259] Ibid.
[260] Ibid.

Once again the Highland Host were flexing their muscle with the threat of secession.[261]

The Sociology of Secession

It can be argued that the Highlander's willingness to secede or separate was born out of a realisation that while he was losing control of many aspects of his life, yet in the one area which probably meant most he could control his own destiny. By the end of the nineteenth century, the Highlands had been 'transformed' socially, politically, and economically,[262] and were allegedly contributing little more than 'romance and rebellion' to the country as a whole.[263] Rebellion had not been a particularly successful field of operation, given the more or less spectacular failures of the eighteenth-century Jacobite rebellions and the nineteenth-century attempts to resist either the Clearances or the Land Laws. The religious Highlander increasingly saw religion as the one area of central importance to his own conception of his life and cultural traditions where he could – and did – exercise significant influence. Political rebellion had not achieved much, but religious rebellion could change the world as he knew it – the Disruption of 1843 was there as evidence for all to see.

As the sociologist Steve Bruce has recently pointed out, religion can have a secular role; religion can act as part of the defence of a culture under real or imagined attack. He argued that religion can 'give beleaguered minorities a sense of self-worth', and that 'where one has a people with a common religion dominated by an external force of a different religion or none, then religious institutions can acquire an

---

261 There has been some debate among sociologists as to why some forms of church government seem to have a propensity to produce secessions. It has been suggested that the theoretical Protestant reliance on personal interpretation of Scripture and the priesthood of all believers, with the accompanying lack of stress on the authority of the Church as an institution, has made Protestantism more schismatic than, e.g., Roman Catholicism or Eastern Orthodoxy. This is heightened when members of a denomination are what sociologists of religion call 'sectarian': i.e., they believe that they alone are right and everyone else is wrong. As Steve Bruce argued: 'Conservative Protestants have no centralised church organisations to settle arguments about precisely what the correct teaching is on any issue, yet they are vitally concerned to know what is the correct teaching. As a result, conservative Protestants are perpetually dogged by internal disagreements': Bruce, *No Pope of Rome*, pp. 113–16, citing R. Wallis, *Salvation and Protest: Studies of Social and Religious Movements* (London, 1979). And it only takes a glance at the famous denominational 'map' of Scotland to see that Scotland's religious history has produced a disproportionate number of secessions. A recent summary of the argument is found in S. Bruce, *A House Divided: Protestantism, Schism, and Secularization* (London and New York, 1990), pp. 37–47.

262 Withers, *Gaelic Scotland*, p. 338. Withers called it 'the imposition of a different ideology and a new way of life': ibid., p. 329. While the transformation which took place in the Highlands was not unique, it was unusually abrupt: Bruce, 'Social change and collective behaviour', p. 558.

263 Drummond and Bulloch, *Church in Late Victorian Scotland*, p. 195.

additional purpose as defenders of the people'.[264] Charles Withers saw the Highland attitude to religion as being a protest against the dominant hegemony in the Highlands; a theme which Callum Brown has also touched upon. Brown referred to protests which took place in eighteenth-century Scotland over the removal of the traditional giving out of the line as 'resistance to the innovations of the social elites', arguing that 'for many, the removal of "the line" symbolised alien "liturgy", elite proprietorship of worship, and loss of popular control of the kirk itself'.[265] Religious dissent was not always a form of opposition, but there would seem to be little doubt that, on occasions, that was precisely what it was. In the words of Charles Withers:

> physical resistance as counter-hegemony was not the only means of opposition. To an extent, both the retention of Gaelic as the language of spiritual worship and the significance attached to religion in the Highlands may be considered expressions of opposition. It is possible to suggest that both in their retention of Gaelic and, more strongly, in their turning to spiritual comforts at times of material hardship as many did in the nineteenth century, the Highland people were exercising a form of alternative hegemony, albeit that it was largely tacit opposition to externally-derived material change.[266]

Withers regarded evangelical revivals as one of the two principal religious reactions to the transformation of the Highlands (the other being the Disruption of 1843),[267] and it is certainly possible to see secessionism in this 'rebellious' light also.

Moreover, it might be useful at least to consider whether religious rebellions of this sort were, as well as individual responses to individual situations, part of what had become almost a 'ritual of secession'. The American Church historian Leigh Eric Schmidt has put forward the suggestion that revivals in Scotland should be seen as part of what had become a 'ritual'.[268] It might be helpful to ask whether the questions Schmidt asked about revivals could be asked about the 'endemic' secessions of the Scottish Highlands in the nineteenth century and before. Ethnographic questions along the lines of how secession helped the religious Highlander to explain his world, what these rebellions meant to those taking part, and how much were they a part of the

---

264 S. Bruce, 'Out of the ghetto: the ironies of acceptance', *Innes Rev.*, xliii (2) (1992), pp. 146–7.
265 C. G. Brown, 'Protest in the pews: interpreting Presbyterianism and society in fracture during the Scottish Economic Revolution', in T. M. Devine (ed.), *Conflict and Stability in Scottish Society, 1700–1850* (Edinburgh, 1990), pp. 96–7.
266 Withers, *Gaelic Scotland*, p. 328.
267 Ibid., p. 338.
268 L. E. Schmidt, 'Sacramental occasions and the Scottish context of Presbyterian Revivalism in America', in R. B. Sher and J. R. Smitten (eds.), *Scotland and America in the Age of the Enlightenment* (Edinburgh, 1990), p. 73.

culture of those who joined the rebellions might all be worth asking.[269] Religion was such a central part of life to the pious Highlander that it would seem fair to surmise that being able to control his religious destiny was a vitally important plank in the maintenance of personal esteem and dignity.

This could be the case even if that was not the reason given for religious rebellion. Those who took part in the Evangelical Revival in the Highlands in the eighteenth century would doubtless have stressed the power of the Holy Spirit as the 'cause'; yet as Steve Bruce has cogently argued, a phenomenon like the Revival is far from being unique to the Western Highlands of Scotland. He cites the chiliastic movements of medieval Europe and the cargo-cults of Polynesia, and deduces that 'people respond to rapid social and economic change by participating in enthusiastic religious activity with a millenarian cast'.[270] 'There is no doubt,' said Bruce of the Evangelical Revival in the Scottish Highlands, 'that it was a reaction to the social dislocation of the clearances and "modernisation".'[271] The Second Disruption was one in a long line of Highland secessions, and its roots go much deeper than mere sociology; for that matter, its roots go deeper than mere history or mere geography or mere religion. But it is only when the causes of this movement are considered from every available perspective, with the resultant answers being processed honestly and diligently, that an explanation will begin to emerge. With this in mind, the approach of the sociologists should not be ignored.

* * *

It can be seen, then, that the Highland–Lowland division was an important factor in the nineteenth-century Free Church. It is undoubtedly true that for an influential section of the Free Church in the Lowlands, the Highland interpretation of religion and the resultant attitude to change was obscurantist, inexcusable and extremely exasperating. It is therefore hard to believe that many of them were too sad to see the 'Highland Host' go their own way in the two breaks of the last decade of the nineteenth century.

In some ways, this was much more than a disagreement over modes of worship, or 'love of dogma', or Westminster Calvinism. Arguably it was a nineteenth-century manifestation of ancient Lowland prejudices transposed to an ecclesiastical setting. The divide between Highland and Lowland Scotland assumed a racial character fairly early on, with the Gaelic language being seen as the critical dividing-line, and to this must be added the immense influence of scientific racism and Anglo-Saxonist

---

[269] Ibid.
[270] Bruce, 'Social change and collective behaviour', p. 559.
[271] Bruce, *No Pope of Rome*, p. 22. It was, though, a more complex phenomenon than that; for a fine brief analysis, see Durkacz, *Decline of the Celtic Languages*, pp. 126–33.

historiography, signs of which appear almost constantly throughout contemporary Lowland analyses of Highland religion.

Having said that, it has also to be stated that there was precious little Christian love and brotherly understanding flowing south from the Highland part of the Free Church. The Highlanders felt themselves both beleaguered and wronged, facing what they considered to be the virtual tyranny of the majority; this helped to produce what can be called a 'laager mentality'. The situation worried the Highlanders, but they were either unaware or unconcerned that their own attitude, of holding what they had at all costs, was contributing in large measure to the impending rupture in the Free Church. Ultimately, if the price for purity of worship and the Old Paths as they saw them was to be the splitting up of the Free Church of Scotland, it was to them a price worth paying.

Thus it can be seen that the pressures for division in the Free Church were coming from both sides of the Highland Line. In order for the Free Church of 1843 to remain intact, some way had to be found to keep both Highlanders and Lowlanders content; the fact is that by the 1880s the mutual antagonism had reached such a height that this was beginning to seem impossible. Both sides looked with suspicion on the other, and it seems clear that neither side considered the loss of the other to be worth shedding tears. The unity of the Free Church and the preservation of Chalmers's dream was less important than the advance of the interests of one side or the other. By the late 1880s, all that was needed was something to formalise the divide, and a split – a second disruption – would be unavoidable. As will be seen, something did come to formalise the divide, and that was the Declaratory Act of 1892.

CHAPTER FOUR

The Declaratory Act of 1892

Although the many factors already discussed contributed to the Second Disruption, in the eyes of the men who took part in it, one consideration outweighed all others: this was what Donald Beaton called 'the framing and passing of the Declaratory Act'.[1] The conservatives in the Free Church were undeniably extremely gloomy about the developments which were taking place both within and without the Church; crucially, however, the position of the Free Church of Scotland remained formally unchanged until 1892. This was a highly significant fact, and was accepted by the Free Presbyterian fathers despite the fact that the history of the Free Church was summarised by one of them as follows:

> For the greater part of the 53 years which have elapsed since then [1843], her history has been one of declension and departure from her original position and standards ... the Free Church failed to bear testimony to doctrines which lie at the foundation of the Christian faith. She has delighted to honour men who have cast aside the Bible as the Word of God, and who treat it as a common book. In a word, she has become known throughout the world as the pioneer of heresy, and has earned the unenviable distinction of being foremost in undermining the foundation truths of the Gospel.[2]

For a Church which was formally the same as that of Chalmers and Cunningham, this was a serious indictment. Given that the Free Presbyterians were frequently accused of being hasty in their secession in 1893, this paragraph indicates that they were in fact willing to tolerate a great deal of what they saw as doctrinal degeneration within their Church before they took what was for them the ultimate step of secession.

The final and formal act which eventually forced them to make their decision to split the Free Church was the passing of the Declaratory Act. In the words of the same Free Presbyterian writer:

> the crisis came when the case for separation seemed no longer doubtful. In 1892 the Church passed the Declaratory Act. This Act

---

[1] This phrase occurs in D. Beaton, 'The story of the Oban Free Presbyterian congregation' (n.p., n.d.), p. 1. Although the formal title of the Free Church Declaratory Act of 1892 is given as the 'Act anent Confession of Faith (No. 8 of Class II.)': *AGAFC*, 478–479; almost everyone who made reference to this Act, whether formally or otherwise, called it 'the Declaratory Act'. See, e.g., *PDGAFCS*, 1892, pp. 145–71.

[2] 'Introductory', *FPM*, i (1) (1896), pp. 1–3.

is the formal reason for our separation. Departures, innovations and errors prevailed on all hands, but it seemed the duty of the ministry, so long as the constitution was intact, to remain in the Church, and to protest by every means in their power against the prevalent declension. When, however, the Church, through a majority of her Presbyteries, and by the vote of the Assembly in 1892, passed the Declaratory Act, we felt that now not only the innovating majority, but all who remained in their fellowship would be involved by this Act in the guilt of past and present declensions.[3]

'The Declaratory Act,' commented one Free Churchman to the General Assembly in 1894, 'had provoked the flower of the Church into secession.'[4] It is with the debate over the Declaratory Act of 1892 and its immediate repercussions that this chapter is chiefly concerned. But before looking in detail at the controversy which surrounded the modification of the Westminster Confession of Faith in the nineteenth century, it is worth looking at the origins of the Confession itself.

The Westminster Assembly and the Origins of the Westminster Confession of Faith

If the Free Presbyterians were the product of a battle over the Westminster Confession of Faith, then that document was itself the product of a time of bitter conflict. It was, in the words of one Free Church commentator, William Beveridge, 'the child of its age'.[5] There is certainly some substance in the statement of the Free Church professor William Hetherington, who said that 'in order to form a right conception of the Confession of Faith, it is absolutely necessary to have some acquaintance with the history of the period in which it was composed'.[6] It was not an event of great dramatic excitement – Robert Paul commented that 'few events would appear to be more essentially sedentary than a conclave of seventeenth century clergymen debating theology'[7] – but the Westminster Assembly was unquestionably an event of great ecclesiological importance, and its background is worth examining briefly.

When Charles I ascended to his late father's throne in 1625, he faced a Scottish Church resentful at what it regarded as the imposition of Episcopacy, reintroduced for political as much as religious reasons by

---

3 Ibid., p. 3.

4 McNeilage, in *PDGAFCS*, 1894, p. 87.

5 W. Beveridge, *A Short History of the Westminster Assembly* (Edinburgh, 1904), p. 3. Beveridge was the Free Church minister of New Deer: Ewing, *Annals of the Free Church of Scotland*, i, p. 95.

6 W. M. Hetherington, 'Introductory essay', in R. Shaw, *The Reformed Faith: An Exposition of the Westminster Confession of Faith* (Edinburgh, 1845; repr. Inverness, 1974), p. xxiii. Hetherington, who started the *Free Church Magazine* and edited it for four years, was appointed Professor of Apologetics and Systematic Theology in the Free Church College, Glasgow, in 1857: Ewing, *Annals of the Free Church of Scotland*, i, pp. 55–6.

7 R. S. Paul, *The Assembly of the Lord: Politics and Religion in the Westminster Assembly and the 'Grand Debate'* (Edinburgh, 1985), p. 1.

James VI and I in 1610. Charles made a difficult situation worse by his clumsy introduction of various Anglicised religious forms, including ecclesiastical canons, the English Prayer Book and the prohibition of extempore prayer. Most Scots overwhelmingly opposed all this, and in 1637 the National Covenant was signed; the result was war. By 1640 the Covenanting army held much of the north of England, and Charles was forced to summon the Long Parliament.[8]

The situation in England was such that, from at least the time of the Union of 1603, the Crown had become increasingly allied with the Episcopate, while Parliament became more and more associated with the Puritan, anti-Episcopal forces. This process was accelerated sharply under Charles, particularly after his appointment of Laud as Archbishop of Canterbury in 1633, and it led eventually to the situation which William Beveridge picturesquely summarised:

> the result was 'political and ecclesiastical absolutism'. From 1629 to 1640 there was no Parliament. The Star Chamber and High Commission Court were supreme. Ecclesiastically, the Puritan demands for reformation in doctrine, discipline, government and worship, were ignored. The leaders of the Puritan revolt were silenced, imprisoned, fined, or done to death. The consequence was that everywhere in England indignation, contempt, and ridicule broke forth. Puritanism was on all sides in revolt against the High Church party ... Clearly, the established order was doomed. England was in a dangerous state.[9]

England was indeed in a dangerous state; the Presbyterian Puritans held a majority in the Long Parliament and when Charles tried to use force against the Parliamentary leaders the result was Civil War. The Parliamentarian leaders turned to the Scottish Covenanting army for support, signing the Solemn League and Covenant, which was ratified by the English Parliament in 1643.[10] A political and military treaty as well as a religious one, the Solemn League and Covenant committed the signatories to 'endeavour to bring the Churches of God in the three kingdoms to the nearest conjunction and uniformity in religion, confession of faith, form of Church government, [and] directory for worship'.[11] In the words of Benjamin Warfield:

---

8 J. S. McEwen, 'How the Confession came to be written', in A. I. C. Heron, *The Westminster Confession in the Church Today* (Edinburgh, 1982), pp. 7–10; Paul, *Assembly of the Lord*, pp. 37–8.

9 Beveridge, *Short History of the Westminster Assembly*, p. 13.

10 McEwen, 'How the Confession came to be written', pp. 12–13. With typical hyperbole, William Hetherington called the Solemn League and Covenant 'a document which we cannot help regarding as the noblest and best, in its essential nature and principles, of all that are recorded among the international transactions of the world': Hetherington, 'Introductory essay', pp. xxv–xxvi.

11 'The Solemn League and Covenant', in Beveridge, *Short History of the Westminster Assembly*, App. III, p. 159.

the significance of the Solemn League and Covenant was, therefore, that it pledged the two nations to uniformity in their religious establishments and pledged them to a uniformity in the model of the establishment already existing in the Church of Scotland.[12]

'The Scots,' commented Robert Paul, 'had it all wrapped up.'[13] The result was the Westminster Confession of Faith.

Although it was the Solemn League and Covenant that gave the Assembly its remit to produce what was eventually to become known as the Westminster Confession of Faith, the idea of the Assembly itself predated that particular treaty. From the earliest days of the Long Parliament it became clear that the advice of a Synod of Divines would be needed to produce a suitable constitution for the national Church which replaced the abolished episcopacy. The Assembly was summoned by an Ordinance of Parliament passed on 12 June 1643,[14] and its role was solely as an advisor to Parliament; it was, in B. B. Warfield's words, 'merely the creature of Parliament'.[15] It started work on the revision of the Thirty-Nine Articles, but the Solemn League and Covenant wholly changed the Assembly's role, and on 12 October 1643 the members were instructed by Parliament to 'set themselves to the task of draughting [*sic*] an entirely new Confession of Faith'.[16]

The men who produced the Westminster Confession of Faith were members of an Assembly made up of around one hundred and twenty ministers and thirty laymen selected by Parliament, along with a handful of Scottish commissioners who could advise and debate, but not vote.[17] They convened on 1 July 1643 with sixty-nine of them being present – this was the average daily attendance but forty would have constituted a quorum – and the real business began a week later. There were 1,163 numbered sessions between 1643 and 1649, and three more years of irregular meetings thereafter; the final minute entry is for 25 March 1652.[18] The Assembly was made up of Presbyterians, Episcopalians and

---

[12] B. B. Warfield, 'The Westminster Assembly and its work, pt. 1', *Princeton Theological Rev.*, vi (2) (1908), p. 200.

[13] Paul, *Assembly of the Lord*, p. 97.

[14] Its formal title was 'An Ordinance of the Lords and Commons assembled in Parliament, for the calling of an Assembly of learned and godly Divines, and others, to be consulted with by the Parliament, for the setting of the Government and Liturgy of the Church of England; and for vindicating and clearing of the doctrine of the said Church from false aspersions and interpretations': quoted in full in A. F. Mitchell, *The Westminster Assembly: Its History and Standards* (London, 1883), pp. ix–xii.

[15] Warfield, 'Westminster Assembly and its work, pt. 1', p. 190.

[16] T. C. Pears, in S. W. Carruthers, *The Everyday Work of the Westminster Assembly* (Philadelphia, 1943), p. vi.

[17] The Ordinance named 10 members of the House of Lords, 20 members of the Commons, and 121 divines: Pears, in Carruthers, *Everyday Work of the Westminster Assembly*, p. v. Their names, along with those of the Scottish commissioners, are listed in Beveridge, *Short History of the Westminster Assembly*, App. II, pp. 151–7.

[18] Warfield, 'Westminster Assembly and its work, pt. 1', pp. 177, 191; McEwen, 'How the Confession came to be written', pp. 13–14; Paul, *Assembly of the Lord*, pp. 70–1.

Independents, of whom the vast majority, not altogether surprisingly, were Presbyterians. And, as Carruthers has wittily observed, 'it is plain that this Assembly, like any consultative body, contained at least three groups of men, the business-like, typified by Burges, the diffuse, by Goodwin, and the inert, by the majority'.[19]

The Assembly has had its critics; Milton, in *Paradise Lost*, penned the following lines:

> Others apart sat on a hill retired
> In thoughts more elevate and reasoned high
> Of Providence, Fore-knowledge, Will and Fate –
> Fixed Fate, Freewill, Foreknowledge absolute,
> Had found no end in wandering mazes lost.[20]

Clarendon said of the divines that most of them were 'of very mean parts, if not of scandalous ignorance; and of no other reputation but of malice to the Church of England'.[21] On the other hand they have had extravagant tributes heaped upon them; James Reid called the Westminster Assembly 'the bright, learned, and pious constellation, which adorned that very active period of the Reformation ... they were zealous advocates for all that liberty wherewith Christ has made his people free.'[22] Of the period of Puritan ascendancy which produced the Westminster Assembly, the Free Presbyterian, Donald Beaton, said: 'history has seldom witnessed such a spectacle when learning borrowed her light from eternal truth and piety lent her grace to genius',[23] and his friend Neil Cameron was applauded when he told the Kilmallie congregation in 1892 that 'for learning and piety these men were the most conspicuous who ever assembled in any age of the Church to systematise the doctrines of the Word of God'.[24] Whatever the truth of the matter – and opinions on the scholarly qualities of the Westminster Divines seem to be closely related to the commentators' theological positions – the fact is that the Assembly did succeed in producing the five documents known as The Westminster Confession of Faith, the Larger and Shorter Catechisms, the Form of Government and the Directory for the Worship of God. The Confession and the Shorter Catechism, in

[19] Carruthers, *Everyday Work of the Westminster Assembly*, p. 3.
[20] Milton: quoted in R. G. Crawford, 'The revolt against creeds and confessions of faith', *Scottish Journal of Theology*, xxix (1) (1976), p. 14. Milton also described the Assembly as 'a certain number of divines, neither chosen by any rule or custom ecclesiastical, nor eminent for either piety or knowledge above others left out': quoted in Beveridge, *Short History of the Westminster Assembly*, pp. 22–3.
[21] Quoted in Beveridge, *Westminster Assembly*, p. 22.
[22] J. Reid, *Memoirs of the Lives and Writings of those Eminent Divines, Who Convened in the Famous Assembly at Westminster, in the Seventeenth Century* (Paisley, 1811 and 1815; repr. Edinburgh, 1982), i, p. vii; ii, p. iii.
[23] D. Beaton, 'The Westminster Assembly and the Confession of Faith', *FPM*, iv (1) (1899), p. 17.
[24] Cameron in 'Report of public meeting held at Kilmallie Free Church', *Oban Express*, 13 May 1892.

particular, were to be books of immense influence throughout the world and, whether loved or loathed, provide a lasting and living epitaph to the men who produced them.[25]

A treaty forged in the intense passion of civil war led to a revolutionary parliament instructing an ecumenical assembly to begin the long and complex process of credal formation. The creed which the Westminster Assembly produced was one of the most famous creeds in Christian history, and one whose history could take up a book in itself.[26] But by the late nineteenth century, many voices were being raised in protest at the doctrines of the Westminster Confession of Faith, both at home and abroad, and to many the Confession's days seemed numbered.

The Free Church and the Confession up to the 1880s

There can be little doubt that the Free Church of the Disruption Fathers was a Church which broadly adhered to the Westminster Confession.[27] A. C. Cheyne, for example, has suggested that the Evangelicals' loyalty to the Calvinism of the Westminster Divines was one of their most obvious enthusiasms carried into the Free Church in 1843,[28] and he has contended that even into the 1860s and 1870s theological conservatism held the balance of power in terms of numbers, not only in the Free Church but also 'in every Presbyterian communion'.[29] The Scottish Church historians, Drummond and Bulloch, went as far as to say that, 'The most obvious respect in which the claim of the Free Church to stand for Calvinism [was shown] was its strict adherence to the doctrines

[25] As Robert Paul observes, the influence of the Westminster Confession of Faith alone 'extends far beyond the Presbyterian churches that have become its primary inheritors', although there has been a particular influence on 'Scottish Presbyterianism and its ecclesiastical progeny throughout the world': Paul, *Assembly of the Lord*, p. 2; see also the footnotes on that page. Neil Cameron called the Confession of Faith 'the most famous book in the English language': 'Report of public meeting held at Kilmallie Free Church', and the Oban Free Church elder Duncan Mackenzie said: 'The equal of the Shorter Catechism had not yet been produced and probably it never would be ... The ministers of Canada and the British Colonies acknowledge that the making of these colonies was the Bible and the Shorter Catechism': quoted in 'Report of meeting held at Kilmallie Free Church in connection with the Free Church Declaratory Act', *Oban Express*, 13 May 1893.

[26] See, e.g., A. C. Cheyne, 'The place of the Confession through three centuries', in Heron, *Westminster Confession in the Church Today*, p. 17.

[27] The Rev. Henry Anderson of Partick, speaking in 1893, described the Westminster Confession of Faith as 'one of the bulwarks of our beloved Free Church': Anderson, in the *Free Church Declaratory Act: A Criticism and Protest*, p. 3. Robert Candlish said, in a lecture at New College in March 1864: 'By all means, let them [the Westminster Standards] stand untouched, as monuments of the vast erudition and mental power of other days, and as safeguards of truth and bulwarks against error for ages yet to come': R. S. Candlish, *The Fatherhood of God: Being the First Course of the Cunningham Lectures Delivered Before the New College, Edinburgh, in March 1864* (2nd edn, Edinburgh, 1865), p. 285.

[28] A. C. Cheyne, 'The Westminster Standards: a century of re-appraisal', *RSCHS*, xiv (1963), p. 202.

[29] Cheyne, 'The place of the Confession through three centuries', p. 22.

of predestination and the Divine Decrees'[30] – the doctrines which were arguably at the centre of the Westminster Confession of Faith and which were to be at the heart of the liberal attack on the theology of Westminster in the later nineteenth century. As late as 1875 – a mere eighteen years prior to the passing of the Declaratory Act – the Church had, according to the Free Churchman Norman L. Walker, a reputation for being extremely orthodox: 'other churches had their Broad Schools but in it [the Free Church] there was hardly one man who had shown a disposition to leave the old paths'.[31] The General Assembly of 1866 was opened by the moderator, William Wilson of Dundee, declaring of the Confession that: 'We have embodied in that document that which we believe the Lord is teaching us in his Word',[32] and he was applauded when he stated resoundingly that the Westminster Confession of Faith

> speaks of things which do not wax old and vanish away, and I can rejoice, and give thanks to the Lord, that my free adoption of it identifies me with those witnesses for the truth, who, amid a great fight of afflictions, had obtained grace to be faithful.[33]

Similar remarks were made by both Cunningham and Candlish.[34]

This all gave the Confession greatly increased authority within the Free Church; for a Church which would have scoffed at Roman Catholic 'appeals to tradition', the perceived position of the Disruption Fathers and others took on an extraordinary significance. One defender of the Westminster Confession referred to alteration of the Confession by the Free Church as an action 'which would amount to a virtual surrender of her proud boast that she was the Church of Knox, Melville, Henderson and Chalmers'.[35] At a meeting in Glasgow in February 1893, Henry Anderson of Partick expressed it in this way:

> The truth in the Confession of Faith we receive as the truth of God's Word. That truth formed a rallying-ground in 1643, when the Westminster Assembly was convened. That unchanging truth

[30] Drummond and Bulloch, *Church in Victorian Scotland*, p. 11.

[31] Walker, *Chapters from the History of the Free Church of Scotland*, p. 272.

[32] Wilson: quoted in Withrington, 'Churches in Scotland', p. 161.

[33] *PDGAFCS*, 1866, p. 7.

[34] William Cunningham referred to 'its whole substance and leading features' being 'far too firmly rooted in the Word of God and ... far too conclusively established to be ever again seriously endangered': quoted in Cheyne, 'Westminster standards', p. 207. Robert Candlish said in an address to students at New College, Edinburgh, in 1864: 'I yield to no man in my admiration of the Westminster Assembly and its symbolical books. I doubt if ever synod or council sat, to which the Church catholic will ultimately acknowledge herself to be more, if so much, indebted. I believe that its doctrinal decisions, on all the questions fairly before it, will stand the test of time, and ultimately command the assent of universal Christendom ... as the only safe anchorage in any and in every storm': Candlish, *Fatherhood of God*, p. 289.

[35] William Balfour, in *PDGAFCS*, 1889, p. 133. Supporters of the Westminster Confession were frequently willing to enlist the blessing of men who predated that document and whose approval of Westminster Theology was by no means certain.

proved the rallying ground of the Disruption worthies in 1843. I think I see Chalmers, and Welsh, and Cunningham, and Candlish, and Gordon, and a host of other mighties who were valiant for the truth, standing shoulder to shoulder defending this standard, and saying to us, 'Destroy it not, for a blessing is in it.'[36]

The Signal cast its net even further for a list of ghostly anti-revisionists; the Westminster Confession, it claimed, contained doctrines held

> by Luther and Calvin and Knox and all the Reformers, by all the fathers of the Scotch Presbyterian Church, by Henderson and Gillespie and Rutherford and all the Covenanters, by all the English Puritans, by Boston and the Erskines and Chalmers and Cunningham and Candlish and Gordon and all the Evangelical divines of Scotland down to the present day, by all who have contributed to make the Presbyterian Church great and fruitful of good in America, by Hervey and Romaine and the Venns and Cecil and Ryle and all the missionaries who have planted Christian Churches in heathen lands, and by a great majority of those who have contributed to the support of Missions.[37]

Despite this alleged 'cloud of witnesses', though, not everybody in the Free Church of 1843 was an out-and-out conservative: the Glasgow Free Church College case of 1856–9 showed that fairly far-reaching disagreement could and did occur.[38] But it seems fair to say that in its early years there were relatively few Free Churchmen who would have disagreed radically with Dr Buchanan's claim in the Disruption General Assembly that they were

---

[36] *Free Church Declaratory Act: A Criticism and Protest*, p. 3.
[37] 'The Free Church General Assembly of 1889: what ought it to do?', *The Signal* (Jun. 1889), p. 164.
[38] This case involved Professor James Gibson's accusation that seven of his students held unsound views on the doctrine of human depravity. As Kenneth Ross commented: 'What was significant was that the students were evidently quite out of sympathy with Gibson's high, unyielding, dogmatic Calvinism and that the Assembly, following Candlish, was more disposed to censure Gibson than his students': Ross, *Church and Creed*, p. 170. See also *PDGAFCS*, 1859, pp. 75–146; and Strahan, *Andrew Bruce Davidson*, pp. 60ff. The Free Presbyterians themselves saw an even earlier sign of declension in the case of the Rev. Jonathan Ranken Anderson who, they said, 'so early as 1852 ... withdrew from her [the Free Church's] communion for this, among other reasons, that Arminianism was tolerated in some of her pulpits': 'Introductory', p. 1. The official record, however, tells a very different story. The Free Church never accepted Anderson's resignation, which Dr Candlish described with some indignation as 'one of the clearest and most unequivocal instances that ever occurred of fleeing from discipline'. Candlish and Cunningham both accused him of deliberately misrepresenting the truth and described Anderson's conduct as 'contumacy'; Candlish said that it was 'more shuffling, more evasive ... more painfully disingenuous' than any he had ever met with: *PDGAFCS*, 1852, pp. 270–1; see also pp. 48–9, 53, 178, 263–6, 269–77. The various complex charges against him were found proven by the Commission in August 1852 and he was suspended *sine die* and his charge declared vacant: *AGAFC*, 1853, p. 70. In March 1853 he was 'declared no longer a minister or member of this Church': *AGAFC*, 1853, p. 73.

teaching the pure doctrines of the Scriptures as embodied in the Confession of Faith ... We do not separate from the Confession of Faith, which we do truthfully and assuredly regard as the sound and scriptural exposition of the word of God.[39]

As Kenneth Ross has perceptively observed, although there might have been disagreement among the Disruption Fathers as to what precisely was implied by confessional subscription, 'it was not pressed, since all were equally warmly attached to the Calvinism of Westminster'.[40]

There were, however, signs of unease present from the early years. Thomas Chalmers was hardly an avid proponent of the Westminster Confession; as S. J. Brown has remarked of Chalmers as a young divinity student:

> the systematic exposition of Calvinism was to him sterile. He objected to Christianity being presented as a system to be accepted upon authority, rather than as a faith to be nurtured through personal experience in an organic community.[41]

He was, perhaps, a reluctant Westminster Calvinist even in his later years:

> the Institutes [of Theology] reveals a mind struggling against doubts about some of the harsher doctrines of scholastic Calvinism and seeking a more personal form of Christianity – while at the same time concerned not to challenge openly the Calvinist orthodoxy of the Westminster Confession which he was bound by his professorial office to uphold.[42]

Even William Cunningham was not unequivocal about the Confession. As early as 1828 an apparently ringing defence of the Confession betrayed some ambivalence:

> I think I can safely say sincerely, that I believe the whole doctrine contained in it. I believe to be true every doctrine which is really and expressly asserted in it, though I don't feel myself called upon to maintain that all its statements are expressed in the most strictly correct and appropriate language.[43]

[39] *PDGAFCS*, 1843, pp. 26–7.
[40] Ross, *Church and Creed*, p. 196.
[41] Brown, *Thomas Chalmers*, pp. 7–8.
[42] Ibid., p. 377.
[43] Quoted in R. Rainy, *Life of William Cunningham, D.D.* (Edinburgh, 1871), p. 39. In contrast, B. B. Warfield spoke of the Confession's 'pre-eminence among Reformed Confessions, not only in fullness but also in exactitude and richness of statement': Warfield, 'Westminster Assembly and its work, pt. 1', p. 377. William Hetherington called it 'almost perfect, both in its arrangement and in its completeness': Hetherington, 'Introductory essay', p. xvi; and Neil Cameron declared that 'The Confession of Faith was the most famous book in the English language on account of the labour taken to construct every proposition in it, for the conclusion which was drawn from the premises of each proposition was strictly in accordance with the laws of reasoning': Cameron, in 'Report of public meeting held at Kilmallie Free Church' (1892).

Principal Candlish of New College was said to have believed that the Formula of subscription to the Confession 'did not bind so much to every separate constituent of the Confession as to the resulting "whole"'.[44] and even John 'Rabbi' Duncan was apparently in favour of a long creed for himself and a shorter one for others.[45]

By 1860 Principal Cunningham of New College – hardly an arch radical – was suggesting in the *British and Foreign Evangelical Review* that it was perhaps time at least to start looking at the subject of the Confession and he expressed doubts as to the rectitude of binding everyone to such a long and minutely detailed confession:

> It is a doubt, at least, whether creeds and confessions, which are to be made terms of ministerial communion, and, of course, grounds of division among churches, should be so long and so minute as some of them are. We have noticed of late some indications of this feeling in men who are far superior to the vulgar aversion to creeds, and whom there is no reason to suspect of unfaithfulness to their own confession. We admit that this is a fair and reasonable topic for discussion ... and it may be well that men should be turning their thoughts to it.[46]

As he wittily remarked in another place:

> Calvin would probably have made a difficulty about adopting precise and definitive deliverances on some points concerning the truth of which the great Calvinistic divines of the Seventeenth Century had no hesitation. But it will probably be admitted that he was qualified for the office of minister in the Calvinistic church, even in this advanced Nineteenth Century.[47]

Candlish, in the very same 1864 lecture in which he made the complementary comments about the Westminster Confession mentioned above, said:

> I am not one of those who would lay an arrest on progress in the science of divinity, and compel it to be stationary ... I do not call for any revision of our creeds, confessions, and catechisms ... But it is no disparagement to these symbols to say of them that they do not exhaust the whole volume of revelation. For that is simply saying

---

[44] W. G. Blaikie, 'The revision of the Westminster Confession (I)', *British Weekly*, 22 Apr. 1887, p. 2.

[45] Ibid.

[46] W. Cunningham, *The Reformers and the Theology of the Reformation* (Edinburgh, 1862), p. 52. This is a reprint of his article, 'Review of John Tulloch, *Leaders of the Reformation: Luther, Calvin, Latimer and Knox*', which appeared in the *British and Foreign Evangelical Review* in 1860.

[47] Cunningham, *Reformers and the Theology of the Reformation*, p. 412. This essay appeared originally in the *British and Foreign Evangelical Review* in July 1861.

that the compilers were uninspired men, and that 'the riches of Christ are unsearchable'.[48]

He then went on a few weeks later to clarify his precise meaning:

I assert the right of respectful comment on the Westminster Standards, as on all human compositions; believing, on the one hand, that a man's reverence for these noble documents may be not the less sincere for its being intelligent and discriminating; and, on the other hand, that the more they are subjected to the light of growing and advancing theological science, the more will their excellency and value appear.[49]

It is also worth noting that two years later, in the Moderator's Address which has been mentioned already, William Wilson went on to say this:

No Confession of Faith can ever be regarded by the Church as a final and permanent document. She must always vindicate her right to revise, to purge, to add to it. We claim no infallibility for it ... nay, we believe in the progressive advancement of the Church into a more perfect knowledge of the truth. It is the Word of God only which abideth for ever.[50]

He concluded these remarks on the Confession with an unambiguous statement of his understanding of the relationship between the Free Church and the Westminster Confession of Faith:

It is open to the Church at any time to say, we have obtained clearer light on one or other or all of the propositions contained in this Confession, we must review it, the time has come for us to frame a new bond of union with each other, a new testimony to the world. If this freedom do not belong to us, then indeed we are in bondage to our Confession, and renounce the liberty wherewith Christ has made us free.[51]

Clearly, then, there were signs even before the 1870s that there was some disquiet about the Westminster Confession of Faith within the Free Church. From the 1870s, and certainly from the 1880s, though, this disquiet became more obvious, more widespread and more far-reaching.

William Garden Blaikie, in 1873, produced a clearly reasoned explanation of the problem as he saw it, gently criticising some aspects of the

---

48 Candlish, *Fatherhood of God*, pp. 284–5. On the particular subject of his lectures, Candlish said: 'I never had any scruple to affirm that their statements on the subject of adoption are by no means satisfactory. No doubt all that they say is true; but it amounts to very little': ibid., p. 285.

49 Ibid., p. 289.

50 *PDGAFCS*, 1866, p. 7.

51 Ibid., p. 8. Cheyne described this as being 'surprisingly near Macleod Campbell's position after the trial in 1831' (John Macleod Campbell had been tried before the Synod of Glasgow for heresy): Cheyne, 'Place of the Confession', p. 23.

Confession while mourning the loss of highly qualified young men who would have been ministers or elders but for the 'dread of a subscription' to the whole of the Westminster Confession. At the same time he frankly admitted the lack of easy solutions and his own lack of stomach for tampering with what was a revered document.[52] Among other topics, Blaikie raised the subject of the Confession's treatment of the Civil Magistrate, a section which has seldom been without its stern critics, but which he thought was an outrageous stance to have as an article of faith:

> to elevate such a question to the rank of an article of faith, the denial of which is to separate men from one another's ecclesiastical communion, as really as the denial of the divinity or the atonement of our Lord, is surely an outrage to our Christian instincts, which cannot but revolt the unprejudiced mind.[53]

Even James MacGregor, himself a conservative theologian and not the sternest of confessional critics, conceded four years later that the time had come to face up to the question of revision. He believed that the Westminster Confession itself was a testament to the willingness to replace old with new,[54] while conceding that there were those who said: 'O woodman, spare that tree. Touch not a single bough. / In Youth it sheltered me, And I'll protect it now.'[55] He did not, however, foresee that change would be a source of any great difficulty:

> It would not be too difficult to put into a very few sentences the substance of the faith confessed by the Westminster Divines, in such a way that no able honest man would endorse these sentences without in substance accepting that faith.[56]

Whatever the problems were which might flow from creed revision, MacGregor for one was confident that the advantages would outweigh the disadvantages.

One of the most important Free Church declarations on the subject had been made by Robert Rainy in 1873. In his Cunningham Lecture on 'Creeds', the man who was to be widely seen as the architect of the Declaratory Act made an unambiguous statement of his position. Rainy acknowledged that creeds had been in use in the Christian church from its earliest era and 'in almost every age of the Church',[57] and while he himself approved of their use, he candidly conceded that it was possible

---

[52] W. G. Blaikie, 'On the proper limit of creeds', *British and Foreign Evangelical Rev.*, xxii (1873), pp. 61ff.

[53] Ibid., p. 67.

[54] J. MacGregor, 'On the revision of the Westminster Confession', *British and Foreign Evangelical Rev.*, xxvi (1877), p. 692.

[55] Ibid., p. 696. MacGregor, though, did not approve of giving undue place to the Westminster Confession; he believed that it was apt to become the rule of faith and, in his words, 'the result is bondage, a sort of evangelical popery': ibid., p. 712.

[56] Ibid., p. 698.

[57] R. Rainy, *Delivery and Development of Christian Doctrine* (Edinburgh, 1874), p. 247.

for a Church to 'maintain scriptural doctrine and effective discipline without the aid of documents of this kind'.[58] Where Rainy saw a potential problem was in the binding contents of a creed, accepting as he did that

> according to the different points of view which may be assumed, men may differ in their appreciation of what is fundamental in Christianity ... The Church does not exact, and ought not to exact, of her office-bearers complete uniformity of belief. Points are and ought to be left open on which men might differ; agreed in receiving the same rule of faith, they may differ in their understanding of some parts of its teaching.[59]

This, Rainy believed, posed a problem from the point of view of those who had to exercise discipline:

> In order, then, to justify disciplinary procedure, it is not enough to show that a minister holds views which the Church in general, if called to decide, would judge to be not scriptural. It must also be shown that they are views which ought not to be borne with in a minister ... The ... question is often a delicate and difficult one.[60]

The very process of a Church selecting what did and what did not necessitate the exercise of discipline was, he said, 'virtually a creed'.[61] The problem as Rainy saw it was that creeds did not deal solely with these fundamentals of the Faith. As will be seen, this belief lay at the core of the Declaratory Act and was to be the source of much of the debate surrounding it.

For creeds, asserted Rainy, contained 'two strata of confessional matter', although at the core lay those sections which had to do with the very essence of belief:

> there were also those articles which are not of this character [which] may reasonably be regarded as the more variable element, which circumstances might require to be extended at one time and contracted at another.[62]

In Rainy's opinion this was partly as a result of the denominational differences which existed in this imperfect world; Churches stated their own position in such a way as to exclude those who would feel more comfortable in some other ecclesiastical home. This was all very well, as was the antiquity of most of the creeds and confessions, as long as one principle was never forgotten:

[58] Ibid., pp. 250–1.
[59] Ibid., pp. 257, 261.
[60] Ibid., p. 261.
[61] Ibid., p. 262.
[62] Ibid., p. 263.

with all this, it must be affirmed unequivocally, that all these [creeds] exist subject to correction. This concession must not be a mere idle flourish; it must exist in the Church as a living, practical, powerful principle. Loyalty to God's supreme word requires it; and where it is withdrawn or denied, the defence of creeds, on Protestant principles, becomes impossible.[63]

While the principle that correction of the creed was not just a right but a duty was freely accepted in theory, Rainy saw that things were different in practice. The tendency was to leave well alone. But, he argued, regular revision should be seen as the norm – 'something belonging to her [the Church's] ordinary and recognised responsibilities' – rather than as 'a revolutionary proposal, opening the way to unimaginable possibilities'.[64] Far from weakening the confession, this process would add to its weight and authority, resulting in a creed which more accurately reflected the 'actual and living mind of the Church', while at the same time emphasising the creed's subordinate position before Scripture.

Robert Rainy was under no illusion as to the ease with which a confession could be revised, but he remained adamant that difficulties should not be allowed to stop revision taking place: 'we shall not be always able to escape questions because the solution of them involves difficulties'.[65] Although he considered it to be extremely important to maintain the confession as it was 'except for grave causes' and that even then change was to be in 'the calmest and most deliberate manner', nevertheless he was convinced that it was wrong and, indeed, dangerous to regard revision as 'something strange, monstrous, almost sacrilegious.'[66] Ultimately, Rainy believed that God would guide the Church along these difficult paths, and he closed his lecture with these words:

Christ has always had a Church on the earth, and He has never forsaken it. Through the whole train of works and functions in which the Church has been engaged, amid all the marks of human shallowness, waywardness, and error, we may yet trace the tokens of One who blesses. So, though we may not overlook the Church's failings, we may not deny the Lord's gifts. We must not deny them in His own hands; neither may we deny them in the hands of those on earth whom He has enabled to follow and to serve Him.[67]

Tragically for the Free Church, all such signs of Christian magnanimity and compromise disappeared over the next twenty years.[68]

---

63 Ibid., pp. 273–4.
64 Ibid., pp. 276–7.
65 Ibid., p. 281.
66 Ibid., p. 283.
67 Ibid., p. 287.
68 As Kenneth Macdonald said of the Declaratory Act: 'What was meant for giving relief ... had a different effect in some quarters. It made for disturbance and not for peace, especially in the Highlands. It was the means of breaking up congregations, of dividing

All these árguments were to appear repeatedly up to 1892 (and after), and, as Kenneth Ross observed, 'in the 1880s, when more clamant calls for revision began to be made, there was a history of thought to be appealed to'.[69] They did not emerge out of nothing, though, and therefore before moving on to look at the increasing bitterness of the divide within the Free Church which culminated in the Second Disruption of 1893, it might be helpful to have a brief glance at the wider context of confessional revision, both in and out of Scotland.

Confessional Revision in Other Denominations – 'The Advancing Tide'

A. C. Cheyne has styled the years between around 1860 and around 1910 as the time of 'the Great Confessional Controversy'.[70] The American theologian, B. B. Warfield, wrote in 1889:

> The last few years have been marked, throughout the Presbyterian world, by a widespread agitation regarding the relation of the churches to the Westminster Standards, which has seemed to culminate during the ecclesiastical year which has just closed.[71]

Around 1890, Charles Briggs, Professor of Hebrew and Cognate Languages at Union Theological Seminary, New York, and co-editor with Warfield of the *Presbyterian Review*,[72] described the revision of the Westminster Confession as

> a product of the evolution of Christian thought in our century. It is the swell on the wave of the advancing tide of Christianity ... It was but a spark last April ... and now the whole church is ablaze ... We

---

families and of separating friends': Macdonald, *Social and Religious Life*, p. 240. Ronald Dingwall, Poolewe, said that he could speak of how 'the Declaratory Act ... had divided friends ... had set households, as it were, against each other, and of how congregations were rent': *PDGAFCS*, 1894, p. 88.

69 Ross, *Church and Creed*, p. 197.

70 Cheyne, 'Place of the Confession through three centuries', p. 125.

71 B. B. Warfield, 'The Presbyterian Churches and the Westminster Confession', *Presbyterian Rev.*, x (40) (1889), p. 646.

72 Charles Augustus Briggs was one of the leaders of the revisionist movement in the United States and was involved in a vigourous debate with his more conservative compatriots Archibald Alexander Hodge and Benjamin Breckinridge Warfield (both of whom edited the *Presbyterian Review* with Briggs). The debate produced a multitude of interesting publications, including: C. A. Briggs, *Whither? A Theological Question for the Times* (New York, 1889); C. A. Briggs (ed.), *How Shall We Revise? A Bundle of Papers* (New York, 1890); Warfield, 'Presbyterian Churches and the Westminster Confession'; and B. B. Warfield, *Ought the Confession to be Revised?* (New York, 1890). Another great Union scholar who became involved was Philip Schaff, the Professor of Church History at Union. He was said to be 'overjoyed' when the General Assembly of the Presbyterian Church in the United States seemed set to revise the Westminster Confession in 1889, and was 'gravely disappointed that the revision was not adopted in his lifetime': Shriver, *Philip Schaff*, pp. 87–8. He wrote several articles on the subject, as well as an influential book: P. Schaff, *Creed Revision in the Presbyterian Church* (New York, 1890).

are in the beginnings of a theological reformation that can no more
be resisted than the flow of a great river.[73]

Revision became the norm, and what was seen as the 'harsh' Calvinism
expressed in the Westminster Confession was under attack the world
over.

In Australia, for example, the case of Charles Strong divided the
Presbytery of Melbourne, Victoria; among other things, Strong was
accused of failing to 'assert, maintain and defend the doctrines of the
Confession', and he was ultimately expelled from the Church in 1883.[74]
A draft Declaratory Act, qualifying the Westminster Confession, soon
followed however, and, after consideration by the Presbyterian Church
of Victoria in 1882, it was incorporated into the 'Basis of Union' which
united the Presbyterian Churches of Australia in July 1901.[75] In line with
other declaratory statements, this 'allowed liberty of conscience in those
matters which did not enter into the substance of the faith, and gave the
Assembly the right to determine what these matters could be in any
given case'.[76] Some Free Church conservatives, incidentally, much
preferred it to their own Declaratory Act; Kenneth Moody-Stuart
described it as an Act 'which would relieve weak conscience, but would
exclude those who held really heretical doctrine'.[77] In New Zealand, too,
Declaratory Acts very similar to those in Scotland were passed in order
that 'difficulties and scruples felt by not a few in signing the Confession
of Faith would be removed'.[78]

The Presbyterian Church in Canada also found itself having to

[73] C. A. Briggs, 'The advance towards revision', in Briggs, *How Shall We Revise?*, pp. 1–2.
The article was based on an address before the Presbyterian Union of New York in
December 1899. By 1893, Briggs had been tried for heresy and on 1 June he was
formally suspended by the General Assembly of the American Presbyterian Church.
He was eventually defrocked. See, e.g., *British Weekly*, 15 Jun. 1893, p. 115; and
Shriver, *Philip Schaff*, pp. 88–93.

[74] R. S. Ward, *The Bush Still Burns: The Presbyterian and Reformed Faith in Australia,
1788–1988* (Brunswick, 1989), pp. 250–69.

[75] Ibid., pp. 276–82. The Free Church was well aware of this development, and the
Victorian Church's Act appeared in full in an appendix to the *Report of the Committee
on Confession of Faith*: 'Declaratory Act of the Presbyterian Church of Victoria,
Approved by the Victorian General Assembly in November 1882', *PDGAFCS*, 1890,
Report XLII, App. III, pp. 24–5. The report is a valuable gathering of materials concerning
creeds and creed subscription from around the world.

[76] G. S. S. Yule, 'The Westminster Confession in Australia', in Heron, *Westminster Confession in
the Church Today*, p. 102.

[77] Moody-Stuart, in *The Free Church Declaratory Act and Proposed Alterations to the Questions
and Formula: Report of discussions in the Free Presbytery of Lockerbie* (Glasgow, 1893), p. 9.
On another occasion he said: 'a Declaratory Act is simply an Act explanatory ... the
Australian Church of Victoria conformed exactly to this ideal': K. Moody-Stuart, *The
New Declaratory Act and Proposed New Formula of the Free Church of Scotland: A Lecture
Delivered in Hope Street Free Church, Glasgow, on 28th February, 1893* (Moffat, 1893), p. 4.

[78] J. Dickson, *History of the Presbyterian Church of New Zealand* (Dunedin, 1899), p. 296.
See also J. R. Elder, *The History of the Presbyterian Church of New Zealand, 1840–1940*
(Christchurch, 1940), pp. 169–70; and I. Breward, 'The Westminster Standards in
New Zealand', in Heron, *Westminster Confession in the Church Today*, p. 104.

confront the issue of whether the Westminster Confession was a suitable creed for the late nineteenth century. The case of Daniel James Macdonnell in the mid-1870s which almost split the newly united Canadian Church, and that of Professor John Campbell in the 1890s, indicated that the traditional view of the Confession was changing. Macdonnell accused some members of the Church of treating the Confession 'not as a subordinate standard but as superior to the Scripture itself'; Campbell described sections of the Confession as 'exhibiting utter ignorance of biblical criticism and [being] itself unscriptural'.[79] Both men were largely vindicated in their trials, and although the Confession was not modified in Canada at this time by an actual Declaratory Act, the attitude towards it had clearly changed to such an extent that a *de facto* modification had taken place.

The United Presbyterians had set what was at the very least a Scottish precedent of confessional revision with their Declaratory Act of 1879.[80] In the words of C. G. McCrie: 'to the United Presbyterian Church belongs the distinction of being the first Scottish presbyterian Church to engage in this kind of reconstruction'.[81] The acquittal of the Rev. Fergus Ferguson on charges of holding erroneous doctrines in 1878 indicated that the United Presbyterian Church was moving away from a strict adherence to the Calvinism of Westminster.[82] Formal moves began at the Synod of 1877, when a number of overtures were tabled 'anent the Revisal of the Subordinate Standards'. Although the overtures were not accepted at the time, the Synod concluded as follows: 'In respect ... of the great importance of the question raised, and difficulties attending it requiring grave deliberation, the Synod appoints a Committee to consider the whole subject.'[83] The middle course between the 'conservative party, favouring no change' and the 'progressive or aggressive wing which favoured a shortening and simplification of the Confession of Faith' was to frame a declaratory statement.[84] The final stage was reached in 1879 with the passing of the United Presbyterian Declaratory Act, which sought to 'explain' the Confession's position on such points of doctrine as the love of God, the divine decrees, man's total depravity, and the eternal destination of the souls of those who die in infancy or

---

79 McNeil, *Presbyterian Church in Canada*, pp. 204–10.
80 Some observers went even further. B. B. Warfield, e.g., attributed the 'formal beginnings' of the worldwide agitation over confessional revision 'to the movement which issued in the adoption by the Scottish United Presbyterian Church, in 1879, of a Declaratory Act': Warfield, 'Presbyterian Churches and the Westminster Confession', p. 646.
81 C. G. McCrie, *The Confessions of the Church of Scotland: Their Evolution in History* (Edinburgh, 1907), p. 279.
82 I. Hamilton, *The Erosion of Calvinist Orthodoxy: Seceders and Subscription in Scottish Presbyterianism* (Edinburgh, 1990), p. 188; 'The trials of Fergus Ferguson, and the subsequent toleration of his views all but signalled the final stage in the erosion of Westminster Calvinism within the United Presbyterian Church': ibid., p. 145.
83 Quoted in C. G. McCrie, *The Church of Scotland: Her Divisions and Her Re-unions* (Edinburgh, 1901), pp. 298–9.
84 Ibid., p. 299.

without hearing the Gospel. It also considered the Confession's teaching
on the Civil Magistrate and, in a celebrated clause, allowed liberty of
opinion on points of the Confession which were 'not entering into the
substance of the faith'.[85] The whole process was masterminded by John
Cairns and was described – in what has to be admitted is a rather
gushing manner – by his biographer:

> when a reform becomes manifestly necessary, and when a man of
> great influence and power acquiesces in the necessary, modifies and
> controls the reform, and presides over the transition ... no sane
> observer will fail to acknowledge that there has been perhaps the
> highest indication of masterful statesmanship and individual
> strength. This undoubtedly was the position held by Dr Cairns
> when, in the years 1877, 1878 and 1879, the Church defined its
> relations to the Confession of Faith.[86]

Cairns himself had been dissatisfied with the Westminster Confession
from at least as early as 1845, when, as a Probationer of the Secession
Church, he subjected the Confession to 'free and pungent' criticism. He
only accepted licence after having stated his 'scruples about assent' to the
presbytery and after he had received verbal statements which satisfied
him.[87] As his biographer observed:

> to the end of his life he maintained a critical sobriety in regard to
> Church creeds, and it is notable that when thirty years later he
> presided over a Committee which relaxed the bonds of the
> Confession, the points upon which relaxation was accorded were
> those which had pressed upon his own conscience.[88]

Considerable attention was given to the United Presbyterian Church
Declaratory Act around the world, but it was particularly influential at
home, in the Free Church.[89]

---

85 *Proceedings of the Synod of the United Presbyterian Church*, 1879, pp. 637–8. As one
member of the Committee commented at the time: 'The great essential truths will, of
course, remain, but there is a strong desire for some declaration that will not make
predestination the beginning and end of our faith, but Christ as the expression of
God's love to the world, putting election in its proper place ... The wish is felt to leave
some of the minor questions for each one to settle in thought by himself': *Letters of the
Rev. John Ker D.D., 1866–1890* (2nd edn, Edinburgh, 1890), pp. 283–4.

86 A. R. MacEwen, *Life and Letters of John Cairns D.D., LL.D.* (London, 1895), p. 664.

87 Ibid., pp. 212, 226.

88 Ibid., p. 213.

89 'The Act,' wrote J. H. Leckie, 'has been much derided; but ... it has been accorded the
flattery of being imitated': Leckie, *Secession Memories*, p. 233, and it was, e.g., cited by
Philip Schaff of Union Theological Seminary, New York, in his 1889 article on revision:
P. Schaff, 'The revision of the Westminster Confession of Faith', *Presbyterian Rev.*, x
(40) (1889), p. 535. Later in the article, however, he dismissed it as something which
produces 'two Confessions which flatly contradict each other in three important
articles': ibid., p. 549. Warfield also noted it, and was similarly unimpressed: 'Its effect
is simply to amend the Confession by indirection in certain specified points (and if
amendment is to be made, why not do it directly?), while leaving the liberty of the

Clearly, then, confessional revision was very much on the agenda in the wider Presbyterian world; as Philip Schaff put it: 'Revision is in the air.'[90] James Candlish pointed out in 1886 that, although every English-speaking Presbyterian Church in Britain, Ireland, the Colonies and the United States, held the Westminster Confession as their creed, 'every single one' had adapted it.[91] Indeed, argued Candlish, the principal of confessional adaptation had been established as early as 1647.[92] As has been seen, the debate during this time included two separate aspects of the Westminster Confession: what could be termed 'non-fundamental' doctrines, such as that of the Civil Magistrate; and what were considered to be 'fundamental' doctrines like the Confession's pronouncements on the Love of God and Predestination. Revision generally involved the teaching on these two sets of doctrines.

It is also worth noting that not all the critiques of Westminster were gentle academic treatises. While men like Rainy and MacGregor within the Free Church were prepared to couch both criticism and defence of the Confession in relatively unconfrontational language, this reserve was not always present elsewhere. In the United States, for example, Charles Briggs suggested with characteristic bluntness that it was both unreasonable and unscriptural to think that Divine Revelation had ceased to be brought to bear on the Bible in the seventeenth century. Creation, for example, he looked upon as 'mere child's play', while he also saw Westminster as being inadequate on the Trinity, on the Being of God and on the Atonement.[93] Philip Schaff described the Confession's teaching on predestination as 'in open contradiction to several of the clearest declarations of the Bible',[94] and said of the statements regarding the Pope and the Roman Catholic Church:

subscriber just as much in bondage to the (now altered) Confession as before; it, therefore, does not in any way supersede the need for a freer formula of subscription': B. B. Warfield, 'The new creed of the Presbyterian Church of England', *Presbyterian Rev.*, x (37) (1889), pp. 115–16. Charles Briggs said of the United Presbyterian Act: 'such an Act only deals with a few of the mooted questions. It virtually sets up two standards of doctrine that are not in harmony. It doubtless has done good service in Scotland, but it would not suit the American Church': C. A. Briggs, 'The General Assembly of the Presbyterian Church in the United States of America', *Presbyterian Rev.*, x (39) (1889), p. 469.

90 Schaff, 'Revision of the Westminster Confession of Faith', p. 529.
91 J. S. Candlish, *The Relations of the Presbyterian Churches to the Confession of Faith* (Glasgow, 1886), p. 3.
92 The General Assembly of the Church of Scotland adopted the Confession in 1647 with some qualifications; according to Candlish the Act of 1647 'implies most distinctly the subordination of the Confession to the Church, and the power of the Church to alter or abrogate her Confession': ibid., p. 4. The Act stated that 'the acceptance of the new Confession did not prejudice the position the Church took on Church government and that the magistrate's authority to call ecclesiastical assemblies applied only to "kirks not settled"': Ross, *Church and Creed*, pp. 194–5.
93 Briggs, 'Advance towards revision', p. 18.
94 Schaff, 'Revision of the Westminster Confession of Faith', p. 539.

I protest against this judgement as untrue, unjust, uncharitable, and unsuitable in any Confession of Faith. It is a colossal slander on the oldest and largest Church of Christendom ... It seems incredible ... It outpopes the Pope.[95]

Llewellyn Evans said that the Confession contained:

statements which are admitted to be non-essential to our system of doctrine; which are not supported by the express declarations of Scripture; which, if not absolutely rejected by the large majority of our ministers, are never preached or urged on others; which are at the best misunderstood by other evangelical believers; and which, as long as they are retained, present our Calvinism to the world as something hard, unsympathetic, unlovely, unattractive, and so far powerless for good.[96]

And Samuel Hamilton, another American Presbyterian, said that the Confession contained 'certain statements that horrify men's ordinary sense of justice'.[97] In the Church of Scotland, too, there were blunt words for the Westminster Confession. James Stark's *The Westminster Confession of Faith Critically Compared to the Holy Scriptures and Found Wanting*, for example, was a long, and at times startlingly brutal, critique of the Confession, practically word-by-word. The Confession's sections on Predestination were described thus:

These clauses, therefore, drawn up on a complete misunderstanding of the Scriptures, are disgraceful perversions of the Scriptures and foul slanders of the God of Love ... In fact, were these clauses of the Confession true, then the Gospel is offered to man in vain.[98]

Stark described the Westminster position on Predestination and Election as 'contrary to the whole tenor of the Gospel scheme of salvation ... thoroughly to be detested and abhorred'.[99] Reference was also made to 'that false doctrine which pervades the whole Westminster Confession', and 'jumbled nonsense [which] is then passed off upon our credulity as if it were the word of God and matter for religious faith'.[100] Stark concluded that 'all its leading doctrines have no support from Scripture, but are the false inferences of a vain scholastic philosophy, founded on detached passages of Scripture whose true meaning was misunderstood'.[101] This

95 Ibid., pp. 547–8.
96 L. J. Evans, 'Dogmatic confessionalism versus revision', in Briggs, *How Shall We Revise?*, p. 46.
97 S. M. Hamilton, 'A non-growing creed', in Briggs, *How Shall We Revise?*, p. 133.
98 J. Stark, *The Westminster Confession of Faith Critically Compared with the Holy Scriptures and Found Wanting; or, A New Exposition of the Doctrines of the Christian Religion in Harmony with the Word of God, and Not at Variance with Modern Science* (London, 1863), pp. 55–6.
99 Ibid., p. 64.
100 Ibid., p. 274.
101 Ibid., p. 285. For a wider, mainly English, context of views on predestination, see

was very far away from being the language of compromise – battle lines were being clearly drawn. It was not really until the 1880s, though, that the more strident voices began to make themselves heard within the Free Church, and it is to this that we shall now turn.

The Revision Movement in the Free Church and the Framing of the Declaratory Act, 1880–1892

During the debate on the Westminster Confession in the Free Church General Assembly on 30 May 1889, Thomas Murray of Midmar, a conservative minister, accused those who sought to revise the Confession of 'theological vandalism'.[102] His speech finally faded out among 'interruptions and signs of impatience' from his opponents.[103] During the same debate, one of the champions of confessional revision, Principal David Brown of Aberdeen, claimed that he had not become disloyal to the faith of the Free Church but that he had merely begun to see the Westminster Confession in a new light; he was, however, still able to use the words 'obnoxious' and 'repulsive'[104] to describe particular details in the Confession. It seems, then, that the Free Church was by 1889 as bitterly divided over the Westminster Confession as it was over many other issues.

Although the movement to revise the Westminster Confession clearly emerged out of a growing disquiet with the doctrines that it contained, it also has to be placed in the context of the growing movement in the Free Church that favoured Union with the United Presbyterian Church. There had been prolonged and determined efforts to secure Union in the 1860s and 1870s, with many of the brightest lights in the Free Church heavily involved.[105] At that time one of the main obstacles to Union had been the fact that the United Presbyterians were Voluntaries while the members of the Free Church were not; in other words, one Church favoured the Establishment principle while the other favoured Disestablishment. Over the course of the 1870s and the 1880s, however, the Free Church, led by Rainy, came increasingly to favour Disestablishment itself, and by the 1890s that subject was no longer a source of serious disagreement between the two denominations.[106] Also by then, as has been seen, the United Presbyterian Church had qualified its terms of subscription to the Westminster Confession, and so a desire on the part

G. Rowell, *Hell and the Victorians: A Study of the Nineteenth-Century Theological Controversies concerning Eternal Punishment and the Future Life* (Oxford, 1974), pp. 26–7. The influence of English views on Scotland in the 19th century should not be underestimated, given that these views permeated into Scotland through what Cheyne has called an 'endless torrent' of 'countless books': Cheyne, 'Bible and Confession in Scotland', p. 29; 'Place of the Confession through three centuries', p. 24.

102 *PDGAFCS*, 1889, p. 146.
103 Ibid.
104 Ibid., p. 138.
105 See Ross, *Church and Creed*, pp. 14–29.
106 Ibid., pp. 119–28.

of the Free Church to do something similar can be seen in the context of desiring to remove one last key difference between the two Churches in order to facilitate Union. It is perhaps significant that within eight years of the passing of the Free Church Declaratory Act, Union with the United Presbyterian Church took place.

Throughout the early 1880s, though, things had seemed all quiet on the Westminster front. General Assemblies during this time debated many of the issues already discussed in this book, but left the Westminster Confession alone. The first overture on the subject did not appear until 1887, a full decade after the United Presbyterians had first formally broached the subject. This overture, from the Free Synod of Glenelg, was in response to James Candlish's move in the Free Presbytery of Glasgow to persuade that Presbytery to overture the Assembly on the subject of revising the Confession. Candlish's proposal had been discussed at a special meeting of the Presbytery on 17 February, and was eventually voted down by the narrow majority of 40 to 37.[107] The Glenelg overture also alleged that some Professors in Glasgow had spoken contrary to the Confession and it concluded in this way:

> Whereas such conduct is truly alarming, and more especially so in those entrusted by the Church with the training of her rising ministers; and whereas if the Church were to legislate in terms of the said overture, such a step would assuredly rend and ruin this Church: It is humbly overtured by the Free Synod of Glenelg to ... the General Assembly ... to adopt such measures as will prevent further procedure in a course that will inevitably issue in most disastrous consequences to this Church.[108]

The response which this overture from a conservative synod provoked is illuminating. Although it was an exact reflection of the conservative position as revealed in the pages of *The Signal*, for example, and while the conservative William Sinclair of Plockton referred to the teaching of Candlish and his fellow professors as 'poison',[109] the mind of the Assembly

---

[107] 'Professor Candlish on the Westminster Confession of Faith', *The Signal* (Mar. 1887), p. 81. Candlish's 'urgent appeal' to the Presbytery did, however, succeed in getting a private conference arranged in order to examine the case. The *British Weekly* commented: 'The down-grade scare may possibly have alarmed some earnest men, but we are sure they need not be at all afraid of anything Dr Candlish may propose': *British Weekly*, 13 Jan. 1888, p. 207. The conference resulted in a decision that it was expedient to take the proposal no further: *British Weekly*, 17 Feb. 1888, p. 299. The Rev. W. W. Peyton of Broughty Ferry also failed to get the Presbytery of Dundee to transmit a similar overture: 'The proposed alteration of the Confession of Faith', *The Signal* (May 1887), p. 129.

[108] 'Overture anent Confession of Faith', from the Free Synod of Glenelg, *Free Church of Scotland Assembly Papers, No. I*, 1887, p. 210. The Free Presbytery of Lochcarron, meeting just over 3 weeks later, overtured the General Assembly in almost identical terms: 'Overture anent Confession of Faith', from the Free Presbytery of Lochcarron, *Free Church of Scotland Assembly Papers, No. I*, 1887, pp. 210–11.

[109] *PDGAFCS*, 1887, p. 212.

was obviously not with them, and Walter C. Smith delivered a ringing statement of the position of the revisionists. Smith claimed that the Glenelg overture was based on the principle of 'no more light' being available once a man had signed the Confession. This, he believed, was wholly incompatible with Protestantism:

> It was an assertation of unchangeableness, and that must always rest upon a claim of infallibility ... which that document itself refused to any book except the Holy Scriptures ... The Church had always claimed a right, and had exercised the right, of changing the formula of adherence to the Confession ... the Word of God ... was from above; the Confession was from beneath. What the Church had created, it could alter too.[110]

Smith, himself the subject of the Free Church's 'first full-scale heresy case'[111] in 1867, went on to vindicate James Candlish and concluded with a fervent appeal for review of the Confession:

> if they found that ... men were standing hesitating upon the threshold, and that that hesitation was caused by this document which the Church called upon them to sign, they would be unfaithful to their duty in training and watching over the students if they did not bring the point under the notice of the Church, and ask the Assembly seriously what was to be done in order to retain the services of those best, richest, and most beautiful spirits who were in training for the work of the ministry.[112]

His speech was frequently interrupted by enthusiastic applause, and the Assembly forthwith voted to pass from the overtures. The writing, it seemed, was beginning to appear on the wall. 'The Presbyterian creed,' commented the *British Weekly* in a review of the year, 'is in the crucible, and will certainly not emerge as it went in.'[113]

Candlish had made his position quite clear the previous year, when he suggested that the Westminster Confession stressed Divine sovereignty to the detriment of Divine love and had argued for some sort of revision. The United Presbyterian Declaratory Act he described as 'a considerable step in the right direction', and he had argued that 'the present form of

---

110 Ibid., p. 213.

111 Ross, *Church and Creed*, p. 172. The Free Presbyterian, Neil Cameron, referred to 'heretical views expressed by him in sermons, in which he manifested how far he had departed from the Confession of Faith and the Holy Scriptures': Cameron, in Beaton, *History of the Free Presbyterian Church*, p. 18. Despite this, Smith was allowed to remain in the Church without retracting his views – an outcome described by Cameron as 'the unconstitutional, irregular, and dangerous course upon which the Free Church had entered': ibid., p. 20.

112 *PDGAFCS*, 1887, p. 213.

113 *British Weekly*, 30 Dec. 1887, p. 171. The Confession was thus being placed alongside the Bible, which was also being 'thrown into the crucible': Dods, *Recent Progress in Theology*, p. 10.

subscription in the Free Church is hardly defensible'.[114] During the
speech in support of his overture before the Glasgow Presbytery in
February 1887, he had said that:

> It would not be at all unlikely that the Confession, granting that it
> was the most suitable for the seventeenth century, should be found
> in this nineteenth century not to be altogether so suitable ... he did
> not think that any one could doubt that there were some points on
> which the statements of the Confession had been proved by the
> progress of knowledge, in the history and experience of the
> Church, to be either inaccurate or at least very doubtful.[115]

Just over a month before the 1887 Assembly another prominent Free
Churchman, W. G. Blaikie, had written in the *British Weekly* of the
Westminster Confession:

> I am ... thoroughly persuaded that that creed is not the kind of
> document to every part of which it is reasonable and scriptural to
> require an absolute assent from every one who is to be a teacher in
> the Church. If what appears to be an absolute assent to every part
> of so comprehensive and minute a document is required, it will
> inevitably give risc to popular 'understandings', which at once hurt
> the conscience and interfere with the binding force which a creed
> ought to have.[116]

This was very close to the stated position of A. T. Innes. In 1867, in
his classic work, *The Law of Creeds in Scotland*, he had stated that

> there is no honest and sane man who will pretend that any proposi-
> tion in religious truth constructed by others exactly expressed his
> own view of that religious truth; and though it may be constructed
> with sufficient care and comprehensiveness to include the views of a
> great number of consentients, it is morally certain that every one of
> these consentients differs from every other, and from the objective
> proposition itself, in the exact sense in which he understands it.[117]

---

[114] Candlish, *Relations of the Presbyterian Churches to the Confession of Faith*, pp. 18, 24–5. On
Candlish's comment that the United Presbyterian Declaratory Act was a 'step in the
right direction', one conservative writer commented: 'we are as far as possible from
believing it to have been [such]': 'Professor Candlish on the Wesminster Confession of
Faith', *The Signal* (Mar. 1887), p. 87.

[115] Candlish: quoted in 'Professor Candlish on the Westminster Confession of Faith.
Second Article', *The Signal* (Apr. 1887), p. 99.

[116] Blaikie, 'Revision of the Westminster Confession', p. 1. Interestingly, Blaikie was at
this time an associate editor of the *Presbyterian Review*, of which the two senior editors
were none other than C. A. Briggs and B. B. Warfield.

[117] A. T. Innes, *The Law of Creeds in Scotland: A Treatise on the Legal Relation of Churches in
Scotland Established and Not Established, to their Doctrinal Confessions* (Edinburgh, 1867),
p. 479. This was very close to the position of the Disruption Father, Robert Candlish,
of whom A. T. Innes said: 'I never heard anything more able or more ingenious than
his demonstration ... that a Confession intended for thousands or millions of men

Marcus Dods was never one to remain silent while others spoke out. He had perhaps gone further than the rest when, in the same week as Blaikie's *British Weekly* article, he had written this:

> It were worthy of any church to consider whether Creeds, used as terms of Office, have not done more harm than good, accentuating peculiarities and perpetuating inconsiderable distinctions ... whether a church is justified in holding a creed which cannot be expected ever to become a creed of the Church Catholic, thus dooming herself to everlasting sectarianism; whether a Church is justified in exacting from her ministry any confession of faith beyond the one article of faith in Christ as the Living Supreme, which she is justified in demanding from her members.[118]

Dods had asked rhetorically at the close of the above article where a Calvinistic ministry was going to come from 'if the pew is gradually drifting from Calvinism'. It was becoming clear, though, that it was many of the most senior and influential figures in the Free Church's pulpits and college chairs who were themselves drifting far from the Calvinist consensus of the Westminster Confession.[119]

By 1888, more signs were appearing that this drift was present if not accelerating. This was despite the fact that the *British Weekly* could comment in March of that year: 'the Church is indisposed to enter into a discussion of doctrines which would be long, difficult and disturbing'.[120] There were attempts to raise the subject of creed revision at that year's Assembly, but, as a later edition of the *British Weekly* observed, 'the attempts to make creed revision a subject of debate at the Inverness Free Church Assembly are failing, as they were pretty sure to fail ... the Highland Assembly is not the occasion; that is now quite clear'.[121] Since much of the reason for holding the Assembly in Inverness had been to placate the Highland conservatives, it would have been folly to raise the

could not be the private confession of any one of them, and could not be written for any one of them. It was written to be embraced by all as the common faith': Innes, *Chapters of Reminiscence*, pp. 199–200.

[118] M. Dods, 'The revision of the Westminster Confession (II)', *British Weekly*, 22 Apr. 1887. His views on the need for a creed to embrace the 'Church Catholic' are an interesting echo of those of, e.g., Philip Schaff, who said: 'We need a theology and a confession that is more human than Calvinism, and more divine than Arminianism, and more Christian and Catholic than either': Schaff, 'Revision of the Westminster Confession of Faith', p. 552.

[119] Dods, it will be remembered, was elected to the Chair of New Testament at New College by the Assembly of 1889, an act by which 'the movement towards a Declaratory Act was greatly encouraged': Innes, *Chapters of Reminiscence*, p. 223. 'Unquestionably,' commented Carnegie Simpson, 'it was a very significant election. For, in appointing Dr Dods the Church knew what she was doing. He had never made any secret of his views or stated them with any ambiguity. The election did not mean that the Church had adapted these views, but it did mean she tolerated them and that even in a teacher of her students': Simpson, *Life of Principal Rainy*, ii, p. 110.

[120] *British Weekly*, 2 Mar. 1888, p. 335.

[121] Ibid., 20 Apr. 1888, p. 467.

topic of creed revision in the Highland capital; 'nobody,' said Principal Brown of Aberdeen, 'could expect a hearing for it there'.[122] In the event, there were eventually only two overtures on the subject at that Assembly, one requesting a committee to 'see whether anything can be done to define more clearly the relation of the Church and her office-bearers to the Confession',[123] and the other seeking that the Assembly 'take this whole subject into earnest consideration, and to do in the matter as may seem good'.[124] No one appeared in support of these overtures, however, and they were immediately departed from.[125] Clearly, the revisionists realised that their day was not going to come in the capital of the Highlands. They were prepared to wait another year, and by 1889 victory was in sight.

The year 1888, though, also saw the publication of a controversial pamphlet on the subject of creed revision by Robert Mackintosh, a Free Church probationer. Its very title – *The Obsoleteness of the Westminster Confession of Faith* – was a clear indication that the temperature of the debate was rising. Among other things, Mackintosh said that

> we know that the Confession was meant to teach persecution – was, indeed, drawn up with that view ... it is plain to us as students of history that persecution was an integral part of the Westminster theology – bone of its bone, and flesh of its flesh.[126]

Of the men who drew up the Confession, than whom few were rated more highly by the conservatives in the Free Church, Mackintosh had nothing but contempt. He described them as 'intellectually babes, and morally diseased ... these blunderers and persecutors', and declared:

> Men all wrong in everything else, where we can test them, are not likely to be at all right in the most important point of all, where we cannot so easily test them. Men ignorant of apologetics, ignorant of toleration, ignorant of scientific interpretation – or, in other words ignorant of truth – men who assumed the Bible to contain what it does not contain – men who failed when tried by tests of practice – are not likely to have been miraculously guided to the truth in their hard and inhuman doctrines.[127]

Not surprisingly, the pamphlet provoked an outraged response from the conservatives. This was partly because they were

---

122 *The Confession of Faith: Proceedings of the Free Presbytery of Aberdeen, on 5th February, 1889. The Speeches of Principal Brown and Mr. J. Murray Garden* (Aberdeen, 1889), p. 4. The Aberdeen Presbytery responded to this remark with laughter.

123 'Overture anent subscription by office-bearers to Standards', from the Free Presbytery of Cupar, *Free Church of Scotland Assembly Papers, No. I*, 1888, p. 215.

124 'Overture anent relation of the Church to the Confession of Faith', from the Free Presbytery of Dalkeith: ibid., p. 215.

125 *PDGAFCS*, 1888, p. 220.

126 R. Mackintosh, *The Obsoleteness of the Westminster Confession of Faith* (Glasgow, 1888), p. 15.

127 Ibid., p. 54.

very much afraid that ... [his views] express the sentiment of not a few of the promising young aspirants to the ministry the benefits of whose services he [Mackintosh] thinks it would be a sad thing for the Free Church to lose.[128]

Sections of the pamphlet were quoted in *The Signal* in order to show conservatives 'what doctrinal views are being entertained by young men in our Divinity Halls, and thence finding their way into the pulpits of our Church'. 'We wish you to see,' continued the author grimly,

the full extent of the evil ... that our congregations be not poisoned with the very worst of false doctrine, and the minds of the rising generation imbued with opinions contrary to true Christianity and directly tending to absolute infidelity.[129]

As can be seen, this was very close to the line taken on the higher criticism; a feeling almost of panic that not only was the present gloomy, but that the future seemed to have even worse in store. The sense of gloom was heightened by *The Signal* publishing, on the very next page, an account of a meeting of the Free Presbytery of Dundee at which an overture in favour of changing the relationship of office-bearers to the Confession was defeated by only 21 votes to 15 – a meeting at which the Rev. D. M. Ross asserted that 'The Westminster Creed was no longer a faithful reflection of the living faith of the Church.'[130] The conservatives did not like it, but events were soon to prove Ross right.

For, by the summer of 1889, the trickle of overtures regarding the Confession of Faith had been transformed into a deluge. The General Assembly of that year received no fewer than thirty-three of them. About one third of these were in favour of retaining the existing relationship between Church and Confession but, significantly, all the rest betrayed more or less hostility towards Westminster.[131] The movement towards revision had picked up momentum between 1888 and 1889, with some of the most senior men in the Church working together towards that end. A. T. Innes had helped to set up what he called a 'caucus' of senior revisionists, partly in response to one young student's 'desperate state of

128 'A Free Church Probationer on the Westminster Confession of Faith', *The Signal* (Aug. 1888), p. 229.
129 Ibid., p. 231.
130 'Free Presbytery of Dundee and the Confession of Faith', p. 237.
131 They were divided, predictably, as follows: those in favour of the Confession as it stood were from the Synods of Glenelg, Moray, and Sutherland and Caithness, and the Presbyteries of Abertarff, Breadalbane, Chanonry, Dornoch, Inverness, Islay, Lochcarron, Skye and Uist; those in favour of some change in the position of the Confession came from the Synod of Fife and from the Presbyteries of Aberdeen, Alford, Auchterarder, Brechin, Cupar, Dalkeith, Dumfries, Dundee, Edinburgh, Ellon, Garioch, Glasgow, Greenock, Irvine, Kincardine O'Neil, Kirkaldy, Kirkcudbright, Linlithgow, St Andrews and Turriff: *Free Church of Scotland Assembly Papers, No. I*, 1888, pp. 329–46.

mind' regarding subscription to the Westminster Confession.[132] In the words of one young discontented Free Churchman:

> I myself, ill affected towards the Confession of Faith, had got into touch with a band of younger men, theological students, who felt with unusual keenness the reluctance all students feel towards pledging themselves to the doctrine of former centuries. Our movement would have made little headway if we had not found support from Dr. Lindsay and the late Dr. James Candlish ... Ultimately, the official leaders took up the proposal.[133]

This group of 'official leaders' was made up of men like Walter C. Smith, A. B. Bruce, T. M. Lindsay, James Candlish, Marcus Dods, Ross Taylor and, of course, A. T. Innes himself; significantly, it did not at this time include Robert Rainy who, in late 1888, had indicated his own reluctance that the Church embark on such a course. He had written in November of that year:

> I could conceive myself declining to support the movement unless I saw it to be strongly called for in the Church. The difficulties which may beset the handling of the question, if we agree to take it up, are of course most formidable.[134]

Rainy, ever the aware ecclesiastical politician,[135] knew that action to revise the Westminster Confession would lead to division in the Church. 'And', commented one biographer, 'the Free Church was divided enough. She sorely needed rest.'[136]

---

[132] Innes, *Chapters of Reminiscence*, pp. 219–20. Innes described this (unnamed) student as 'a brilliant theological student, who has since amply fulfilled his early promise': ibid., p. 219. The Free Presbyterian, Donald Beaton, on the other hand, referred to 'the fiery but misguided zeal of the student who was driven by the explosive rashness of youth without compass or guiding star': Beaton, 'Story of the Oban Free Presbyterian congregation', p. 2.

[133] R. Macintosh, *Principal Rainy: A Biographical Study* (London, 1907), pp. 67–8. Mackintosh was the author of *The Obsoleteness of the Westminster Confession of Faith*, and had, during his time at New College (1877–81), lost his belief in at least one Confessional statement – the doctrine of eternal punishment: ibid., pp. 73–5.

[134] Rainy: quoted in Simpson, *Life of Principal Rainy*, ii, p. 122.

[135] Rainy was, of course, frequently mentioned in the same breath as Gladstone, of whom he was a distant cousin: Simpson, *Life of Principal Rainy*, ii, pp. 4–5. His adversary Donald Beaton commented that 'both were born leaders of men and their similarity in other respects was characterised by discerning observers by the phrase 'Gladstone in the State and Rainy in the Church': Beaton, 'Story of the Oban Free Presbyterian congregation', p. 3. 'Which,' continued Beaton, 'was not meant to be complimentary ... It was the opinion of not a few that there was a strong streak of the schemer in his make-up which was intensely distasteful to those who desired above-board dealings in church matters. It was owing to this feature that he was characterised by one northern elder as Rainy without the principle!': ibid., p. 3. Such burlesque apart, there is little doubt that Rainy was, in the words of another biographer, 'the constitutional statesman, opportunist in tactics to his fingertips ... his instinctive caution revolted from every needless frankness': Macintosh, *Principal Rainy*, p. 56.

[136] Simpson, *Life of Principal Rainy*, ii, p. 122.

Rainy was in Australia as the Free Church delegate at the Jubilee of the Presbyterian Church of Victoria when the 'caucus' were planning their action; their activities, said Innes, took place 'with a queer feeling of uneasiness almost as of mice while the cat was away'.[137] The Assembly of 1889 took place in Rainy's absence, but it was no less significant for that. Indeed, the debate in the 1889 Free General Assembly on the Confession was a clear indication of the wide gulf that had come to exist within the Free Church. When William Balfour 'trembled' lest the Church took steps 'which would amount to a virtual surrender of her proud boast to be the church of Knox, Melville, Henderson and Chalmers',[138] the response was applause from the conservatives but laughter from his opponents. He was fearful of a kind of Trojan Horse of revision:

> the advocates of change began by stating that there were one or two little things which required to be rectified, but when they got elsewhere the little things swelled into almost the whole Confession, therefore the members of the House required to be very cautious how they moved in this matter.[139]

On the other hand, to James Smith the Westminster Confession was like an old navigational chart which had long outlived its usefulness. If revision revealed divisions within the Free Church, he believed, it would be because these divisions already existed.[140] Orrock Johnson could argue that all they were doing was changing 'trivialities',[141] but at the same time Sheriff Cowan of Paisley believed that 'Predestination ... was a repulsive doctrine which kept back many who were attracted by the offer of universal salvation which was to be found in the Bible.'[142]

Several speakers – and indeed several of the overtures being considered – made reference to bringing the Confession into line with the 'Living Faith' or 'present Faith' of the Church,[143] and this seemed to be the heart of the matter. To conservatives the 'Present Faith' was exactly the same as the faith of 1843 – and of the Apostles and of the Reformers – and as Alex Forbes put it, the process should have been to revise the

---

[137] Innes, *Chapters of Reminiscence*, p. 223.
[138] *PDGAFCS*, 1889, p. 133.
[139] Ibid.
[140] Ibid., p. 143.
[141] Ibid., p. 145.
[142] Ibid., p. 150.
[143] 'It is humbly overtured by the Free Presbytery of Dalkeith, to the Venerable the General Assembly, to ... secure fuller harmony between the subordinate standards on the one hand, and the spirit and teaching of Scripture and the living faith of the Church on the other hand': 'Overture anent Confession of Faith', from the Free Presbytery of Dalkeith, *Free Church of Scotland Assembly Papers, No. I*, 1889, p. 336. David Macrae's plea for revision of the United Presbyterian Church's relationship with the Confession had also – partly – been for this reason. He said: 'the professed [creed] is not the actual creed of the Church ... our Church is professing one creed while holding, and to a large extent preaching, another': *Mr Macrae and the Confession of Faith* (London, 1877), p. 5.

'Living Faith' to fit the Confession, not the reverse. If not, then faith was regulated by 'the wayward and ever-shifting imagination of each man's heart'.[144] *The Signal*, never a magazine to make use of much circumlocution when blunt terms could be employed, expressed it thus:

> The living faith of the Church! Say rather, the actual unbelief of the Church, – or of some in the Church, who ought not to be in it at all, even as members, much less as ministers or elders ... God forbid that it should change its Confession to bring it into accordance with their views, or to give them a legitimate standing-place within its pale.[145]

Soon after the debate, James Gibson of Perth said this of the phrase, 'living faith': 'It is no secret that for some of the advocates of revision the words mean that they no longer hold (if they ever did hold) certain of the leading doctrines of the Confession.'[146] And in an abrasive pamphlet published that year Kenneth Moody-Stuart declared:

> Even now it is difficult to gather from their pleadings how many have changed their faith, and how long they have changed their faith, and how deliberately they have changed their faith ... [but] they overestimate their numbers when they assert that the whole Church has changed its living faith.[147]

Clearly, then, there were perceived to be two distinct 'living faiths' within the Free Church, and towards the end of the debate, Dr Scott of Aberlour made an explicit statement of this fact:

> it had been made clear that they were by no means a united Church. They were, in fact, nearly as far divided as they could be, not only in regard to Biblical criticism, but in regard to such primary doctrines as the plenary inspiration, infallible truth, and divine authority of Scripture.[148]

What it also illustrated, of course, was the age-old divide in the Free Church between the Highlands and the Lowlands, with the Highlanders voting overwhelmingly against any change.[149]

---

[144] *PDGAFCS*, 1889, p. 142.

[145] 'Free Church General Assembly of 1889: what ought it to do?', pp. 165–6.

[146] J. Gibson, *'Buy the Truth': Thoughts on Creeds and Creed Revision* (Edinburgh, 1889), p. 33, note 3.

[147] K. Moody-Stuart, *Why We Do Not Mean to Change Our Confession of Faith* (Edinburgh, 1889), p. 4.

[148] *PDGAFCS*, 1889, p. 150.

[149] Of the 130 votes for the anti-revision motion, 55 came from four Synods: Glenelg, Ross, Sutherland and Caithness, and Moray. The 13 presbyteries of Inverness, Nairn, Chanonry, Dingwall, Tain, Dornoch, Tongue, Caithness, Lochcarron, Abertarff, Skye, Uist, and Lewis voted against any revision by 56 votes to 16. In contrast, the Presbytery of Aberdeen voted in favour of revision by 23 votes to none; Glasgow by 40 votes to 2; Edinburgh by 23 votes to 12; Stirling by 8 votes to 1; Paisley and Greenock combined by 20 votes to none; and the Synod of Galloway by 12 votes to none. The final margin was a crushing 413 to 130: ibid., pp. viii–xxvi, 154.

The revisionists who spoke in the debate took great care to stress their own conservatism and to deny being revolutionaries. This was an understandable approach; as W. G. Blaikie had said in 1873, although there was a theoretical right to alter the Confession, 'in practice this liberty is next to a nullity ... any material alteration of the creed would be nearly tantamount to a revolution'.[150] This was also echoed by the conservatives, who nearly all paid lip-service to the theory of revision but denied that it was necessary at this particular juncture. One long overture is worth quoting at length in order to convey something of their tone:

It is hereby overtured ... that, while recognising the abstract right of the Church to revise its subordinate standards in circumstances of peculiar urgency, so as to adapt them to the special exigencies of the times, yet, in view of the unrest which prevails, and the indefinite-ness of the theological belief characteristic of the times, the extremely difficult and delicate nature of the task, the great danger lest the Church's testimony in support of fundamental truths should be weakened instead of strengthened, along with the absence of any well-founded call to engage in the work of revision, or agents specially fitted to carry such an undertaking to such an issue as should prove conservative of all essential truth, and an antidote to all prevailing errors, that the Assembly decline to consider the overtures sent up from Presbyteries on this subject.[151]

Or, as William Balfour put it a little more succinctly: 'Truth does not change with the times.'[152] Some conservatives were prepared to go even further: 'We very much doubt if it is competent for the General Assembly ... to entertain any proposal for a change in the Confession of Faith as to any doctrine whatsoever.'[153] The conservative side in the Free Church were determined, but were heavily outnumbered; at the end of the 1889 debate the anti-revisionists lost by over three votes to one. While the argument over confessional revision continued, the battle was all but over. The way had been cleared for the Declaratory Act.

The motion which won the day in 1889 made no mention of a Declaratory Act, and indeed did no more than set up a committee whose remit was

to consider carefully what action it is advisable for the Church to take, so as to meet the difficulties and relieve the scruples referred to in so large a number of overtures – it being always understood, that this Church can contemplate the adoption of no change which

---

150 Blaikie, 'On the proper limit of creeds', p. 26.
151 'Overture anent Confession of Faith', from the Free Synod of Sutherland and Caithness, *Free Church of Scotland Assembly Papers, No. I*, 1889, p. 331.
152 *PDGAFCS*, 1889, p. 134.
153 'Free Church General Assembly of 1889: what ought it to do?', p. 162.

shall not be consistent with a cordial and steadfast adherence to the
great doctrines of the Confession.[154]

The Committee consisted of fifty ministers and twenty-five elders, and
even its composition was a source of disagreement. Rainy said that its
members were 'carefully chosen from men of various shades of opinion
on Church questions',[155] but the conservatives were not convinced; *The
Signal* commented:

> of these about ten represent what may be called the orthodox or
> conservative party in the Church ... It will be observed that those
> who at different times have had doubts cast on their orthodoxy are
> mostly on the Committee.[156]

Over the next two years, the Committee – which had an average
attendance of 'little more than a half' of the original seventy-five[157] –
deliberated as to the best way forward, and by the Assembly of 1891 its
convener, Robert Rainy, was able to put forward a draft Declaratory Act
which was, in the opinion of the Committee, 'the mildest, the least
startling, the least offensive way ... of taking in hand the duty which was
committed to them'.[158] Rainy argued that the proposed Act did not
amount to much:

> The truth was, they were not anxious to do exceedingly much.
> They were not anxious to do anything that was revolutionary, and
> they were very well aware that if they had gone a little further, the
> ... critics would have said that the committee had now gone over to
> rationalism, and had deserted the evangelical faith.[159]

Rainy stressed that what they were proposing would do no more than
put the Free Church in line with 'those sister Churches' which had
already taken similar steps. He went on to recommend the Act, in a
speech which was received most enthusiastically, and proposed that the
Act be sent down to the presbyteries of the Church under the Barrier
Act. After a short debate, during which Murdo Macaskill's main anti-
Declaratory Act speech was interrupted by a large number of members
noisily leaving the Assembly hall, the motion was overwhelmingly passed

---

154 *PDGAFCS*, 1889, p. 137.
155 R. Rainy, *Explanatory Notes on the Declaratory Act of the Free Church of Scotland* (Edin-
	burgh, 1894), p. 1.
156 'Revision of the Confession of Faith', *The Signal* (Jul. 1889), p. 213. The same article
	names all the members of the Committee.
157 Several members never appeared at all, and others only presented themselves 'on a
	very few occasions': J. McEwan, *The Proposed Free Church Declaratory Act, and the Duty of
	the General Assembly of 1892 Thereanent: Being the Substance of a Speech Delivered in the
	Free Presbytery of Edinburgh on Wednesday, the 24th February 1892, in support of the Follow-
	ing Overture* (Edinburgh, 1892), p. 11.
158 *PDGAFCS*, 1891, p. 78.
159 Ibid.

by a majority of over 6 to 1.[160] Having gone through the presbyteries the Act came back to the Assembly and, after a debate in which Murdo Macaskill's speech was again interrupted by the noisy departure of many members, it was passed on 26 May 1892 by a majority of 346 to 195. The Declaratory Act was now part of the law of the Free Church.[161] For the sake of clarity, the Act will now be quoted in full:

> Whereas it is expedient to remove difficulties and scruples which have been felt by some in reference to the declaration of belief required from persons who receive licence or are admitted to office in this Church, the General Assembly, with consent of Presbyteries, declare as follows:–

> 1. That, in holding and teaching, according to the Confession, the Divine purpose of grace towards those that are saved, and the execution of that purpose in time, this Church most earnestly proclaims, as standing in the forefront of the revelation of Grace, the love of God – Father, Son, and Holy Spirit – to sinners of mankind, manifested especially in the Father's gift of the Son to be the Saviour of the world, in the coming of the Son to offer Himself a Propitiation for sin, and in the striving of the Holy Spirit with men to bring them to repentance.

> 2. That this Church also holds that all who hear the Gospel are warranted and required to believe to the saving of their souls; and that in the case of such as do not believe, but perish in their sins, the issue is due to their own rejection of the Gospel call. That this Church does not teach, and does not regard the Confession as teaching, the fore-ordination of men to death irrespective of their own sin.

> 3. That it is the duty of those who believe, and one end of their calling by God, to make known the Gospel to all men everywhere for the obedience of faith. And that while the Gospel is the ordinary means of salvation for those to whom it is made known, yet it

---

[160] The 13 Highland Presbyteries cited above only voted against the motion by 35 votes to 28, which seems to cast some doubt on the claim that the geographical divide was significant. This figure must be seen, though, in the context of an absolutely crushing defeat for the anti-revisionists (428 to 66) and it should be noted that these Highland Presbyteries provided over half of the total votes cast against the Act. This is put into some perspective by the Synod of Glasgow and Ayr, whose members voted in favour of Rainy's motion by 114 votes to 4; and by the combined votes of the Synods of Lothian and Tweeddale, Merse and Teviotdale, Dumfries, and Galloway, where the voting was 89 to 6 in favour of the Act. The Synods of Perth and Stirling, Fife, and Angus and Mearns voted for the motion by 95 votes to 7: *PDGAFCS*, 1891, pp. viii–xxvii.

[161] *PDGAFCS*, 1892, pp. 145–72. Macaskill said that 'this just showed that when anybody stood up there in defence of the truth and of the Confession, that was the treatment that was always given them': ibid., p. 159. The 13 Highland presbyteries did what they could, voting against the Act by 49 to 8; but the Synod of Glasgow and Ayr, e.g., voted in favour by 96 votes to 23: ibid., pp. xi–xxvii.

does not follow, nor is the Confession to be held as teaching, that any who died in infancy are lost, or that God may not extend His mercy, for Christ's sake, and by His Holy Spirit, to those who are beyond the reach of these means, as it may seem good to Him, according to the riches of His grace.

4. That, in holding and teaching, according to the Confession of Faith, the corruption of man's whole nature as fallen, this Church also maintains that there remain tokens of his greatness as created in the image of God; that he possesses a knowledge of God and of duty; that he is responsible for compliance with the moral law and with the Gospel; and that, although unable without the aid of the Holy Spirit to return to God, he is yet capable of affections and actions that in themselves are virtuous and praiseworthy.

5. That this Church disclaims intolerant or persecuting principles, and does not consider her office-bearers, in subscribing the Confession, committed to any principles inconsistent with liberty of conscience and the right of private judgement.

6. That while diversity of opinion is recognised in this Church on such points in the Confession as do not enter into the substance of the Reformed Faith therein set forth, the Church retains full authority to determine, in any case which may arise, what points fall within this description, and thus to guard against any abuse of this liberty to the detriment of sound doctrine, or to the injury of her unity and peace.[162]

The Declaratory Act: The Free Presbyterian Response

The Declaratory Act of 1892 was the single cause of the Second Disruption in 1893. Other conservatives lambasted the Act and its framers with strong words but ultimately took the decision to remain in the Free Church and live with the Act. The Free Presbyterians, on the other hand, took the very difficult step of secession, and their specific reasons must be examined here.

In only the second edition of the *Free Presbyterian Magazine*, the following statement can be found:

the Act ... [is] the formal reason for our separation from the Free Church ... [because] by the adoption of this Act the constitution of the Free Church is now changed, and ... no one who holds the principles of this Church as settled in 1843 can consistently remain in fellowship with the body that now bears that name.[163]

---

162 'Act anent Confession of Faith (No. 8 of Class II.)', *AGAFC*, 1889–1893, pp. 478–9. The clauses were not originally numbered, and in some places the numbering varies according to different subdivisions of the clauses.

163 'The Declaratory Act', *FPM*, i (2) (1896), p. 41.

It was, in a nutshell, the argument which was to be repeated throughout the history of the Free Presbyterian Church and from which that Church has never wavered. The Free Presbyterians argued that their Disruption of 1893 was to preserve the Free Church of 1843, and that the Church from which they seceded contained in fact the 'real' seceders. As Donald Macfarlane put it in his diary:

> Some call us 'Seceders', but we are not seceders. The word 'seceder', according to the literal meaning, is to step aside from a position. We have not stepped aside from the position of the Church of Scotland for centuries. It is those who have left that position who are seceders from God's Word and worship.[164]

The position of the Free Church Constitution was, in their eyes, very simple. Prior to 1892, the Constitution

> mainly consisted in unreserved adherence to the principles and doctrines embodied in the Confession of Faith as the chief subordinate standard of the Church ... But now, by the passing of the Declaratory Act, that relation has been changed into a modified acceptance of Confessional doctrine. In fact a new standard of doctrine has been set up ... This change of standard we hold is an obvious change in the constitution.[165]

Far from seeing the Declaratory Act as a 'relieving' Act, the early Free Presbyterians saw it as something which went very much further. 'The Act,' continued the same writer, 'is in reality a new creed, and by its own terms is evidence that the Church has now changed her constitution.'[166] According to the Free Presbyterian argument, the fact that the Act had been sent down to presbyteries, and had been approved under the Barrier Act, immediately made it a different proposition from other so-called examples of declension in the Church:

> the Declaratory Act has passed through all the forms of procedure necessary to make it a law in the Church. It therefore forms a part of the constitution, and if so, the constitution of the Free Church is now essentially changed ... We hold, therefore, that the constitution of the Free Church is essentially changed when this Act that opposes and sets aside the Confession is a standing law and constitution in the Church.[167]

The revisionists hotly disputed such a view. Rainy in particular, as will be seen, was at pains to stress that the Act was indeed merely a 'relieving act'. As Kenneth Macdonald of Applecross put it:

---

164 Beaton, *Donald Macfarlane*, p. 55.
165 'Declaratory Act', p. 42.
166 Ibid.
167 Ibid., pp. 43–4.

the Act is not binding ... it is a permissive Act ... that is, I am not bound to accept the explanations given in it. I am free to hold my own view on the topics explained ... A man who takes office ... must subscribe the Confession of Faith. If he does so with or without the explanation given in the Declaratory Act, the Church is satisfied.[168]

Another part of the Free Presbyterian apologia was that, as Presbyterians, each individual was responsible for the actions of the Church as a whole. If the action was good, each member shared in the benefits; but if the corporate action of the Church was bad, then each member shared 'the dishonour, guilt and loss'.[169] This was exactly what Neil Cameron was talking about when he argued in 1920 that the Act had the effect of imputing the corporate guilt of the Free Church on to the individuals within it. Of the liberals in the Church he said: 'The Confession of Faith was no longer their confession of faith, and all the changes they had made were now to be bound on the neck of the Free Church.'[170] Those who left at the Second Disruption had been prepared to accept what had happened within the Free Church up to 1892 because they did not see these developments as having a direct effect upon them. The Declaratory Act, according to Cameron, changed all that:

When they had filled the Church with the flood of heresies, carnality in worship and practice, the infamous Declaratory Act was duly passed into 'a binding law and constitution in the Church'. This meant that all the innovations contained in that Act were to be bound on all who would continue in future fellowship with that Church. We refused to put our necks under this Satanic yoke, so we separated in 1893 in order ... to continue the existence of the Free Church of Scotland as that Church was settled in 1843.[171]

The Free Presbyterians, then, believed that dissociation from a flawed denomination was their only scriptural option.

Part of the reason for the Free Presbyterians' aggressive defence of their actions in 1893 was that they found themselves under attack from the very beginning. One Free Presbyterian writer spoke of 'the shout of scorn and censure that greeted the Disruption of 1893, as contrasted with the shout of acclamation and praise that filled the air at the Disruption of 1843'.[172] And it has already been seen that many commentators saw the Second Disruption as yet another example of Highlanders being led astray by silver-tongued villains. 'Those who have seceded from the Church,' wrote Kenneth Macdonald, 'must have acted in ignorance.'[173] Rainy made the distinction very clear:

---

168 Macdonald, *Social and Religious Life*, p. 237.
169 'Declaratory Act', p. 44.
170 Cameron, 'New Year's Day Lecture, 1920', p. 156.
171 Cameron, 'New Year's Day Lecture, 1926', p. 174.
172 'Separation from an unsound Church', *FPM*, i (12) (1897), p. 441.
173 Macdonald, *Social and Religious Life*, p. 238.

Every man in that Assembly knew that there was not a benighted parish in the Lowlands in which it would be possible to possess the minds of the people with the exaggerations and the impressions that had been spread abroad in many parts of the Highlands. Nobody could do it.[174]

It was not just those who took part in the Second Disruption that Rainy believed were misled; of the two ministers formally at the head of the movement, the Principal said this:

He believed that both of them had been laid hold of, and exploded, as it were, into space by forces with the origination of which they had nothing very specially to do, and for the effects of which they had no very special responsibility.[175]

Even the leading anti-Declaratory Act minister, William Balfour, told a laughing General Assembly that some of the Highlanders

said things in Gaelic which he sometimes thought they did not understand themselves ... They were a very generous, noble, and sound-principled people, very steadfast in defending their views of what they believed to be the truth, and all he knew of them had been in their praise; but still they were a peculiar people in many ways.[176]

Dugald MacLachlan of Portree said that he condemned

those ministers and others who had, in a manner injudicious and one-sided, brought the Declaratory Act to the judgement of the people of the Highlands, who, to say the least of it, had not sufficient knowledge of the English language fully to understand what had been said on the subject in this Assembly ... He knew of meetings at which motions condemnatory of the Act, of the Church and her professors, and of every progressive movement within the Church in recent years, had been put in English to an audience who were all but ignorant of that language, and of course carried.[177]

This all fits into the stereotypical portrayal of the Highlanders as ill-informed and uneducated opponents of all progress.[178] In the face of a

---

174 *PDGAFCS*, 1894, p. 81.
175 Ibid., 1894, p. 53.
176 Ibid., 1894, pp. 83–4.
177 Ibid., 1894, p. 87.
178 This is in contrast to one statement in the Assembly of 1894, when William Sinclair of Plockton said that 'hundreds, if not thousands, of the Church's firmest and most loyal adherents had left it on account of the Act': *PDGAFCS*, 1894, p. 78. Archibald McNeilage made the controversial remark that 'the Declaratory Act had provoked the flower of the Church into secession. Take away the millionaires who made their wealth grinding the flesh of the poor, and the Free Church would still be as rich as ever – but take away the people who lived by faith, and who were truly religious and godly people, then, he said, the Free Church would be poor': ibid., 1894, p. 87.

secession which was overwhelmingly Highland, it was, perhaps, an understandable response.

The Free Presbyterians responded to this criticism in three ways. The first, as has been shown, was to seek to prove that the Free Church, by changing her constitution, had ceased to be the Church of Scotland, Free, of 1843. The second was to argue that the Act tied them to all the ills of the Free Church and that it was their duty to separate from such an 'unsound Church'. This was the position advanced by Cameron in the lectures quoted above, and was also argued at great length in a series of editorial articles in the *Free Presbyterian Magazine*, presumed to be written by James S. Sinclair, one of the students who left the Free Church in 1893 and a man who became one of the Free Presbyterian Church's longest-serving and best-loved ministers. He used a variety of biblical examples to assert that 'it is unscriptural, and, therefore, sinful, for the followers of Christ to have fellowship with those who are not His followers, or those who are unfaithful to His Word in any way that would compromise divine truth'.[179] He cited the cases of such people as Abraham, Lot, Achan, and the Children of Israel in Egypt and concluded that when ungodly men rose to dominate a Church, it was time for 'the faithful' to 'go forth out of this bondage'.[180] Those who remained in the Free Church were accused of being like

> children who remained in the house, [who] received ... robbers as brethren, gave them everything in it, allowed them to usurp the parental place of authority, and submitted to see their parents thrust into a corner, there to live or die, at the mercy of those robbers ... That is the exact state of the case of those who remain in the Free Church.[181]

Reference was made to 'corrupt bodies such as the Free Church',[182] and in a later argument on the same theme Sinclair argued that:

> Infidelity has gone to a greater height in the Free Church of today than ever it did since the Christian era began in any body professing to be part of Christ's visible Church. If the ... command – 'come out from among them and be ye separate, saith the Lord' – does not apply to people within her pale, we confess we don't know where to apply it.[183]

It was a truly remarkable allegation, and one which illustrates explicitly

---

[179] 'Separation from an unsound Church', *FPM*, i (12) (1897), pp. 441–2. The article, although probably written by Sinclair, was unsigned.

[180] Ibid., pp. 442–3.

[181] 'Separation from an unsound Church viewed in the light of Scripture', *FPM*, ii (1) (1897), p. 2.

[182] Ibid., p. 4.

[183] 'Separation from an unsound Church viewed in the light of Scripture', *FPM*, ii (2) (1897), p. 43.

the unbridgeable gulf which had come to exist within the Free Church. It is often the closest of friends who become the bitterest of enemies.

The third strand in the Free Presbyterian policy of aggressive defence was a clause-by-clause critique of the Declaratory Act itself. This has continued to the present day, and still remains an integral part of the traditional New Year's Day Lecture, but its most celebrated initial exponent was James Sinclair, in a series of articles in the *Free Presbyterian Magazine*.[184] Published over five months in the second half of 1896 and running to some twenty-six pages, his 'Explanatory Criticism on the Declaratory Act' remains as one of the clearest testaments to the original position of the Free Presbyterian Church. While it is a fairly intricate refutation of what was itself an intricate Act, the 'Explanatory Criticism' is a fascinating glimpse inside the minds of the men who led the Second Disruption in 1893.

There is no need here to do more than summarise briefly the essence of these articles. If James Stark's critique of the Westminster Confession was notable for its thoroughness, then the same can certainly be said for Sinclair's treatment of the Declaratory Act. One speaker at 'a great public meeting' in Oban of April 1892, suggested that the only word of the Declaratory Act which did not require amendment was 'whereas',[185] and Sinclair seemed to come close to that stance in his 'Explanatory Criticism'. Section by section the Declaratory Act was mercilessly attacked, and if he did not go as far as to say, as one enemy of the Act allegedly observed, that it was 'the blackest Act that had ever been cooked in the devil's kitchen',[186] he was not far from it.

He believed that the situation demanded a clear statement of 'the great unchanging and unchangeable doctrines of the Word of God as embodied in the Confession'. But, said Sinclair,

> instead of this, the Free Church, in order to please the fickle tastes of carnal men has traitorously lowered the standard of accepted truth, and weakened down the saving doctrines of the Gospel, so that they shall be powerless for any spiritual good to this or future generations.[187]

He accused the Declaratory Act of being Arminian – 'the remedy that has thus been provided for difficulties and scruples,' said Sinclair, 'is more dangerous than the disease'.[188] The Act, he argued, 'practically affirms a

---

184 When Beaton's *History of the Free Presbyterian Church* was reprinted and updated in the early 1970s, Sinclair's series of articles was reprinted in full as an appendix: A. McPherson (ed.), *History of the Free Presbyterian Church (1893–1970)* (Inverness, n.d.), pp. 385–427.

185 John Kennedy, in *Free Church Declaratory Act of 1891. Report of Speeches: Delivered at a Public Meeting ... Oban ... 13th April, 1892*, p. 6.

186 Dugald MacLachlan, in *PDGAFCS*, 1894, p. 88.

187 'Explanatory criticism on the Declaratory Act', *FPM*, i (4) (1896), p. 121.

188 Ibid., p. 122.

universal atonement ... the love spoken of is *universal in character*.[189] As
Calvinists to the very marrow, there were few epithets in the Free
Presbyterian vocabulary more pejorative than 'Arminian'; the Act was
described as such, and repeatedly so.[190]

The Act was further accused, in part of its second clause ('That this
Church does not teach, and does not regard the Confession as teaching,
the fore-ordination of men to death irrespective of their own sin'), of
being

> in direct contradiction to the truth as stated in the 5th chapter of the
> Romans ... it denies that the spiritual death under which all men
> are born is in consequence of the imputation of Adam's first sin. It
> may even be taken as denying that we are born in a state of spiritual
> death at all ... the Act, by implication, denies that Adam stood for
> his posterity ... [and] if it is unwarrantable to say that Adam stood
> for his seed, it is equally so to say that Christ stood for his people.[191]

Again, it is for theologians to argue over these niceties; it is at least
debatable whether the Act was intended to teach anything of the kind,
and its architects certainly denied it.[192] What is important to emphasise,
however, is that the conservatives interpreted it in this way, and by
doing so made a cleavage in the Free Church more likely.[193]

The third clause of the Act was alleged by Sinclair to teach that it was
the duty of all men and women to preach the Gospel. This would seem
to be, to say the least, a somewhat imaginative reading of the words in
question: 'That it is the duty of those who believe, and one end of their
calling by God, to make known the Gospel to all men everywhere for the
obedience of faith.' It was, however, enough evidence for Sinclair to
detect 'the essence of Plymouth Brethrenism', and so another heresy
could be ascribed to the Declaratory Act.[194] The Act did not specify
'preaching', and it would seem to be pedantry in the extreme to argue as
Sinclair did, and, indeed, as Murdo Mackenzie did when he asked: 'If
they all became ministers, where would their congregations be?'[195] With
conservatives picking holes in the Act where it could well be argued, with
Rainy, that all it was doing was asserting that 'all believers have a calling

---

[189] Ibid., p. 124. Emphasis his.
[190] 'The Arminian Gospel ... is almost verbally the Gospel we find in the Declaratory Act':
ibid., i (5) (1896), p. 161. Most of the Act's conservative critics said much the same
about that clause.
[191] Ibid., pp. 162–3.
[192] Rainy, e.g., said that 'This clause is to show that ... those who shall be condemned are
ordained to dishonour and wrath for their sins': Rainy, *Explanatory Notes on the Declaratory
Act*, p. 4.
[193] J. C. Robertson of Rayne, for one, held that the final part of Clause 2 seemed quietly
to 'set aside the great principles of representative responsibility and imputation': *The
Free Church Declaratory Act: A Criticism and Protest*, p. 11.
[194] 'Explanatory criticism on the Declaratory Act', *FPM*, i (5) (1896), pp. 163–4.
[195] *Free Church Declaratory Act: A Criticism and Protest*, p. 12.

and a duty to set the Gospel forth as the way of salvation to those who sit in darkness',[196] it was clear that a bitter battle was imminent.

Sinclair went on to criticise the Act's section about the salvation of infants and 'those who are beyond the reach' of ordinary means of grace. It was, he said, 'a dagger into all true missionary effort'.[197] Clause 4, which, according to Rainy, merely asserted 'the reality of the natural virtues that are found in unregenerate men',[198] was described in the following terms:

> Instead of a bold, clear, and truthful statement of man's total depravity by nature ... we have a statement which is fitted to gratify the pride and self-righteousness of the age, and is not wanting in serious deviations from essential and vital truth.[199]

Sinclair argued that by speaking of the 'corruption of man's whole nature as fallen' but not of the 'total corruption', the Act, in which 'every word is of value', was preparing its readers for 'the light and erroneous views of man's fallen estate that follow'.[200] He concluded his attack on clause 4 with these words: 'we affirm that it is drugging souls with sweet poison to make them believe they are capable of affections and actions that have any real virtue or praiseworthiness in the sight of God'.[201] Sinclair and his colleagues who went out at the Second Disruption believed absolutely in the total depravity of man by nature; that there was 'none that doeth good, no, not one'.[202] Believing as they did that the Declaratory Act contradicted this doctrine, it is understandable that they saw it as subversive of their interpretation of the Westminster Confession.

Clause 5, which said that the Church 'disclaims intolerant or persecuting principles, and does not consider her office-bearers, in subscribing the Confession, committed to any principles inconsistent with liberty of conscience and the right of private judgement', was described by Kenneth Ross as being 'not disputed'.[203] Sinclair in fact spent four pages disputing this part of the Act, in which he said that the Free Church 'tacitly abandons the principle of national religion, one of the most important principles in her constitution'.[204] The fact that the Act did not here mention the doctrine of the Civil Magistrate or the Establishment principle did not deflect Sinclair from producing a lengthy defence of the principle of national Establishments.

The final clause of the Declaratory Act stated:

---

196 Rainy, *Explanatory Notes on the Declaratory Act*, p. 5.
197 'Explanatory criticism on the Declaratory Act', *FPM*, i (5) (1896), p. 167.
198 Rainy, *Explanatory Notes on the Declaratory Act*, p. 6.
199 'Explanatory criticism on the Declaratory Act', *FPM*, i (6) (1896), p. 201.
200 Ibid., pp. 201–2.
201 Ibid., p. 205.
202 Psalms liii.3.: quoted in ibid.
203 Ross, *Church and Creed*, p. 205.
204 'Explanatory criticism on the Declaratory Act', *FPM*, i (7) (1896), p. 241.

That while diversity of opinion is recognised in this Church on such points in the Confession as do not enter into the substance of the Reformed Faith therein set forth, the Church retains full authority to determine, in any case which may arise, what points fall within this description, and thus to guard against any abuse of this liberty to the detriment of sound doctrine, or to the injury of her unity and peace.

This clause was described by James Sinclair as 'though last ... probably the most important section of all'.[205] He said that there was reason to believe that here a door was 'opened that may admit heresy without end'.[206] As Ross has pointed out, other Free Church conservatives also reacted violently to this final clause,[207] but Sinclair seemed to see more than most within its phrases. He said that 'heresy and sound doctrine are awarded an equal platform', and that the people who held that diversity of opinion as an ideal

plainly set aside the Bible as an infallible and authoritative standard of belief, and in fact deny that any such standard is to be found ... The Free Church, by this clause in her Act, impugns the perfection and authority of the Bible, and opens a door for Romanism and Rationalism, the two greatest enemies of mankind.[208]

He further argued that nobody had the right to 'cut and carve the Faith', claiming that it was the duty of the Church to profess 'the whole revealed will of God'.[209] He saw this clause as permissive in the extreme, permitting doubts as to the infallibility of the Bible, the divinity of Christ, the divine decrees, particular atonement and total depravity; evolution too, said Sinclair, was covered by this clause. 'This section,' he said,

in fact shelters all the errors that up till now have crept into the Free Church. How many more will find shelter under the ample folds of this Act we cannot say, but provision is made for just as many as the Church cares to accept. If she acts in the future as she has done in the past ... we tremble for the terrible effects of such conduct upon the rising generation. They will get an inheritance of evil more extensive and soul-destroying in its influence than any generation in the past.[210]

As far as can be ascertained, Sinclair never said, as one anti-Declaratory Act speaker was alleged to have claimed: 'there is a street in hell which is paved ... with the skulls of those who have signed the Declaratory Act'.[211]

205 Ibid., i (8) (1896), p. 281.
206 Ibid.
207 Ross, *Church and Creed*, p. 205.
208 'Explanatory criticism on the Declaratory Act', *FPM*, i (8) (1896), p. 282.
209 Ibid., p. 284.
210 Ibid., p. 285.
211 Macdonald, *Social and Religious Life*, p. 221. It should be borne in mind that this is the account of an extremely prejudiced witness; Macdonald's book bristles with personal hostility to the Second Disruption.

But the arguments just cited show that there was no doubt in the Free Presbyterians' minds that the Act was one which they believed would bear fruit more terrible than had ever been seen before. They saw it as being literally 'soul-destroying'; an Act which would condemn future generations to eternal damnation. The stakes could not have been any higher.

The final criticism of the Act from Sinclair's pen was that in the words 'the Church retains full authority to determine ... what points fall within' the substance of the Faith, the Church was taking to herself improper powers. It was seen as being tainted with Roman Catholicism; in Sinclair's words: 'the section [is] essentially Popish in its character'.[212] Given the stance of conservative Free Churchmen on Roman Catholicism, this was a serious charge indeed. There was almost a sense of glee in Sinclair's writing when he declared:

> the Free Church claims full authority to determine the substance of the Faith. It plants itself thereby on the same pedestal of supremacy with the Pope of Rome over the Word of God. The Church or the framers of the Act may attempt to deny this, but no denial can make void what is so manifestly the truth.[213]

The terms being used in the debate were about as serious and derogatory as a nineteenth-century Free Churchman could muster. It was far from being a gentle academic disagreement. Sinclair's last word continued the tone, and made it clear that the Second Disruption, in some form anyway, was inevitable:

> The creed of the Church is practically at the feet of a backsliding majority. The original standards are divested of all authority or power. No one knows where such a church may drift. She will probably land on the rocks of Romanism or Atheism, or both.[214]

Four years' later, an editorial in the *Free Presbyterian Magazine* summed up their stance, in devastating terms:

> In 1892 the Free Church passed a Declaratory Act, which tells us what 'the Church holds' on very important points. According to this Act, 'the Church holds' Arminian views about the love of God, the Atonement and the work of the Holy Spirit, Pelagian views about our relation to Adam and state by nature, Voluntary views about the Establishment principle, and Popish views about the authority of the Church.[215]

---

212 'Explanatory criticism on the Declaratory Act', *FPM*, i (8) (1896), p. 286.
213 Ibid.
214 Ibid., p. 287.
215 'The Free Church anti-Unionists: a criticism of some of their views', *FPM*, v (6) (1900), pp. 201–2.

The issue which must now be examined is why, despite agreeing with almost all that has just been quoted, so many conservatives chose not to join the Second Disruption.

The Split in the Conservative Ranks

James Sinclair and the Free Presbyterians were not alone in their criticism of the Act. Virtually all conservatives in the Free Church were outraged by the passing of an Act which contained, in their opinion, 'errors of Arminianism, Pelagianism, Voluntaryism, and Romanism'.[216] Neil Cameron called it 'this pernicious Act',[217] and John R. Mackay, another Free Church student who left the Church over the Act, said: 'I have never shaken in my opinion that the Act was meant to promote doctrines which were specially used by the Kingdom of darkness in promoting that Kingdom in our day.'[218] Murdo Macaskill called it 'a most defective piece of legislation, and most dangerous',[219] while James Scott said that it 'not only minimised and even caricatured several prime doctrines of the Confession, but also altered some of them.'[220] Sir William Mackinnon described it in 1892 as 'the cunningly devised Declaratory Act ... which, in my opinion, is calculated to undermine and destroy the principles and constitution of our church',[221] while at the same Glasgow meeting John McNeilage said that the Confession was 'perverted and undermined' by the Declaratory Act.[222]

It seemed, then, that the conservatives within the Free Church were united in their opposition to the Act. The ministers and students had argued their case up and down the country, and they were not going to give up merely because a battle had been lost. Pamphlets were written, and a considerable amount of money was spent.[223] Laymen too had their opinions; as Donald Munro wrote to John Macleod:

> I had a long 'chat' with our friend ... John MacKenzie, as he was breaking stones at the road side. His plan was to send some of the leading ministers through all the Highlands, bringing before the people the perils of the Dec[laratory] Act and then to get every one, in every parish, above 18 years of age, who was determined not to

---

[216] 'Introductory', p. 4.

[217] Cameron, 'Report of meeting held at Kilmallie Free Church' (1893).

[218] J. R. Mackay to John Macleod, 23 Feb. 1893, *John Macleod Collection*, 3e.

[219] *PDGAFCS*, 1892, p. 161.

[220] Ibid., p. 164.

[221] *Free Church Declaratory Act: A Criticism and Protest*, p. 2.

[222] Ibid., p. 28.

[223] Archibald MacNeilage was the Honourary Secretary of the 'Glasgow Committee of Ministers and Office-bearers Opposed to the Free Church Declaratory Act'. This committee spent between £200 and £300 on publishing literature opposed to the Declaratory Act: *PDGAFCS*, 1894, p. 87. This included such pamphlets as the *Free Church Declaratory Act ... Report of discussions in the Free Presbytery of Lockerbie*, which has been cited above.

pay a penny to [the] sustentation fund, except where the ministers proved themselves to be thoroughly opposed to the Act.[224]

Certainly in 1892, it seemed that the conservatives were presenting a united front, and that opposition was just about as thorough as it was possible to be. Murdo Macaskill of Dingwall, an indefatigable figure in the battle at this time, said this of the debate over the Declaratory Act:

> It is one of the most important questions which has ever come before this Free Church of ours. It is one of the most important questions which has ever come before Scotland. I believe, since the days of the Reformation, there has been no question at all equal in importance to the questions that are now being agitated within this Free Church.[225]

He acknowledged that the issues of the Disruption of 1843 had been fundamental ones, and that the sacrifices of the time had been great. But, he said, the questions raised by the Declaratory Act were still more fundamental: 'The questions today are these:– Bible or no Bible. Atonement or no Atonement. Salvation for a perishing world on the basis of the finished work of Christ, or Salvation by Works.'[226] These were not the words of men who could be expected easily to find common ground with the architects of the Declaratory Act. These were the words of men preparing for battle. 'We are,' warned Macaskill grimly, 'only getting our weapons in order.'[227]

Archibald Bannatyne, at the same Oban meeting, declared that the Declaratory Act would destroy the old system of doctrine as taught in Scotland in the past 'as surely as the tree withers to its outmost branch and twig from whose base the circling bark has been stripped'.[228] His stance was an uncompromising assault on the doctrines which he believed the Declaratory Act to teach, and when he went so far as to accuse its framers of promulgating, in the clause on the salvation of infants, a 'doctrine [which] does not run far off from an encouragement to infanticide', his audience responded with applause.[229] Allan MacKenzie, another of the Free Church divinity students who left over the Declaratory Act, delivered an impassioned and effective speech that night in Oban. 'The fight,' he said, 'was really around the Bible, not around the Confession. And if the Confession was built around the Word of God surely it was worth fighting for.'[230] Amid what the report of the meeting described as 'sensation', with women weeping and strong men sobbing, MacKenzie ringingly declared that

224 Donald Munro to John Macleod, 9 Jun. 1893, *John Macleod Collection*, 1c.
225 *Free Church Declaratory Act of 1891. Report of Speeches: Delivered at a Public Meeting ... Oban ... 13th April, 1892*, p. 7.
226 Ibid.
227 Ibid., p. 11.
228 Ibid., p. 12.
229 Ibid., p. 14.
230 Ibid., p. 21.

they would never, God giving them grace to resist, sign such a document as the Declaratory Act. Their consciences would not let them. As they had to stand before the bar of God's Judgement, and as they hoped to see Christ, they could not go on to be ministers of the Free Church to proclaim the extraordinary doctrines of this Declaratory Act ... Are you prepared to sacrifice us?[231]

And Kenneth Moody-Stuart said grimly of the Act in a popular pamphlet: 'The Convener stated that this Act was an expression of the living faith of the Church, but it would have been more correct to call it an indication of her dying faith.'[232]

Crucially, however, between May 1892 and May 1893 the conservative opponents of the Declaratory Act split among themselves. Men who at one stage shared platforms and seconded each other's motions came to disagree over what concrete action was to be taken. Men like William Balfour and Murdo Macaskill, who seemed certain to leave in May 1893 if the Act were not rescinded, chose not to do so.

Initially convinced that all the conservatives would leave the Free Church over the Act in May 1893, Neil Cameron became increasingly depressed as the intervening year passed. He wrote mournfully to his friend and confidant John Macleod in February of 1893:

It is greatly to be feared that none of the ministers intend to make a stand upon the old ways and principles at first Assembly. 'Help Lord, because the godly man doth daily fade away.' May the everlasting arms of the God of Joshua be underneath you and around you continually.[233]

Tempted though he was with atheism, he still had the faith to pray on behalf of his friend. He believed that his Lord would be constant, but doubted almost everyone else. Allan MacKenzie was almost as despondent the same month, writing as he did to John Macleod:

I am told that the ministry are dead against a disruption save should the Formula be changed. Macfarlane, Kilmallie, and Dr Balfour are the only two known to be for a disruption at all. Bannatyne Rothesay of course would join. The rest are all against a disruption. Will the two mentioned act? ... Evidently dark times are at hand. I do not expect the testimony of the past to be renewed.[234]

---

[231] Ibid.

[232] K. Moody-Stuart, *Letter to a Friend Regarding the Free Church Declaratory Act* (Moffat, 1892), p. 15.

[233] Neil Cameron to John Macleod, 13 Feb. 1893, *John Macleod Collection*, 2b. The same letter contained the plea: 'My beloved John don't forget me ... as I am sorely tried with Atheism and thick darkness of mind.'

[234] Allan MacKenzie to John Macleod, 1 Feb. 1893, *John Macleod Collection*, 6d.

In Cameron's eyes, though, even Donald Macfarlane, the eventual father of the Free Presbyterian Church, was under suspicion:

I am very much afraid that the ministers will do nothing at the coming Assembly. It is more than probable (I understand) that Mr Macfarlane will accept the call to Raasay. If he will he cannot consistently break off at the Assembly according to his public declaration.[235]

His fellow student Neil McIntyre had exactly the same worries. He wrote this to John Macleod on 5 April 1893:

I have no doubt but that you heard about McFarlane [*sic*]. I was very sorry when I heard it, for if he intends to act on his statements it will put him in a very delicate position and I cannot see how he can take any public action by the step he has taken.[236]

The month before the Assembly of 1893, the fact that Macfarlane had moved to Raasay and been inducted there – in Cameron's view, under the Declaratory Act – was causing Cameron great worries. He wrote in April 1893:

I cannot understand Mr Macfarlane for he said to me distinctly that he intended to stand at the Assembly and to declare himself and those who might follow him the F[ree] Ch[urch]. How can he do so after signing the Formula under the present jurisdiction I cannot conceive.[237]

By 9 May, the very eve of the Assembly, Cameron was getting very anxious, and wrote a very human letter to his friend. 'My Dear John,' wrote Cameron,

The Assembly time is nearly upon us. What is to take place is getting darker. There is a painful silence on the part of those who were expected to do something, but that may not be the worst sign. I am getting very doubtful in my own mind about Mr Macfarlane. He must feel that it changed his relation to the Act his having taken induction under it. The Lord alone can lead his poor church out of this perplexity.

As you may have such little time at your disposal you might be framing something in the shape of such a statement as you would like to see issued from our party: for I am very much afraid it will come to that ...

Rev. Mr Geddes is not so promising now, and we are getting suspicious that after all he will do nothing.

235 Cameron to Macleod, 24 Feb. 1893, *John Macleod Collection*, 2c.
236 Neil MacIntyre to John Macleod, 5 Apr. 1893, *John Macleod Collection*, 8b.
237 Cameron to Macleod, 7 Apr. 1893, *John Macleod Collection*, 2d.

The people in the gaelic congregations are pretty much awake to the danger of truth in the land, but I am afraid the elders are not for the most part so zealous as the people are; though of course there are some of the people who care nothing about it. So far as can be understood there will be a most serious breaking up in our congregation.[238]

With that Cameron signed off, clearly a deeply troubled man.

He was not the only one to have worries of this kind, as has been seen. The role of their friend and fellow student John R. Mackay seemed to cause these men a great deal of heart-searching in the troubled period of 'phoney war' before the Second Disruption of May 1893. Mackay had come to the view that as long as the Questions and Formula remained unchanged, they were not justified in leaving the Free Church. As he wrote in February 1893:

I did think that there was so much to be said for the opinion that the Act was not just now in the constitution of the Free Church, that I found the minority ministers as a body manfully taking up that attitude and at the same time making it most plain that if the Questions and formula were interfered with to suit the Act they were at once two Churches. I should at least hope that it was my duty still to seek to abide by them ... [F]or the minority to say publicly that because every Presbytery in the church is yet bound to administer the question 'Do you promise to maintain etc. the whole doctrine etc.' to every candidate for the ministry, therefore they held the constitution of the Church yet intact, I would consider an honourable proceeding, inasmuch as of course I should mean them to add that once that state of things was changed they were at once two Churches.[239]

Mackay was during this time assailed by poor health which, combined with depression, made him fear that, in his own words, 'a malady had taken hold of me which would make my days few indeed'.[240] More than that, though, he felt the pain of criticism from old friends. As he wrote to Macleod:

when I was at home I had your most kind and soothing letter; and soothing truly it was and I had need of it; for I feel more Neil Cameron's and others' standing in suspicion of me than I would a stab from most other men.[241]

and he concluded the same letter with the remark that 'notwithstanding

---

[238] Cameron to Macleod, 9 May 1893, *John Macleod Collection*, 2c.
[239] J. R. Mackay to John Macleod, 23 Feb. 1893, *John Macleod Collection*, 3c.
[240] Ibid.
[241] Ibid.

my regard for many others of the students, of you only did I feel as though you were a Jonathan towards me'.[242]

George MacKay, another of the students, referred to J. R. Mackay's scheme as going through him 'like an arrow',[243] while Allan MacKenzie, who had moved strong men to tears with his denunciation of the Act and his own unwillingness to stay in a Church which had adopted it, said of Mackay's position: 'I cannot understand how he managed to drift into mid-channel.'[244] Cameron, perhaps, felt it most of all:

> Mr J. R. MacKay's new scheme has caused me so much trouble that it left me no heart to do anything. The last letter he wrote me upon the subject grieved me very much owing to the manner in which he seems to have taken my criticism of his scheme ... I do earnestly hope and pray that we have heard the last of it. If Mr MacKay goes of [sic] the rails we must all feel it keenly.[245]

Later in the month he confessed that he was 'quite astonished' at J. R. MacKay,[246] and even on the eve of the Assembly was still unsure:

> I do not fully understand what JR intends to do, though we spent the best of a week together. I asked him, should none of the ministers stand, would he join us and he left me without answering the question. I feel exceedingly for poor dear John, for he is very much perplexed over this matter, but the Lord, in His good time, will make his way straight before him.[247]

As letters of men who have been portrayed as standing shoulder to shoulder, under the leadership of Donald Macfarlane, this correspondence makes interesting reading.

Cameron's biographer, his fellow student Donald Beaton, wrote in 1932 that Cameron had been a great help to Donald Macfarlane in the crisis of 1893 and that 'his fearless disposition, his earnest concern for God's truth, and his strong attachment to the Scriptures and the doctrines of the Confession of Faith, made him a tower of strength'.[248] What these letters indicate with rare clarity is that in the period between the Declaratory Act being accepted by the Free Church and the Second Disruption taking place, Cameron and the other students were besieged by worries, doubts and fears about their allies, their friends and even their God. Cameron, for example, was far from being the 'fearless' figure of Free Presbyterian hagiology. He was, in fact, more in need of a 'tower of strength' than he was one himself. Ironically, the man to whom

242 Ibid.
243 George MacKay to John Macleod, 23 Jan. 1893, *John Macleod Collection*, 7c.
244 Allan MacKenzie to John Macleod, 24 Jan. 1893, *John Macleod Collection*, 6c.
245 Neil Cameron to John Macleod, 13 Feb. 1893, *John Macleod Collection*, 2b.
246 Cameron to Macleod, 24 Feb. 1893, *John Macleod Collection*, 2c.
247 Cameron to Macleod, 9 May 1893, *John Macleod Collection*, 2e.
248 Beaton, *Neil Cameron*, p. 52.

he turned when he had these serious doubts over the intentions of Donald Macfarlane, was John Macleod – a brilliant student who joined the Free Presbyterians in 1893 but who left them soon after to join the Free Church (continuing), and who was never really forgiven for this betrayal. Macleod listened to the complaints and worries of most of the students and, from these letters at any rate, seems to have been an integral figure in the Second Disruption. Given his eventual place of honour in the Free Church (as Principal of the Free Church College, Edinburgh), it is perhaps understandable that his role has not been stressed enough before; clearly, though, he was a steady linchpin while others wavered, and his function in helping the Second Disruption to succeed should not be forgotten.[249]

Macleod, for all his academic brilliance, was just a student at the time; Macfarlane, though respected in the Highlands, was not a national figure. What the Free Presbyterians needed was for one of the major conservative leaders to have come out in 1893. That would have transformed the whole nature of the Second Disruption. For the role of individual ministers was absolutely critical in the numerical scale of the Second Disruption; had men like Gustavus Aird, Creich, Murdo Mackenzie, Inverness, or John Noble, Lairg, 'come out', the Free Presbyterian movement would undoubtedly have been much larger. As the student Alexander Stewart wrote in June 1893:

> Sutherlandshire is very dead to the issues at stake: but the fault is almost entirely with the ministers. I am convinced that in the parish of Lairg, for instance, if Mr Noble were to join the Separatists, not half a dozen would remain behind.[250]

His fellow student Donald Munro analysed the situation in almost exactly the same way in a letter one month later:

> I don't know in the world what the 'Con' [Constitutionalist] ministers mean. The Sutherland 'men', I'm glad to say, are for separation – at least nearly all save the Voluntary elders. Geo[rge] MacDonald, Lairg, is at heart a seceder, but he is so much governed by his minister that he does not openly profess to be a Macfarlanite. If Mr Noble were to come out he w[oul]d not leave many, if any, of

---

[249] John Macleod's summary of the Free Presbyterian position as opposed to the Declaratory Act Free Church, which appeared in the *Free Presbyterian Magazine* in 1901 in Gaelic, was reprinted at length in a chapter of the *History of the Free Presbyterian Church of Scotland* written over 30 years later by his old friend Donald Beaton. The passage was accompanied by a footnote attributing it to Macleod, who, it was acknowledged, had by then changed both his views and his Church. It was stressed that it was not being printed 'to gain a controversial advantage' but simply because of the clarity and simplicity with which Macleod had stated what was still the Free Presbyterian position. The matter was handled with a gentleness which, perhaps, indicated that old friendships had not been entirely forgotten in the sometimes-bitter conflict between the Free Presbyterians and the Free Church.

[250] Alexander Stewart to John Macleod, 20 Jun. 1893, *John Macleod Collection*, 5a.

his congregation, but seeing Dr Aird is for staying in, I don't think Mr Noble will go out.[251]

In the event, the conservatives divided, and divided bitterly. 'The Cons,' wrote Allan MacKenzie bitterly in February 1893, 'hate us more than the Act itself.'[252]

This was echoed by several of the other earliest members of the fledgling denomination. Cameron was devastated by what he saw as the betrayal of the cause by former friends:

> Things are now more like fighting than ever they were since the beginning of the Church controversy but what grieves us very much is that friends are fighting against us and have made some truce with the common enemy in order to prove that we are wrong ... It grieves me very much that these men are so weak and that they are doing their utmost now to carry out Dr Rainy's plans. 'Tell it not in Gath and declare it not in the streets of Askilon!' Every calumny is brought against us that can be invented and every base motive. The judge of all the earth shall do justice.[253]

Donald Beaton wrote in his biography of Donald Macfarlane:

> The effort to check the [Free Presbyterian] movement was not confined to the out-and-out advocates of the new order of things, for among some of the most bitter opponents to the Free Presbyterian movement were former friends ... There are no opponents so envenomed and fierce in their attacks as those who were at one time active and strong supporters.[254]

Cameron wrote to John Macleod:

> It grieves my very soul that our dearest friends have become our bitterest enemies. Mr MacCaskill [*sic*], Onich, I understand, is entirely against our position and does not intend to do anything. He grieves me more than all the rest ... [but] Peace of Conscience and Peace with God is of more value than the good-will of all the men of this world and I must say as Luther did 'I cannot otherwise.' Should He give grace I feel that though I were to die I could not take any other course in this controversy.[255]

Murdo Macaskill of Dingwall had attended the same anti-Declaratory Act meetings as those who joined the Free Presbyterians and, like Macaskill of Onich, he heard Neil Cameron declare in April 1892 that there were those who would leave the Church if the Declaratory Act was

251 Donald Munro to John Macleod, 10 Jul. 1893, *John Macleod Collection*, 1f.
252 Alan MacKenzie to John Macleod, 1 Feb. 1893, *John Macleod Collection*, 6d.
253 Neil Cameron to John Macleod, 22 Jun. 1893, *John Macleod Collection*, 2f.
254 Beaton, *Donald Macfarlane*, p. 31.
255 Neil Cameron to John Macleod, 22 Jun. 1893, *John Macleod Collection*, 2f.

passed by the Free Church.[256] Yet he became what Beaton called 'one of the chief critics of the new movement'. He was quoted as saying that the Free Presbyterian movement was 'the most mischievous movement of modern times and calculated only to do most serious harm to the cause of truth and godliness in our beloved Highlands'.[257] J. R. Mackay felt that the misrepresentation he received in the press was so bad that he wrote to his parents to clarify matters in July 1893. 'My dear father and mother,' wrote Mackay,

> There are so many accounts in the papers about my doings and in some of them given by enemies so that they are altogether unfair that I am afraid you may be much troubled about me. Don't be so at all. I was never calmer all the days of my life.[258]

Given the depth of feeling involved, perhaps such eventualities were inevitable.

What the difference came down to, ultimately, was how far the Declaratory Act was believed to alter the constitution of the Free Church. To men like Murdo Macaskill of Dingwall or Murdo Mackenzie of Inverness, the Act came to be what they considered a 'dead letter'. They accepted that, in the words of an 1894 Assembly Act, 'the statements of doctrine contained in the said [Declaratory] Act are not thereby imposed upon any of the Church's office-bearers as part of the Standards of the Church'.[259] They held to what was J. R. Mackay's position at one stage, as outlined above, that as long as the Questions and Formula remained unchanged, so too did the constitution. As Dugald Matheson of Tarbat put it:

> I have always held that this Act, with all that is objectionable about it, is not a ground for leaving the Free Church; but, were it binding upon any of the church's office-bearers, or imposed upon him as a part of the Standards of the Church, I could then see cause to leave a Church asking me to put myself under a yoke I was not willing to endure. But matters have not come to such a pass in our Church.[260]

Rainy argued at the 1894 Assembly, as he had done in 1892 and 1893, that 'the Declaratory Act imposed no personal belief in the line of its doctrinal statements on any individual. It was a relieving Act.'[261] and prior to the Assembly he had written: 'The object in view was to relieve difficulties and scruples, so far as that could be done, but not to lay a

---

256 This was at the meeting in Oban, on 13 April 1892.
257 Quoted in Beaton, *History of the Free Presbyterian Church*, p. 117, note.
258 J. R. Mackay to his parents, 11 Jul. 1893. *John Macleod Collection*, 3f.
259 'Act anent Declaratory Act 1892 on Confession of Faith (No. 5 of Class II.)', *AGAFC*, 1894, p. 6.
260 *PDGAFCS*, 1894, p. 85.
261 *PDGAFCS*, 1894, p. 91; *PDGAFCS*, 1893, pp. 166–7; *PDGAFCS*, 1892, p. 170.

new burden on anyone.'[262] Rainy appeared to be both genuinely surprised by the reaction to the Act and not a little irritated; he said at the close of the somewhat ill-tempered debate in the 1894 Assembly:

> it was with a sense of discouragement, and almost of humiliation, that he found himself in broad daylight at this time of day engaged in these discussions in the manner in which they were engaged upon them ... and when he considered the great and grave questions which were rising all over the world ... it was with a sense of humiliation that he felt they were spending so much time on these pin-points of difference in the way of understanding Scripture doctrine. Let there be a way of right and a way of wrong in regard to them, but surely the right and the wrong lay within so narrow a compass that they might really bear with one another in a very different manner to that in which they had been doing.[263]

As Dods had done some years before, Rainy seemed to be asking himself 'whether the game was worth the candle'.[264]

Crucially, men like William Balfour and Murdo Macaskill came to accept the argument that the Declaratory Act did not tie them to any particular doctrine or interpretation of a doctrine. It seems to have been a remarkable about-face on their part. Macaskill had said in Oban in the hearing of Donald Macfarlane, Neil Cameron, Neil McIntyre, Alex MacRae and George MacKay, that he could not understand how men whom he respected (on the Confession of Faith Committee) 'could ever have accepted such a production as this Act'. He had told Robert Rainy that night that if the Act became law, Rainy would have to 'take the responsibility of laying the first stroke upon the demolition of the Free Church of Scotland'.[265] As the letters quoted above show, Balfour was one minister whom the young conservative students were confident would leave the Church in the event of the Declaratory Act remaining on the Church statute books. In February 1892, he had called the Act a 'Jesuitical Act', adding:

> It was difficult to understand how it could proceed from a body of office-bearers in the Free Church, who have declared the Westminster Confession of Faith 'to be the confession of their faith'. It was so palpably inconsistent with it, that he had no hesitation in saying the Free Church of Scotland would require to be sought for elsewhere than within the body which adopted this Act.[266]

Macaskill and Balfour consulted with Neil Cameron prior to May 1893,

262 Rainy, *Explanatory Notes on the Declaratory Act*, p. 2.
263 *PDGAFCS*, 1894, p. 91.
264 Dods, 'Revision of the Westminster Confession'.
265 *Free Church Declaratory Act of 1891. Report of Speeches: Delivered at a Public Meeting ... Oban ... 13th April, 1892*, pp. 10–11.
266 *Free Church Declaratory Act: A Criticism and Protest*, p. 6.

and Cameron was said to have had the 'greatest respect' for William Balfour.[267] Yet by 1893 they had come to the view that the Free Church of Scotland was, after all, still to be found within the body that had overwhelmingly adopted the 'Jesuitical Act'. No longer was it an issue to fight over; no longer was it a case of 'bible or no bible'. It was certainly not an issue over which they were going to risk losing Church, manse and stipend.

For Donald Macfarlane on the other hand that was precisely what it was. He may not have been a highly communicative leader between 1892 and 1893, and his position may have remained in doubt right up to the final days before the Assembly; yet on 25 May 1893, he advanced to the table of the Assembly and read the protest by which he severed his connection with the Free Church.[268] On 28 July, in the company of Donald Macdonald, minister of Sheildaig, and Alexander Macfarlane, schoolmaster of Raasay, he formed the 'Free Church Presbytery of Scotland' and the Free Presbyterian Church was born.[269] What he did on that May day in 1893 took courage, and it is rightly remembered as a formative moment in Free Presbyterian history. In a letter of 1894, Allan MacKenzie denounced those who accused the Free Presbyterian movement of 'moral cowardice':

> there is no moral cowardice in a man's conduct when he goes to the table of Assembly, and without a single ministerial friend, submits a protest, in which he declares before hundreds of enemies that he cannot any longer submit to their jurisdiction, since they have departed from the truth of God. There is no moral cowardice in a man's conduct when he says that he is to do a certain act, and then does it, without turning his back on the path of duty ... For his pains he has been eased of his church and his home, and driven miles apart from his congregation to get shelter for himself and his family from rain and storm, and some would relieve him of his reputation if they could.[270]

The Second Disruption had taken place. Already, it seemed, the accompanying martyrology was being created.

[267] Beaton, *Neil Cameron*, p. 52.
[268] *PDGAFCS*, 1893, p. 183.
[269] Records of the Free Church Presbytery of Scotland (27 Jul. 1893–31 Aug. 1894), pp. 1–4.
[270] Allan MacKenzie, letter of Jun. 1894, Private Collection.

CHAPTER FIVE

Conclusion

The rest of the story can be very briefly told. Donald Macfarlane and Donald Macdonald were followed by some dozen students and by thousands of the Free Church's most loyal members and adherents throughout Scotland. Whatever might be said about the importance of leadership, the fact is that the Second Disruption was a movement of the people, some of whom acted before they even knew what Donald Macfarlane had done.[1] There was much bitterness and ill feeling in the Highlands over the Second Disruption, with precious little brotherly love on view; the Rev. Angus Galbraith of Lochalsh asserted in 1896 that the Declaratory Act had produced 'family divisions, congregations divided, friends alienated, and a state of things which was simply deplorable'.[2] One Free Presbyterian's daughter spoke of her father never having forgotten the embittered reaction he and his family received on choosing to follow 'the seceders' in Lochcarron in 1893. Much mud, by no means all metaphorical, was slung in their direction.[3]

Although there were soon congregations in such Lowland places as Greenock, Dumbarton, Glasgow and Edinburgh, the vast bulk of the new denomination's congregations were north of the Highland line. While it is difficult to provide certain statistical evidence, it is very probable that the majority of those in the 'Lowland' congregations would have been immigrant Highlanders; the Greenock congregation, for example, emerged out of the Free Gaelic congregation. The Free Presbyterians were, almost exclusively, a Highland denomination. It is

---

[1] One notable example was the Greenock elder John Urquart, who made his decision to leave the Free Church while quite unaware that any others had made the same decision. As Lachlan MacLeod has recently observed: 'it was not a case of following Mr Macfarlane': L. MacLeod, 'Formation of the Greenock Free Presbyterian Congregation', *FPM*, xcviii (9) (1993), p. 265. Urquart and some friends had resolved never to worship in the Free Church again and, according to the writer of his obituary, 'great was the joy of John Urquart and the rest of the Lord's people in this town, who separated for ever from the Declaratory Act Free Church, when they became acquainted with the fact that the late Rev. Donald Macfarlane had also severed connection with that Church': 'Late Mr John Urquart, Elder, Greenock', pp. 264–5.

[2] *PDGAFCS*, 1896, p. 199. In the same debate, the Rev. Murdo MacQueen of Kiltearn said that it was alleged that members of the same family would not speak to one another on account of the Second Disruption and commented: 'It was said of old, "Behold these Christians, how they love one another." Alas! alas! that at the end of the nineteenth century they should expose themselves to the taunt of the enemy, who might say now, "Behold these Christians, how they hate one another!"': ibid., p. 198.

[3] Interview with Mrs Jessie MacLeod (nee MacRae), of Lochcarron, 20 Dec. 1992.

very difficult to speculate on the numbers involved, and these clearly varied very much from place to place. Estimates on the size of the Secession varied hugely, and the Free Presbyterians' own official history never gave a figure, preferring to refer to 'the little band who faced a hostile world'.[4] Donald Macfarlane, however, claimed that the number was 'about 20,000' and that they had 'amongst that 20,000 the brightest men of God to be found in the Highlands'.[5] It was not until 1896 that the Free Church managed to produce their own statistics on the Second Disruption and this delay is perhaps itself an indication of the problems of collecting reliable figures in such circumstances. Rainy told the Free Church General Assembly of that year that Presbyteries had been asked to provide numbers of those who had left as a result of the Second Disruption and, he said, 'were especially asked not to underrate the amount of the Secession'.[6] The total number, according to these official Assembly returns, was 6,756 elders, deacons, communicants and adherents over the age of eighteen; this was considerably less than many estimates but is almost impossible to evaluate.[7]

There remains the question of why a greater number of the Highlanders did not leave. The prejudice that was souring the relationship between north and south surely affected all Highland Free Church people, and not just those who left in 1893. The truth is that while the Highland–Lowland hostility contributed to the eventual rending of the Free Church, it was not in itself enough to provoke a schism. The same can be said of revision of the Westminster Confession; relaxation in the terms of subscription to creeds and confessions was taking place in Protestant Churches all over the world, and yet there does not seem to have been a response anywhere else to equal the Second Disruption. And the changes detailed in Chapter 1 could be said to affect people in many places; it would be parochial in the extreme to say that the Scots had an experience in the nineteenth century which was not felt anywhere else. Moreover, biblical criticism was also an international movement; Europe and North America contained scholars saying much the same as Marcus Dods, A. B. Davidson and A. B. Bruce. Indeed, there were many going a great deal further, and evolution, for example, was for many not the 'method God chose for creation' but the very proof that God was dead. And yet in the late 1890s, there does not seem to be a movement comparable to the Second Disruption. The Second Disruption was exceptional.

The reasons for this are certainly open to debate, but at least one thing seems clear. It would seem fair to say that there was probably no

[4] Beaton, *History of the Free Presbyterian Church*, p. 118.

[5] Macfarlane, in 'Secessionist conference at Inverness: the progress of the movement', Free Presbyterian Church Newspaper Cuttings (1986 version), p. 3.

[6] *PDGAFCS*, 1896, p. 91.

[7] Ibid., p. 91. A recent writer gave the number as being 17,000: J. Macleod, *Highlanders: A History of the Gaels* (London, 1996), p. 282.

denomination throughout the world in which the matters discussed in this book coalesced so dramatically as in the Free Church in the nineteenth century. The crucial point is that the background of social and economic flux, the perceived assault on the Scriptures from criticism and science, the movement to revise the Westminster Confession and the underlying hostility between two regions were all present in the Free Church at this time. One alone could not produce schism; two or even three in harness were not able to split the Free Church; but when the four developments converged, the result was dramatic. If the Second Disruption was exceptional, so too was the combination of factors that made it happen.

It is even possible to argue that in some ways a schism in the Free Church was inevitable. It has been demonstrated that it was a Church which was divided between the rural north and the urban south; between a region at the periphery of Scottish affairs and one which was at the very centre; between a Gaelic-speaking population and one which spoke English; between people who could be called peasantry and those who were increasingly middle class and bourgeois; between the relatively uneducated and the university-educated intelligentsia; between rich and poor; and, crucially, between the 'old paths' and the 'new theology'. Underlying all this was the fact that the later nineteenth century was a time of unprecedented social dislocation and great uncertainty, particularly for the rural peasantry in the Highlands; this was, as has been seen, coupled with revolutionary developments in academic and intellectual life which cast great doubt on many old certainties and which placed the Bible in the 'crucible of criticism'. The whole situation was aggravated enormously by the intensity given to the divide by the influence of contemporary theories of race. When a constitutional issue emerged to formalise the divide (the Declaratory Act), the result was the Second Disruption.

In some senses explaining the Second Disruption is thus quite straightforward; given what has just been said and the high level of commitment by Highland conservatives both to an inspired and inerrant Bible and an unqualified Westminster Confession, a separation between the Highland conservatives and the Lowland liberals seems to have been almost inescapable. The question that remains, however, is why all, or even most, of the Highland conservatives did not secede in 1893. It would seem fair to say that most of the factors analysed in this book applied equally to all the Highland conservatives, and yet the majority of them chose, despite their previous protestations, to remain in the Free Church. Most remained in until 1900, and many even went into the United Free Church at that time. Away from the petty name-calling of bitter interdenominational rivalries, there is no simple answer; but it has to be remembered that for people who believed that schism was a sin, and that the Free Church was a true Church of Christ which had been richly blessed, secession was not a step to be taken lightly. The sacrifices of the Disruption of 1843 were still well remembered. It took a remarkable combination of events to provoke secession from a group of people for whom loyalty to the Free Church was one of life's highest priorities.

This goes a long way to explain why the secession was not universally supported, even in the Highlands. One hundred years on, when church affairs seldom generate the passion which they did then, it is easy to forget the magnitude of what the Free Presbyterians did. The Free Church was a denomination that was recognised throughout the Protestant world as an orthodox and conservative Church. It was considered to be the Church of the Covenanters, of the Reformers and of the Disruption heroes. Above all it was believed to be a Church which had enjoyed an abundant divine blessing. All this was particularly true in the Highlands of Scotland where the Free Church was generally the Church of the people – where the Church of Scotland was, in many places, the 'Invisible Church'. The Second Disruption challenged this comfortable consensus, setting up an alternative Church which in places devastated Free Church membership and which throughout the Highlands was an ever-present reminder that the bride of Christ, His Church, was divided. The Free Presbyterians' step was bitterly lamented by those who disagreed with them, and it was a step that nobody could take lightly. In the year of the Free Church's Jubilee, fifty years after the Disruption of 1843, the Second Disruption changed forever the Free Church of 1843. Yet with delegates present from all over the Protestant world carrying messages of congratulation to the Free Church on her Jubilee, it is perhaps understandable that more did not leave. The mood of the 1893 Assembly was described by an official source as being one of 'undisguised enthusiasm', and given the sense of achievement felt by the Church, dissension and disruption was certain to be unpopular.[8]

Donald Macfarlane and Donald Macdonald both lost their churches and their manses. They were vilified in the press and at the Free Church General Assembly. Those who followed them had a far from easy time of it, worshipping as they did on occasions with, as the Free Presbyterian folklore had it, the snowflakes falling on the leaves of their bibles:

> One of the sufferers from these discreditable proceedings ... was the Rev. D. Macdonald, Shieldaig ... He was an old man at the time, his years having almost reached the allotted three score and ten. Ordained in 1872, he had been the first Free Church minister settled in Shieldaig since the Disruption ... This man had borne the burden and the heat of the day for long years among the solitude of the Ross-shire hills. When he came to Shieldaig there was neither

---

[8] *PDGAFCS*, 1893, p. 1. See also 'Letter from Edinburgh', *British Weekly*, 25 May 1893, p. 73. Congratulations were received from at least 27 other church groupings, and delegates were present from at least 24; the Assembly also received a letter of congratulation from Gladstone: *PDGAFCS*, 1893, pp. 103–5.

church nor manse awaiting him ... For five years he laboured among circumstances of peculiar difficulty, preaching on the hill-side in all kinds of weather, exposed to summer heat and winter cold, within sound of the Atlantic breakers. Sometimes he had to brush the snowflakes off his Bible before he could see his text. And after twenty-one years of faithful service this was his reward; he was turned adrift from church and home once more to face the rigours of an inhospitable climate! ... The minister of Shieldaig had consented to the spoiling of his goods without making any noise or attempting the least resistance.[9]

The step of secession was for them an ultimate step, and from this standpoint it is understandable that more did not follow. As was said at the time, leadership was crucial. When men like Murdo Mackenzie, Murdo Macaskill and Gustavus Aird, who were looked up to as leaders and, more than that, as men of God, came to the decision that the Declaratory Act was not something which justified secession, people were relieved to follow their lead. It is not to denigrate them to say that this was, relatively, the path of least resistance; there are many occasions when such a path has proved to be the right path, and this is not the place to pronounce on the rightness or wrongness of other people's conscience-based decisions. The circumstances detailed in this book combined to produce an extraordinary situation in which the Free Church could have lost the vast majority of its Highland membership; as it happens, the decision of two or three significant figures to stay in the Church and fight the Declaratory Act from within, coupled with an understandable reluctance to face the disagreeable consequences of secession, limited the Second Disruption to moderate proportions. Given the difficulties they faced and the unhappiness engendered by any schism in the Church, the real question is perhaps why so many chose to join the secession and face the unappealing consequences. Both sides acted in the belief that they were doing God's service; they would not be the first, nor have they been the last, to come to disagreement with that end in view.

To explain why the individual conservative leaders who remained in the Free Church chose to do so despite their previous strong words is clearly a complex problem; in many respects it is possible only to speculate. Gustavus Aird, for example, was an eighty-year-old man in 1893, having left the Church of Scotland at the Disruption of 1843 and having ministered in the Free Church in Creich for fully fifty years. He had been a victim of the petty persecution that followed the Disruption, and was in fact one of only thirty-four surviving ministers of the 1843

---

[9] This, one of the most colourful accounts of the treatment meted out to the early Free Presbyterian ministers, can be found in a later piece of Free Church polemic, ironically written by Alexander Stewart, one of the original Free Presbyterians, who joined the Free Church in 1905: Stewart and Cameron, *Free Church of Scotland*, pp. 80–2.

Disruption (out of 474).[10] The year 1893 was therefore his own Jubilee, during which he was presented with money and was honoured with a special service of tribute which 'deeply affected' him.[11] Perhaps it was asking too much for a man at his stage in life to forsake everything and to go out into the wilderness for a second time, especially since he had been chosen for the great honour of being moderator of the Inverness Assembly of 1888.[12] It is also worth noting that he was one of the nine prominent Free Churchmen – described as 'some of the men among us to whom the Church has been accustomed to listen' – to whom the *Free Church of Scotland Monthly* turned in early 1893 for their opinion on how best the Free Church's Jubilee should be marked.[13]

As has been seen, Murdo Macaskill of Dingwall was another figure whose decision to remain in the Free Church was the source of bitter controversy. Macaskill's son John described the Second Disruption as 'this extreme step', but his retrospective defence of his father's position does convey a slight note of embarrassment.[14] Murdo Macaskill argued that the Act was a 'dead letter' and that 'there is no law of my Church that compels me to administer it',[15] but it is hard not to see a certain adjustment of his stance in the period between 1892 and 1893, and those who left were bitterly disappointed at his decision. Remarkably, the same Murdo Macaskill not only stayed in the Free Church but went into the United Free Church in 1900;[16] for the opponents of Union, this 'defection' was described as 'probably the sorest blow of all'.[17] As his son put it, somewhat delicately, when discussing Macaskill's stance on Union: 'He was in the position of a man who, being pitched by the force of circumstances into a new point of view, comes to see things in a different perspective.'[18] The same could be said of James MacDonald, whose protest against the Declaratory Act had been to insert a rider when he signed the Confession of Faith (which the Synod of Sutherland and Caithness ordered to be removed from the records).[19] He not only stayed in the Free Church and joined the United Free Church, but went into the Church of Scotland at the Union of 1929.[20]

---

10 Brown, *Annals of the Disruption*, pp. 492–3, 815–16.
11 Mackenzie, *Murdo Mackenzie*, pp. 47–8; Ewing, *Annals of the Free Church of Scotland*, i, p. 78.
12 Gustavus Aird had been proposed as Moderator by none other than Robert Rainy, who described him as 'a man of tried wisdom and tried fidelity in the work in which he had laboured so long': *PDGAFCS*, 1888, p. 2.
13 'The Jubilee', *Free Church of Scotland Monthly* (Mar. 1893), pp. 55–7. Aird was being placed in distinguished company; among the nine were Alexander Whyte, Thomas Brown, author of the *Annals of the Disruption*, and Robert Rainy.
14 Macaskill, *Highland Pulpit*, p. xix.
15 Quoted in Ross, *Church and Creed*, p. 210.
16 Drummond and Bulloch, *Church in Late Victorian Scotland*, p. 272.
17 G. N. M. Collins, *The Heritage of Our Fathers. The Free Church of Scotland: Her Origin and Testimony* (Edinburgh, 1974), p. 99.
18 Macaskill, *Highland Pulpit*, p. xxv.
19 *PDGAFCS*, 1893, p. 55.
20 Drummond and Bulloch, *Church in Late Victorian Scotland*, p. 272.

The Rev. Murdo Mackenzie of Inverness was another conservative leader who surprised many by remaining in the Free Church. His wife explained his position as follows:

> Needless to say, he was strongly opposed to the Act, and vehemently opposed it in the Church Courts. While the Act gave individual liberty to those who revolted from what they considered the Ultra-Calvinism of the Confession of Faith, it was in no way binding upon those who did not desire any such liberty. So long as the subscription to the Confession remained unaltered, he regarded it as a dead letter ... Having taken up his position, he ignored the Secession movement, and neither then nor at any other time took cognisance of it.[21]

What she failed to mention in this context was that her husband had spent the previous four years overseeing the financing and construction of a new church at the gigantic cost of £11,000. A new manse had been purchased in 1892 and money had been spent on 'making it suitable for a family'. Mackenzie's own personal friends contributed large amounts of money towards the church building, and the new place of worship was due to open on 7 June 1893.[22] Mackenzie would have been an exceptional man to contemplate secession in such a situation. Something similar could be said about Kenneth Moody-Stuart. He had been minister of Moffat for twenty-five years since being ordained there in 1868. His manse had been extended in the early 1880s, and a brand-new church building, complete with stained-glass windows, was opened in 1892.[23]

It would be most unfair to suggest that these and other men were motivated wholly by the factors mentioned here, and it might be uncharitable to reflect that, in the words of the Free Presbyterians' official history, 'no juggler ever excelled them in the way they made out that their present position was in keeping with the whirling words they used in the past'.[24] It is important, however, to provide a context; decisions are frequently made for reasons very different to those which are admitted publicly and some mundane factors might have come into play in the difficult summer of 1893. To explain why the entire 'Highland Host' did not leave in 1893 is problematic, but it seems perhaps to lie in a combination of two factors – one of which is laudable, the other less so. On the one hand it reflected an unwillingness to fragment further the Church of Christ and a tenacious willingness to lick wounds and return to the fray after previous battles had been lost. Most of the Highland conservatives who remained in the Free Church continued to fight what they saw as the damaging liberalisation of

---

21 Mackenzie, *Murdo Mackenzie*, pp. 79–80.
22 Ibid., pp. 35–7.
23 Ewing, *Annals of the Free Church of Scotland*, i, p. 42; ii, p. 334.
24 Beaton, *History of the Free Presbyterian Church*, p. 118.

doctrine and practice over the next seven years until the Union of 1900 finally forced them to take their own step of secession. However, their reluctance to move in 1893 also reflects an unwillingness to face very unpleasant consequences, which would mean turning their backs on a comfortable and prestigious life and going out into the denominational wilderness to face an unknown future. The founding fathers of the Free Presbyterian Church can be accused of many things, but they certainly cannot be accused of taking the easy way out.

For, as has been seen already, the early years of the life of the Free Presbyterian Church were not easy, and there was bitterness throughout the Highlands. The denomination initially survived with just the two ministers, Macdonald in Sheildaig and Macfarlane in Raasay, backed up by the immense amount of work carried out by the students and the 'men', who 'were accustomed to speaking, and in the hour of need they presided at the public means'.[25] John R. Mackay and Allan Mackenzie were the first two ministers licensed by the Free Presbyterian Church; Mackay was ordained and inducted in Gairloch in October 1893, and Mackenzie in Inverness just over a month later. They were followed by Alexander Macrae at Tighnabruaich in 1894, Neil Cameron at St Jude's, Glasgow in January 1896, Roderick Mackenzie at Portree in March 1896, and James S. Sinclair at John Knox's, Glasgow, in April 1896.[26] On 15 June 1896 the single Free Presbyterian presbytery was divided into a northern and a southern presbytery 'for the better management of her affairs ... [and] to embrace the congregations south of the Grampians'.[27] In July the synod of the Free Presbyterian Church met for the first time with Donald Macfarlane as moderator and J. R. Mackay as clerk; in the same year came the first issue of the *Free Presbyterian Magazine*, edited by James Sinclair. Its stated purpose was to maintain the Church's doctrines and

> for bearing testimony against the erroneous tendencies of the times in which we live. We shall endeavour to combine with the magazine, a record of events among our own congregations, and also brief notices of current events of special religious interest taking place in Church and State.[28]

By 1900 the number of congregations in the Free Presbyterian Church had reached a total of seventy-five. Of these seventy-five, seventy of them were north of the Highland line: Lewis and the Uists (four in Lewis, three in North Uist, one in South Uist), Harris (five), Skye (twelve), Ross and Cromarty (sixteen), Caithness (five), Sutherland (eleven), Inverness-shire (seven), Argyllshire (five) and Aberdeenshire

---

[25] Ibid., pp. 123–4.
[26] Records of the Free Church Presbytery of Scotland, p. 17.
[27] 'New Presbytery and Synod', *FPM*, i (3) (1896), p. 120.
[28] 'Introductory', pp. 4–5.

(one). The other five were in Glasgow (two), Greenock, Edinburgh and Dumbarton. The split is 93.3% 'Highland' and 6.7% 'Lowland'.[29] Of these seventy-five congregations, twenty-one of them, some 28%, were without either a minister or missionary by 1900, while ten congregations were served by a minister, twenty-six by a missionary, ten by an elder, three by a probationer, two by a student and three by one of the 'men'.[30] To the ministers already mentioned had been added John Macleod in Lochbroom, Neil McIntyre in Duirinish, Alexander Stewart in Oban and George Mackay in Stornoway, while Allan Mackenzie had departed from the Church in 1897.[31]

There is no single explanation as to why the Free Presbyterian Church survived its difficult birth and early problems. Rainy, for one, believed that the effect of the Second Disruption was to remove what he considered to be 'troublesome' people.[32] He told the annual congregational meeting of the Free Church College, Glasgow, in April 1896 that

> there was no doubt at all that the effect of that movement was to disembarrass a number of the Free Church congregations of impracticable elements – those elements which from conscientious conviction led men to set themselves against everything like the active and vigorous developments of Christian life in modern times.[33]

And yet these 'troublesome' and 'impracticable' people managed to pull together with sufficient force to build a denomination that has lasted for over one hundred years. Despite the poverty of many of its members, the Church embarked immediately on a church-building programme and took steps to ensure the supply of preachers to fill pulpits. The students were stretched to their very limits – when John Macleod asked J. R. Mackay to help him in Lewis in December 1893, he got this reply:

> I should have been most willing to cross the Minch ... but for the present it is I think quite unseemly and impolite on my part to leave Gairloch so soon. I have been here only three Sabbaths for the past three months, and the battle is fought here quite as keenly as it can be anywhere else ... But let me tell you lest you be at more expenses in the way of wiring that I am under promise to go a Sabbath to Portree, and a Sabbath to Lochinver as soon as possible, and how can I do that as soon as possible if I now allow the claims of Stornoway to precede?[34]

---

29 'Tabular view of the sustentation fund and special collections of the Free Presbyterian Church of Scotland: for the year from 31st March, 1899, to 31st March, 1900', *FPM*, v (4) (1900), pp. 136–7; Withers, 'Scottish Highlands outlined', xcviii, p. 155.
30 'Tabular view of the sustentation fund', pp. 136–7.
31 Beaton, *History of the Free Presbyterian Church*, pp. 124–7.
32 *PDGAFCS*, 1896, p. 91.
33 'Principal Rainy on the Free Presbyterian Church', *FPM*, i (2) (1896), p. 75.
34 J. R. Mackay to John Macleod, 1 Dec. 1893, *John Macleod Collection*, 3f.

Almost one year later, J. R. Mackay's workload had obviously not lessened:

> My dear friend ... After being nearly a month [except a day or two] away during which time I visited Ullapool, Lochinver, Coigach, Lochcarron, North and South Harris, Inverness, Tighnabruaich and Glasgow, I arrived here only late on Saturday night. I had been away three Sabbaths in succession and the last Sabbath the Missionary even was not able to turn out so I was considerably cheered at the prospect of having you here next Sabbath when I must be in Applecross myself.[35]

Given the enormous amount of work which had already been done in travelling around the country speaking out against the Declaratory Act, it is clear that the vigour of the students and the ministers was a significant factor in the success of the Free Presbyterian Church. Beaton commented more than once that had the Free Presbyterians had more ministers they would have had more congregations,[36] but what seems equally clear is that the few they did have did a disproportionate amount of work, and to their sacrifices must go a lot of the credit for the survival of the Free Presbyterian Church.

It is also clear that the spirit of the people was of profound importance. One writer, looking back in 1933 on the early days, commented thus:

> the criticisms of former friends and the frowns of those in high ecclesiastical positions did not interfere with the warmth and unity that characterised the little band that faced a hostile world with neither great leaders, nor men of social standing and wealth to support them. Those who are still living and who remember the early years of the movement will readily bear witness to this statement.[37]

Donald Beaton wrote in another place: 'to many the separation was like deliverance from Egyptian bondage. There was a unity, zeal and warmth among those that left the Declaratory Act Church which makes that time one of the green spots in their memories.'[38] Allied closely to this was a very profound sense that, however difficult their situation might be, they were doing God's work. As Neil Cameron expressed it in June 1893:

> Peace of Conscience and Peace with God is of more value than the good-will of all the men of this world and I must say as Luther did

---

[35] Mackay to Macleod, 18 Sep. 1894, *John Macleod Collection*, 3i.
[36] E.g. Beaton, *History of the Free Presbyterian Church*, p. 118; and Beaton, *Donald Macfarlane*, p. 32.
[37] Beaton, *History of the Free Presbyterian Church*, p. 118.
[38] Beaton, *Donald Macfarlane*, p. 31.

'I cannot otherwise.' Should He give grace I feel that though I were to die I could not take any other course in this controversy.[39]

J. R. Mackay had similar sentiments; he wrote to his parents in July 1893: 'Almost all the praying people of Gairloch are with us; and what need we fear. "My sheep hear my voice, and a stranger's voice will they not follow" ... We never had more pleasant times many of us in Gairloch.'[40] Donald Macfarlane was another who felt assured that the Free Presbyterians were doing the Will of God, noting in his diary:

> It appears to me that one reason why Satan attacks me so much and so often is that I took a lead in raising a testimony in defence of God's truth at a time when the faith once delivered to the saints was in danger of being overthrown in Scotland ... the Lord's cause was dear to me, and I could not see it fall to the ground without putting my weak shoulder to it to hold it up as an unworthy instrument in His mighty hand ... I suffer for a good cause – the best cause.[41]

In many ways this strong sense of being right and of fulfilling a divine destiny was crucial to the survival of the Free Presbyterians as a separate body.

This also helps to explain why the Free Presbyterian Church never took on a conscious 'Gaelic' identity. The overwhelmingly Highland nature of their Disruption did provide an identity, but this 'Gaelic' and 'Highland' identity was never allowed to obscure what was seen as the far more important 'Presbyterian', 'Calvinist', 'Scriptural' identity which the Church possessed and which made possible, for example, a successful missionary effort in Southern Africa. A Highland Gaelic denomination could have had no pretensions to be a national Church in Scotland, let alone an international Church ministering throughout the world. The Free Presbyterians were and are doubtless aware of the importance of the Highlands, but they have always been loathe to accept that they are merely a Highland Church. The Highland nature of the Free Presbyterian Church was an almost inevitable product of the circumstances in which that Church was born; but that Highland nature was never made the focal point of the Church's identity, and the concentration in wider Gaelic culture on secular poetry, on song and on dance, ensured that ceilidh-culture would become anathema to a Church which looked more to English Puritans than to Gaelic poets. Donald Macfarlane, for instance, appreciated the aim of those who sought to promote Gaelic, such as An Cumunn Gaidhealach, but opposed their method; he wrote in his diary:

> the people of Dingwall were today very busy, and in high glee at their own Vanity Fair – the Mod. The Mod has for its object the

---

[39] Neil Cameron to John Macleod, 22 Jun. 1893, *John Macleod Collection*, 2f.
[40] J. R. Mackay to his parents, 11 Jul. 1893, *John Macleod Collection*, 3f.
[41] Quoted in Beaton, *Donald Macfarlane*, pp. 30–1.

teaching of Gaelic and to keep up that language among the Highlanders. This is a commendable object, but there are many objectionable things in connection with it, such as vain songs and dancing, which must have a deteriorating effect upon the moral and religious character of those connected with it.[42]

The ceilidh was associated with drinking, dancing and immorality, while much of Gaelic folklore was seen as superstition and was perceived as being detrimental to religion. Indeed the wider attitude of antipathy towards Highland culture in general – folklore, music, songs, the ceilidh – has continued to be a badge of the Free Presbyterians up to the end of the twentieth century.[43]

The Free Presbyterian Church of Scotland has been distinct over the past century by maintaining positions on all the issues already discussed which have remained wholly unchanged in that time. As Lachlan MacLeod, the moderator of the Free Presbyterian Synod, put it in 1989: 'we hold on to our positions while the rest of society goes away from [them]'.[44] The Free Presbyterian response to change has been unswerving continuity, earning them the title of 'one of the strictest churches in Britain'.[45] Their position is that, while changes occur in every other walk of life, the fundamental truths of the Bible never change, and neither should the Church; as 'the whole Bible is a mine of unchanging truth', so the Church should be a mine of unchanging doctrine and practice.[46] It seems clear that this resistance to change is a direct response to the ferment of change that created the circumstances of the Church's birth: born out of seemingly unending change, the Free Presbyterians have subsequently staked their identity on resisting change.

This can be seen, first, on the issue of the rejection of instrumental music and hymns in public worship; the Free Presbyterian position on this has never changed, with another call to 'defend and continue this hallowed tradition' being issued in March 1997.[47] In their centenary volume, the following statement was made in a chapter entitled 'Our Enduring Testimony': 'as for our worship, we do not allow what is of the world or of man's invention to adulterate it; hence no place is given to instrumental music and hymns of human composition'.[48] The Free Presbyterian position now is the same as it was in 1893; continuity is

42 Ibid., p. 46.
43 D. Meek, 'Saints and scarecrows: the Churches and Gaelic culture in the Highlands since 1560', *Scottish Journal of Evangelical Theology*, xiv (1), Internet http://www.rutherfordhouse.org.uk/meek.htm, p. 4 of 14.
44 L. MacLeod, 'Free Church's key player', *Greenock Telegraph*, 28 Jun. 1989.
45 G. Paterson, 'Church too pure even for a Lord Chancellor', *Daily Express*, 26 May 1989.
46 K. Macleod, 'Changes', *Young People's Magazine*, ci (12) (1996), p. 224.
47 G. Hutton, 'Why psalms only?', *FPM*, cii (3) (1997), p. 74.
48 J. Macleod, 'Our enduring testimony', in D. B. MacLeod (ed.), *One Hundred Years of Witness* (Glasgow, 1993), pp. 212–13.

seen as the only valid response to change, and that continuity goes back much further than just one hundred years:

> If we go to the suffering church in the past and enquire, Why Psalms only? we will hear the French Huguenots, the persecuted Waldenses of the Alps, the suffering Covenanters from Scotland and Ireland, and many others, give their unhesitating answer with one voice, as David said to Ahimelech concerning the sword of Goliath; 'There is none like that; give it me.' Why Psalms only? The answer is clear. There is no substitute.[49]

The Free Presbyterians clearly feel a sense of continuity with the men who founded their denomination one hundred years ago, but their sense of continuity goes much further than that. In an age of change, it has only grown stronger.

Secondly, there can be no doubt that the Free Presbyterians hold a staunchly Sabbatarian position. This was well summarised by one observer:

> members adhere strictly to the sabbath; there can be no work on a Sunday and even children's play is frowned upon. Newspapers cannot be read and even these on a Monday are often shunned because they would have been produced on a Sunday. The stricter elements will shave on a Saturday night to avoid doing so on Sunday ... All food is prepared in advance.[50]

In 1996, the *Free Presbyterian Magazine* carried a series of articles on Sabbath observance – originally written seventy years earlier, which concluded on this note:

> We are guilty as a people, in what used to be called Sabbath-loving Scotland but now may be called Sabbath-hating Scotland, of ... the desecration of the Sabbath ... Therefore let us beware lest our Sabbath desecration bring down the wrath of God upon us as a country: and let Free Presbyterians take to heart that God will not connive at sin in them in the day of judgement.[51]

The Free Presbyterians still hold that it is 'the Lord's requirement to do no work on the first day of the week other than works of necessity and mercy'.[52] 'The Sabbath,' said the Free Presbyterian Sabbath Observance Committee in 1995, 'is God's gift to man, but it is a gift which most people today despise.'[53] On this, as on other issues, the Free Presbyterian stance has not changed since their birth in 1893. As the traditional Sabbath is increasingly undermined from many directions, the Free

49 Hutton, 'Why psalms only?', p. 115.
50 K. Gill, 'A church bound by doctrine of 1643', *The Times*, 5 Nov. 1988.
51 N. Cameron, 'Lecture on the Sabbath', *FPM*, ci (3) (1996), p. 74.
52 K. Watkins, 'Saying no to Sabbath work', *Young People's Magazine*, lxi (12) (1996), p. 226.
53 Sabbath Observance Committee's Report, *Free Presbyterian Church of Scotland Proceedings of Synod*, May 1995, p. 18.

Presbyterians seem more and more alone in Scotland in their absolute Sabbatarian stance. As their position becomes more isolated, however, it becomes more distinctive and identifiable; Sabbatarianism, it seems, is a major part of the Free Presbyterians' 'brand identity'.

Thirdly, the Free Presbyterians have retained their attitude to Scripture, again making no compromise or adjustment in the past one hundred years. One Free Presbyterian writer described the Church's 'initial pledge' as being 'to hold unswervingly, and with unremitting vigilance, to that testimony bequeathed to us',[54] and clearly the maintenance of the belief that 'the Bible is the Word of God, inspired and infallible, from beginning to end'[55] has been an essential part of that. The attitude of the nineteenth-century Free Church to the Bible was a primary cause of the Free Presbyterians leaving in 1893; one Free Presbyterian writer in 1996 referred to the Free Church of 1893 as having been a 'spiritually diseased body' because of its attitude to Scripture. Evolution, he argued, 'has played a strong part in the decline of ... [biblical Christianity] and the strengthening of Satan's kingdom', while biblical critics he described as 'the servants of Satan'.[56] These words are distinct echoes of the Free Presbyterian position one hundred years earlier. Neil Cameron, one of the Free Presbyterians' founding fathers, referred to critics of the doctrine of 'the absolute infallibility and inerrancy of the Bible, as being the Word of God' as 'traitors to God and men',[57] while evolution was described as 'an absurd God-dishonouring theory, the product of irreverent imagination, destitute of any foundation in fact, and contrary to the clearest testimony of the Word of God'.[58] A speaker at a Free Presbyterian conference spelled out the modern Free Presbyterian view of the Bible in December 1994: 'There is one Author throughout Scripture, a Divine Author who determined the very words as well as the thoughts. In the fullest possible sense, Scripture is the Word of God. It is God who speaks to us through it.'[59] The level of continuity is again illustrated in this paper by the fact that the speaker actually quoted two nineteenth-century Free Presbyterian ministers, writing in 1896, to support his argument. While in the rest of the Christian world, critical attitudes to Scripture have ebbed and flowed, in the Free Presbyterian Church, the attitude has remained unadjusted and unaltered. The Bible, then as now, is believed to contain nothing but the Word of God, and to be entirely free from error. As others have altered their position on the Bible and its status, the Free Presbyterians' position has remained unchanged.

54 F. Macdonald, 'Continuing the struggle, 1920–1960', in MacLeod, *One Hundred Years of Witness*, p. 108.
55 'Which Church?', *FPM*, ci (7) (1996), p. 212.
56 A. McPherson, 'Synod sermon', *FPM*, ci (7) (1996), p. 201.
57 Beaton, *Neil Cameron*, p. 20.
58 'Bruce's new book', p. 342.
59 K. Watkins, 'The inspiration of Scripture', *FPM*, c (2) (1995), p. 46.

And finally, the Free Presbyterian attitude to the Westminster Confession of Faith has not undergone any changes in the past century either. As creeds and confessions have become less popular with many denominations, and as the Westminster Confession of Faith in particular has come to be seen as outdated and obsolete, the Free Presbyterian Church has clung resolutely to every single aspect of that controversial document. The *Free Presbyterian Magazine* said in 1996:

> A creedless church is an absurdity. The Free Presbyterian Church of Scotland maintains a wholehearted allegiance to the Westminster Confession of Faith – a confession which, for scripturalness, comprehensiveness, and precise definition, has not been bettered.[60]

One year later the same magazine described the Westminster Confession of Faith as 'the product of the collective learning and wisdom of some of the ablest and most spiritual men in England and Scotland in any generation. They possessed almost unrivalled acumen and judgement.'[61] While most Churches that subscribed to the Westminster Confession have changed their terms of subscription or abandoned them altogether in the past hundred years, the Free Presbyterians have not. On the contrary, they have gripped it with unfaltering strength and held it high as a symbol of their identity. Continuity on this issue has been one of the Free Presbyterians' most unshakeable emblems, and that has also contributed to their distinctive identity.

To sum up, the Free Presbyterian Church has remained virtually unchanged over the past century because the circumstances of its birth made an unbending and inflexible stance almost inevitable. As a Church which emerged in response to and, more importantly, as a protest against change, change became anathema to it. If most Christian Churches have the choice between continuity or change, it is clear that the Free Presbyterians fundamentally have no choice – as one writer in their centenary publication put it: 'The responsibility for adhering faithfully to the testimony raised in 1893 was inherent in the very constitution of the Free Presbyterian Church of Scotland.'[62] Above all else, the Free Presbyterian Church of Scotland fears losing sight of what is seen as its 'special commitment to conserve and transmit intact the goodly heritage transmitted to them by the founding fathers of the Church'.[63] This reluctance to change in any way has given the Free Presbyterian Church a remarkable level of continuity, and with that continuity has come a clear and distinctive identity. The implication of many Free Presbyterian statements on the subject is that *unlike everyone*

---

60 'Which Church?', p. 211.
61 E. Chacko, 'A tribute to the Westminster Confession of Faith (1646)', *FPM*, cii (5) (1997), p. 144.
62 Macdonald, 'Continuing the struggle', p. 78.
63 Ibid., p. 79.

else they have not changed their position . The Free Presbyterians reject change on the grounds that it is change, and hold unswervingly to the position of their founding fathers over a century ago; this of course brings problems and conflicts, but it also brings advantages. By stressing absolute continuity, the Free Presbyterians have carved themselves a unique niche among modern Protestant Churches. It is certainly not a niche that is likely to change.

There were from the beginning moves to bring the Free Presbyterians and the more conservative part of the Free Church back together again. This intensified with the split in the Free Church over the Union with the United Presbyterians in 1900, when the more conservative section of the Free Church, mainly in the Highlands and including many of the Free Presbyterians' ex-allies in the battle against the Declaratory Act, chose to remain outside the Union. The Free Presbyterians gave this decision a guarded welcome, but declared that 'the ecclesiastical position of the Anti-Unionists' was 'still unsatisfactory'.[64] The Free Church minority rescinded the Declaratory Act and took other steps that, by 1905, had raised a very real possibility of reunion between the erstwhile allies, but although some of the Free Presbyterians' most eminent ministers did rejoin the Free Church, the majority remained separate.[65]

To the Free Presbyterians, the key issue was the form of words of the Preamble to the Act with which the Free Church rescinded the Declaratory Act, where it was said that 'this Church adheres, as she has always adhered, to her subordinate standards'. In a motion at the Free Presbyterian Synod of 1905, Neil Cameron stated bluntly that:

> By this statement the Free Church seem to justify their own actions since 1893, and by implication to condemn the separate position taken up then by the Free Presbyterian Church of Scotland. This action on their part makes it impossible for this Church to view the terms of said preamble in any other light than as fixing these Churches in their present separate positions.[66]

The key phrase 'as she has always adhered' implied that those who remained in the Free Church after the Declaratory Act had not been affected by it; by implication the Free Presbyterians were wrong to quit the Church at that time. The phrase was seen to be troublesome before it ever made it into the Preamble – one of the members of the Free Church committee that framed it, Donald Munro, wrote in a letter to his old friend John Macleod, by then of course a leading figure in the Free Presbyterian Church:

---

[64] Records of the Synod of the Free Presbyterian Church, 13 Nov. 1900: quoted in Beaton, *History of the Free Presbyterian Church*, p. 133.

[65] Ibid., pp. 140–8; Collins, *Heritage of Our Fathers*, 130–2.

[66] Quoted in Beaton, *History of the Free Presbyterian Church*, p. 141.

at our firśt meeting we sat for nearly 24 hours discussing matters. To remove the dead lock in which we were someone unfortunately introduced the phrase in the beginning, 'as she has always adhered', making the overture run – 'Whereas this Church adheres, as she has always adhered, to her Subordinate Standards' etc. ... I think I am the only member who objected to it.[67]

He then explained his objections:

My objection to the phrase is this – We adhered to the Subordinate Standards before the Union only as individuals, or as a minority. If you have time I should like to hear what you think of the phrase. I am afraid it will be regarded as quite objectionable, by some of your men ... The older ministers ... will insist on some such phrase, and will carry the day.[68]

To defend the decision made by one side in 1893, either to secede or to stay in and fight the Declaratory Act from within the Free Church, involved, almost inevitably, a degree of denigration of the other side. The position of one side was virtually defined by what the other side did not do. To those concerned the issues were stark, and their own rightness was defined by the other's wrongness; a man had either committed the sin of schism or the sin of being content to dwell in Sodom. To many the whole issue became crystallised in that one phrase in the Preamble, a phrase that crept into the document in the course of an extremely long committee meeting, when men's minds could not possibly have been fresh.

In truth, both sides felt bitter in 1905. The Free Presbyterians never forgave their erstwhile allies for what they saw as desertion in the heat of battle in 1893, while the conservatives who had remained in the Free Church at that time, and who then stayed out of the Union of 1900, felt that the Free Presbyterians had gone too soon. Blame for this bitterness can be attached to both sides. Today, little has changed. The Free Presbyterians would stress important differences between the two denominations, and there are probably too many people in both denominations who are happy to remain separate for a formal reunion to take place. Crucially, much of the ill feeling that still exists between the two Churches stems from the bitterness that surfaced in the years after the Second Disruption of 1893.

Fifty-seven years on, Chalmers's great dream at the Disruption of 1843 lay in tatters, the Free Church of 1843 torn apart by the two secessions of 1893 and 1900. The inherent tension in the Church between its twin power bases – one in the Highlands and another in the Lowlands – had proved to be too powerful to resist. The forces pulling

---

[67] Donald Munro to John Macleod, 8 May 1905, *John Macleod Collection*, 1k.
[68] Ibid.

the Church apart proved to be stronger than any of the forces – or individuals – trying to hold it together. The Free Presbyterian secession – the Second Disruption – was the first great crack to appear in the Free Church, and it was this crack that was to lead irrevocably to the destruction of Chalmers's dream in 1900. By then the Highlanders were in effect separate and they have remained so ever since. The Great Disruption had not been a final schism – a 'Disruption to end all Disruptions' – instead it had been merely the biggest and most dramatic of what has been a long and sad history of Disruptions in Scotland. Ultimately, the dream of holding together a Church that comfortably represented both the Highlands and the Lowlands in a time of revolutionary change proved to be an impossible dream.

Bibliography

MANUSCRIPT SOURCES

Glasgow, St Jude's Free Presbyterian Church of Scotland Library
Records of the Free Church Presbytery of Scotland (27 Jul. 1893–31 Aug. 1894).
Records of the Presbytery of the Free Presbyterian Church of Scotland (13 Sep. 1894–15 Jun. 1896).
Free Presbyterian Synod Minute Book, vol. I (7 Jul. 1896–5 Jul. 1904).
Minutes and Records of the Southern Presbytery of the Free Presbyterian Church of Scotland, Book 1 (22 Jun. 1896–4 Mar. 1901).
Minute Book of the Southern Presbytery of the Free Presbyterian Church of Scotland, Book 2 (1 Apr. 1901–8 Nov. 1907).

Privately held, John Macleod Collection
Letters of Neil Cameron to John Macleod, 6 Jun. 1892–26 Mar. 1901.
Letters of John R. Mackay to John Macleod, 14 Sep. 1891–7 Apr. 1905.
Letters of Donald Munro to John Macleod, 30 Jan. 1890–8 May 1905.
Letters of James S. Sinclair to John Macleod, 6 Aug. 1892–17 Aug. 1896.
Letters of Allan MacKenzie to John Macleod, 13 Sep. 1892–22 Nov. 1905.
Letters of Alexander Stewart to John Macleod, 30 Jun. 1890–18 Apr. 1899.
Letters of George MacKay to John Macleod, 8 Jun. 1892–14 Sep. 1894.
Letters of Neil McIntyre to John Macleod, 24 Jul. 1891–18 Sep. 1896.
Letters of Donald Beaton to John Macleod, 21 May 1895–19 Nov. 1896.
Letter of reference for John Macleod, written by Donald Macfarlane, 19 Oct. 1891.
Private Invitation to 'A Convention of Ministers and other Office-bearers of the Free Church, who concur in disapproving of the passing of the Declaratory Act', dated 29 Jun. 1892.
Documents from the General Assembly's College, Belfast, 1894–6.

Privately held, Lexy Gillies Collection of Letters and Cuttings
Privately held, Free Presbyterian Newspaper Cuttings, 1986 Reproduction

PRINTED PRIMARY SOURCES

SELECTED PUBLISHED SERMONS AND ARTICLES BY THE FOUNDERS OF THE
FREE PRESBYTERIAN CHURCH OF SCOTLAND
(Author's name will only be given if it was given at the time)

A. SERMONS

CAMERON, N., 'Psalms lxxx.12,13.', *FPM*, i (4) (1896).
——, 'Jude 3.', *FPM*, ii (9) (1898).
MACDONALD, D., 'Luke x.30–35. (notes from Gaelic)', *FPM*, i (2) (1896).
——, 'Luke vii. 37–38.', *FPM*, ii (1) (1897).
MACFARLANE, D., 'Exodus xxxiii.14.', *FPM*, i (1) (1896).
——, '2 Chronicles xxxiv.1–2.', *FPM*, ii (12) (1898).
——, 'Isaiah xxi.11–12.', in Beaton, *Donald Macfarlane*.
——, 'Isaiah xxviii.16.', *FPM*, i (10) (1897).
——, 'Haggai ii.4.', in Beaton, *Donald Macfarlane*.
——, 'Micah iv.1–2.', in Beaton, *Donald Macfarlane*
——, 'Luke xiii.18,19.', *FPM*, iv (2) (1899).
——, '2 Corinthians iii.3.', in Beaton, *Donald Macfarlane*.
MACKAY, J. R., 'Psalms l.5.', *FPM*, i (5) (1896).
——, 'Romans iv.5.', *FPM*, i (12) (1897).
MACKENZIE, A., 'Hebrews v.7.', *FPM*, i (6) (1896).
MACLEOD, J., 'Psalms li.7.', *FPM*, ii (7) (1897).
MACRAE, A., 'Matthew iii.12.', *FPM*, i (3) (1896).
——, 'John xvi.8.', *FPM*, ii (3) (1897).
SINCLAIR, J. S., 'John iii.16.', *FPM*, i (11) (1897).

B. ARTICLES

BEATON, D., 'The late Rev. Professor Watts, D.D., LL.D.', *FPM*, i (1)
(1896).
——, 'The Westminster Assembly and the Confession of Faith', *FPM*, iv
(1) (1899).
——, 'The story of the Oban Free Presbyterian congregation' (n.p., n.d.).
CAMERON, N., 'The late Alexander Cameron, Aharacle, Argyllshire',
FPM, i (3) (1896).
——, 'The late Mr John Campbell', *FPM*, i (10) (1897).
——, 'The late Mr. John Hamilton, Oban', *FPM*, ii (10) (1898).
——, 'The late Donald Macmaster, Strontian', *FPM*, ii (5) (1897).
——, 'New Year's Day Lecture, 1920', in Beaton, *Neil Cameron*.
——, 'New Year's Day Lecture, 1926', in Beaton, *Neil Cameron*.
MACFARLANE, D., 'Notes of lecture delivered at Portree on 14th March,
1898', *FPM*, ii (12) (1898).
MACKAY, J. R., 'Inspired psalmody', *FPM*, i (1) (1896).

MACKENZIE, A., 'The Sabbath Day', *FPM*, i (4) (1896).

[——] '£154,000,000', *FPM*, iv (3) (1899).

[——] 'An Address and letters of the late William Sinclair, of Wick', *FPM*, i (12) (1897).

[——] 'The Assemblies (Free Church)', *FPM*, iv (2) (1899).

[——] 'Dr. Barnardo on Romanism', *FPM*, i (4) (1896).

[——] 'Professor Bruce's new book: "The Providential Order"', *FPM*, ii (9) (1898); (10) (1898); (11) (1898); (12) (1898).

[——] 'The burning of Bibles', *FPM*, i (8) (1896).

[——] 'Pastor Chiniquy and the challenge by a priest', *FPM*, i (8) (1896).

[——] 'Pastor Chiniquy in Edinburgh', *FPM*, i (8) (1896).

[——] 'Pastor Chiniquy threatened by the Romanists', *FPM*, i (10) (1897).

[——] 'Rev. Thos. Connellan on the Jesuits', *FPM*, i (10) (1897).

[——] 'Converts from Rome', *FPM*, i (1) (1896).

[——] 'Death of Sir William Dawson', *FPM*, iv (9) (1899).

[——] 'The Declaratory Act', *FPM*, i (2) (1896).

[——] 'The Declaratory Act and admission into office in the Free Church', *FPM*, i (11) (1897).

[——] 'The Declaratory Act and its consequences', *FPM*, i (10) (1897).

[——] 'Professor Drummond's theology', *FPM*, i (12) (1897).

[——] 'Explanatory criticism on the Declaratory Act', *FPM*, i (4) (1896); (5) (1896); (6) (1896); (7) (1896); (8) (1896).

[——] 'The farmer and the Romish relic-monger', *FPM*, i (5) (Sep., 1896).

[——] 'The franchise in bad hands', *FPM*, iv (6) (1899).

[——] 'The Free Assembly', *FPM*, ii (3) (1897).

[——] 'The Free Church anti-Unionists: a criticism of some of their views', *FPM*, v (6) (1900).

[——] 'A Free Church professor on the twelve prophets', *FPM*, i (2) (1896).

[——] 'Free Church Moderator's Address', *FPM*, v (2) (1900).

[——] 'F. P. Students at the Assembly's College, Belfast', *FPM*, i (2) (1896).

[——] 'Glasgow Sabbath Protection Association', *FPM*, i (7) (1896).

[——] 'The Gospel changes not', *FPM*, iv (4) (1899).

[——] 'Insane Liberalism', *FPM*, ii (6) (1897).

[——] 'Introductory', *FPM*, i (1) (1896).

[——] 'Dr. Kennedy and separation from the Free Church', *FPM*, ii (5) (1897).

[——] 'The late Dr. Kennedy on Union between the Free and U.P. Churches', *FPM*, iv (6) (1899).

[——] 'The latest opinion of Free Presbyterianism', *FPM*, iv (11) (1900).

[——] 'A loud voice', *FPM*, iv (4) (1899).

[——] 'Mr M'Caskill's [*sic*] strange development', *FPM*, ii (12) (1898).

[——] 'Cardinal Manning's fanatical zeal', *FPM*, i (5) (1896).

[——] 'More labour in the fire', *FPM*, i (5) (1896).

[——] 'New Presbytery and Synod', *FPM*, i (3) (1896).

[——] 'Open letter to the editor of the "British Weekly"', *FPM*, ii (9) (1898).

[——] 'Open letter to Rev. Alex. Whyte, D.D.', *FPM*, i (5) (1896).

[——] 'The opening of museums on Sabbath sanctioned by Parliament', *FPM*, i (1) (1896).

[——] 'Principal Rainy on the Free Presbyterian Church', *FPM*, i (2) (1896).

[——] 'Principal Rainy on Union with the U.P. Church', *FPM*, i (9) (1897).

[——] 'A sentence from the "Review of Reviews"', *FPM*, ii (9) (1898).

[——] 'Professor G. A. Smith on the twelve prophets: unsound views on fundamental doctrines', *FPM*, i (3) (1896).

[——] 'Professor G. A. Smith on the twelve prophets: erroneous views of the Word, the Love of God, the Atonement, and Hell', *FPM*, i (4) (1896).

[——] 'The progress of Rome', *FPM*, i (2) (1896).

[——] 'The restoration of the Jesuits', *FPM*, iv (3) (1899).

[——] 'Review of *The Higher Criticism: The Greatest Apostasy of the Age, by D. K. Paton*', *FPM*, ii (2) (1897).

[——] 'Sabbath desecration', *FPM*, ii (7) (1897).

[——] 'Separation from an unsound Church viewed in the light of Scripture', *FPM*, i (12) (1897); ii (1) (1897); (2) (1897); (4) (1897).

[——] 'Some features of present-day preaching', *FPM*, ii (8) (1897).

[——] 'The late Mr. Spurgeon and the Free Church', *FPM*, ii (5) (1897).

[——] 'The supreme need of the times', *FPM*, ii (5) (1897).

[——] 'The suppression of convents: startling incident', *FPM*, i (9) (1897).

[——] 'The Union debate in the Free Assembly', *FPM*, v (3) (1900).

[——] 'The West Highland Commission of the Established Church and the Communion', *FPM*, ii (3) (1897).

C. NEWSPAPERS

British Weekly
Daily Express
Dundee Advertiser
Greenock Telegraph
London Daily Chronicle
North British Daily Mail
Northern Chronicle
Oban Express
The Times
United Free Church Magazine

D. CONTEMPORARY COMMENTARIES AND HISTORIES (PRE-1920)

AULD, A., *Ministers and Men in the Far North* (Wick, 1896).

——, *Life of John Kennedy, D.D.* (London, 1887).

BAYNE, P., *The Life and Letters of Hugh Miller* (London, 1871).

BEGG, J., *A Handbook of Popery; or, Text Book of Missions for the Conversion of Romanists: being Papal Rome Tested by Scripture, History, and its Recent Workings* (Edinburgh, 1852).

BETTANY, G. T., 'Robert Knox (1791–1862)', in *Dictionary of National Biography*, xxxi (London, 1892), pp. 331–3.

BEVERIDGE, W., *A Short History of the Westminster Assembly* (Edinburgh, 1904).

BLACK, J. S. and CHRYSTAL, G. W., *The Life of William Robertson Smith* (London, 1912).

BLAIKIE, W. G., 'On the proper limit of creeds', *British and Foreign Evangelical Rev.*, xxii (1873), pp. 51–83.

——, 'The revision of the Westminster Confession (I)', *British Weekly*, 22 Apr. 1887.

——, *After Fifty Years or Letters of a Grandfather on Occasion of the Jubilee of the Free Church of Scotland in 1893* (London, 1893).

——, *An Autobiography: Recollections of a Busy Life* (London, 1901).

BLIND, M., *George Eliot* (London, 1883).

BONAR, H., *The Old Gospel: Not 'Another Gospel' but the Power of God Unto Salvation. A Reply to Dr. Kennedy's Pamphlet, 'Hyper-Evangelism'* (Edinburgh, 1874).

BONNEY, T. G., 'Sir John William Dawson (1820–1899)', *Dictionary of National Biography*, Supplement, vol. II (London, 1901), pp. 120–2.

BRIGGS, C. A., *Whither? A Theological Question for the Times* (New York, 1889).

—— 'The General Assembly of the Presbyterian Church in the United States of America', *Presbyterian Rev.*, x (39) (1889), pp. 464–74.

—— (ed.), *How Shall We Revise? A Bundle of Papers* (New York, 1890).

——, 'The advance towards revision', in Briggs, *How Shall We Revise?*

BROWN, D., *Life of the Late John Duncan LL.D.* (2nd edn, Edinburgh, 1872).

BROWN, T., *Annals of the Disruption; with Extracts from the Narratives of Ministers who Left the Scottish Establishment in 1843* (Edinburgh, 1893).

BRUCE, A. B., *The Kingdom of God: or Christ's Teaching According to the Synoptic Gospels* (Edinburgh, 1889).

——, *The Providential Order of the World* (London, 1897).

BRYCE, J., 'Edward Augustus Freeman', *Eng. Hist. Rev.*, vii (1892), pp. 497–509.

BUCHANAN, R., *The Ten Years' Conflict*, 2 vols. (Glasgow, 1852).

BURT, E., *Letters from a Gentleman in the North of Scotland to his Friend in London*, 2 vols. (London, 1754; 5th edn, London, 1818).

CANDLISH, J. S., *The Relations of the Presbyterian Churches to the Confession of Faith* (Glasgow, 1886).

CANDLISH, R. S., *Examination of Mr Maurice's Theological Essays* (London, 1854).

——, *The Fatherhood of God: Being the First Course of the Cunningham Lectures Delivered Before the New College, Edinburgh, in March 1864* (2nd edn, Edinburgh, 1865).

CAVE, A., 'The Old Testament and the critics', *Contemporary Rev.*, lvii (Apr. 1890), pp. 537–51.

CREIGHTON, M., 'John Richard Green (1837–1883)', in *Dictionary of National Biography*, xxiii (London, 1890), pp. 46–9.

CROSKERY, T., 'Conversions to Romanism', *Presbyterian Rev.*, vi (22) (1885), pp. 201–25.

CUNNINGHAM, W., *The Reformers and the Theology of the Reformation* (Edinburgh, 1862).

DALES, J. B., and PATTERSON, R. M. (eds.), *Report of Proceedings of the Second General Council of the Presbyterian Alliance Convened at Philadelphia, September 1880* (Philadelphia, 1880).

DARWIN, C., *The Origin of Species by Means of Natural Science; or, The Preservation of Favoured Races in the Struggle for Life* (London, 1859).

DAVIES, T., *Answer to Hugh Miller and Theoretic Geologists* (New York, 1860).

DAWSON, J. W., 'The Deluge: biblical and geological', *Contemporary Rev.*, lvi (Dec. 1889), pp. 884–900.

DICKSON, J., *History of the Presbyterian Church of New Zealand* (Dunedin, 1899).

DODDS, J., 'A day with Hugh Miller', in *Personal Reminiscences and Biographical Sketches* (Edinburgh, 1887).

DODS, M., *The Book of Genesis: With Introduction and Notes* (Handbooks for Bible Classes Series, Edinburgh, 1882).

——, 'The revision of the Westminster Confession (II)', *British Weekly*, 22 Apr. 1887.

——, *The Book of Genesis* (Expositor's Bible Series, London, 1888).

——, *Recent Progress in Theology: Inaugural Lecture at New College Edinburgh, 1889* (Edinburgh, 1889).

——, *What is a Christian?* (Edinburgh, 1889).

——, *An Introduction to the New Testament* (London, 1892).

——, Letter to the *Dundee Advertiser*, 24 Oct. 1900.

——, *The Bible: Its Origin and Nature* (Edinburgh, 1905).

DODS (JNR), M. (ed.), *The Early Letters of Marcus Dods, D.D.* (London, 1910).

——, *The Later Letters of Marcus Dods* (London, 1911).

DRIVER, S. R., 'The critical study of the Old Testament', *Contemporary Rev.*, lvii (Feb. 1890), pp. 215–231.

DRUMMOND, H., 'Mr. Gladstone and Genesis: articles by T. H. Huxley and Henry Drummond', *Nineteenth Century*, xix (1886), pp. 206–18.

——, 'The evolution of Man: being the First Lowell Lecture delivered at Boston, April 4th, 1893', *British Weekly*, 20 Apr. 1893.

——, 'Temptations (an address to the students of Amherst College)', *British Weekly*, 22 Jun. 1893.

——, *The Lowell Lectures on the Ascent of Man* (London, 1894).

——, 'Survival of the fittest', in *The New Evangelism and Other Papers* (London, 1899).

ELDER, J. R., *The Highland Host of 1678* (Glasgow, 1914).

EVANS, L. J., 'Dogmatic confessionalism versus revision', in Briggs, *How Shall We Revise?*

EWING, W. (ed.), *Annals of the Free Church of Scotland, 1843–1900*, 2 vols. (Edinburgh, 1900).

GIBSON, J., *'Buy the Truth': Thoughts on Creeds and Creed Revision* (Edinburgh, 1889).

GORDON-GORMAN, W., *Converts to Rome: A List of over Three Thousand Protestants who have become Catholics since the Commencement of the Nineteenth Century* (London, 1884).

GRAY, W. F., 'John Watson (1850–1907)', *Dictionary of National Biography*, 2nd Supplement, vol. III (London, 1912), pp. 605–7.

GUINNESS, A. H., 'The Jesuits and social morality', *The Papacy of Modern Times: Report of the National Convention of Protestants held in Glasgow, December, 1886* (Glasgow, 1887).

GUTHRIE, T., *Autobiography of Thomas Guthrie and Memoir by his sons, the Revd David K. Guthrie, and Charles J. Guthrie, M.A.*, 2 vols. (London, 1874–5).

HAMILTON, S. M., 'A non-growing creed', in Briggs, *How Shall We Revise?*

HETHERINGTON, W. M., 'Introductory essay', in R. Shaw, *The Reformed Faith: An Exposition of the Westminster Confession of Faith* (Edinburgh, 1845; repr. Inverness, 1974).

HODGE, A. A., and WARFIELD, B. B., 'Inspiration', *Presbyterian Rev.*, ii (6) (1881), pp. 225–60.

HUNT, W., 'Edward Augustus Freeman (1823–1892)', *Dictionary of National Biography*, Supplement, vol. II (London, 1901), pp. 247–51.

INNES, A. T., *The Law of Creeds in Scotland: A Treatise on the Legal Relation of Churches in Scotland Established and Not Established, to their Doctrinal Confessions* (Edinburgh, 1867).

——, 'The religion of the Highlands', *British and Foreign Evangelical Rev.*, xxi (Jul. 1872), pp. 413–46.

——, *Studies in Scottish History Chiefly Ecclesiastical* (London, 1892).

——, *Chapters of Reminiscence* (London, 1913).

INVERACH, J., 'Professor Drummond's new book', *British Weekly*, 24 May 1894.

——, *Evolution and Christianity* (London, 1894).

KENNEDY, J., *The Days of the Fathers in Ross-shire* (Inverness, 1861).

——, *Hyper-Evangelism 'Another Gospel', Though a Mighty Power: A Review of the Recent Religious Movement in Scotland* (Edinburgh, 1874).

——, *The Distinctive Principles and Present Position and Duty of the Free Church* (Edinburgh, 1875).

——, *A Reply to Dr. Bonar's Defence of Hyper-Evangelism* (Edinburgh, 1875).

——, 'Speech on Union by the late Rev. Dr. John Kennedy, of Dingwall: at an anti-Union meeting at Inverness', *FPM*, iv (11) (1900), pp. 409–14.

Letters of the Rev. John Ker, D.D., 1866–1890 (2nd edn, Edinburgh, 1890).

KERR, J., *Vivisection in Theology, and its Chief Apologist, Prof. Dods, D.D.* (Glasgow, 1890).

——, *The Higher Criticism: Disastrous Results. Professors Smith, Dods and Denney* (Glasgow, 1903).

KNIGHT, W. (ed.), *Colloquia Peripatetica: Notes of Conversations with John Duncan* (Edinburgh, 1879).

KNOX, R., *The Races of Men: A Philosophical Enquiry into the Influence of Race over the Destinies of Nations* (2nd edn, London, 1862).

LEASK, W. K., *Dr Thomas McLauchlan* (Edinburgh and London, 1905).

LENNOX, C., *Henry Drummond: A Biographical Sketch* (London, 1901).

LIDDON, H. P., *The Life of Edward Bouverie Pusey*, vol. (London, 1893).

LONSDALE, H., *A Sketch of the Life and Writings of Robert Knox the Anatomist* (London, 1870).

MACASKILL, J., *A Highland Pulpit: Being Sermons of the Late Rev. Murdoch Macaskill* (Inverness, 1907).

MACASKILL, M., *Report of a Committee of the Presbytery of Dingwall Appointed to Consider the Appointment of Dr Dods ...* (Edinburgh, 1889).

——, *The New Theology in the Free Church* (Edinburgh, 1892).

MACBEAN, L., *Dugald Buchanan, the Sacred Bard of the Scottish Highlands* (London, 1919).

MCCRIE, C. G., *The Church of Scotland: Her Divisions and Her Re-unions* (Edinburgh, 1901).

——, *The Confessions of the Church of Scotland: Their Evolution in History* (Edinburgh, 1907).

MACDONALD, K., *Social and Religious Life in the Highlands* (Edinburgh, 1902).

MCEWAN, J., *The Proposed Free Church Declaratory Act, and the Duty of the General Assembly of 1892 Thereanent: Being the Substance of a Speech Delivered in the Free Presbytery of Edinburgh on Wednesday, the 24th February 1892, in support of the Following Overture* (Edinburgh, 1892).

MACEWEN, A. R., *Life and Letters of John Cairns, D.D., LL.D.* (London, 1895).

MACFARLANE, D., *Memoir and Remains of the Rev. Donald Macdonald, Sheildaig, Ross-shire* (Dingwall, 1903).

MACFARLANE, M., 'The Gaelic language and the people who speak it', in *The Old Highlands: Papers Read Before the Gaelic Society of Glasgow 1895–1906* (Glasgow, 1908).

MACGREGOR, J., 'On the revision of the Westminster Confession', *British and Foreign Evangelical Rev.*, xxvi (1877), pp. 692–713.

MACKENZIE, E. M., *Rev. Murdo Mackenzie: A Memory* (Inverness, 1914).

MACKENZIE, W. M., *Hugh Miller: A Critical Study* (London, 1905).

MACKINTOSH, R., *The Obsoleteness of the Westminster Confession of Faith* (Glasgow, 1888).

——, *Principal Rainy: A Biographical Study* (London, 1907).

MACLAREN, I. [J. WATSON], *Beside the Bonnie Briar Bush* (London, 1895).

——, *St. Jude's* (London, n.d.).

MCLAUCHLAN, T., *Celtic Gleanings; or, Notices of the History and Literature of the Scottish Gael* (Edinburgh, 1857).

MACLEOD, D., *Gloomy Memories in the Highlands of Scotland* (Glasgow, 1892).

MAITLAND, F. W., 'William Stubbs, Bishop of Oxford', *Eng. Hist. Rev.*, xvi (1901), pp. 417–26.

MILLER, H., *My Schools and Schoolmasters* (Edinburgh, 1854).

——, The *Testimony of the Rocks* (Edinburgh, 1857).

MITCHELL, A. F., *The Westminster Assembly. Its History and Standards* (London, 1883).

MITCHELL, D. G., *The Life of Robert Rainy* (Glasgow, n.d.).

MOFFAT, J. (ed.), *Letters of Principal James Denney to his Family and Friends* (London. n.d.)

MOODY-STUART, A., *Recollections of the Late John Duncan, LL.D.* (Edinburgh, 1872).

MOODY-STUART, K., *Why We Do Not Mean to Change Our Confession of Faith* (Edinburgh, 1889).

——, *Letter to a Friend Regarding the Free Church Declaratory Act* (Moffat, 1892).

——, *The New Declaratory Act and Proposed New Formula of the Free Church of Scotland: A Lecture Delivered in Hope Street Free Church, Glasgow, on 28th February, 1893* (Moffat, 1893).

MURRAY, T., *Heretical Declamation in the Free Church Brought to the Test of Argument* (Edinburgh, 1890).

NICOLL, W. R., *'Ian Maclaren': Life of Rev. John Watson, D.D.* (London, 1908).

ORR, J. B., *Scotch Church Crisis* (Glasgow, 1905).

PATERSON, J. A. (ed.), *The Called of God, by the late A. B. Davidson, with a Biographical Introduction by A. Taylor Innes* (Edinburgh, 1905).

PATON, D. K., *The Higher Criticism: The Greatest Apostasy of the Age, with Notable Examples and Criticisms of Several Scottish Theological Professors* (2nd edn, London, 1898).

RAINY, R., *Life of William Cunningham, D.D.* (Edinburgh, 1871).

——, *Delivery and Development of Christian Doctrine* (Edinburgh, 1874).

——, *Evolution and Theology* (Edinburgh, 1874).

——, *Explanatory Notes on the Declaratory Act of the Free Church of Scotland* (Edinburgh, 1894).

REID, J., *Memoirs of the Lives and Writings of those Eminent Divines: Who Convened in the Famous Assembly at Westminster, in the Seventeenth Century*, 2 vols. (Paisley, 1811 and 1815; repr. Edinburgh, 1982).

ROSS, J. M. E., *William Ross of Cowcaddens* (London, 1905).

ROSS, W., *Dwight Lyman Moody the Prince of Evangelists* (London, n.d.).

RUNCIMAN, J., 'The ethics of the drink question', *Contemporary Rev.*, lvi (Oct. 1889), pp. 539–54.

SALMOND, C. A., 'Romish ascendancy versus British ascendancy', in *The Papacy of Modern Times: Report of the National Convention of Protestants held in Glasgow, December 1886* (Glasgow, 1887).

SAYCE, A. H., *The 'Higher Criticism' and the Verdict of the Monuments* (London, 1893).

SCHAFF, P., 'The revision of the Westminster Confession of Faith', *Presbyterian Rev.*, x (40) (1889), pp. 529–52.

——, *Creed Revision in the Presbyterian Church* (New York, 1890).

SCOTT, WALTER, *Manners, Customs and History of the Highlanders of Scotland* (Glasgow and London, 1893).

SIMPSON, P. C., *Life of Principal Rainy*, 2 vols. (London, 1909).

SMEATON, O., *Thomas Guthrie* (Edinburgh, 1900).

SMITH, G., *The Life of Dr Alexander Duff, D.D., LL.D.* (4th edn, London, 1900).

SMITH, G. A., *Modern Criticism and the Preaching of the Old Testament: Eight Lectures on the Lyman Beecher Foundation, Yale University, U.S.A.* (London, 1901).

——, *The Life of Henry Drummond* (London, 1905).

SMITH, J., *The Integrity of Scripture: Plain Reasons for Rejecting the Critical Hypothesis* (London, 1902).

STARK, J., *The Westminster Confession of Faith Critically Compared with the Holy Scriptures and Found Wanting; or, A New Exposition of the Doctrines of the Christian Religion in Harmony with the Word of God, and Not at Variance with Modern Science* (London, 1863).

STEWART, A., and CAMERON, J. K., *The Free Church of Scotland, 1843–1910: A Vindication* (Edinburgh and Glasgow, 1910).

STRAHAN, J., *Andrew Bruce Davidson* (London, 1917).

TOUT, T. F., 'William Stubbs (1825–1901)', *Dictionary of National Biography*, 2nd Supplement, vol. III (London, 1912), pp. 444–51.

WALKER, N. L., *Chapters from the History of the Free Church of Scotland* (Edinburgh, 1895).

WARFIELD, B. B., 'The new creed of the Presbyterian Church of England', *Presbyterian Rev.*, x (37) (1889), pp. 115–24.

WARFIELD, B. B., 'The Presbyterian Churches and the Westminster Confession', *Presbyterian Rev.*, x (40) (1889), pp. 646–57.

——, *Ought the Confession to be Revised?* (New York, 1890).

——, 'The Westminster Assembly and its work, pt. 1', *Princeton Theological Rev.*, vi (2) (1908), pp. 177–210; 'pt. 2', vi (3) (1908), pp. 353–91.

WATTS, R., *Dr. Dods' St. Giles Sermon on the Essentials of Christianity: or, the New Scottish Homiletic* (Edinburgh, 1890).

WILSON, W., and RAINY, R., *Memorials of Robert Smith Candlish, D.D.* (Edinburgh, 1880).

YOUNG, R., *Hyper-Criticism: An Answer to Dr. Kennedy's 'Hyper-Evangelism'* (Edinburgh, n.d.)

[——] 'The late Dr. Begg', *The Signal* (Nov. 1883), pp. 169–72.

[——] *British Weekly, Free Church Jubilee Supplement*, 18 May 1893.

[——] 'The Chair of Natural Science in Glasgow Free Church College and Mr. H. Drummond', *The Signal* (Feb. 1884), pp. 38–43.

[——] 'The coming struggle in the Free Church Assembly and its issues', *The Signal* (May 1883), pp. 65–70.

[——] *The Confession of Faith: Proceedings of the Free Presbytery of Aberdeen, on 5th February, 1889. The Speeches of Principal Brown and Mr. J. Murray Garden* (Aberdeen, 1889).

[——] 'Culloden Papers', *Quarterly Rev.*, xiii (28) (1816), 283–333.

[——] 'Darwin and Darwinism', *The Signal* (Feb. 1883), pp. 29–30.

[——] 'The Rev. Dr. Marcus Dods on Genesis and at the Pan-Presbyterian Council', *The Signal* (Jul. 1888).

[——] 'Drunkenness, abstinence, and restraint', *Edinburgh Rev.*, cxxxvii (280) (1873), pp. 398–421.

[——] 'Effects of Free Church training for the Ministry', *The Signal* (Jun. 1888), pp. 183–4.

[——] *The 'Essays and Reviews' Examined on the Principles of Common Sense* (London, 1861).

[——] 'Events of the year', *The Signal* (Jan. 1886), pp. 1–6.

[——] 'The Expositor's Bible: *The Book of Genesis*, by Marcus Dods, D.D.', *The Signal* (Jun. 1888), pp. 176–81.

[——] *Faith and Criticism: Essays by Congregationalists* (London, 1893).

[——] *The Free Church Declaratory Act. A Criticism and Protest: Being the Speeches Delivered at a Public Meeting Held in Glasgow On Thursday, 18th February, 1892* (Glasgow, 1892).

[——] *The Free Church Declaratory Act and Proposed Alterations to the Questions and Formula: Report of discussions in the Free Presbytery of Lockerbie* (Glasgow, 1893).

[——] *The Free Church Declaratory Act of 1891: Report of Speeches Delivered at a Public Meeting held in the Free Church Mission Hall, Oban, Against this Act, on Wednesday, 13th April, 1892* (Oban, 1892).

[——] 'Free Church Defence Association', *The Signal* (Aug. 1883), pp. 127–9.

[——] 'The Free Church General Assembly of 1889: what ought it to do?', *The Signal* (Jun. 1889), pp. 161–8.

[——] '"The Free Church Monthly" and Dr. Marcus Dods', *The Signal* (May 1888), pp. 146–9.

[——] 'A Free Church Probationer on the Westminster Confession of Faith', *The Signal* (Aug. 1888), pp. 229–34.

[——] *Free Church of Scotland Assembly Papers, No. I*, 1887; *No. I*, 1888; *No. I*, 1889; *No. II*, 1890.

[——] 'Free Church students and orthodoxy', *The Signal* (Feb. 1888), p. 58.

[——] 'The Free Presbytery of Dundee and the Confession of Faith', *The Signal* (Aug. 1888), pp. 234–8.

[——] 'The Gaelic record of the Free Church', *The Signal* (Nov. 1888), pp. 337–41.

[——] 'Gaelic versus English', *The Signal* (Jan. 1889), p. 32.

[——] 'Genesis, by Marcus Dods, D.D.', *The Signal* (Dec. 1882), pp. 3–5.

[——] 'How far is the Church responsible for present scepticism?', *The Signal* (Sep. 1888), pp. 267–72.

[——] 'Infidelity in the Church', *The Signal* (Jul. 1882), p. 9.

[——] 'The Jubilee', *Free Church of Scotland Monthly* (Mar. 1893), pp. 55–7.

[——] 'Dr. Kennedy and separation from the Free Church', Letter from C. R. Auld of 10 Nov. 1894, sent to the *Northern Chronicle*, *FPM*, ii (5) (1897), pp. 179–80.

[——] 'The late Dr Kennedy of Dingwall', *The Signal* (Jun. 1884), pp. 161–7.

[——] 'Letter to the editor', *The Signal* (Jun. 1888), p. 192.

[——] *Mr Macrae and the Confession of Faith* (London, 1877).

[——] 'Members of the Free Church Assembly alleged to have travelled on Sabbath', *The Signal* (Jul. 1888).

[——] *Narrative and Engagement Adopted at a Meeting of Ministers and Elders in Inverness* (Inverness, 1893).

[——] 'Parliamentary Sabbath breaking', *The Signal* (Oct. 1883).

[——] 'The present crisis in Scotland', *The Signal* (Feb. 1883), pp. 17–19.

[——] *The Presently Controverted Opinions of Professor Marcus Dods, D.D. on The Inspiration of Holy Scripture, Refuted by the Rev. Marcus Dods, Belford, Northumberland, in 'Remarks on the Bible' (publ. 1828)* (Edinburgh and Glasgow, 1890).

[——] *Proceedings of the Synod of the United Presbyterian Church*, 1879.

[——] 'Professor Candlish on the Westminster Confession of Faith', *The Signal* (Mar. 1887), pp. 81–7; '... Second article' (Apr. 1887), pp. 97–104.

[——] 'Proposals for extending the Irish Poor-Law', *Edinburgh Rev.*, lxxxiv (170) (1846), pp. 267–314.

[——] 'The proposed alteration of the Confession of Faith', *The Signal* (May 1887), p. 129.

[——] 'Puritanism in the Highlands: "The Men"', *Quarterly Rev.*, lxxxix (Sep. 1851), pp. 307–32.

[——] 'Dr Rainy's sermon at opening of Assembly', *The Signal* (Sep. 1888), pp. 257–61.

[——] 'Rationalism and moderatism', *The Signal* (Oct. 1883), pp. 162–3.

[——] 'The rationalism of Wellhausen and Robertson Smith', *The Signal* (Mar. 1886), pp. 65–71.

[——] 'Realities of Irish life', *Quarterly Rev.*, cxxvi (251) (1869), pp. 61–80.

[——] *Report of Proceedings of the Second General Council of the Presbyterian Alliance Convened at Philadelphia, September 1880* (Philadelphia, 1880).

[——] 'Report of Public Meeting held at Kilmallie Free Church', *Oban Express*, 13 May 1892.

[——] 'Review of *The Constitutional History of England in its Origins, by William Stubbs*', *Edinburgh Rev.* (307) (Jul. 1879), pp. 1–40.

[——] 'Review of *Scotland As It Is and As It Was, by the Duke of Argyll*', *Edinburgh Rev.* (338) (Apr. 1887), pp. 532–62.

[——] 'Revision of the Confession of Faith', *The Signal* (Jul. 1889), p. 213.

[——] 'Sabbath-breaking in Forfar', *The Signal* (Oct. 1883).

[——] 'Sabbath desecration', *The Signal* (Sep. 1887), pp. 257–68.

[——] 'The Scottish Episcopal Church', *The Signal* (Oct. 1887), pp. 312–20.

[——] 'Mr. Spurgeon on Professor Bruce', *The Signal* (Sep. 1882), pp. 10–12.

[——] *Statement by ministers and other office-bearers of the Free Church of Scotland in regard to the decisions of the last General Assembly in the cases of Doctors Dods and Bruce* (Edinburgh, 1890).

[——] 'The story of the Grange Free Church: a tragedy', *The Signal* (May 1884), pp. 152–9.

[——] 'The Strome Ferry Case', *The Signal* (Oct. 1883), pp. 161–2.

[——] 'The Strome Ferry prisoners', *The Signal* (Sep. 1883), pp. 147–8.

[——] 'Tabular view of the sustentation fund and special collections of the Free Presbyterian Church of Scotland: for the year from 31st March, 1899, to 31st March, 1900', *FPM*, v (4) (1900), pp. 136–7.

[——] 'The truth about Ireland', *Quarterly Rev.*, cli (301) (1881), pp. 242–84.

[——] , *The Westminster Confession of Faith* (Edinburgh, 1877).

[——] 'What will the Assembly do?', *The Signal* (Jun. 1883), pp. 96–8.

[——] 'Where are the Highlands drifting to?', *The Signal* (Mar. 1888), pp. 86–9; (Jun. 1888), pp. 170–4.

SECONDARY SOURCES

ACQUAVIVA, S. S., *The Decline of the Sacred in Secular Society* (Oxford, 1979).

ALTHOLZ, J. L., 'The mind of Victorian orthodoxy: Anglican responses to "Essays and Reviews", 1860–1864', *Church History*, li (2) (1982), pp. 186–97.

ANSDELL, D. B. A., 'The 1843 Disruption of the Church of Scotland in the Isle of Lewis', *RSCHS*, xxiv (2) (1992), pp. 181–97.

ASPINWALL, B., 'Some aspects of Scotland and the Catholic Revival in the early nineteenth century', *Innes Rev.*, xxvi (1975), pp. 3–19.

——, 'Popery in Scotland: image and reality, 1820–1920', *RSCHS*, xxii (1986), pp. 235–58.

BANTON, M., *Race Relations* (London, 1967).

BARBOUR, G. F., *The Life of Alexander Whyte* (London, 1923).

BAUCKHAM, R. J., 'Sabbath and Sunday in the Protestant tradition', in D. A. Carson (ed.), *From Sabbath to Lord's Day: A Biblical, Historical, and Theological Investigation* (Grand Rapids, Mich., 1982).

BEATON, D., *Memoir, Diary and Remains of the Rev. Donald Macfarlane, Dingwall* (Inverness, 1929).

——, *Memoir, Biographical Sketches, Letters, Lectures and Sermons (English and Gaelic) of the Revd Neil Cameron, Glasgow* (Inverness, 1932).

—— (ed.), *History of the Free Presbyterian Church of Scotland, 1893–1933* (Glasgow, 1933).

BEBBINGTON, D., 'Religion and national identity in nineteenth-century Wales and Scotland', *Studies in Church History*, xviii (1982), pp. 489–503.

——, *Evangelicalism in Modern Britain: A History from the 1780s to the 1980s* (London, 1989).

BIDDISS, M. D., 'The politics of anatomy: Dr Robert Knox and Victorian racism', *Proceedings of the Royal Society of Medicine*, lxix (1976), pp. 245–50.

BISHOP, D. H., 'Church and Society: A Study of the Social Work and Thought of James Begg, D.D. (1808–1883), A. H. Charteris, D.D., LL.D. (1835–1908) and David Watson, D.D. (1859–1943)' (Edinburgh University, Ph.D. thesis, 1953).

BLAKEY, R. S., *The Man in the Manse* (Edinburgh, 1978).

BRADLEY, I., '"Having and holding": the Highland Land War of the 1880s', *History Today*, xxxvii (Dec. 1987), pp. 23–8.

BREWARD, I., 'The Westminster Standards in New Zealand', in Heron, *Westminster Confession in the Church Today*.

BRIDIE, J., *The Anatomist* (London, 1931).

BROOKE, J. H., *Science and Religion: Some Historical Perspectives* (Cambridge, 1991).

BROWN, C. G., *The Social History of Religion in Scotland since 1730* (London, 1987).

——, 'Religion, class and Church growth', in W. H. Fraser and R. J. Morris (eds.), *People and Society in Scotland, 1830–1914* (Edinburgh, 1990).

——, 'Protest in the pews: interpreting Presbyterianism and society in fracture during the Scottish economic revolution', in T. M. Devine (ed.), *Conflict and Stability in Scottish Society, 1700–1850* (Edinburgh, 1990).

BROWN, J. H., 'The Contribution of William Robertson Smith to Old Testament Scholarship, with Special Emphasis on Higher Criticism' (Duke University, Ph.D. thesis, 1964).

BROWN, S. J., *Thomas Chalmers and the Godly Commonwealth* (Oxford, 1982).

——, '"Outside the Covenant": the Scottish Presbyterian Churches and Irish immigration, 1922–1938', *Innes Rev.*, xlii (1) (1991), pp. 19–45.

——, 'Thomas Chalmers and the communal ideal in Victorian Scotland', in T. C. Smout (ed.), *Victorian Values: A Joint Symposium of the Royal Society of Edinburgh and the British Academy, December 1990* (Oxford, 1992).

——, 'Martyrdom in early Victorian Scotland: Disruption Fathers and the making of the Free Church', in D. Wood (ed.), *Martyrs and Martyrologies* (Oxford, 1993).

——, 'The Ten Years' Conflict and the Disruption', in Brown and Fry, *Scotland in the Age of the Disruption*.

——, 'The Disruption and the dream: the making of New College, 1843–1861' in Wright and Badcock, *Disruption to Diversity*.

——, and FRY, M. (eds.), *Scotland in the Age of the Disruption* (Edinburgh, 1993).

BRUCE, S., 'Social change and collective behaviour: the Revival in eighteenth-century Ross-shire', *British Journal of Sociology*, xxiv (4) (1983), pp. 554–72.

——, *No Pope of Rome: Militant Protestantism in Modern Scotland* (Edinburgh, 1985).

——, *A House Divided: Protestantism, Schism, and Secularization* (London and New York, 1990).

——, 'Out of the ghetto: the ironies of acceptance', *Innes Rev.*, xliii (2) (1992), pp. 145–54.

—— (ed.), *Religion and Modernization: Sociologists and Historians debate the Secularization Thesis* (Oxford, 1992).

BURLEIGH, J. H. S., *A Church History of Scotland* (Oxford, 1960).

BURNETT, G. B., *The Story of Quakerism in Scotland* (London, 1952).

——, *The Holy Communion in the Reformed Church of Scotland* (Edinburgh and London, 1960).

CAMERON, N., 'Lecture on the Sabbath', *FPM*, ci (3) (1996).

CAMERON, N. M. DE S., *Biblical Higher Criticism and the Defence of Infallibilism in Nineteenth-Century Britain* (Lewiston, NY, 1987).

CARRUTHERS, S. W., *The Everyday Work of the Westminster Assembly* (Philadelphia, 1943).

CHACKO, E., 'A tribute to the Westminster Confession of Faith (1646)', *FPM*, cii (5) (1997).

CHADWICK, O., *The Victorian Church*, pt. 2 (2nd edn, London, 1972).

CHECKLAND, S. and O., *Industry and Ethos: Scotland, 1832–1914* (London, 1984).

CHEYNE, A. C., 'The Westminster Standards: a century of re-appraisal', *RSCHS*, xiv (1963), pp. 199–214.

——, 'The place of the Confession through three centuries', in Heron, *Westminster Confession in the Church Today*.

——, *The Transforming of the Kirk. Victorian Scotland's Religious Revolution* (Edinburgh, 1983).

——, 'Bible and Confession in Scotland: the background to the Robertson Smith Case', in W. Johnstone (ed.), *William Robertson Smith: Essays in Reassessment* (Sheffield, 1995).

——, 'Thomas Chalmers: then and now', in A. C. Cheyne (ed.), *The Practical and the Pious: Essays on Thomas Chalmers (1780–1847)* (Edinburgh, 1985).

COLLINS, G. N. M., *'Whose Faith Follow'* (Edinburgh, 1943).

——, *Donald Maclean, D.D.* (Edinburgh, 1944).

——, *John Macleod, D.D.* (Edinburgh, 1951).

——, *The Heritage of Our Fathers. The Free Church of Scotland: Her Origin and Testimony* (Edinburgh, 1974).

COLLINSON, S., 'Robert Knox's anatomy of race', *History Today*, xl (Dec. 1990), pp. 44–9.

CRAWFORD, R. G., 'The revolt against creeds and confessions of faith', *Scottish Journal of Theology*, xxix (1) (1976), pp. 13–25.

CROWLEY, D. W., 'The "Crofters' Party", 1885–1892', *Scot. Hist. Rev.*, xxxv (1956), pp. 110–26.

CURRIE, A. S., 'Robert Knox, anatomist, scientist and martyr', *Proceedings of the Royal Society of Medicine*, xxvi (1933), pp. 39–46.

CURTIN, P. D., *The Image of Africa: British Ideas and Action, 1780–1850* (Madison, 1964).

CURTIS, L. P., *Anglo-Saxons and Celts: A Study of Anti-Irish Prejudice in Victorian England* (Bridgeport, Conn., 1968).

——, *Apes and Angels: The Irishman in Victorian Caricature* (Newton Abbot, 1971).

DARLOW, T. H., *William Robertson Nicoll: Life and Letters* (London, 1925).

DAVIS, D., 'Contexts of ambivalence: the folkloristic activities of nineteenth-century Scottish Highland ministers', *Folklore*, ciii (2) (1992), pp. 207–21.

DAWSON, J. E. A., 'The origin of "The Road to the Isles": trade, communications and Campbell power in early modern Scotland', in R. Mason and N. Macdougall (eds.), *People and Power in Scotland: Essays in Honour of T. C. Smout* (Edinburgh, 1992).

DELANEY, J. J., and TOBIN, J. E. (eds.), *Dictionary of Catholic Biography* (London, 1962).

DEVINE, T. M., 'Highland migration to the Lowlands of Scotland', *Scot. Hist. Rev.*, lxii (1985), pp. 137–49.

——, *The Great Highland Famine: Hunger, Emigration and the Scottish Highlands in the Nineteenth Century* (Edinburgh, 1988).

DONNACHIE, I., "'The Enterprising Scot'", in I. Donnachie and C. Whatley (eds.), *The Manufacture of Scottish History* (Edinburgh, 1992).

DRUMMOND, A. L., and BULLOCH, J., *The Church in Victorian Scotland, 1843–1874* (Edinburgh, 1975).

——, *The Church in Late Victorian Scotland, 1874–1900* (Edinburgh, 1978).

DURKACZ, V. E., *The Decline of the Celtic Languages: A Study of Linguistic and Cultural Conflict in Scotland, Wales and Ireland from the Reformation to the Twentieth Century* (Edinburgh, 1983).

EDWARDS, S. J. (JNR), 'Marcus Dods: With Special Reference to his Teaching Ministry' (Edinburgh University, Ph.D. thesis, 1960).

ELDER, J. R., *The History of the Presbyterian Church of New Zealand, 1840–1940* (Christchurch, 1940).

ELLIS, I., *Seven Against Christ: A Study of 'Essays and Reviews'* (London, 1980).

FERGUSON, M., and MATHESON, A., *Scottish Gaelic Union Catalogue* (Edinburgh, 1984).

FERGUSON, W., *Scotland: 1689 to the Present* (Edinburgh, 1978).

FLEMING, J. R., *A History of the Church in Scotland, 1875–1929* (Edinburgh, 1933).

GALLAGHER, T., *Glasgow: The Uneasy Peace. Religious Tension in Modern Scotland* (Manchester, 1987).

GAMMIE, A., *Dr. George H. Morrison. The Man and his Work* (London, 1928).

GILBERT, A. D., *Religion and Society in Industrial England: Church, Chapel and Social Change, 1740–1914* (London and New York, 1976).

GILL, K., 'A church bound by doctrine of 1643', *The Times*, 5 Nov. 1988.

GOSSET, T. F., *Race: The History of an Idea in America* (Dallas, 1973).

GRIGOR, I. F., *Mightier Than A Lord: The Highland Crofters' Struggle For the Land* (Stornoway, 1979).

HALES, E. E. Y., *Pio Nono: A Study in European Politics and Religion in the Nineteenth Century* (London, 1954).

HALLER, W., *Foxe's Book of Martyrs and the Elect Nation* (London, 1963).

HAMILTON, I., *The Erosion of Calvinist Orthodoxy: Seceders and Subscription in Scottish Presbyterianism* (Edinburgh, 1990).

HANHAM, H. J., 'The problem of Highland discontent, 1880–1885', *Trans. of the Royal Hist. Soc.*, 5th ser., xix (1969), pp. 21–65.

HENDERSON, D. M., 'The Scottish soldier abroad: the sociology of acclimatization', in G. G. Simpson (ed.), *The Scottish Soldier Abroad, 1247–1967* (Edinburgh, 1992).

HERON, A. I. C., *The Westminster Confession in the Church Today* (Edinburgh, 1982).

HUNTER, J., 'The emergence of the crofting community: the religious contribution, 1798–1843', *Scottish Studies*, xviii (1974), pp. 95–116.

——, *The Making of the Crofting Community* (Edinburgh, 1976).

——, 'The politics of Highland land reform, 1873–1898', *Scot. Hist. Rev.*, liii (1976), pp. 45–68.

HUTTON, G., 'Why psalms only?', *FPM*, cii (3) (1997).

JARVIE, G., 'Culture, social development and the Scottish Highland Gatherings', in D. McCrone, S. Kendrick and P. Shaw (eds.), *The Making of Scotland: Nation, Culture and Social Change* (Edinburgh, 1989).

JAY, E., *Faith and Doubt in Victorian Britain* (London, 1986).

KENNA, R., and MOONEY, A., *People's Palaces: Victorian and Edwardian Pubs of Scotland* (Edinburgh, 1983).

LATOURETTE, K., *Christianity in a Revolutionary Age* (New York, 1959).

LAVERDURE, P., 'Creating an anti-Catholic crusader: Charles Chiniquy', *Journal of Religious History*, xv (1) (1988), pp. 94–108.

LEAKEY, R. E., and LEWIN, R., *Origins: What New Discoveries Reveal about the Emergence of our Species and its Possible Future* (London, 1977).

LECKIE, J. H., *Secession Memories: The United Presbyterian Contribution to the Scottish Church* (Edinburgh, 1926).

LINDBERG, D. C., and NUMBERS, R. L., 'Beyond war and peace: a reappraisal of the encounter between Christianity and science', *Church History*, lv (3) (1986), pp. 338–54.

LIVINGSTONE, D. N., *Darwin's Forgotten Defenders: The Encounter Between Evangelical Theology and Evolutionary Thought* (Grand Rapids and Edinburgh, 1987).

LYNCH, M., *Scotland: A New History* (London, 1992).

MACCUISH, D. J., 'Crofting legislation since 1886', *Scot. Geog. Magazine*, ciii (2) (1987), pp. 90–4.

MACDONALD, D., *Lewis: A History of the Island* (Edinburgh, 1978).

MACDONALD, R., 'The Catholic Gaidhealtachd', *Innes Rev.*, xxix (1978), pp. 56–72.

MACDONALD, S., 'Crofter colonisation in Canada, 1886–1892: the Scottish political background', *Northern Scotland*, vii (1986–7), pp. 47–59.

MCEWEN, J. S., 'How the Confession came to be written', in Heron, *Westminster Confession in the Church Today*.

MCFARLAND, E. W., *Protestants First: Orangeism in Nineteenth-Century Scotland* (Edinburgh, 1990).

MACHAFFIE, B. Z., '"Monument Facts and Higher Critical Fancies": archaeology and the popularization of Old Testament criticism in nineteenth-century Britain', *Church History*, l (3) (1981), pp. 316–28.

MACINNES, A. I., 'Evangelical Protestantism in the nineteenth-century Highlands', in Walker and Gallagher, *Sermons and Battle Hymns*.

MACINNES, J., *The Evangelical Movement in the Highlands of Scotland* (Aberdeen, 1951).

——, 'The origin and early development of "The Men"', *RSCHS*, viii (1944), pp. 16–41.

——, 'Religion in Gaelic society', *Trans. of the Gaelic Soc. of Inverness*, lii (1980–2), pp. 222–42.

MACLEOD, D. B. (ed.), *One Hundred Years of Witness* (Glasgow, 1993).

MACLEOD, D. J., 'Gaelic prose', *Trans. of the Gaelic Soc. of Inverness*, xlix (1974–6), pp. 198–230.

MACLEOD, J., *Scottish Theology in Relation to Church History Since the Reformation* (Edinburgh, 1943).

——, *By-Paths of Highland Church History* (Edinburgh, 1965).

MACLEOD, J., 'Our enduring testimony', in MacLeod, *One Hundred Years of Witness*.

MACLEOD, J., *Highlanders: A History of the Gaels* (London, 1996).

MACLEOD, K., 'Changes', *Young People's Magazine*, ci (12) (1996).

MACLEOD, L., 'Free Church's key player', *The Greenock Telegraph*, 28 Jun. 1989.

——, 'Formation of the Greenock Free Presbyterian congregation', *FPM*, xcviii (9) (1993), pp. 263–6.

MACLEOD, N., 'A letter addressed to the Rev. John Kennedy, author of *The Days of the Fathers in Ross-shire*, by a New Zealander', in Macleod, *By-Paths of Highland Church History*.

MCNEIL, J. T., *The Presbyterian Church in Canada, 1875–1925* (Toronto, 1925).

MACPHAIL, I. M. M., 'Prelude to the Crofters' War, 1870–1880', *Trans. of the Gaelic Soc. of Inverness*, xlix (1974–6), pp. 159–88.

——, 'The Highland elections of 1884–86', *Trans. of the Gaelic Soc. of Inverness*, l (1976–8), pp. 368–402.

——, 'Gunboats to the Hebrides', *Trans. of the Gaelic Soc. of Inverness*, liii (1982–4), pp. 531–67.

MCPHERSON, A., 'Synod sermon', *FPM*, ci (7) (1996).

——, *History of the Free Presbyterian Church (1893–1970)* (Inverness, n.d.).

MANGAN, J. A., *The Games Ethic and Imperialism: Aspects of the Diffusion of an Ideal* (Harmondsworth, 1986).

MARWICK, W. H., 'Social heretics in the Scottish Churches', *RSCHS*, xi (3) (1953), pp. 227–39.

MARX, K., *Capital: A Critique of Political Economy* (London, 1976).

MAXWELL, I., 'Alexander Duff and the Theological and Philosophical Background to the General Assembly's Mission in Calcutta to 1840' (Edinburgh University, Ph.D. thesis, 1995).

MEEK, D. E., 'Gaelic poets of the land agitation', *Trans. of the Gaelic Soc. of Inverness*, xlix (1974–6), pp. 309–76.

——, '"The Land Question Answered From the Bible": the land issue and the development of a Highland theology of liberation', *Scot. Geog. Magazine*, ciii (2) (1987), pp. 84–9.

——, 'Evangelical missionaries in the early nineteenth-century Highlands', *Scottish Studies*, xxviii (1987), pp. 1–34.

——, 'The Gaelic Bible', in Wright, *Bible in Scottish Life and Literature*.

——, 'The Bible and social change in the nineteenth-century Highlands', in Wright, *Bible in Scottish Life and Literature*.

——, 'Saints and scarecrows: the Churches and Gaelic culture in the Highlands since 1560', *Scottish Journal of Evangelical Theology*, xiv (1), Internet http://www.rutherfordhouse.org.uk/meek.htm, 4 of 14.

MILLER, A. A., *Alexander Duff of India* (Edinburgh, 1992).

MILLER, R. S., 'Greatheart of China: a brief life of William Chalmers Burns, M.A.', in S. M. Houghton (ed.), *Five Pioneer Missionaries* (London, 1965).

MOORE, J. R., *The Post-Darwinian Controversies: A Study of the Protestant Struggle to come to terms with Darwin in Great Britain and America, 1870–1900* (Cambridge and New York, 1979).

MURDOCH, A., and SHER, R. B., 'Literary and learned culture', in T. M Devine and R. Mitcheson (eds.), *People and Society in Scotland, 1760–1830* (Edinburgh, 1988).

NELSON, R. R., 'The Life and Thought of William Robertson Smith, 1846–1894' (Michigan University, Ph.D. thesis, 1969).

NORMAN, E. R., *Anti-Catholicism in Victorian England* (London, 1968).

O'NEIL, J., 'New Testament', in Wright and Badcock, *Disruption to Diversity*.

PAGE, L. E., 'Diluvialism and its critics', in Russell, *Science and Religious Belief*.

PARKER, K. L., *The English Sabbath: A Study of Doctrine and Discipline from the Reformation to the Civil War* (Cambridge, 1988).

PARSONS, G., 'Biblical criticism in Victorian Britain: from controversy to acceptance?', in Parsons, *Religion in Victorian Britain*, vol. II.

——, 'Victorian Roman Catholicism: emancipation, expansion and achievement', in Parsons, *Religion in Victorian Britain*, vol. I.

—— (ed.), *Religion in Victorian Britain*, 2 vols. (Manchester and New York, 1988).

PATERSON, G., 'Church too pure even for a Lord Chancellor', *Daily Express*, 26 May 1989.

PAUL, R. S., *The Assembly of the Lord: Politics and Religion in the Westminster Assembly and the 'Grand Debate'* (Edinburgh, 1985).

PHILLIPS, A., *My Uncle George: The Respectful Recollections of a Backslider in a Highland Manse* (London, 1984).

PITTOCK, M. G. H., *The Invention of Scotland: The Stuart Myth and the Scottish Identity, 1638 to the Present* (London and New York, 1991).

PREBBLE, J., *The Highland Clearances* (Harmondsworth, 1963).

——, *The King's Jaunt: George IV in Scotland, August 1822. 'One and Twenty Daft Days'* (London, 1988).

RAE, I., *Knox the Anatomist* (Edinburgh and London, 1964).

REARDON, B. M. G., *Religious Thought in the Victorian Age: A Survey from Coleridge to Gore* (London, 1980).

RHODES, A. C., *The Power of Rome in the Twentieth Century, the Vatican in the Age of Liberal Democracies* (London, 1983).

RICHARDS, E., 'The "Moral Anatomy" of Robert Knox: the interplay between biological and social thought in Victorian scientific naturalism', *Journal of the History of Biology*, xxii (3) (1989), pp. 373–436.

RIESEN, R. A., '"Higher Criticism" in the Free Church Fathers', *RSCHS*, xx (1980), 119–42.

——, *Criticism and Faith in Late Victorian Scotland: A. B. Davidson, William Robertson Smith and George Adam Smith* (Lanham, MD, 1985).

ROBB, G., 'Popular religion and the Christianization of the Scottish Highlands in the eighteenth and nineteenth centuries', *Journal of Religious History*, xvi (1) (1990), pp. 18–34.

ROGERSON, J. W., *The Bible and Criticism in Victorian Britain: Profiles of F. D. Maurice and William Robertson Smith* (Sheffield, 1995).

RORDORF, W., *Sunday: The History of the Day of Rest in the Earliest Centuries of the Christian Church* (London, 1962).

ROSIE, G., *Hugh Miller: Outrage and Order* (Edinburgh, 1981).

ROSS, A., 'The development of the Scottish Catholic community, 1878–1978', *Innes Rev.*, xxix (1978), 30–55.

——, *The Root of the Matter: Boyhood, Manhood and God* (Edinburgh, 1989).

ROSS, A. C., *John Philip (1775–1851): Missions, Race and Politics in South Africa* (Aberdeen, 1986).

——, *Livingstone: The Scot and the Doctor* (Glasgow, 1990).

ROSS, K. R., 'The Free Church Case, 1900–4 and its Origins: A Study in the Relation of Church and Creed' (Edinburgh University, Ph.D. thesis, 1987).

——, *Church and Creed* (Edinburgh, 1988).

——, 'Calvinists in controversy: John Kennedy, Horatius Bonar and the Moody Mission of 1873–74', *Scottish Bulletin of Evangelical Theology*, ix (1) (1991), pp. 51–63.

ROWELL, G., *Hell and the Victorians: A Study of the Nineteenth-Century Theological Controversies concerning Eternal Punishment and the Future Life* (Oxford, 1974).

RUDWICK, M. J. S., 'The principle of Uniformity', in Russell, *Science and Religious Belief*.

RUSSELL, C. A. (ed.), *Science and Religious Belief: A Selection of Recent Historical Studies* (London, 1973).

SABBATH OBSERVANCE COMMITTEE'S REPORT, *Free Presbyterian Church of Scotland Proceedings of Synod*, May 1995.

SCHMIDT, L. E., 'Sacramental occasions and the Scottish context of Presbyterian Revivalism in America', in R. B. Sher and J. R. Smitten (eds.), *Scotland and America in the Age of the Enlightenment* (Edinburgh, 1990).

SCOTLAND, N. A. D., 'Essays and reviews (1860) and the reaction of Victorian Churches and Churchmen', *Downside Rev.*, cviii (371) (1990), pp. 146–56.

SEFTON, H. R., 'Free Presbyterian Church of Scotland', in J. Douglas (ed.), *The New International Dictionary of the Christian Church* (Grand Rapids, 1978).

SETON-WATSON, H., *Language and National Consciousness* (London, 1981).

SHORTLAND, M., *Hugh Miller's Memoir: From Stonemason to Geologist* (Edinburgh, 1995).

SHRIVER, G. H., *Philip Schaff: Christian Scholar and Ecumenical Prophet* (Macon, Georgia, 1987).

SINCLAIR, J. S. (ed.), *Rich Gleanings After the Vintage from 'Rabbi' Duncan* (London, 1925).

SINGLETON, J., 'The Virgin Mary and religious conflict in Victorian Britain', *Journal of Ecclesiastical History*, xliii (1) (1992), pp. 16–34.

SMITH, D. C., *Passive Obedience and Prophetic Protest: Social Criticism in the Scottish Church, 1830–1945* (New York, 1987).

SMITH, R. M., *The History of Greenock* (Greenock, 1921).

SMOUT, T. C., *A History of the Scottish People, 1560–1830* (London, 1969).

——, *A Century of the Scottish People, 1830–1950* (London, 1986).

—— (ed.), *Victorian Values: A Joint Symposium of the Royal Society of Edinburgh and the British Academy December 1990* (Oxford, 1992).

THURSTON, H., *No Popery: Chapters on Anti-Papal Prejudice* (London, 1930).

TREVOR-ROPER, H., 'The invention of tradition: the Highland tradition of Scotland', in E. Hobsbawm and T. Ranger (eds.), *The Invention of Tradition* (Cambridge, 1983).

VIDLER, A. R., *The Church in an Age of Revolution* (London, 1961).

WAGNER, G., *Barnardo* (London, 1979).

WALKER, G., '"There's not a team like the Glasgow Rangers": football and religious identity in Scotland', in Walker and Gallagher, *Sermons and Battle Hymns*.

——, and GALLAGHER, T. (eds.), *Sermons and Battle Hymns: Protestant Popular Culture in Modern Scotland* (Edinburgh, 1990).

WALLIS, R., *Salvation and Protest: Studies of Social and Religious Movements* (London, 1979).

WARD, R. S., *The Bush Still Burns: The Presbyterian and Reformed Faith in Australia, 1788–1988* (Brunswick, 1989).

WATKINS, K., 'The inspiration of Scripture', *FPM*, c (2) (1995).

——, 'Saying no to Sabbath work', *Young People's Magazine*, lxi (12) (1996).

WATT, H., *New College Edinburgh: A Centenary History* (Edinburgh, 1946).

WHEELER, M., *Heaven, Hell and the Victorians* (Cambridge, 1994).

WIGLEY, J., *The Rise and Fall of the Victorian Sunday* (Manchester, 1980).

WILKIE, J. S., 'Buffon, Lamarck and Darwin: the originality of Darwin's Theory of Evolution', in Russell, *Science and Religious Belief*.

WILLIAMS, C. P., 'British religion and the wider world: mission and Empire, 1800–1940', in S. Gilley and W. Sheils (eds.), *A History of Religion in Britain* (Oxford, 1994).

WITHERS, C. W. J., 'The Highland Parishes in 1698: an examination of sources for the definition of the Gaidhealtachd', *Scottish Studies*, xxiv (1980), pp. 63–88.

——, 'The Scottish Highlands outlined: cartographic evidence for the position of the Highland–Lowland boundary', *Scot. Geog. Magazine*, xcviii (3) (1982), pp. 143–57.

——, 'Education and Anglicization: the policy of the SSPCK towards Gaelic in the Highlands, 1709–1825', *Scottish Studies*, xxvi (1982), pp. 37–56.

WITHERS, C. W. J., *Gaelic in Scotland, 1698–1981* (Edinburgh, 1984).

——, 'Kirk, club and culture change: Gaelic chapels, Highland societies and the urban Gaelic subculture in eighteenth-century Scotland', *Social History*, x (1985), pp. 171–92.

——, 'Highland–Lowland migration and the making of the crofting community, 1775–1891', *Scot. Geog. Magazine*, ciii (2) (1987), pp. 76–83.

——, *Gaelic Scotland: The Transformation of a Culture Region* (London and New York, 1988).

——, 'The historical creation of the Scottish Highlands', in I. Donnachie and C. Whatley (eds.), *The Manufacture of Scottish History* (Edinburgh, 1992).

WITHRINGTON, D. J., 'The Churches in Scotland, c.1870–c.1900: towards a new social conscience?', *RSCHS*, xxix (1977), pp. 155–68.

——, '"A Ferment of Change": aspirations, ideas and ideals in nineteenth-century Scotland', in D. Gifford (ed.), *The History of Scottish Literature*, vol. III (Aberdeen, 1988).

——, 'Non-church-going, church organisation and "crisis in the church", c.1800–c.1920', *RSCHS*, xxiv (2) (1992), pp. 199–236.

WOLFFE, J., *The Protestant Crusade in Great Britain, 1829–1860* (Oxford, 1991).

WOMACK, P., *Improvement and Romance: Constructing the Myth of the Highlands* (London, 1989).

WOOD, J. D., 'Transatlantic land reform: America and the Crofters' Revolt, 1878–1888', *Scot. Hist. Rev.*, lxiii (1984), pp. 79–104.

WRIGHT, D. F. (ed.), *The Bible in Scottish Life and Literature* (Edinburgh, 1988).

—— (ed.), *Chosen By God: Mary in Evangelical Perspective* (London, 1989).

——, and BADCOCK, G. D. (eds.), *Disruption to Diversity: Edinburgh Divinity, 1846–1996* (Edinburgh, 1996).

YOUNGSON, A. J., *Beyond the Highland Line. Three Journals of Travel in Eighteenth-Century Scotland: Burt, Pennant, Thornton* (London, 1974).

YULE, G. S. S., 'The Westminster Confession in Australia', in Heron, *Westminster Confession in the Church Today*.

[——] 'The late Mr. John Urquart, Elder, Greenock', *FPM*, xxxix (6) (1934), pp. 259–68.

[——] 'Which Church?', *FPM*, ci (7) (1996).

Index

2